Arabic Poetics

What makes language beautiful? *Arabic Poetics* offers an answer to what this pertinent question looked like at the height of the Islamic civilization. In this novel argument, Lara Harb suggests that literary quality depended on the ability of linguistic expression to produce an experience of discovery and wonder in the listener. Analyzing theories of how rhetorical figures, simile, metaphor, and sentence construction are able to achieve this effect of wonder, Harb shows how this aesthetic theory, first articulated at the turn of the eleventh century CE, represented a major paradigm shift from earlier Arabic criticism, which based its judgment on criteria of truthfulness and naturalness. In doing so, this study poses a major challenge to the misconception in modern scholarship that Arabic criticism was "traditionalist" or "static," exposing an elegant, widespread conceptual framework of literary beauty in the post-tenth-century Islamicate world that is central to poetic criticism, the interpretation of Aristotle's *Poetics* in Arabic philosophy, and the rationale underlying discussions about the inimitability of the Quran.

Lara Harb is Assistant Professor of Near Eastern Studies at Princeton University where she specializes in classical Arabic literature. She is the author of articles in journals such as *Journal of American Oriental Society* and *Middle Eastern Literatures*. Her PhD was awarded the S. A. Bonebakker Prize for the best thesis in Classical Arabic Literature in 2014.

Cambridge Studies in Islamic Civilization

Other titles in the series are listed at the back of the book.

Arabic Poetics

Aesthetic Experience in Classical Arabic Literature

LARA HARB
Princeton University

CAMBRIDGE
UNIVERSITY PRESS

CAMBRIDGE
UNIVERSITY PRESS

University Printing House, Cambridge CB2 8BS, United Kingdom

One Liberty Plaza, 20th Floor, New York, NY 10006, USA

477 Williamstown Road, Port Melbourne, VIC 3207, Australia

314-321, 3rd Floor, Plot 3, Splendor Forum, Jasola District Centre, New Delhi - 110025, India

103 Penang Road, #05-06/07, Visioncrest Commercial, Singapore 238467

Cambridge University Press is part of the University of Cambridge.

It furthers the University's mission by disseminating knowledge in the pursuit of education, learning and research at the highest international levels of excellence.

www.cambridge.org
Information on this title: www.cambridge.org/9781108748292
DOI: 10.1017/9781108780483

First published 2020
First paperback edition 2021

A catalogue record for this publication is available from the British Library

Library of Congress Cataloging in Publication data
Names: Harb, Lara, 1981 author.
Title: Arabic poetics : aesthetic experience in classical Arabic literature / Lara Harb.
Description: Cambridge, UK ; New York, NY: Cambridge University Press, 2020. | Series: Cambridge studies in Islamic civilization | Includes bibliographical references and index.
Identifiers: LCCN 2019051666 (print) | LCCN 2019051667 (ebook) | ISBN 9781108490214 (hardback) | ISBN 9781108780483 (ebook)
Subjects: LCSH: Poetics – History – To 1500. | Arabic poetry – 750–1258 – History and criticism. | Arabic poetry – 1258–1800 – History and criticism. | Arabic language – Versification – History.
Classification: LCC PN1049.A7 H37 2020 (print) | LCC PN1049.A7 (ebook) | DDC 808.10917/5927–dc23
LC record available at https://lccn.loc.gov/2019051666
LC ebook record available at https://lccn.loc.gov/2019051667

ISBN 978-1-108-49021-4 Hardback
ISBN 978-1-108-74829-2 Paperback

To my parents

Contents

Preface

How was classical Arabic poetry evaluated by medieval critics? This is the question motivating this study. We can search for the answer in a large body of texts that has come down to us from the Islamic Middle Ages concerned with issues of eloquence and poetic beauty. These texts may be described as "medieval" or "classical" Arabic literary theory. Before we delve into this literature, however, let me take a moment to qualify this description. Each word in this label is problematic.

The term "medieval" is borrowed from the European context, which designates a middle period between the collapse of the Western Roman Empire and the Renaissance. Broadly speaking, this period, which stretches between the fifth and the fifteenth centuries CE, does correspond more or less to the period one refers to when designating the term medieval to the Arabo-Islamic world. However, with the rise of Islam in the seventh century, the expansion of the Islamic Empire soon after, and its dominance over a territory stretching from Spain to the Indus Valley for centuries to follow, this period marks the beginning and height of the Islamic civilization.[1] To modern Arabic culture, the literary production of that period also constitutes its "classical" heritage. Hence, the literature of the

[1] For the case against using the term "medieval" to describe the old Islamic world, see Thomas Bauer, *Warum es kein islamisches Mittelalter gab: das Erbe der Antike und der Orient* (Munich: C.H. Beck, 2018). One way scholars have circumvented using the term "medieval" to describe the Islamic civilization is by referring to dynasties in power and speaking of the Umayyad, Abbasid, and Mamluk eras. However, this periodization rarely corresponds to intellectual trends and developments. It is therefore sometimes still necessary to resort to the term medieval in order to describe a period spanning dynasties and territories.

period is also – although not less problematically – referred to as "classical."[2]

The term "Arabic" can also be problematic. In this context, the texts that I will be analyzing in this book were all written in Arabic and all deal with literary works written in Arabic. However, it is important to note that many of the authors came from regions well beyond what we would consider the Arab world today, including one of the main theorists discussed in this book, ʿAbd al-Qāhir al-Jurjānī, who was from Gorgan (in modern-day Iran). I use the term "Arabic" strictly to describe the language of the scholarship I am analyzing. Any mention of "Arab critics" or "Arab philosophers" is intended as a designation of the linguistic medium in which they were writing and not their ethnic background.

The concept of the "literary" is problematic because it does not map onto how we today, and particularly in the West, would necessarily define "literature."[3] As we will see, the literary in the Arabic critical tradition operates at the level of stylistics and the verbal arts. Critical engagement with larger structures such as plot or even content is less prominent.[4] The poetic examples analyzed in Arabic sources are most often limited to single verses or even fragments of verses. Moreover, the literary subject of the critical tradition is not limited to verses of poetry. Verses from the Quran, as well as phrases in prose, are evaluated using the same criteria as poetry. The "literary," therefore, is discussed in reference to poetry, the Quran, and artistic prose regardless of larger structures. The literary thus

[2] While the entire "medieval" period can be regarded as classical, there are periods of "classicism" and "post-classicism" within it as well. In the early Abbasid period (late second/eighth century), for example, a new style of poetry started developing, as we will see in Chapter 1, that contrasted with a pre-Islamic and early Islamic poetic tradition that had already come to represent a "classical" heritage for the Abbasids. Sometimes everything up to the end of the Abbasid period (656/1258) is described as "classical" and what follows as "post-classical." For a critique of this periodization, see Thomas Bauer, "In Search of 'Post-Classical Literature': A Review Article," *Mamlūk Studies Review* 11, no. 2 (2007). I loosely use the label "classical Arabic literary theory" in this book to describe "old Arabic criticism" (*al-naqd al-ʿArabī al-qadīm*), as it is sometimes described in Arabic scholarship. The texts I discuss happen to range from the third/ninth to the eighth/fourteenth century because I look at the development of aesthetic ideas over the centuries up to and including the standardization of the study of eloquence as a scholastic discipline in the seventh/thirteenth and eighth/fourteenth century.

[3] For a discussion of the meaning of "literature" and the "literary" in the classical Arabic context and how they might differ from modern-day assumptions, see Julie Scott Meisami's introduction in *Structure and Meaning in Medieval Arabic and Persian Poetry: Orient Pearls* (London; New York: Routledge, 2003).

[4] Geert Jan van Gelder has tackled the treatment of larger structures of poems in classical Arabic criticism in his *Beyond the Line: Classical Arabic Literary Critics on the Coherence and Unity of the Poem* (Leiden: E.J. Brill, 1982).

encompasses both poeticity (*shiʿriyya*) and eloquence (*balāgha*). In the Arabic context, both revolve around the question of the beauty of speech, not its persuasive power. Although eloquence (*balāgha*) is a more frequently used term than poeticity (*shiʿriyya*) and entails a broader category that can describe the Quran as well as poetry, what is meant by *balāgha* is closer to poetics in English than rhetoric, as it is sometimes described.[5] Thus, for our present purposes, I will be using the terms "poeticity" and "eloquence" interchangeably to describe literary aesthetics. Popular narratives such as the *Arabian Nights*, dramatic performances, and storytelling, as well as anecdotal literature (*adab*), which constitute important components of classical Arabic literature, never enjoyed the attention of the critical tradition that poetry, the Quran, and artistic prose did.[6]

On a related note, the poet himself or the poem from which a verse is quoted rarely plays a role in their analyses. Poets certainly had reputations that sometimes come into play. Nevertheless, critics were generally more concerned with the specific images they want to discuss, not the poet. Moreover, while in some cases the quoted verses are taken from famous poems, which the medieval reader would have undoubtedly recognized, the poem as a whole is rarely relevant to the point the critics try to illustrate. In many cases, the verses only survive as isolated quotations with their original literary context lost. Moreover, many of the verses and examples quoted in the critical tradition become a standardized canon of their own. Specific verses become famous in and of themselves as illustrations of one or another poetic device and are repeatedly discussed over the centuries.

Finally, the term "theory" is an anachronistic application of a modern concept. Using it to describe medieval Arabic discussions of poetry and

[5] While the term *balāgha*, meaning eloquence in Arabic, is often translated as "rhetoric," it must be distinguished from rhetoric (*khaṭāba*) in the ancient Greek sense of argumentation and oratory, which aims at persuasion. The goal of *balāgha* is distinctly aesthetic, not persuasion, even if the former can benefit the latter. (See Pierre Larcher, "Mais qu'est-ce donc que la balâgha?," in *Literary and Philosophical Rhetoric in the Greek, Roman, Syriac, and Arabic Worlds*, ed. Frédérique Woerther (Hildesheim, Zürich, New York: Georg Olms Verlag, 2009); and Filippomaria Pontani, "Inimitable Sources: Canonical Texts and Rhetorical Theory in the Greek, Latin, Arabic and Hebrew Traditions," in *Canonical Texts and Scholarly Practices: A Global Comparative Approach*, ed. Anthony Grafton and Glenn W. Most (Cambridge: Cambridge University Press, 2016).)

[6] Some anecdotal literature was written in highly stylized language, such as the *maqāmāt*. These do become the subject of literary criticism. However, also in this case, the focus of the criticism tends to be on the verbal arts employed in them, not larger structures such as the plot. See Matthew Keegan, "Commentarial Acts and Hermeneutical Dramas: The Ethics of Reading al-Ḥarīrī's Maqāmāt" (PhD Dissertation, New York University, 2017).

eloquence might lead one to have certain modern expectations that the sources do not fulfill.[7] However, I use the term deliberately because I believe, as I hope to show, that the critical texts that have come down to us from the Islamic Middle Ages do provide us with general principles that can explain phenomena beyond the specific examples of Arabic literature.

Keeping these qualifications in mind, the body of texts that can be described as "classical Arabic literary theory" is enormous and multifaceted.[8] Much of it has been published in easily accessible modern printed editions and many of these are even searchable online. However, many manuscripts remain much less accessible in libraries around the world. Far less is accessible in English translation.[9] This book is an attempt to shed light on some of these texts and to uncover some salient aspects that define classical Arabic literary aesthetics.

[7] Modern expectations of medieval Arabic literary theory form the basis of Meisami's critique of modern scholarship on the topic (Julie Scott Meisami, "Arabic Poetics Revisited," *Journal of the American Oriental Society* 112, no. 2 (1992)).

[8] For an analysis of the Arabic critical tradition as a discipline, see Wen-chin Ouyang, *Literary Criticism in Medieval Arabic-Islamic Culture: The Making of a Tradition* (Edinburgh: Edinburgh University Press, 1997).

[9] English translations of selections and excerpts can be found in Vicente Cantarino, *Arabic Poetics in the Golden Age: Selection of Texts Accompanied by a Preliminary Study* (Leiden: Brill, 1975); Geert Jan van Gelder and Marlé Hammond, eds., *Takhyīl: The Imaginary in Classical Arabic Poetics* (Cambridge, UK: Gibb Memorial Trust, 2008). Information about other translations is provided where relevant throughout the book.

Acknowledgments

This project has been long in the making. Its flame was sparked and kindled by my advisers, classmates, and friends in graduate school at New York University, especially Philip F. Kennedy, Everett K. Rowson, and Tamer el-Leithy. I owe much of this book to them. I would also like to thank Hala Halim, Mohammad Mehdi Khorrami, Marion Katz, and Zachary Lockman for their support and guidance, and Jeannie Miller, Eman Morsi, Zainab Mahmood, Robyn Creswell, Amir Moosavi, Omar Cheta, Ryvka Barnard, Leena Dallasheh, Allison Brown, and Ali Akhtar for the conversations and friendship. The completion of the first iteration of this project was made possible by the Lane Cooper Fellowship and Dean's Dissertation Fellowship at NYU. I am grateful to Wen-chin Ouyang for her support and feedback from very early stages of the project. The book looks the way it does today thanks to the generous comments, corrections, and questions I received at various stages of the project from numerous scholars who made the time to read complete drafts or sections, including Julia Bray, Hilary Kilpatrick, Li Guo, Antonella Ghersetti, Dimitri Gutas, Frank Griffel, and Devin Stewart. A special thanks to Geert Jan van Gelder, who caught more errors in the book than I care to admit, and Alexander Key for his meticulous feedback and for being such an engaging interlocutor. I owe much to Elliott Colla for taking me under his wing from my first days on this side of the ocean. I am grateful to my colleagues and friends at Dartmouth College for giving me my first home after graduate school and making it such a welcoming and inspiring one, including Jonathan Smolin, Kevin Reinhart, Yasser el-Hariry, and Katie Hornstein. I am thankful to my friends and mentors at Princeton, and especially to my colleagues at the Near Eastern Studies Department who made the completion of this book possible. Special thanks go out to Marina Rustow for her unwavering support and friendship, Michael Cook for his generous guidance, Andras Hamori for his warm welcome and insightful feedback, Anna Shields for her unhesitant readiness to engage with my work, Daniel Heller-Roazen for inspiring conversations, and Qasim Zaman for his model leadership. I am also grateful to Ekaterina Pukhovaia and Anna Bailey for their help, and the reliable staff at the Near Eastern Studies Department and Firestone library, whose support was a real luxury to have. Finally, I am thankful to the editors and staff at Cambridge University Press for providing a final home for this project.

The writing process was only possible thanks to the love and support of my family and friends. I am grateful to Omar and Gerlinde, for always being there for me in more ways than can be described; Firas and Tareq, for their love and support that I always felt despite the geographical distance; and Alba and Nereo, for helping in ways that went beyond anything I could have wished for. I thank Justine and Ioanna for their readiness to listen at any moment. I am especially grateful to Zeina, whose steadfast support and enviable humanity were without fail a phone call away ready to encourage and inspire at a moment's notice. My deepest gratitude goes to my husband, Fulvio, without whose admirable serenity, inspiring curiosity, and stimulating conversations this book would not be what it is. I am thankful for our daughter, Dalia, who was born at the inception of this project and has been growing up with this book, for keeping things in joyful perspective. Finally, I have my mother to thank for instilling in me a sense of wonder and my father for filling my ears with Arabic poetry growing up. To them I dedicate this book.

Princeton, 2019

Note on Dates, Translations, Transliterations, and Names

All dates are given in the Islamic Hijri calendar, a lunar system that begins in 622 CE, followed by the corresponding Common Era date. Death dates are based on those reported in the *Encyclopedia of Islam*, Second and Third Editions (Brill Online). Arabic terms are provided in transliteration in cases where they are noteworthy, following the IJMES transliteration system. Poetic and Quranic quotations are provided in Arabic script alongside their translations. Verses in classical Arabic poetry are conventionally made up of two hemistichs. I preserve this structure in the English translations. I use the term "listener," as opposed to "reader" or "audience," when discussing the reception of poetry or eloquent speech as this is how medieval critics themselves spoke of the person experiencing the poetic speech. Finally, the epithet "al-Jurjānī" is shared by several critics whose works are discussed in this book. When I speak of "al-Jurjānī," without any further specification, I refer to ʿAbd al-Qāhir al-Jurjānī (d. 471/1078 or 474/1081), the author of *Asrār al-balāgha* (*The Secrets of Eloquence*) and *Dalāʾil al-iʿjāz* (*The Signs of the Inimitability of the Quran*). He is not to be confused with al-Qāḍī al-Jurjānī (d. 392/1001), author of *al-Wasāṭa bayn al-Mutanabbī wa-khuṣūmih* (*The Mediation between Mutanabbī and His Opponents*); Muḥammad ibn ʿAlī al-Jurjānī (d. 729/1329), who wrote *al-Ishārāt wa-l-tanbīhāt fī ʿilm al-balāgha* (*Pointers and Reminders on the Science of Eloquence*); and ʿAlī ibn Muḥammad (al-Sayyid al-Sharīf) al-Jurjānī (d. 816/1413), who wrote a commentary on al-Sakkākī's *al-Miftāḥ* (*The Key*) and glosses on al-Taftāzānī's *al-Muṭawwal*, a commentary on the *Miftāḥ*. Furthermore, Jalāl al-Dīn al-Qazwīnī (d. 739/1338), known as al-Khaṭīb al-Qazwīnī, the author of two important commentaries on the *Miftāḥ*, is also not to be confused with Zakariyyā al-Qazwīnī (d. 682/1283), the author of *ʿAjāʾib al-makhlūqāt* (*The Wonders of Creations*).

Introduction

The sixth-/twelfth-century Andalusian philosopher Ibn Rushd, or Averroes as he is known in Latin, cites the following early Islamic-era verse in his commentary on Aristotle's *Poetics*. In it, the poet describes having a conversation with his fellow caravan travelers (or beloved) on camelback on their way home after they have fulfilled their pilgrimage duties in Mecca:[1]

أَخَذْنا بأطرافِ الأحاديثِ بيننا   وسالتْ بأعناقِ المَطِيِّ الأباطحُ

We took to the choicest of speech between us
as the broad valleys flowed with the necks of camels
~ Kuthayyir ʿAzza (d. 105/723)

Ibn Rushd cites this verse as an example of rendering poetic the simple idea of "we spoke and we traveled." While it might seem intuitively obvious in this case that one way of expressing the idea is more poetic than the other, this book seeks to explore the theoretical reasoning classical Arabic literary theory provided for poeticity. The question is not what defines poetry as verse, the answer to which entails a description of the formal structure of a poem, its rhyme and meter. Rather, the inquiry of this study is what defines language as *poetic* or *eloquent*, whether in the form of verse, prose, or the

1 Ibn Rushd, *Talkhīṣ kitāb al-shiʿr* (Cairo: Markaz Taḥqīq al-Turāth, 1986), 122. This verse is frequently discussed in medieval Arabic literary criticism. It is variously understood as being about pilgrimage or love. As is often the case with early Arabic poetry, the verse is attributed to several poets, among them the famous Kuthayyir ʿAzza, or quoted without any attribution. See my discussion of the verse in Chapter 2, under the section "Alteration (*Taghyīr*),"and in Chapter 4, under "What Makes One Metaphor Better than Another?"

Quran.[2] The answer to this question is an aesthetic one and requires an understanding of the criteria employed in classical Arabic theory when evaluating poetic speech.[3]

This leads us to a less obvious question: On what basis did medieval Arabic critics evaluate the *relative* merit of two poetic statements? ʿAbd al-Qāhir al-Jurjānī, the great fifth-/eleventh-century literary theorist, for example, compares the following two verses by two preeminent Abbasid poets. Both verses describe a similar battle scene, observing the shining flashes of metal in the dust of combat.[4]

يزورُ الأعادي في سَماءِ عَجاجَةٍ   أسِنَّتُهُ في جانِبَيها الكَواكِبُ

He visits the enemies in the dust-clouded sky
his spears stars in its midst

~ al-Mutanabbī (d. 354/965)

كأنَّ مُثارَ النَّقْعِ فوْق رُؤوسِنا   وأسْيافَنا ليْلٌ تَهاوَى كَواكِبُهْ

The dust, stirred up over our heads,
and our swords [in its midst] were like a night with shooting stars

~ Bashshār ibn Burd (d. c. 167/784)

Al-Jurjānī found Bashshār ibn Burd's verse superior to al-Mutanabbī's. How and why does he come to this conclusion? To what does he attribute the aesthetic superiority of Bashshār's rendering of the image? Is there a universal aesthetic sensibility that governed his and other critics' judgments of poetic beauty at the time or is it simply a matter of personal taste? In sum, what criteria did medieval Arab thinkers consider when evaluating literary quality?

While Ibn Rushd, the philosopher, and al-Jurjānī, the literary theorist, wrote in different disciplines, in disparate corners of the Islamicate world, and lived a century apart, I believe they shared a common aesthetic outlook drawn from the same literary heritage that shaped their ideas about poetry. In this book, I argue that this aesthetic outlook is defined by

[2] Language can be metered and rhymed but not be poetic, like the famous instructive thousand-line poem (*Alfiyya*) by Ibn al-Mālik (d. 672/1274) on grammar, the purpose of which was to aid the memorization of grammatical rules. At the same time, speech can be poetic even when not written in verse. As a result, the question of poeticity was discussed in prose and in the Quran, as well as in poetry.

[3] As discussed in the Preface, eloquence (*balāgha*) and poeticity both refer to the beauty of speech. That is, discussions of eloquence (*balāgha*) do not assess the persuasive power of speech, rather its beauty.

[4] ʿAbd al-Qāhir al-Jurjānī, *Asrār al-balāgha*, ed. Hellmut Ritter (Istanbul: Government Press, 1954), 159.

a statement's ability to evoke wonder in the listener. By analyzing the explanations they offer for the capacity of speech to arouse wonder, a sophisticated theory of aesthetic experience comes to light. This theory begins to be articulated at the turn of the fifth/eleventh century, marking a major paradigm shift from earlier Arabic criticism and representing an adaptation to the stylistics of *muḥdath* poetry, the "modern" style of the early Abbasid period (late second/eighth and third/ninth centuries).

The application of the concept of aesthetics to medieval Arabic thought is anachronistic. Aesthetics as a branch of philosophy that looks into the nature of art and beauty is a modern concept that developed in Europe in the eighteenth century.[5] However, as José Miguel Puerta Vílchez has shown in his *Aesthetics in Arabic Thought*, there is no paucity of discussions of beauty in the medieval Arabic context.[6] Nevertheless, the goal of this study is not merely to determine what they perceived as beautiful, but to investigate their justifications for this perception as well.[7] As such, our inquiry touches on three central aspects of aesthetics as a philosophical inquiry: aesthetic judgment, aesthetic experience, and the aesthetic object.

5 The term was coined by the German philosopher Alexander Gottlieb Baumgarten in the eighteenth century and then developed by Edmund Burke and Immanuel Kant.

6 José Miguel Puerta Vílchez, *Aesthetics in Arabic Thought: From Pre-Islamic Arabia through al-Andalus* (Leiden: Brill, 2017). Puerta Vílchez discusses aesthetics in various fields, including art, the Quran, and mysticism, as well as literary theory. Another important work on medieval Arabic aesthetics is a work by ʿIzzuddīn Ismāʿīl first published in 1955 entitled *al-Usus al-jamāliyya fī al-naqd al-ʿArabī* (*The Aesthetic Foundations in Arabic Criticism*). His analysis of the purely aesthetic aspects of poetry is limited to sound, on the one hand, and sentence construction, on the other. In both cases, he comes to the conclusion that beauty for the medieval critics lies in meter and proportionate relationships between parts of a sentence (p. 208). While I do not address questions of sound and meter in this book, my conclusions about the beauty of sentence construction are very different, as we will see in Chapter 5.

7 Discussions of beauty (*jamāl* and *ḥusn*) per se in medieval Arabic generally revolved around physical human beauty or spiritual forms of goodness (see S. Kahwaji, *ʿIlm al-Djamāl*, in *EI*[2]; Puerta Vílchez, *Aesthetics*, 66). The concepts of beauty and ugliness are also used in an ethical sense. These nevertheless could serve aesthetic purposes as well. Sarah R. bin Tyeer, for example, analyzes concepts of beauty (*ḥusn*) and ugliness (*qubḥ*) in Arabic prose based on the Quranic idea of justice and injustice (*The Quran and the Aesthetics of Premodern Arabic Prose* (London: Palgrave Macmillan, 2016). For a brief sketch of aesthetics in the medieval Islamicate world, see Doris Behrens-Abouseif, "Aesthetics," in *Encyclopedia of Islam, THREE*, ed. Gudrun Krämer, et al. (Leiden: Brill, 2010). Conceptions of beauty in medieval Arabic culture have been discussed in the realm of art and architecture. See Doris Behrens-Abouseif, *Beauty in Arabic Culture* [Schönheit in der arabischen Kultur] (Princeton, NJ: Markus Wiener Publishers, 1999); and Valerie Gonzalez, *Beauty and Islam: Aesthetics in Islamic Art and Architecture* (London: I.B. Tauris in association with the Institute of Ismaili Studies, 2001).

The three are intertwined in classical Arabic discussions of poetic excellence: The effect of poetic speech on the listener's emotions (aesthetic experience) is regularly cited as the reason for their evaluation of something as beautiful (aesthetic judgment). The causes they cite for this emotional reaction, in turn, identify what aspects of poetic speech (the aesthetic object) render it beautiful (i.e., enable it to move the listener).

Arabic sources do not identify and classify these various aesthetic aspects as such. However, by gauging the kinds of characteristics they typically find commendable in poetry and the reasons they give for this, in addition to their general descriptions of poetic beauty and eloquence, the various pieces of the puzzle begin to expose a picture of classical Arabic literary aesthetics. I contend that this aesthetic is centered on an experience of wonder. In exposing the ways in which they explain the production of wonder through language, an aesthetic theory becomes visible, which identifies the principles that render the aesthetic object (which is poetic/eloquent speech in this case) worthy of being deemed beautiful.

Discussions of the aesthetic in the European context typically revolved around conceptions of the beautiful and the sublime. Before the eighteenth century, sublimity was assumed to be "either complementary to or identical with beauty."[8] In the eighteenth century, however, Edmund Burke and Immanuel Kant distinguished between the two aesthetic qualities, which Alan Singer and Allen Dunn describe as follows: "Beauty is the product of harmony, symmetry and wholeness, while sublimity is generated by the experience of power and magnitude. Beauty is usually credited with producing feelings of pleasure, well-being, and integration with nature and society, while sublimity is said to inspire feelings of empowerment, autonomy, and even isolation."[9] Some studies have identified classical Arabic conceptions of beauty in the sense of "harmony, symmetry, and wholeness."[10] While these characteristics may contribute to the pleasure of poetic speech, I argue that wonder was the aesthetic on which classical Arabic criticism was anchored, at least after the fourth/tenth century. Wonder does not depend on characteristics of harmony, symmetry, and wholeness; neither is it an experience generated by power and magnitude. It is an aesthetic that is altogether different from the European conceptions of beauty and the sublime.

[8] Alan Singer and Allen Dunn, eds., *Literary Aesthetics: A Reader* (Oxford, UK; Malden, MA: Blackwell, 2000), 6.

[9] Ibid., 5. [10] See, for example, Puerta Vílchez, *Aesthetics*; Ismāʿīl, *al-Usus al-jamāliyya*.

Classical Arabic texts abound with statements that credit a verse or a phrase's excellence to its ability to "move the soul." Medieval authors use a wide range of terms to describe this "movement to the soul." Among these, one finds explicit descriptions of the effect of poetic speech as one of wonder (*taʿajjub*), strangeness (*istighrāb*), and finding it novel (*istiṭrāf*).[11] However, medieval authors also describe the poetic effect as one of splendor (*rawnaq*), pleasure (*ladhdha/iltidhadh*), *ṭarab*, which roughly translates as delight resulting particularly from music, or simply as the effect of being moved (*hazza/ihtizāz*), and cheerfulness/liveliness (*aryaḥiyya*), among many others. Despite the wide range of adjectives used to describe the effect of poetic speech, the explanations they give for the arousal of all these various kinds of pleasurable emotions are consistent with those that lead to an effect of wonder. (This is true at least in post-fourth-/tenth-century criticism.) The various descriptions of the effect of poetic and eloquent speech on the listener, therefore, can be collectively characterized by wonder.[12] It is important to note that this inquiry does not simply look

[11] The concept of wonder is usually expressed using the terms *ʿajab* (wonder), *ʿajīb* (wonderful), *taʿjīb* (the evocation of wonder), and *taʿajjub* (wonderment). These terms are often used in conjunction with expressions coming from the root *gh-r-b*, including: *gharāba* (strangeness), *gharīb* (strange/foreign), *ighrāb* (the evocation of strangeness and unfamiliarity), and *istighrāb* (finding something strange). *Istiṭrāf* (finding something strange and novel) and *badīʿ* (innovative, original, and marvelous) also convey a sense of wonder and are also employed. While *taʿajjub*, *istiṭrāf*, and *badīʿ* usually (though not always) have positive connotations, *gharīb* can have both positive and negative connotations depending on the context. It is typically used in a negative sense, for example, when critics discourage the use of strange, unusual, unfamiliar vocabulary. In this case it is often paired with *waḥshī* (uncultivated) (see Khalil Athamina, "*Lafẓ* in Classical Poetry," in *Israel Oriental Studies XI: Studies in Medieval Arabic and Hebrew Poetics*, ed. Sasson Somekh (Leiden: Brill, 1991), 49–50). However, it can also be employed neutrally, as in discussions of "*gharīb al-Qurʾān*" (the strange or uncommon words of the Quran). It is usually clear from the context if the description is intended positively or negatively (for discussions of the distinctions between *ʿajīb* and *gharīb*, see Nasser Rabbat, "*ʿAjāʾib* and *Gharīb*: Artistic Perception in Medieval Arabic Sources," *The Medieval History Journal* 9, no. 1 (2006): 106–7; and Kamal Abu Deeb, *al-Adab al-ʿajāʾibī wa-l-ʿālam al-gharāʾibī fī kitāb al-ʿAẓma wa-fann al-sard al-ʿArabī* (Beirut: Dār al-Sāqī, 2007), introduction). Ultimately, however, the exact employment of the *term* for wonder is not as important for our purposes as the presence of the *concept* of wonder, as I will clarify in the next section. The presence of the term *taʿajjub,* in turn, does not in and of itself signal an aesthetic of wonder.

[12] Wonder does not necessarily have to be pleasurable. Sophia Vasalou has pointed out the feelings of pain and fear that could be associated with wonder in Western Philosophy (Sophia Vasalou, *Wonder: A Grammar* (Albany, NY: State University of New York Press, 2015), ch. 2). However, the effect of beautiful poetry that our medieval authors describe is always something positive and pleasing. I am trying to pinpoint more specifically the nature of this pleasure by narrowing it down to wonder. Therefore, the wonder we will be talking about in the context of the experience of poetry must be pleasurable as well.

for moments where the *term* wonder (*taʿajjub*) is employed in medieval texts when describing poetry. Rather, it seeks to expose the presence of wonder as an aesthetic underlying Arabic criticism. This aesthetic is implicit in the logic of their explanations of poetic beauty and eloquence.

WONDER

Wonder has a complex and variegated global history. One must be cautious in assuming that it is a universal singular human experience. Nevertheless, there seem to be certain basic ingredients that one consistently finds in relation to wonder in terms of its triggers and the ensuing consequences: (a) It is an experience evoked by matters that are judged to be novel, strange, out of the ordinary, and/or inexplicable, which (b) consequently provide the impetus to search for a clarification. Attitudes toward this two-layered experience of wonder have varied across time and place. While it is an emotional experience that can be delightful, it can also involve pain and fear. While it can be associated with knowledge, it can also be associated with ignorance. Wonder can be a positive incentive to contemplate and reflect and advance human knowledge. It could also play out negatively as a desire to control and dominate. In the Islamic Middle Ages, wonder was largely spoken of as a positive experience triggered by the strange and mysterious, which also drove one into an intellectual search to discover the meaning behind such matters. This meaning could be religious, involving the mysteries of God's creations; or, it could be poetic.[13]

Much modern scholarship on wonder has rightly highlighted the negative aspects of wonder, especially with respect to the age of exploration and discovery of the New World and the beginning of Enlightenment. As Caroline Bynum has delineated in her presidential address to the American Historical Association in 1997, modern scholarship has described wonder in three main ways: as the impulse to collect and control, serving as an agent for colonial appropriation;[14] as associated with ignorance that can

[13] The poetic could be religious of course, especially when it comes to mystical poetry, which was an important genre in Arabic poetry. However, I will not be discussing mystical poetry in this book mainly because it was not the focus of classical Arabic literary theory as such. However, this does not preclude the applicability of the aesthetics of wonder to mystical poetry as well.

[14] Early modern European fascination with the marvelous led to the emergence of the museum in the form of the *Wunderkammer* (wonder cabinet). See Joy Kenseth, ed., *The Age of the Marvelous* (Hanover, NH: Hood Museum of Art, 1991), 81–102. See also

be eliminated through rational thought; or as a purely physiological Darwinian startle response to the unfamiliar and potentially dangerous.[15] Bynum, however, calls for reclaiming a more positive view of wonder and reaches back to medieval European understandings of the concept for inspiration. She reminds us that the capacity to wonder at that which cannot be explained is a proof of our humanity and that, rather than being appropriative, wonder can also simply signal one's amazement at the inimitable and the singular. Wonder, therefore, has the potential to be a magical, respectful, and humbling experience of matters that are beyond our grasp, rare, and unfamiliar.[16]

In the medieval Islamic world, wonder also had positive connotations. In fact, marveling at God's creations was a spiritual duty.[17] Everything in the world, from the most despicable to the most marvelous, was considered a sign of God deserving our wonder. This was one of the factors motivating encyclopedic writing as early as al-Jāḥiẓ's (d. 255/868–9) *Kitāb al-ḥayawān* (*Book of the Living*).[18] Encyclopedic descriptions of the world and its creations were also the subject of a number of later works sometimes described collectively by modern scholars as a genre of *ʿajāʾib* (marvels). In one of the most prominent examples of this genre, *ʿAjāʾib al-makhlūqāt wa-gharāʾib al-mawjūdāt* (*The Wonders of Created [Things] and the Oddities of Existing [Things]*), Zakariyyā al-Qazwīnī (d. 682/1283) exclaims that the world is filled with wonders. The only reason we are not constantly in awe is that "wonder fades [...] as a result of familiarity and frequent observation."[19]

Stephen Greenblatt, *Marvelous Possessions: The Wonder of the New World* (Chicago: University of Chicago Press, 1991), who argues that wonder was a useful concept for the early encounters with the New World that allowed for the mediation between the unknown and the known, ultimately serving to control and appropriate the former.

15 Caroline Walker Bynum, "Wonder," *The American Historical Review* 102, no. 1 (1997): 4–5.

16 More recent studies have recuperated the concept of wonder, namely: Philip Fisher, *Wonder, the Rainbow, and the Aesthetics of Rare Experiences* (Cambridge, MA: Harvard University Press, 1998), who defines wonder as "a sudden experience of an extraordinary object that produces delight"; and Vasalou, *Wonder*, who builds on Fisher's definition.

17 For an analysis of wonder in classical Arabic thought, see Fāṭima Mubārak, *al-ʿAjab fī adab al-Jāḥiẓ: Dirāsa sīmyāʾiyya fī Kitāb al-ḥayawān* (Tunis: al-Dār al-Tūnisiyya li-l-Kitāb, 2015), 47–83.

18 See James E. Montgomery, *Al-Jāḥiẓ: In Praise of Books*, ed. Wen-chin Ouyang and Julia Bray, Edinburgh Studies in Classical Arabic Literature (Edinburgh: Edinburgh University Press, 2013). For a study of wonder specifically in al-Jāḥiẓ's *Kitāb al-ḥayawān* (*The Book of the Living*), see also Mubārak, *al-ʿAjab fī adab al-Jāḥiẓ*.

19 Zakariyyā al-Qazwīnī, *ʿAjāʾib al-makhlūqāt wa-gharāʾib al-mawjūdāt*, ed. Fārūq Saʿd (Beirut: Dār al-Āfāq al-Jadīda, 1973), 35. On al-Qazwīnī's monumental encyclopedia of

Wonder is therefore an emotional reaction that is triggered by unfamiliarity and infrequent observation, as we learn from al-Qazwīnī. A near contemporary of his, Ibn Manẓūr (d. 711/1311), the author of one of the most comprehensive medieval Arabic dictionaries, *Lisān al-ʿArab* (*The Tongue of the Arabs*), lists the factors that trigger wonder in his definition of the term as:[20] (a) being in denial of an occurrence due to its infrequency (*qillat iʿtiyadih*); (b) seeing that which is rare (*yaqill mithluh*), unfamiliar (*ghayr maʾlūf*), or unusual (*lā muʿtād*); (c) being in awe of that whose cause is hidden (*khafiya sababuhu*) and unknown (*lam yuʿlam*); or (d) being in awe of something if its stature is great (*ʿaẓuma mawqiʿuhu*) and its cause hidden (*khafiya sababuhu*). Wonder is therefore defined as the reaction of awe and disbelief one experiences as a result of seeing something unexpected, rare, unfamiliar, unusual, mysterious, magnificent, or obscure whose cause is unknown. In short, wonder is an emotional reaction triggered by the strange and inexplicable.

Yet, wonder is also a cognitive experience. The endeavor to document the marvels of the world in the Arabic *ʿajāʾib* genre was not motivated by a desire to give the reader the thrill of witnessing the strange and the rare, but it was a call to contemplate God's creations. Ultimately, the disparate features listed by Ibn Manẓūr as triggers of wonder represent only part of the story. Wonder is an intellectual search for an explanation of the extraordinary and for the hidden through what is visible, as Fāṭima Mubārak has argued.[21] God's creations are things medieval authors like Zakariyyā

the world, see Syrinx von Hees, *Enzyklopädie als Spiegel des Weltbildes: Qazwinis Wunder der Schöpfung: Eine Naturkunde des 13. Jahrhunderts* (Wiesbaden: Harrassowitz, 2002). See also her discussion of the significance of *ʿajāʾib* in classical Arabic literature and of the shortcomings of classifying it as a genre in "The Astonishing: A Critique and Re-reading of *ʿAjāʾib* Literature," *Middle Eastern Literatures* 8, no. 2 (2005). For the role of wonder in *ʿajāʾib* manuscripts, see Persis Berlekamp, *Wonder, Image, and Cosmos in Medieval Islam* (New Haven, CT: Yale University Press, 2011). For a discussion of *ʿajaʾib* discourse in descriptive geography in the medieval period, see Travis Zadeh, *Mapping Frontiers across Medieval Islam: Translation, Geography, and the ʿAbbāsid Empire* (London; New York: I.B. Tauris, 2011). On the concept of wonder in al-Qazwīnī's *Wonders of Creation*, see also Zadeh's article "The Wiles of Creation: Philosophy, Fiction, and the *ʿAjāʾib* Tradition," *Middle Eastern Literatures* 13, no. 1 (April 2010). More generally, on the rise of encyclopedism in the Islamic world, see Elias Muhanna, *The World in a Book: al-Nuwayri and the Islamic Encyclopedic Tradition* (Princeton, NJ: Princeton University Press, 2018).

20 Ibn Manẓūr, *Lisān al-ʿArab* (Beirut: Dār Ṣādir, 1955), s.v. *ʿ-j-b*. This definition is repeated in a similar fashion in the other major medieval Arabic dictionaries, as well as in *ʿajāʾib* literature.

21 Mubārak, *al-ʿAjab fī adab al-Jāḥiẓ*, 37–8. Mubārak distinguishes between the marvelous as a genre that seeks to astound and instill awe and the intellectual engagement with these marvels through contemplation found in classical Arabic texts (ibid., 75).

al-Qazwīnī and al-Jāḥiẓ believed we ought to wonder at in order to contemplate God and his munificence. Even those man-made marvels of past civilizations left behind in ruins were wonders to medieval Islamic geographers and travelers to be reflected upon and learned from.[22]

"Wonder," as John Llewelyn explains, "is one of those wonderful words that face in opposite directions at one and the same time."[23] While it results from a state of ignorance, it is "not any absence of knowledge, but an ignorance that challenges us to dispel it [. . .]."[24] It is due to wonder, after all, that Man began to philosophize, as Aristotle tells us.[25] The elimination of this ignorance through discovery is also part of the experience of wonder. Linking wonder to learning, Fisher describes this moment of discovery as "the moment when the puzzling snaps into sharp focus and is grasped with pleasure."[26] The strange, unusual, and extraordinary, the unexpected, the inexplicable and puzzling, and the unfamiliar, and the rare all entail a kind of ignorance that leads us to pause, examine, and contemplate in order to grasp and bring to light the unusual or unclear meaning. While ignorance might be the impetus for wonder initially, it is the eventual discovery of the meaning and its clarification that also evokes wonder. As such, wonder is an emotional experience that is highly cognitive in nature.

The literary arts can also have the capacity to evoke wonder. In this case, the conditions that lead to wonder in nature are reproduced through language. Characteristics such as strangeness, unexpectedness, and obscurity in language can evoke wonder in the listener. Significantly, what renders it wonder in the full sense, however, (rather than mere surprise or shock and awe) is the consequent search for and discovery of the meaning hidden behind the strange, unexpected, and obscure. What these conditions look like in language, according to classical Arabic literary theory, and how they lead to an experience of discovery is the subject of this study.[27]

[22] As Elliott Colla has argued, medieval geographers saw value in marveling at ruins of past civilizations, such as the pyramids, not for their greatness, but as signs of the hubris of those who built them (*Conflicted Antiquities: Egyptology, Egyptomania, Egyptian Modernity* (Durham; London: Duke University Press, 2007), 72–120).

[23] John Llewelyn, "On the Saying that Philosophy Begins in Thaumazein," *Afterall: A Journal of Art, Context, and Inquiry* 4 (2001): 48.

[24] Ibid., 51. [25] Aristotle, *Metaphysics*, 982b13–14.

[26] Fisher, *Wonder, the Rainbow, and the Aesthetics of Rare Experiences*, 7. Fisher explains that "wonder and learning are tied by three things: by suddenness, by the moment of first seeing, and by the visual presence of the whole state or object" (ibid., 21).

[27] One can draw parallels between the literary arts and the visual arts, where wonder has also been the subject of analysis in scholarship on medieval Islamic art. Matthew D. Saba, for example, has argued that the evolution of lusterware during the Abbasid period was also

The role of wonder and strangeness in classical Arabic literature has received some attention in modern scholarship as a narrative technique in the tales of the *Thousand and One Nights* and anecdotal literature.[28] The place of wonder in classical Arabic literary theory, however, remains largely overlooked. While its significance in the philosophical understanding of the function of poetry is acknowledged,[29] its role in nonphilosophical literary theory, instead, has been at best relegated to being of "an anecdotal nature," describing the "reaction of the listener to a poem."[30] As I hope to show, the triggers of wonder coupled with the ensuing experience of discovery form the basis of a sophisticated aesthetic theory evident in medieval Arabic explanations of the reaction poetic speech produces in the listener.

It is important to note some caveats here. This study is not an inquiry into the artificial expression of wonder in poetry, which the Arabic critical tradition identified as a type of rhetorical figure known as *taʿajjub*

driven by the desire to produce wonder in the viewer. In an artistic craft like lusterware, Saba argues that this effect is achieved through "surface effects like reflection, sheen, and iridescence," as well as "the use of complex, difficult-to-decipher motifs, the creation of a sense of motion, and the juxtaposition of dissimilar patterns, textures, and forms" (Matthew D. Saba, "Abbasid Lusterware and the Aesthetics of *ʿAjab*," *Muqarnas* 29 (2012): 206). He also draws astute parallels between this development in lusterware and the contemporaneous evolution of *badīʿ* in *muḥdath* poetry (ibid., 202–3). The theories that subsequently develop in the Arabic critical tradition to describe this aesthetic of wonder in language is what this book tries to uncover.

28 Roy Mottahedeh has examined the role of wonder as a narrative technique in the *Thousand and One Nights* where he relates it to irony ("*ʿAjāʾib* in *The Thousand and One Nights*," in *The Thousand and One Nights in Arabic Literature and Society*, ed. Richard C. Hovannisian and Georges Sabagh (Cambridge, New York: Cambridge University Press, 1997)). Abdelfattah Kilito also discusses the concept of strangeness in a variety of classical Arabic literary genres in *al-Adab wa-l-gharāba: Dirāsāt bunyawiyya fī al-adab al-ʿArabī* (Beirut: Dār al-Ṭalīʿa, 1983), including its treatment by the literary theorist ʿAbd al-Qāhir al-Jurjānī (ibid., 62–75).

29 The place of wonder in the philosophical discussions of Aristotle's *Poetics* has been considered by some scholars, though in passing: Salim Kemal discusses the place of wonder in Ibn Sīnā's treatment of the poetic syllogism in Salim Kemal, "Aristotle's *Poetics*, the Poetic Syllogism, and Philosophical Truth in Averroes's Commentary," *The Journal of Value Inquiry* 35 (2001): 169–76. See also Deborah L. Black, "Aesthetics in Islamic Philosophy," in *Routledge Encyclopedia of Philosophy*, vol. 1, ed. Edward Craig (London and New York: Routledge, 1998), 1:75–9. More recently, the role of wonder in Naṣīr al-Dīn al-Ṭūsī's Persian commentary on the *Poetics* has also been discussed in Justine Landau, "Naṣīr al-Dīn Ṭūsī and Poetic Imagination in the Arabic and Persian Philosophical Tradition," in *Metaphor and Imagery in Persian Poetry*, ed. Ali Asghar Seyed-Gohrab (Leiden; Boston: Brill, 2012).

30 Wolfhart Heinrichs, "Taʿjīb," in *Encyclopedia of Arabic Literature*, ed. Julie Scott Meisami and Paul Starkey (London: Routledge, 1998).

(amazement).[31] Rather, I focus on wonder as an effect of poetic speech on the listener, whether it happens by means of the literary figure of *taʿajjub* or otherwise. Furthermore, I would also like to emphasize that this study is not an inquiry into medieval discussions of the nature of wonder itself. Rather, it is an inquiry into the nature of the aesthetic experience resulting from poetic speech. This aesthetic experience, it is worth reiterating, is not described exclusively using the word for wonder (*taʿajjub*). Rather, I use wonder as an umbrella term to incorporate a variety of adjectives medieval literary theorists used to describe the listener's experience of poetic speech. It is a notion implicit in their writings. This study brings it to light by showing that the aspects of poetic speech to which they attribute poetic excellence involve a process that can be described as an experience of wonder, as I have described it here. That is, poetic speech is described in classical Arabic texts as having the capacity to arouse intellectual curiosity through strangeness, unexpectedness, or obscuration, which leads the listener to reflect and search for the meaning, allowing him to go through an experience of discovery.

Furthermore, the focus of this study is not the expression of awe and admiration at a poet's skill and ability. Rather, it is the production of an experience of wonder through language; that is, an experience of having one's curiosity aroused because of some strangeness (or unexpectedness or unclarity) in the language that leads to one's search for the meaning. While this leads to a value judgment of a work that calls for its admiration, the experience of wonder as an aesthetic experience results from the impetus to contemplate and the ensuing discovery that the poetic language accomplishes in the listener through its particular formulation. Wonder may also result from one's admiration of the poet's ability to produce such language. This wonder, however, is external to the poetic process itself and can be the result of nonpoetic factors, such as the poet's status and one's expectations in a particular context.

For example, one of the earliest elaborations on the emotional impact of speech on the listener is given by al-Jāḥiẓ in his work on eloquence entitled *al-Bayān wa-l-tabyīn* (*Elucidation and Exposition*). Al-Jāḥiẓ relates that Sahl ibn Hārūn (a literary personality often cited by him) said that if two

[31] The medieval Arabic (and Persian) literary figure known as "wonderment" (*taʿajjub*) is sometimes conflated with the poetic effect of evoking wonder (*taʿjīb*) (see, for example, Geert Jan van Gelder, *Taʿadjdjub*, in *EI*^{2}; and Landau, "Naṣīr al-Dīn Ṭūsī," 53n105). *Taʿajjub*, as a rhetorical (*badīʿ*) figure, amounts to a poet's expression of feigned amazement at a make-believe image (see my discussion of the figure in Chapter 1, as well as a technique of reinforcement of metaphor in Chapter 4).

people spoke equally as eloquently, but one donned elegant expensive clothing and the other was in rags, people would be much more in awe of the speech of the one in rags because it is unexpected:

> the beauty of his speech would double in their hearts and increase in their eyes. This is because that which is outside of its element is stranger. The stranger something is, the further it is from one's imagination. The further it is from the imagination, the more novel (*aṭraf*) it seems. The more novel something is, the more wonderful (*aʿjab*) it is. The more wonder-evoking, the more eloquent/innovative (*abdaʿ*) it is. [. . .] People are inclined to exalt the strange and find novel the far-fetched [. . .][32]

Although al-Jāḥiẓ identifies several elements that explain the arousal of wonder, namely, the unexpected, the strange, the novel, and the far-fetched, he places these factors outside the realm of speech itself. We will be looking at how these elements can be created *within* speech. Before we embark on this journey, let me first give a brief sketch of classical Arabic literary theory, its main strands and actors, the literary canon that was subject to their criticism, and the literary units that were subject to their analysis.

CLASSICAL ARABIC LITERARY THEORY

Wonder was not always a defining criterion of poetic beauty in classical Arabic literary theory. The first two centuries of criticism primarily evaluated poetry based on its truthfulness and naturalness. I describe this early approach as the "old school of criticism." This framework began to be replaced with an aesthetic of wonder around the turn of the fifth/eleventh century. This "new school of criticism" was spearheaded by ʿAbd al-Qāhir al-Jurjānī (d. 471/1078 or 474/1081). His theories formed the basis of what al-Sakkākī (d. 626/1229) and al-Khaṭīb al-Qazwīnī (d. 739/1338) standardized as a "science of eloquence" (*ʿilm al-balāgha*) in the seventh/thirteenth and eighth/fourteenth centuries. This new school of criticism was inspired by purely poetic concerns, but was also concerned with the discussions of eloquence more generally, the miraculousness of the Quran, and was influenced by Aristotelian Arabic poetics. The treatment of Aristotle's *Poetics* in Arabic philosophy, in turn, also exhibited the same aesthetic of wonder.

[32] al-Jāḥiẓ, *al-Bayān wa-l-tabyīn*, ed. ʿAbd al-Salām Hārūn, 7th ed., 4 vols. (Cairo: Maktabat al-Khānjī, 1998), 1:89–90.

One can identify four different clusters of critical texts that developed in the third/ninth and fourth/tenth centuries, each with its own foci and motivated by its own questions: (1) Poetic criticism was concerned with the debates about the new style of poetry that developed in the early Abbasid period and its use of rhetorical figures (*badīʿ*). (2) Discussions of Aristotle's *Poetics*, which took place in philosophy, were concerned with making sense of poetry as part of logic. Their discussions focused primarily on simile and metaphor. (3) Works on eloquence more generally, driven by the question of *bayān* (elucidation) or how meaning is made manifest, incorporated discussions of figurative expressions and implicit meaning. Their approach to such rhetorical figures as simile, metaphor, and metonymy was distinct from that of poetic criticism. (4) Works concerned with showing the miraculousness of the Quran, in turn, added to the discussion the effect of sentence construction (*naẓm*) on eloquence.

In the fifth/eleventh century, ʿAbd al-Qāhir al-Jurjānī took elements from each of these approaches in his two monumental works, *Asrār al-balāgha* (*The Secrets of Eloquence*) and *Dalāʾil al-iʿjāz* (*The Signs of the Inimitability [of the Quran]*). These two works went on to form the basis of what became a formal discipline known as the "science of eloquence" (*ʿilm al-balāgha*). Its three branches cover the following aspects of language: (i) The science of meanings (*ʿilm al-maʿānī*) focuses on sentence construction and the impact of syntactical choices on the meaning, (ii) the science of elucidation (*ʿilm al-bayān*) focuses on figures that signify their meaning indirectly, including metaphor and metonymy, as well as simile; (iii) the science of rhetorical figures (*ʿilm al-badīʿ*) focuses on rhetorical figures.

The philosophical engagement with Aristotle's *Poetics*, which developed its own unique vocabulary to describe poeticity, also betrays an underlying aesthetic of wonder. Rather than representing unrelated disciplines, Aristotelian Arabic poetics and *balāgha* together reflect what we could describe as a "new school of criticism." Despite their different approaches, they both develop theories of poeticity and eloquence based on an aesthetic of wonder.

Poetic Criticism and Badīʿ

The use of Arabic as a literary language dates back to pre-Islamic Arabia, when by the sixth century CE, a well-established poetic form was already in place.[33] After the rise of Islam and the expansion of the Islamic Empire, pre-Islamic poetry became an important lexical and grammatical resource for the new empire that very quickly incorporated large areas of non-Arabic-speaking territories. This primarily oral pre-Islamic tradition began to be collected and recorded systematically in the second/eighth century, as a writerly culture began to develop.[34] While these anthologies do not represent treatises on poetics per se, they do fashion a classical canon, which came to constitute the yardstick by which poetry was evaluated.[35] Moreover, they represent some of the earliest recorded statements in Arabic about poetry.

As poetry connoisseurs were collecting old poetry, a new style of poetry started to develop. With the rise of the Abbasid Empire in Iraq in the mid-second/-eighth century, poets like Bashshār ibn Burd (d. c. 167/784) and Abū Nuwās (d. c. 198/813) began to innovate in their poetic style. This new style, known as *muḥdath* (modern) poetry, poked fun at and reinvented old Arabian poetic conventions, and used more ornate language, rhetorical figures, and imagery. It was not to the liking of everyone, however, and sparked a debate between those who preferred the classical style of the "ancients" and those who defended the new style of the "moderns." The star poets of the third/ninth century, al-Buḥturī (d. 284/897) and Abū Tammām (d. c. 232/845), engendered further debate about the comparative merits of the old and new as the two poets exemplified a more classical style and a more modern one respectively. The controversy culminated with the rise of another star poet in the fourth/tenth century, al-Mutanabbī (d. 354/965), whose poetry provided fodder for much discussion.

33 The dating of this early poetry is difficult to determine with certainty since it was initially transmitted orally and mostly documented in writing only after the rise of Islam. For a sketch of Arabic literature, its development, and genres, from the fifth to the twentieth century, see Pierre J. Cachia, "Arabic Literature," in *Encyclopaedia of Islam, THREE*. Some of the earliest statements about poetic quality date back to these pre-Islamic times when poets would compete and be judged at the ʿUkāẓ market near Mecca.

34 For a discussion of the development of prose writing and book production in early Islam, see Gregor Schoeler, *The Genesis of Literature in Islam: From the Aural to the Read*, ed. and trans. Shawkat M. Toorawa, revised ed. (Edinburgh: Edinburgh University Press, 2009).

35 The designation of the *muʿallaqāt* as the select, best pre-Islamic odes seems to have taken place around the mid-second/-eighth century (see Andras Hamori, "Anthologies, Arabic Literature (Pre-Mongol Period)," in *Encyclopaedia of Islam, THREE*). Among the earliest extant anthologies are the well-known *al-Mufaḍḍaliyyāt* and *al-Aṣmaʿiyyāt*, which date to the second/eighth and perhaps early third/ninth century (*al-Mufaḍḍaliyyāt*, ed. Aḥmad Muḥammad Shākir and ʿAbd al-Salām Muḥammad Hārūn (Cairo: Dār al-Maʿārif, 1963); al-Aṣmaʿī, *al-Aṣmaʿiyyāt*, ed. Aḥmad Muḥammad Shākir and ʿAbd al-Salām Hārūn (Cairo: Dār al-Maʿārif, 1963)).

This tension between the old and the new was a fruitful one in terms of the development of critical ideas, as medieval scholars began to articulate more elaborately their views on poetic ideals. Because one of the main features of the new style of poetry was a more deliberate use of rhetorical figures, one of the first major treatises written on poetics dealt precisely with these literary devices. Written in 274/887, this treatise by Ibn al-Muʿtazz, entitled *Kitāb al-badīʿ* (*The Book of Rhetorical Figures*), identified these rhetorical figures as "innovations" (*badīʿ*).[36] This work provided for the first time a taxonomy of such figures and it established *badīʿ* figures as a unit of analysis. This initial attempt included seventeen figures, which in later works continued to increase in number.[37] These include figures familiar to the Western context such as metaphor, paronomasia, antithesis, and simile, as well as less familiar ones, such as "affirming praise with what resembles rebuke" (*taʾkīd al-madḥ bimā yushbih al-dhamm*), "feigned ignorance" (*tajāhul al-ʿārif*), and having the end of a verse echo the beginning (*radd al-ʿajuz ʿalā al-ṣadr*).[38]

The debate about the new style continued in the fourth/tenth century with a major treatise written by Abū al-Qāsim al-Āmidī (d. 370/980 or 371/981) dedicated to the comparison of the two star poets of the preceding century, entitled *al-Muwāzana bayn shiʿr Abī Tammām wa-l-Buḥturī* (*The Weighing of the Poetry of Abū Tammām and al-Buḥturī*). This was followed by another major treatise dedicated to al-Mutanabbī by al-Qāḍī al-Jurjānī (d. 392/1002), entitled *al-Wasāṭa bayn al-Mutanabbī wa-khuṣūmih* (*The Mediation between al-Mutanabbī and his Opponents*). Other noteworthy works on literary criticism from the fourth/tenth

[36] Ibn al-Muʿtazz, a poet who wrote in the style of the "moderns" himself, mentions the date of writing his book in his *Kitāb al-badīʿ*, ed. Ignatius Kratchkovsky, 3rd ed. (Beirut: Dār al-Masīra, 1982), 58.

[37] The number seventeen is taken from Ibn Abī al-Iṣbaʿ's (d. 654/1256) assessment, although one could arrive at a different number depending on how one counts (Ibn Abī al-Iṣbaʿ, *Taḥrīr al-taḥbīr fī ṣināʿat al-shiʿr*, ed. Ḥifnī Muḥammad Sharaf (Cairo: al-Majlis al-Aʿlā li-l-Shuʾūn al-ʿArabiyya, Lajnat Iḥyāʾ al-Turāth al-Islāmī, 1963), 83–5). The list continues to expand as authors after Ibn al-Muʿtazz continue to identify new ones or more specific ones. Ibn Abī al-Iṣbaʿ himself identifies up to 125 rhetorical figures (ibid., 94).

[38] Ibn al-Muʿtazz established five main *badīʿ* figures and classified the rest under "beautifying" elements. This distinction was not upheld by later authors, who consider them all "*badīʿ*" (see ibid., 83–5). See also Seeger Adrianus Bonebakker, "Ibn Abi'l-Iṣbaʿ's Text of the *Kitāb al-badīʿ* of Ibn al-Muʿtazz," *Israel Oriental Studies* 2 (1972); Seeger Adrianus Bonebakker, "Reflections on the *Kitāb al-badīʿ* of Ibn al-Muʿtazz," in *Atti del terzo congresso di studi arabi e islamici (Ravello, 1966)* (Naples: Istituto Universitario Orientale, 1967). For an expanded list of the standard Arabic rhetorical figures with definitions in English, see Wolfhart Heinrichs, "Rhetorical Figures," in *Encyclopedia of Arabic Literature*, ed. Julie Scott Meisami and Paul Starkey (London; New York: Routledge, 1998).

century include Ibn Ṭabāṭabā's (d. 322/934) *ʿIyār al-shiʿr* (*The Standard of Poetry*) and Qudāma ibn Jaʿfar's (d. 337/948; other earlier dates also reported) *Naqd al-shiʿr* (*The Assaying of Poetry*). Whether directly or not, the concern with the old and new styles is evident in many of the critical works of this period.

The main criteria on which this early criticism based its judgment of poetry were its truthfulness and naturalness. The degree of a poet's employment of rhetorical figures was one of the main reasons critics deemed poetry "natural" or "artificial." How far these rhetorical figures took the poetry away from literal accuracy, whether through hyperbole or fantastic imagery, determined the poetry's "truthfulness" or "falsehood." Caught up in the debate about *muḥdath* poetry, therefore, critics were either proponents of truthfulness and naturalness, characteristics exemplified by the pre-Islamic "ancient" poets (*al-mutaqaddimūn*), or proponents of falsehood and mannerism, typified in the *badīʿ*-filled style of the new poets (*al-muḥdathūn*). Despite difference in opinion, the underlying framework that both sides relied on was essentially a classical aesthetic of truthfulness and naturalness. The ideals of this classical aesthetic informed what came to be known as the "the fundaments of poetry" (*ʿamūd al-shiʿr*), which were most explicitly formulated by al-Marzūqī (d. 421/1030) in the introduction to his commentary on Abū Tammām's well-known anthology of early Arabic poetry called *al-Ḥamāsa* (*Bravery*).[39] No sooner did al-Marzūqī outline these fundaments than a new aesthetic framework began to take hold. As we will see in Chapter 1, "Wonder: A New Paradigm," instead of truth and naturalness, this "new school of criticism" based its evaluation of poetic speech on the ability of *badīʿ* figures to evoke wonder in the listener.

Aristotelian Arabic Poetics

Another arena that witnessed discussions about the poetic presented itself in philosophy with the translation of Aristotle's *Poetics* in the third/ninth century. Philosophers of the Islamicate world were interested in the work from the perspective of logic, however. This was because they understood Aristotle's *Poetics* and *Rhetoric* as belonging to the logical sciences, a classification they inherited from late antiquity. Like their predecessors writing commentaries on the Aristotelian corpus in Greek and Syriac,

[39] A thematically based anthology of poetry, starting with the theme of "bravery" (*ḥamāsa* – hence the title) collected by Abū Tammām.

philosophers writing in Arabic tried to explain poetry and rhetoric as forms of syllogistic reasoning. As a result, they had their own unique concerns (and vocabulary) when it came to describing what renders speech poetic. Nevertheless, as we will see in Chapter 2, "Wonder in Aristotelian Arabic Poetics," their solution to the problem of fitting poetic speech into the logical sciences echoes developments in Arabic literary criticism at the time. Early solutions to the philosophical problem distinguished poetic speech from other forms of syllogistic reasoning based on a truth scale in which the poetic was defined by its falsehood, paralleling debates in the old school of criticism that evaluated poetry based on its truthfulness or falsehood. However, like in the nonphilosophical critical tradition, this framework was soon replaced by another, which defined the poetic by its ability to evoke wonder.

The earliest commentaries on the *Poetics* dating from the third/ninth century have not survived.[40] Some short commentaries by Abū Naṣr al-Fārābī (d. 339/950, known as Alfarabius or Avennasar in the medieval Latin West) give us a glimpse of early attempts to describe poetry from the point of view of logic. However, the discussion of the *Poetics* reached a new height with Ibn Sīnā (Avicenna, d. 428/1037) in the early fifth/eleventh century and Ibn Rushd (Averroes, d. 595/1198), a century later. A strand of philosophical literary theory continued to develop in the centuries that followed in the West of the Islamicate world with the Andalusian Ḥāzim al-Qarṭājannī (d. 684/1285) and the Moroccan al-Sijilmāsī (d. after 704/1304) in the seventh/thirteenth and eighth/fourteenth centuries respectively.

The philosophical strand did have its own idiosyncratic way of describing poetic speech. Nevertheless, their take on Greek poetics was very much influenced by the conventions and concerns of Arabic poetry and poetics. While Aristotle primarily discusses the dramatic genres of tragedy and comedy, the Arab philosophers base their analysis on Arabic poetry. Instead of being concerned with the literary units that Aristotle discusses in his *Poetics* such as a plot and characters, Aristotelian Arabic poetics focused on simile and metaphor, even applying the fundamental Aristotelian concept of mimesis to these figures, as we will see in Chapter 2.

[40] The philosopher al-Kindī (d. after 256/870) is said to have written commentaries on Aristotle's *Poetics*, but they have not survived (Muḥammad ibn Isḥāq Ibn al-Nadīm, *Kitāb al-fihrist*, ed. Muḥammad Riḍā Tajaddud (Tehran: Amīr Kabīr, 1987), 310).

Eloquence and Bayān *(Elucidation)*

Alongside poetic criticism and philosophy, there was also a concern with eloquence more broadly: in poetry, but also in prose, oratory, and the Quran. One of the earliest works to take such a broad view of eloquence and communication was al-Jāḥiẓ's *al-Bayān wa-l-tabyīn* (*Elucidation and Exposition*). His concern lay in the capacity of all sorts of matters to make something manifest. *Bayān* (lit. elucidation) thus came to refer to the various ways in which meaning is conveyed whether through speech, writing, gesturing, counting, or God's creations. This line of thinking continued in the fourth/tenth century, in a slightly modified way, with Isḥāq ibn Wahb (d. after 335/946–7) in his *Kitāb al-burhān fī wujūh al-bayān* (*The Book of the Demonstration of the Aspects of Bayān*).[41] Eventually, this *bayān* focus narrowed to language in works such as *Kitāb al-ṣināʿatayn: al-kitāba wa-l-shiʿr* (*The Book of Two Arts: [Prose] Writing and Poetry*) by Abū Hilāl al-ʿAskarī (d. after 395/1005), who also saw himself as building on al-Jāḥiẓ's work on *bayān*.[42]

What was significant about the *bayān* approach to language was that it highlighted the communicative aspects of certain rhetorical figures, which were otherwise treated as ornamental in poetic criticism. By addressing the difference between literal and figurative forms of expression, figures like metaphor were approached from the perspective of the semiotic processes they entail, as we will see in Chapter 4, "Metaphor and the Aesthetics of the Sign." Simile also came to be treated from the angle of how it makes meaning manifest, as we will see in Chapter 3, "Discovery in *Bayān*." This discussion is most elaborately forged by ʿAbd al-Qāhir al-Jurjānī and later developed in the science of eloquence by al-Sakkākī and al-Khaṭīb al-Qazwīnī. *Bayān* works were also concerned with how sentence construction influences the communication of meaning. This became one of the focuses of works on the miraculousness of the Quran.

[41] Isḥāq ibn Wahb's book was mistakenly attributed to Qudāma ibn Jaʿfar and published as the latter's work under the title *Naqd al-nathr* (Qudāma ibn Jaʿfar, *Naqd al-nathr*, ed. Taha Hussein and ʿAbd al-Ḥamīd al-ʿAbbādī (Cairo: Dār al-Kutub al-Miṣriyya, 1933)). New accurate editions have since been published, including Isḥāq ibn Wahb, *al-Burhān fī wujūh al-bayān*, ed. Aḥmad Maṭlūb and Khadīja al-Ḥadīthī (Baghdad: Maṭbaʿat al-ʿĀnī, 1967).

[42] See Abū Hilāl al-ʿAskarī, *Kitāb al-ṣināʿatayn*, ed. ʿAlī Muḥammad al-Bijāwī and Muḥammad Abū al-Faḍl Ibrāhīm (Cairo: ʿĪsā al-Bābī al-Ḥalabī, 1952), 5.

The Miracle of the Quran

The Quran was another major catalyst of critical discussions of eloquence. The Quran was the miracle that proved Muhammad's prophethood. The proof of its miraculousness (*iʿjāz*) came to be understood as lying primarily in the inimitability of its eloquence. By the third/ninth century, arguments for its inimitability began to be articulated. The earliest treatises dedicated to the topic that have survived, however, date from the fourth/tenth century and were written by religious scholars, namely, al-Rummānī (d. 384/994), al-Khaṭṭābī (d. 386/996 or 388/998), and al-Bāqillānī (d. 403/1013). They nevertheless were also interested in discussing poetry seeing that it represented the highest degree of eloquence attainable by humans, in contrast with the eloquence of the Quran, which is humanly unattainable.

Unsurprisingly, early works on the inimitability of the Quran were influenced by the poetic criticism that was vibrant at the time. The literary units they analyzed included *badīʿ* figures. However, they were not concerned with the poetic debates of the period (e.g., about *muḥdath* poetry). Rather, their objective was to show the uniqueness of the Quranic text. This led to the incorporation of literary aspects that were largely ignored in the poetic context, namely, discussions of composition and sentence structure (*naẓm*). These were influenced more by the equally vibrant discussions of grammar that were taking place at the time as well. As we will see in Chapter 5, "*Naẓm*, Wonder, and the Inimitability of the Quran," the way a sentence is constructed and the way it conveys a given idea or meaning became the central aspect in which they located the inimitability of the Quran.

*Al-Jurjānī and the Science of Eloquence (*Balāgha*)*

Influence from all the preceding approaches to eloquence and poeticity is evident in the works of ʿAbd al-Qāhir al-Jurjānī. His comprehensive theory addresses *badīʿ* and the question of truth and falsehood in poetry in his *Asrār al-balāgha*, which also contains an extensive analysis of simile, as well as metaphor and figurative speech. In *Dalāʾil al-iʿjāz*, he develops a theory of sentence construction (*naẓm*), as well as indirect signification in metaphor (*istiʿāra*) and metonymy (*kināya*). It took several attempts at reorganizing al-Jurjānī's ideas before its different components became compartmentalized into the three branches of the science of eloquence (*balāgha*). The first notable attempt was by the renowned theologian Fakhr al-Dīn al-Rāzī (d. 606/1209) in his *Nihāyat al-ījāz fī dirāyat al-iʿjāz* (*The Utmost Brevity in Understanding Inimitability*). Though the field was very much influenced by Fakhr al-Dīn al-Rāzī, it was al-Sakkākī in his *Miftāḥ al-ʿulūm* (*The Key to the Sciences*) who laid the foundation of *ʿilm al-balāgha*. The part on the "science of eloquence" (*ʿilm al-balāgha*) in the *Miftāḥ* inspired many commentaries, most notably that of the preacher (*khaṭīb*) of Damascus, Jalāl al-Dīn al-Qazwīnī, in his *Talkhīṣ al-Miftāḥ* (*A Resumé of the Miftāḥ*) and its expanded version, *al-Īḍāḥ fī ʿulūm al-balāgha* (*The Clarification of the Sciences of Eloquence*).[43]

Al-Sakkākī divides the "science of eloquence" into two subfields: (1) the science of meanings (*ʿilm al-maʿānī*), which focuses on the conveying of meaning through syntax and sentence construction, and (2) the science of *bayān*, which focuses on simile, figurative expressions (including metaphor), and metonymy.[44] Al-Sakkākī also includes a relatively brief overview of literary figures (*badīʿ*), although he does not establish it as a "science." Al-Khaṭīb al-Qazwīnī more clearly defines the boundaries between the two sciences of *bayān* and *maʿānī* and establishes the study of rhetorical figures as the third subfield of the science of eloquence, greatly expanding the last. Al-Khaṭīb al-Qazwīnī's organization leaves us with what became the standard tripartite division of the science of *balāgha* as consisting of: *ʿilm al-maʿānī* (the science of meanings), *ʿilm al-bayān* (the science of elucidation), and *ʿilm al-badīʿ* (the science of rhetorical figures).[45]

These works were not the only word on the topic and certainly not the last. Al-Jurjānī's influence is visible in numerous other works starting from the sixth/twelfth century, including exegetical works such as al-Zamakhsharī's

[43] For a list and discussion of the commentaries on al-Sakkākī's *Miftāḥ*, see William Smyth, "Controversy in a Tradition of Commentary: The Academic Legacy of al-Sakkākī's *Miftāḥ al-ʿulūm*," *Journal of the American Oriental Society* 112, no. 4 (1992); Aḥmad Maṭlūb, *al-Qazwīnī wa-shurūḥ al-talkhīṣ* (Baghdad: Maktabat al-Nahḍa, 1967); and Rudolf Sellheim, *Materialien zur arabischen Literaturgeschichte*, 2 vols. (Wiesbaden: Franz Steiner, 1976–87), 1:299–334 and 2:60–84.

[44] The borderline between the two sciences is still not absolutely clear in al-Sakkākī's text. He seems to consider *ʿilm al-bayān* a branch of *ʿilm al-maʿānī* (see Benedikt Reinert, *al-Maʿānī wa'l-bayān*, in *EI*^{2}).

[45] Al-Khaṭīb al-Qazwīnī's near contemporary Badr al-Dīn ibn Mālik (d. 686/1287) was the first to explicitly present *ʿilm al-balāgha* in this tripartite formulation in *al-Miṣbāh fī al-maʿānī wa-l-bayān wa-l-badīʿ*, ed. Ḥusnī ʿAbd al-Jalīl Yūsuf (Cairo: Maktabat al-Ādāb, 1989). Al-Khaṭīb al-Qazwīnī's rendition of the science, however, became the most popular and standard configuration (see William Smyth, "The Canonical Formulation of *ʿIlm al-Balāghah* and al-Sakkākī's *Miftāḥ al-ʿUlūm*," *Der Islam* 72 (1995): 8).

al-Kashshāf and al-Muṭarrizī's commentary on al-Ḥarīrī's *Maqāmāt*.[46] Moreover, while al-Sakkākī and al-Khaṭīb al-Qazwīnī's configuration of *balāgha* became popular, it was not adopted by all their successors. Different systems of organizing discussions on eloquence and poeticity and with different scopes were also forged.[47] An important example includes Ḍiyā' al-Dīn Ibn al-Athīr's (d. 637/1239) al-*Mathal al-sā'ir fī adab al-kātib wa-l-shā'ir* (*The Current Model on the Discipline of the Scribe and the Poet*), which itself was influenced by a contemporary of al-Jurjānī's, Ibn Sinān al-Khafājī (d. 466/1074) in his *Sirr al-faṣāḥa* (*The Secret of Articulateness*).[48]

However, al-Sakkākī's and al-Khaṭīb al-Qazwīnī's works had a major impact on creating a standardized version of the science in terms of its scholastic organization, which was adopted for centuries to follow. Their works were the subject of numerous commentaries up to the twentieth century.[49] Some notable commentaries, which I consult throughout this book, include al-Taftāzānī's (d. 793/1390) *al-Muṭawwal fī sharḥ Talkhīṣ Miftāḥ al-ʿulūm* (*The Long Commentary on the Abridgement of the Key to the Sciences*), which is a commentary on al-Khaṭīb al-Qazwīnī's short commentary (*Talkhīṣ*) of the *Miftāḥ*, and al-Sayyid al-Sharīf al-Jurjānī's (d. 816/1413) *Ḥāshiya* (*Marginal Glosses*) on al-Taftāzānī's work, as well as his own direct commentary on the *Miftāḥ* entitled *al-Miṣbāḥ* (*The Lamp*).

46 For an analysis of al-Zamakhsharī's commentary on the Quran in light of al-Jurjānī's influence, see Badri Najib Zubir, "Departure from Communicative Norms in the Qur'an: Insights from al-Jurjānī and al-Zamakhsharī," *Journal of Qur'anic Studies* 2, no. 2 (2000). For the influence of al-Jurjānī on al-Muṭarrizī's commentary on the *Maqāmāt*, see Keegan, "Commentarial Acts and Hermeneutical Dramas"; and "Throwing the Reins to the Reader: Hierarchy, Jurjānian Poetics, and al-Muṭarrizī's Commentary on the Maqāmāt," in "ʿAbd al-Qāhir al-Jurjānī," ed. Alexander Key, special issue, *Journal of Abbasid Studies* 5 (2018).

47 Notable examples of authors who did not follow this taxonomy include al-Nuwayrī and Ibn Khaldūn (see Gustave E. von Grunebaum, *Bayān*, in *EI*²). Yaḥyā al-ʿAlawī (d. 747/1346), a near contemporary of al-Khaṭīb al-Qazwīnī's, presented yet another division of these sciences of eloquence (Yaḥyā ibn Ḥamza al-ʿAlawī, *al-Ṭirāz al-mutaḍammin li-asrār al-balāgha wa-ʿulūm ḥaqā'iq al-iʿjāz* (Cairo: Dār al-Kutub al-Khidaywiyya, 1914)). These different divisions, however, do not necessarily indicate a great difference in approach.

48 For a study of Ibn al-Athīr's work and its relationship to the science of eloquence, see Avigail Noy, "The Emergence of *ʿIlm al-Bayān*: Classical Arabic Literary Theory in the Arabic East in the 7th/13th Century" (PhD Dissertation, Harvard University, 2016).

49 For a description of the commentary tradition see Smyth, "Controversy in a Tradition of Commentary"; Maṭlūb, *Qazwīnī*; and Sellheim, *Materialien zur arabischen Literaturgeschichte*, 1:299–334 and 2:60–84.

The New Aesthetic

A comprehensive aesthetic theory, therefore, begins to emerge with the works of al-Jurjānī and the science of eloquence (*balāgha*). This theory centered around four linguistic units:[50] (1) sentence construction; (2) simile; (3) metaphor and metonymy; (4) rhetorical figures. Eloquence and beauty in each of these units depend on their ability to move the soul. The explanations given for this movement to the soul are based on the capacity of these linguistic units to convey information in (summarily) an indirect way, requiring the listener to deduce the meaning. This allows the listener to go through an experience of discovery, which speech would otherwise not have the capacity to produce. This experience can be enhanced, as we will see, through characteristics such as farfetchedness, strangeness, rarity, and unexpectedness.

While the old school of criticism evaluated *badīʿ*, including metaphors and similes, based on their closeness to the truth and literal accuracy, the new school justified the beauty of *badīʿ* figures, as we will see in Chapter 1, through their inherent capacity to produce an unexpected discovery of meaning and hence an experience of wonder. This capacity to evoke wonder was also the distinguishing characteristic of poetic speech in

[50] Other linguistic units of poetry were also discussed in classical Arabic literary criticism, including the visual appearance of the poetry, larger elements that structure a poem, as well as the sound and meter (see Lara Harb, "Beyond the Known Limits: Ibn Dāwūd al-Iṣfahānī's Chapter on 'Intermedial' Poetry," in *Arabic Humanities, Islamic Thought: A Festschrift for Everett K. Rowson*, ed. Shawkat Toorawa and Joseph Lowry (Leiden: Brill, 2017), for a discussion of the role of visual appearance in the written poem; van Gelder, *Beyond the Line*, with regard to organic unity; and *Sound and Sense in Classical Arabic Poetry* (Wiesbaden: Harrassowitz, 2012), on the role of meter and rhyme in medieval Arabic poetry). Some of these elements were not standard subjects of literary criticism and any discussions of them give us a rare glimpse into phenomena that nevertheless are witnessed in classical Arabic poetry. Rhyme and meter were the focus of their own dedicated field of study known as *ʿilm al-ʿarūḍ wa-l-qawāfī*. Finally, the sounds of utterances were also discussed and some invested it with much importance (most notably, Ibn Sinān al-Khafājī, who has a long section on the sounds of letters in his treatise on eloquence in *Sirr al-faṣāḥa*, ed. ʿAbd al-Mutaʿāl al-Saʿīdī (Cairo: Maktabat wa-Maṭbaʿat Muḥammad ʿAlī Ṣubayḥ, 1953), 15–25 and 66–101). However, the *balāgha* tradition generally limited their relevance to a beautifying accessory. Fakhr al-Dīn al-Rāzī, for example, acknowledges the potentially beautifying effect of the sounds of words (*Nihāyat al-ījāz fī dirāyat al-iʿjāz*, ed. Nasrullah Hacimüftüoğlu (Beirut: Dār Ṣādir, 2004), 51–8). Al-Jurjānī, however, explicitly argues that the sound of utterances has no role in their eloquence (see Lara Harb, "Form, Content, and the Inimitability of the Qurʾān in ʿAbd al-Qāhir al-Jurjānī's Works," *Middle Eastern Literatures* 18, no. 3 (2015)). As a result, questions of sound, meter, and rhyme, larger poetic structures, and the written appearance of poetry will not be addressed in this book.

Aristotelian Arabic poetics. As we will see in Chapter 2, the beauty of simile and metaphor was variously attributed in philosophical works to their rarity, capacity to defamiliarize language, and simulate an experience of discovery. Discovery is also elaborately theorized in *bayān*, especially with regard to simile. As we will see in Chapter 3, the beauty of simile is attributed to its ability to make something hidden manifest. Metaphor and metonymy are also ways of making meaning manifest (*bayān*). Their beauty and emotional impact go back to the fact that they signify their intended meaning indirectly, as we will see in Chapter 4. As a result, they require the listener to search for and deduce their meaning, allowing him to go through an experience of discovery. Finally, eloquent, moving sentences are ones that are constructed in a way that conveys further meaning about the context or addressee implicitly. As we will see in Chapter 5, here again, the emotional impact is due to discovering this added meaning after reflection.

The focus of medieval criticism on small linguistic units rather than the complex structures of a poem as a whole has led some modern scholars to describe classical Arabic literary theory as "molecular" or "atomistic" and deem this a "deficiency."[51] Far from being a deficiency, however, the discussions of literary figures and linguistic structures constitute a sophisticated theory of aesthetic experience. As I hope to show in this book, literary figures and phrasal constructions are the very elements through which speech evokes wonder. In addition, post-Jurjānian literary theory is often described as ossified and rigid, not producing any new ideas.[52] As I hope to show, quite to the contrary, these later works provide sophisticated advancements to al-Jurjānī's

[51] Wolfhart Heinrichs, "Literary Theory: The Problem of Its Efficiency," in *Arabic Poetry: Theory and Development*, ed. G. E. von Grunebaum, Third Giorgio Levi della Vida Biennial Conference (Wiesbaden: Harrassowitz, 1973). For a critique of this view, see Meisami, "Arabic Poetics Revisited"; and Michael Sells, "The Qasida and the West: Self-Reflective Stereotype and Critical Encounter," *al-ʿArabiyya* 20 (1987). For a discussion of the debate on molecularity and organic unity in modern scholarship on classical Arabic literature, see Adam Talib, *How Do You Say "Epigram" in Arabic? Literary History at the Limits of Comparison* (Leiden: Brill, 2018), 183–212.

[52] See, for example, Aḥmad Maṭlūb, *al-Balāgha ʿind al-Sakkākī* (Baghdad: Maktabat al-Nahḍa, 1964); and Shawqī Ḍayf, *al-Balāgha: Taṭawwur wa-tārīkh*, 9th ed. (Cairo: Dār al-Maʿārif, 1995). This is partly a symptom of a more general attitude in twentieth-century scholarship that regarded the post-Abbasid era as a period of decline. This has been changing in recent decades, with much new scholarship exposing the exciting intellectual developments of the period. For an overview of the breadth of material from this later period, see Muhsin J. al-Musawi, *The Medieval Islamic Republic of Letters: Arabic Knowledge Construction* (Notre Dame, IN: University of Notre Dame Press, 2015).

thinking and to classical Arabic literary theory. Finally, the Aristotelian Arabic tradition of philosophical poetics is often treated as an exceptional anomaly in the critical tradition. While it is idiosyncratic in its approach to poetics, it shares a common aesthetic of wonder with the *balāgha* tradition, as I hope to show.

1

Wonder

A New Paradigm

وإنما مثل القدماء والمحدثين كمثل رجلين: ابتدأ هذا بناءً فأحكمه
وأتقنه، ثم أتى الآخر فنقشه وزيّنه، فالكُلفة ظاهرة على هذا
وإن حسن، والقُدرة ظاهرة على ذلك وإن خشن.

The example of the ancient [poets] and the moderns is like the example of two men: one founded a structure, mastered it and perfected it; the other embellished and decorated it. Affectation is apparent in the latter even when beautiful; aptitude is apparent in the former even when rough.[1]

~ *Ibn Rashīq (d. 456/1063–4 or later)*

With the rise of the Abbasid Empire in the mid-second/eighth century, a new style of poetry started developing. This so-called *muḥdath* (lit. modern/innovated) poetry was new in contrast to the poetic heritage that had been established by the pre-Islamic poets. A variety of factors, including urbanization in cities like Baghdad (as opposed to the primarily nomadic lifestyle of pre-Islamic Arabia), a shift from a tribal to a patron-based society, and the rise of a writerly culture, contributed to the development of a new social and cultural environment with new poetic demands.[2] Perhaps most important, however, was the existence – by

[1] Ibn Rashīq al-Qayrawānī, *al-ʿUmda fī maḥāsin al-shiʿr wa-ādābih wa-naqdih*, ed. Muḥammad Muḥyiddīn ʿAbd al-Ḥamīd, 5th ed., 2 vols. (Beirut: Dār al-Jīl, 1981), 1:92.

[2] For an old yet classic overview of the new style of poetry, see Ignaz Goldziher, "Alte und neue Poesie im Urtheile der arabische Kritiker," in *Abhandlungen zur arabischer Philologie* (Leiden: E.J. Brill, 1896). See also Suzanne Pinckney Stetkevych, *Abū Tammām and the Poetics of the ʿAbbāsid Age* (Leiden: E.J. Brill, 1991). For a discussion of the changing status of the poet, see Beatrice Gruendler, *Medieval Arabic Praise Poetry: Ibn al-Rūmī and the Patron's Redemption* (London; New York: Routledge, 2003), 10ff. For the changing function of poetry in the

then – of an established literary heritage within (and against) which Abbasid poets composed their own poetry.

Poets like Abū Nuwās (d. c. 198/813), the famous wine poet and one of the leading *muḥdath* poets, began pushing for innovation, making fun of the old. Tired of the traditional calls to lament the departure of the beloved on her abandoned encampment (*aṭlāl*), a conventional yet – by his time – outdated motif with which the pre-Islamic ode (*qaṣīda*) traditionally began, Abū Nuwās jokes:

راحَ الشقيُّ على الربوعِ يَهيمُ   والرّاحُ في راحي ورُحْتُ أهيمُ

The wretch went to the *aṭlāl*, wandering
whilst I with wine in my palm went wandering[3]

What was new about Abū Nuwās's verse was not merely that it diverged from the conventions of Arabic poetry at the time, replacing the theme of mourning the departure of the beloved with that of wine, it was also the particular attention given in it to poetic devices. That is, in this case, his construction of paronomasia (*tajnīs*) with the words *rāḥa* (went)/*al-rāḥu* (wine)/*rāḥī* (my palm)/*ruḥtu* (I went) and the anticipation of the rhyme word *ahīmū* (I wander) with *yahīmū* (he wanders) in the first hemistich, a rhetorical figure known as "having the end echo the beginning" (*radd al-ʿajuz ʿalā al-ṣadr*).[4] This is not to say that one cannot find these figures in the old Arabian style of poetry. The increased and conscious employment of rhetorical figures, however, was what medieval critics cited as the distinguishing characteristic of the new Abbasid style.

The association of rhetorical figures with the new style was so firm that the word that came to denote rhetorical figures in classical Arabic criticism was *badīʿ*, which literally means "novel/innovated."[5] This increased use of *badīʿ*

Abbasid period, see Ouyang, *Literary Criticism*, 55–89. Adonis credits the changes in poetic style to a shift from a primarily oral culture in pre-Islamic times to a writerly culture propelled by the Quran in his *al-Shiʿriyya al-ʿArabiyya* (Beirut: Dār al-Ādāb, 1985). I am borrowing the term "writerly culture" from Shawkat Toorawa (*Ibn Abī Ṭāhir Ṭayfūr and Arabic Writerly Culture: A Ninth-Century Bookman in Baghdad* (London: Routledge Curzon, 2005)).

3 Translation from Philip F. Kennedy, *The Wine Song in Classical Arabic Poetry: Abū Nuwās and the Literary Tradition* (Oxford; New York: Clarendon Press; Oxford University Press, 1997), 45, slightly modified to highlight the rhetorical figures.

4 I am adopting Wolfhart Heinrichs's translation of the figure, in "Rhetorical Figures," in *Encyclopedia of Arabic Literature*.

5 The first to employ the word *badīʿ* in the sense of "rhetorical figures" was Ibn al-Muʿtazz in his *Kitāb al-badīʿ*. Before him, al-Jāḥiẓ employed *badīʿ* in reference to metaphor (*istiʿāra*) as Heinrichs has argued in "*Istiʿāra* and *Badīʿ* and Their Terminological Relationship in Early Arabic Literary Criticism," *Zeitschrift für Geschichte der Arabisch-Islamischen Wissenschaften* 1 (1984).

was also what Ibn Rashīq referred to in the passage quoted at the opening of this chapter when describing the ancients (*al-qudamāʾ*) as "builders" and the moderns (*al-muḥdathūn*) as "embellishers." Significantly, however, it was not simply the increased quantity of rhetorical figures that characterized *muḥdath* poetry; it was also the "heightened awareness of a prior tradition," a quality Huda Fakhreddine identifies as "metapoetic,"[6] that led to more abstraction, intellectualism, and metaphorical complexity in poetry.[7]

Like the poets, literary critics were also keenly aware of this prior tradition. However, while *muḥdath* poets sought to innovate and forge their own new path distinct from their predecessors, the critics held up the poetry of the ancients as an idealized model against which they evaluated the new style. With an eye toward the tradition, early critics tended to find the new style distasteful because it deviated from the classical ideals of pre-Islamic poetry. They frequently described the old style with adjectives such as truthful, straightforward, and effortlessly natural, whereas they deemed the new style far-fetched, obscure, contrived, and affected. While the new

[6] Huda J. Fakhreddine, *Metapoesis in the Arabic Tradition: From Modernists to Muḥdathūn* (Leiden: Brill, 2015). Stefan Sperl has described the modern style as one that did not seek to represent a specific physical reality (classical mimesis), but instead an "intralinguistic reality," which he terms "semiological mimesis," directed toward the heritage of poetry using the object of description as a catalyst for metaphorical transformations, rather than being directed at the object of description itself (*Mannerism in Arabic Poetry: A Structural Analysis of Selected Texts (3rd Century AH/9th Century AD–5th Century AH/11th Century AD)* (Cambridge; New York: Cambridge University Press, 1989)). Alternatively, as Heinrichs has described it, the modern style was "literature-oriented" as opposed to the classical style, which was "referent-oriented" ("Mannerism in Arabic Poetry: A Structural Analysis of Selected Texts by Stefan Sperl (Review)," *Middle East Journal* 45, no. 4 (1991): 698).

[7] Suzanne Stetkevych argues that rhetorical figures changed from being straightforward and concrete to being "abstract [and] dialectical," employing a "greater degree of metaphorical manipulation" ("Toward a Redefinition of 'Badīʿ' Poetry," *Journal of Arabic Literature* 12 (1981): 29 and 24, respectively). Muḥammad Mandūr also describes the difference between the old and the new as being a matter of concreteness and abstraction: The style of the ancients "is composed of direct sense perceptions and is far from abstraction and strange-making," while the style of the *muḥdathūn* (the moderns) dwells in "the realm of the abstract" (*al-Naqd al-manhajī ʿind al-ʿArab* (Cairo: Nahḍat Miṣr, 2004), 88–9). Renate Jacobi and Benedikt Reinert have also identified the use of "fantastic imagery" and an increased "intellectualism" as defining features of the new style (Renate Jacobi, "Abbasidische Dichtung (8.-13. Jhdt.)," in *Grundriss der arabischen Philologie. Band II: Literaturwissenschaft*, ed. Helmut Gätje (Wiesbaden: Ludwig Reichert Verlag, 1987), 53; and Benedikt Reinert, "Der Concetto-Stil in den islamischen Literaturen," in *Neues Handbuch der Literaturwissenschaft (Band 5: Orientalisches Mittelalter)*, ed. Wolfhart Heinrichs (Wiesbaden: AULA-Verlag, 1990), 372). For an applied analysis of the new kinds of metaphors that appeared in *muḥdath* poetry, see Wolfhart Heinrichs, "Paired Metaphors in *Muḥdath* Poetry," *Occasional Papers of the School of Abbasid Studies* 1 (1986).

Abbasid style did not lack an appreciative audience, as Beatrice Gruendler has shown,[8] and its reception by critics was not categorically negative, the initial attempts to defend it were weak and were dominated by a classical aesthetic. This has led some modern scholars to conclude that the Arabic critical tradition was not able to adapt to the changes that were taking place in poetic style.[9] As we will see, however, the story of Arabic literary criticism is more complex than this.

It is the contention of this book that a new way of thinking about poeticity began to emerge around the turn of the fifth/eleventh century. This (what can be described as a) "new school of criticism" articulated a more universal conception of poetic beauty. In other words, it sought to explain what makes language poetic in general, thus accounting for the beauty of the old and the new alike. Instead, what we may describe as the "old school of criticism," which crystallized in the fourth/tenth century, treated poetic beauty as a subjective matter of taste based on one's tolerance for untruthfulness and artifice in poetry. While this attitude can still be found in texts dating from the fifth/eleventh century, the new aesthetic framework, spearheaded by ʿAbd al-Qāhir al-Jurjānī but also evident in the philosophical treatments of Aristotle's *Poetics*, began to replace the old critical framework. This framework, as we will see throughout this book, went on to shape what in the seventh/thirteenth century was formalized as the "science of eloquence" (*ʿilm al-balāgha*) by al-Sakkākī and – later – al-Khaṭīb al-Qazwīnī.

Several scholars have shown the significance of ʿAbd al-Qāhir al-Jurjānī's works for changing attitudes towards *muḥdath* poetry. They attribute this change variously to his new conception of *ṣanʿa* (artifice),

[8] Beatrice Gruendler, "Fantastic Aesthetics and Practical Criticism in Ninth-Century Baghdad," in *Takhyīl: The Imaginary in Classical Arabic Poetics*, ed. Geert Jan van Gelder and Marlé Hammond (Cambridge, UK: Gibb Memorial Trust, 2008).

[9] Gustave von Grunebaum has argued, for example, that medieval literary criticism tended to be "traditionalist" and resistant to innovation in his article, "The Aesthetic Foundation of Arabic Literature," *Comparative Literature* IV, no. 4 (1952). Heinrichs has suggested that there was an incongruity in general between the developments taking place in Arabic poetry and the literary theory ("Efficiency," 19). The modern Syrian poet and critic Adonis's thesis in his study entitled *al-Thābit wa-l-mutaḥawwil: Baḥth fī al-ittibāʿ wa-l-ibdāʿ ʿind al-ʿArab* (*The Fixed and the Changing: A Study of Imitation and Innovation among the Arabs*), 7th ed. (Beirut: Dār al-Sāqī, 1994) also centers on the belief that medieval critics tended towards the "fixed" tradition and met "change" with scorn. Even though he singles out ʿAbd al-Qāhir al-Jurjānī as having given legitimacy to Abū Tammām and his innovations, he presents this as an exception in an otherwise classically oriented poetic and critical tradition.

his theory of imagery, and his theory of *naẓm* (sentence construction).[10] I build on this research by showing, first, that a unified aesthetic theory, which I am summarily characterizing as "wonder," underlies al-Jurjānī's treatment of all aspects of poetic language, including *badīʿ*, imagery, and *naẓm*. Second, I show that this theory of wonder is not limited to al-Jurjānī and continues to constitute the aesthetic basis of what later develops into the standardized science of eloquence. Finally, I argue that an aesthetic of wonder also forms the basis of poetic theories developed by the philosophers (also starting in the fifth/eleventh century) in their treatment of Aristotle's *Poetics*. What I am noting here, in other words, is a general shift in paradigm that is evident (a) across the critical treatment of the various aspects of poetic language that concerned Arabic criticism, (b) beyond al-Jurjānī in the science of eloquence, and (c) across disciplines, including philosophy.

Over the course of this book, we will see how the beauty of poetic language began to be attributed in the new school of criticism to factors such as strangeness, farfetchedness, and unexpectedness. Contrary to the ideals of the old school, the truthfulness or falsehood of poetry became inconsequential for poetic beauty. This change was not the result of a subjective shift in taste to an opposite extreme, which embraced artificiality and falsehood. Rather, the critical apparatus changed altogether from a binary system based on personal preference to a paradigm of wonder. Qualities that lead to an experience of wonder, such as strangeness and unexpected, as a result, replaced the concern with the truthfulness and naturalness of poetry. As such, this new school of criticism did not only allow for an articulation of the aesthetics of *muḥdath* poetry, but it also constituted a new comprehensive approach to poetic aesthetics, incorporating both the old style and the new, and as we will see in Chapter 5, the aesthetics of the Quran as well.

This chapter focuses specifically on the treatment of *badīʿ* figures, which were at the center of the *muḥdath* poetry debate. While the old school of criticism assessed *badīʿ* based on its closeness to the truth, the new school of criticism, first, changed the conception of truthfulness and, second,

[10] See especially Mansour Ajami, *The Neckveins of Winter: The Controversy over Natural and Artificial Poetry in Medieval Arabic Literary Criticism*, Studies in Arabic Literature vol. 9 (Leiden: E.J. Brill, 1984), 51–66; Kamal Abu Deeb, *al-Jurjānī's Theory of Poetic Imagery* (Warminster: Aris & Phillips, 1979); Margaret Larkin, *The Theology of Meaning: ʿAbd al-Qāhir al-Jurjānī's Theory of Discourse* (New Haven, CT: American Oriental Society, 1995). See also Abdelfattah Kilito, "Sur le métalangage métaphorique des poéticiens arabes," *Poétique* 38 (1979).

rendered it irrelevant as it attributed the beauty of *badīʿ* to mechanisms that enhance the evocation of wonder in the listener, regardless of its truthfulness. In Section I, we will see how truthfulness in the old school of criticism was based on *extrinsic* considerations that depended on the explicitness, straightforwardness, and plausibility of an image, and an adherence to poetic convention. In Section II, we will first see how this conception of truthfulness changed with ʿAbd al-Qāhir al-Jurjānī, who expands and modifies it to one based on the *internal* logicality of an image with his new category of *takhyīl* (make-believe). Furthermore, we will see how the aesthetic theory he develops to explain the beauty of make-believe imagery is based on the ability of this kind of fantastic imagery to produce an effect of wonder. The same kind of wonder-based logic explains the beauty of *badīʿ* figures in general, as conceived of by al-Jurjānī and his successors, regardless of any closeness to the truth. Poetic beauty across all these cases, as we will see, depended on the linguistic mechanisms that convey meaning in such a way that allows the listener to go through an experience of discovery, which in turn explains the emotional impact poetic language has on the listener. It is this causal link that critics expose between the discovery of meaning and the resulting emotional impact of poetic language that leads me to describe this new aesthetic as one of wonder.[11]

I THE OLD SCHOOL OF LITERARY CRITICISM

Initial divisions between the ancient poets (*al-mutaqaddimūn*) and the moderns (*al-muḥdathūn*) in early Islam were simply based on the eras from which poets hailed. The anthologist Abū ʿAmr ibn al-ʿAlāʾ (d. 144/771 or 147/774), for example, is reported to have said of the famous Umayyad poet al-Akhṭal (d. c. 92/710): "if only he had seen one day of the *Jāhiliyya* [the pre-Islamic era], I would not give any poet precedence over him."[12] Thus, simply having lived in the pre-Islamic period automatically granted a poet a superior status. Pre-Islamic poetry represented for the medieval scholar the repository of pure and authentic Arabic language and poetic form before the era of Islamic expansion that led to contact

[11] As discussed in the Introduction, Arabic criticism did not explicitly or exclusively describe the desired effect of poetic language on the listener as one of "wonder." However, the factors to which they attribute poetic beauty and the explanations they give for their ability to move the listener, as we will see, imply an experience of wonder.

[12] Cited in Goldziher, "Alte und neue Poesie," 135–6.

with foreign languages and cultures. This alone merited it a superior status. Nevertheless, by the late third/ninth century, the debate shifted from chronology to style and quality.[13] *Muḥdath* poets writing in the new *badīʿ* style were compared to their contemporaries writing in the style of the ancients.

Among the Abbasid poets, al-Buḥturī (d. 284/897) came to represent for his contemporaries the ideal classical style in his poetry. His older distant cousin of the same Ṭayyiʾ tribe, Abū Tammām (d. 231/846), on the other hand, came to represent the excesses of the new *badīʿ* style. About a century later, the Kufan poet al-Mutanabbī (d. 354/965) took the new *badīʿ* style to yet another level, his poetry (and persona) earning him the description of the poet who "filled the world [with his fame] and occupied people [with his affairs] (ثم جاء المتنبي فملأ الدنيا وشغل الناس)."[14] The fourth/tenth century witnessed lively debates as a result between proponents of al-Buḥturī and defenders of Abū Tammām and al-Mutanabbī.[15] The classical style of al-Buḥturī was generally described as natural and truthful, while the new style was associated with artificiality and falsehood. As we will see, these assessments ultimately boiled down to a question of truthfulness that depended on the plausibility, explicitness, and straightforwardness of an image, and the adherence to the conventional stock of imagery.

Naturalness and Artificiality

Abū al-Qāsim al-Āmidī (d. 370/980 or 371/981), in his multivolume treatise entitled *al-Muwāzana bayn shiʿr Abī Tammām wa-l-Buḥturī* (*The Weighing of the Poetry of Abū Tammām and al-Buḥturī*), explains that those who prefer al-Buḥturī's style like it because of the "sweetness of [its] utterances, [its] good transitions, the appropriate placement of [its] speech, the correctness of [its] expression, the familiarity and clarity of its

[13] Ibn Qutayba (d. 276/889), for example, in the introduction to his anthology of poets and poetry, *al-Shiʿr wa-l-shuʿarāʾ* (*Poetry and Poets*), rejects the idea of judging a poet purely based on having lived in the *Jāhiliyya* (*al-Shiʿr wa-l-shuʿarāʾ*, ed. Aḥmad Muḥammad Shākir, 2nd ed. (Cairo: Dār al-Maʿārif, 1967), 62–3). On Ibn Qutayba and the state of literary criticism in the third/ninth century, see also Seeger Adrianus Bonebakker, "Poets and Critics in the Third Century A.H.," in *Logic in Classical Islamic Culture*, ed. G. E. von Grunebaum (Wiesbaden: Harrassowitz, 1970).

[14] Ibn Rashīq al-Qayrawānī, *al-ʿUmda*, 1:100.

[15] For a description of the controversy over Abū Tammām and later al-Mutanabbī and an overview of the relevant texts, see Ouyang, *Literary Criticism*, 130–65.

meanings."[16] He goes on to say that al-Buḥturī "is Bedouin in his poetic [style], natural (*maṭbū'*), follows the ways of the progenitors (*al-awā'il*), does not diverge from the known conventions of poetry, and avoids complication, ugly words, and lowly speech."[17] Al-Āmidī goes on to state that for him who prefers "easy and familiar speech, proper style, good expressions, and sweet utterances, [. . .] al-Buḥturī is a must."[18]

Abū Tammām's style, on the other hand, is characterized by "obscure and unapparent meanings, much of it needing deduction, explanation, and reasoning."[19] Abū Tammām "is extremely artificial (*shadīd al-takalluf*), the master of artifice (*ṣan'a*) and despised[20] words and meanings, his poetry is unlike that of the ancients and does not follow their ways for what it contains of far-fetched metaphors (*isti'ārāt ba'īda*) and innovated meanings (*ma'ānī muwallada*)."[21] He goes on to explain that for him who "inclines towards artifice (*ṣan'a*) and obscure meanings that are only deducible after deep delving and thought, then Abū Tammām is no doubt the better poet."[22]

Al-Āmidī declares that "the first group (i.e., those who prefer the Buḥturī style) are the *kuttāb* (secretaries/learned men), Bedouins, poets with natural unaffected style (*al-shu'arā' al-maṭbū'ūn*), and the people of eloquence,"[23] while those who prefer Abū Tammām's style are "exegetes of abstruse meaning (*ahl al-ma'ānī*),[24] poets with an affected artificial

[16] Abū al-Qāsim al-Āmidī, *al-Muwāzana bayn shi'r Abī Tammām wa-l-Buḥturī*, ed. Aḥmad Ṣaqr, 4th ed., 2 vols. (Cairo: Dār al-Ma'ārif, 1961–5), 1:4. The remaining two parts of the work were published later in a separate edition: *al-Muwāzana bayn shi'r Abī Tammām wa-l-Buḥturī*, ed. 'Abd Allāh Ḥamad Muḥārib, vol. 3, i–ii (Cairo: Maktabat al-Khānjī, 1990).

[17] al-Āmidī, *al-Muwāzana*, 1:4. The Bedouins were seen as carrying the repository of pure Arabic language and authentic poetry. Thus, comparing the urban al-Buḥturī to them was an indication of the naturalness and authenticity of his poetry.

[18] Ibid., 1:5. [19] Ibid., 1:4.

[20] I read the variation "*mustakrah*" over the editor's choice of the verb "*yastakrih*" (see ibid., 1:4n10).

[21] Ibid., 1:4–5. [22] Ibid., 1:5. [23] Ibid., 1:4.

[24] I adopt Mansour Ajami's interpretation of the term *ahl al-ma'ānī* as "exegetes of abstruse meaning." Discussing al-Āmidī's use of the term, he explains that they "were the philologists and grammarians who culled out verses that had obscure meanings and subjected them to various interpretations" (Ajami, *Neckveins*, 24n76). The term *abyāt al-ma'ānī* (verses of [abstruse] meanings) came to be associated with strange and difficult poetry that requires explanation. One finds texts dedicated to the clarification of obscure meanings from early on, such as Ibn Qutayba's *Kitāb al-ma'ānī al-kabīr fī abyāt al-ma'ānī* (*The Big Book of Meanings of "Difficult Verses"*) and *Kitāb ma'ānī al-shi'r* (*The Book of the [Difficult] Meanings of Poetry*) of Abū 'Uthmān Sa'īd al-Ushnāndānī (d. 288/901), transmitted by Ibn Durayd (d. 321/933). Much later, in the ninth/fifteenth century, al-Suyūṭī (d. 911/1505) employs the term

style (*aṣḥāb al-ṣanʿa*), and he who inclines towards details and philosophical speech."[25] While al-Āmidī purports to want to be a fair arbiter between the two poets, he clearly sees himself as belonging to the first group.

Al-Qaḍī ʿAlī ibn ʿAbd al-ʿAzīz al-Jurjānī (d. 392/1001), in his *al-Wasāṭa bayn al-Mutanabbī wa-khuṣūmih* (*The Mediation between al-Mutanabbī and His Opponents*), another major treatise comparing the old and modern styles, similarly describes those inclined to the modern style as "the people of strange-making (*ighrāb*) and innovation (*badīʿ*)."[26] He also describes the style of the moderns as artificial and affected (*maṣnūʿ* and *mutakallif*),[27] and by artificiality, he means innovation (*ibdāʿ*), overmeticulousness (*tadqīq*), and strange-making (*ighrāb*).[28] He attributes the artificiality of Abū Tammām to his employment of literary devices wherever possible, his intentional effort to make his poetry difficult, and his seeking of obscure meanings, along with concealing the intention "so that this type of his poetry upon reaching the ear would not touch the heart except after tiresome thought and much effort."[29] He goes on to say, "if he does succeed in this, it is only after much struggle and effort [. . .]. This is a state in which the soul does not eagerly rejoice from hearing something beautiful or enjoying something elegant. This is the flaw of affectedness."[30]

abyāt al-maʿānī in a section on "riddles" (*alghāz*) to refer to poetry that "requires interpretation and could not be comprehended at first sight" (*al-Muzhir fī ʿulūm al-lugha wa-anwāʿihā*, ed. Muḥammad Aḥmad Jād al-Mawlā, Muḥammad Abū al-Faḍl Ibrāhim, and ʿAlī Muḥammad al-Bajāwī, 3rd ed., 2 vols. (Cairo: Maktabat Dār al-Turāth, n.d.), 1:578). For an interesting take on *abyāt al-maʿānī* and the meaning of *maʿnā*, see David Larsen, "Meaning and Captivity in Classical Arabic Philology," in "ʿAbd al-Qāhir al-Jurjānī," ed. Alexander Key, special issue, *Journal of Abbasid Studies* 5 (2018).

[25] al-Āmidī, *al-Muwāzana*, 1:4. Interestingly, al-Fārābī divides poets into "natural" ones and "syllogizing" ones (*musaljisūn*) ("Fārābī's Canons of Poetry," *Rivista degli Studi Orientali* 17 (1938): 271).

[26] al-Qāḍī ʿAlī ibn ʿAbd al-ʿAzīz al-Jurjānī, *al-Wasāṭa bayn al-Mutanabbī wa-khuṣūmih*, ed. Muḥammad Abū al-Faḍl Ibrāhīm and ʿAlī Muḥammad al-Bajāwī (Beirut: al-Maktaba al-ʿAṣriyya, 2006), 354. Note that al-Qāḍī al-Jurjānī (d. 392/1001), the author of *al-Wasāṭa*, is not the same person as ʿAbd al-Qāhir al-Jurjānī (d. 471/1078) who wrote *Asrār al-balāgha* and *Dalāʾil al-iʿjāz*, discussed later in the chapter.

[27] See, for example, his discussion of the effect of "urbanization" on *muḥdath* poetry and its affectedness (ibid., 25).

[28] He lists these adjectives as absent in "natural" poets, such as al-Buḥturī (ibid., 33).

[29] Ibid., 26. [30] Ibid.

The Fundaments of Poetry (ʿAmūd al-Shiʿr)

Critics took a number of elements into consideration in these debates when they evaluated a poet and his poetry, culminating in the articulation of what they called the "fundaments of poetry" (*ʿamūd al-shiʿr*). The fifth-/eleventh-century critic al-Marzūqī summarized these "fundaments" in seven categories: (1) the nobility and correctness of the meaning and idea; (2) the eloquence and soundness of the wording; (3) the accuracy of the description; (4) the closeness of similes; (5) the congruity of the parts of the composition with each other and with the choice of meter; (6) the appropriateness of a word borrowed metaphorically for that which it was borrowed for; and (7) the harmony between the utterance and the meaning, as well as the rhyme word.[31] He goes on to explain that within each of these categories one can find means and extremes with respect to truth and falsehood. A poet's tendency toward truth, hyperbole, or moderation shows through them. Critics' preferences, in turn, follow these tendencies.[32] As a result, critics fell on a spectrum between those who espoused the view that "the best poetry is the most truthful (*aḥsan al-shiʿr aṣdaquhu*)," those who believed "the best poetry is the most untruthful (*aḥsan al-shiʿr akdhabuhu*)," and those who preferred the middle ground (*aḥsan al-shiʿr aqṣaduhu*).[33]

Al-Marzūqī goes on to state that the diverging inclinations toward naturalness (*ṭabʿ*) or artificiality (*ṣanʿa/takalluf*) are a natural consequence of the disagreement about truthfulness (*ṣidq*) and falsehood (*kadhib*).[34] Thus, the debate about truth and falsehood in poetry was ultimately the main underlying issue on which the evaluation of poetry depended. As we will see in the following section, however, even proponents of falsehood qualified their position by limiting untruthfulness to the realm of what is possible, believable, and accurate on a literal level. Thus, the culmination of poetic criticism by the end of the fourth/tenth century, with its establishment of the "fundaments of poetry," was very much an expression of a classical aesthetic of truthfulness, deviations from which were tolerated in limited ways.[35]

[31] Abū ʿAlī Aḥmad ibn Muḥammad ibn al-Ḥasan al-Marzūqī, *Sharḥ Dīwān al-Ḥamāsa*, ed. Aḥmad Amīn and ʿAbd al-Salām Hārūn (Beirut: Dār al-Jīl, 1991), 1:9. On the concept of *ʿamūd al-shiʿr*, see Mansour Ajami, "ʿAmūd al-shiʿr': Legitimization of a Tradition," *Journal of Arabic Literature* 12 (1981); and "Al-Marzūqī's Treatment of *ʿAmūd al-Shiʿr* (The Essentials of Poetry)" (PhD Dissertation, Columbia University, 1976).

[32] al-Marzūqī, *Sharḥ Dīwān al-Ḥamāsa*, 1:8–12. [33] Ibid., 1:11–12. [34] Ibid., 1:12.

[35] Ajami also notes that the *ʿamūd al-shiʿr* project was aimed at legitimizing a tradition in reaction to the new *badīʿ* style ("ʿAmūd al-shiʿr': Legitimization of a Tradition").

Truth and Falsehood

Falsehood (*kadhib*) as a poetic quality to be appreciated (or not) did not mean fiction in the sense of fabricated information. Poetry as a medium of expression was in general acknowledged as fictional in medieval Arabic culture in the sense that it was understood that the information it conveyed did not necessarily exist or happen in real life.[36] As a poetic quality, however, falsehood had to do more with linguistic deviation from literal accuracy in the employment of metaphorical language and hyperbole (*ghuluww*).[37] Al-Marzūqī explains that those who espouse the idea that "the best poetry is the most untruthful" see the work of the poet as lying in "exaggeration (*mubālagha*) and representation through analogy (*tamthīl*), not on coincidence [of description and that which is described] and verification."[38] Discussions of falsehood in the old school of criticism, therefore, typically revolved around the limits of figurative language and hyperbole. Truthfulness (*ṣidq* or *ḥaqīqa*), in turn, was not about the authentic expression of an actual lived experience. Rather, it referred to the accuracy of the literal meaning,[39] the plausibility of ideas, and the adherence to conventional motifs.[40]

[36] See Rina Drory, "Three Attempts to Legitimize Fiction in Classical Arabic Literature," *Jerusalem Studies in Arabic and Islam* 18 (1994): 159–61. Poetry was regarded as fiction especially in contrast with the true (yet poetic) message of the Quran. See Wolfhart Heinrichs, *Arabische Dichtung und Griechische Poetik: Ḥāzim al-Qarṭāğannīs Grundlegung der Poetik mit Hilfe Aristotelischer Begriffe* (Beirut: Franz Steiner Verlag, 1969), 58; and J. Christoph Bürgel, "Die beste Dichtung ist die lügenreichste: Wesen und Bedeutung eines literarischen Streites des Arabischen Mittelalters im Lichte komparatistischer Betrachtung," *Oriens* 23–24 (1974): 25–36.

[37] Cf. Heinrichs's delineation of the various aspects of the truth–falsehood debate (*Arabische Dichtung*, 56–68). On the truth–falsehood debate in general, see also Bürgel, "Die beste Dichtung"; Renate Jacobi, "Dichtung und Lüge in der arabischen Literaturtheorie," *Der Islam* 49 (1972); Mansour Ajami, *The Alchemy of Glory: The Dialectic of Truthfulness and Untruthfulness in Medieval Arabic Literary Criticism* (Washington, DC: Three Continents Press, 1988).

[38] al-Marzūqī, *Sharḥ Dīwān al-Ḥamāsa*, 1:11–12.

[39] As Heinrichs has shown, the term *ḥaqīqa*, when used in juxtaposition with *majāz* (figurative language), referred to the literal meaning ("On the Genesis of the *ḥaqîqa-majâz* Dichotomy," *Studia Islamica* 59 (1984)). Alexander Key has argued for understanding *ḥaqīqa* as "accuracy" in general (*Language between God and the Poets: Maʿnā in the Eleventh Century* (Berkeley, CA: University of California Press, 2018)). I ultimately use the word "truthfulness" to describe the usage of both *ḥaqīqa* and *ṣidq* in the debates of poetic truthfulness, in contrast to *kadhib* (falsehood/mendacity). Nevertheless, the critics' concern, as we will see, does indeed revolve around the "accurate" usage of language, logic, and conventional imagery. Thus, accuracy vs. inaccuracy could be a useful way to think of the truth–falsehood debate in poetic criticism.

[40] There are several important studies cited in this section on the question of truth and falsehood, which the following brief presentation of the topic has benefited from. However, the topic merits to be revisited more extensively in a dedicated study.

Hyperbole

Stretching the truth for the sake of hyperbole (*ghuluww*) was something that the likes of Qudāma ibn Jaʿfar (d. 337/948) considered beautiful in poetry.[41] However, even Qudāma, who famously espoused the view that "the best poetry is the most untruthful,"[42] qualified his position by limiting untruthfulness to the realm of what is possible and believable (even if unlikely).[43] He explains that the difference between impossibility (*istiḥāla*) and self-contradiction (*tanāquḍ*), on the one hand, and unrealizability (*imtināʿ*), on the other, is that the former does not exist and its existence is inconceivable (because it is contradictory, for example), whereas the latter does not exist, but is conceivable. He lists impossible and self-contradictory ideas among the "flaws in meanings (*maʿānī*)."[44] He also lists fantastic or unrealizable matters (*al-mumtaniʿ*) that are presented *as if possible* as a flaw.[45] In other words, unrealistic imagery was fine as long as it did not result in self-contradiction or unviability; and false statements were fine as long as their claims were qualified. As a result, a false hyperbolic claim that is fantastic yet conceivable could be justified if the poet qualifies the idea as a *near* possibility and does not present it as actually possible.

This concern comes through clearly in the discussions surrounding a controversial verse by Abū Nuwās. Critics debated the adequacy of the qualification the poet gives for his hyperbolic praise of the capacity of the Abbasid caliph Hārūn al-Rashīd (r. 170/786 – 193/809) to instill fear in unbelievers:

وأَخَفْتَ أَهلَ الشِّرْكِ حتَّى إنَّهُ لَتَخافُكَ النُّطَفُ الَّتِي لَمْ تُخْلَقِ

You have sown fear among the polytheists so that
even their unformed semen (practically) fears you [long before birth][46]

Al-Qāḍī al-Jurjānī rejects the image outright as an impossibility and lists it among Abū Nuwās's bad poetry.[47] Al-Āmidī cites the argument of the proponents of Abū Tammām and *muḥdath* poetry who regarded the

[41] Qudāma ibn Jaʿfar, *Naqd al-shiʿr*, ed. Muḥammad ʿAbd al-Munʿim Khafājī (Beirut: Dār al-Kutub al-ʿIlmiyya, n.d.), 91–5.
[42] Ibid., 94.
[43] Ibid., 201. See Wolfhart Heinrichs, *Mubālagha*, in *EI*[2]; Bürgel, "Die beste Dichtung," 55–62; Ajami, *Alchemy*, 19–30.
[44] Qudāma ibn Jaʿfar, *Naqd al-shiʿr*, 195. [45] Ibid., 202.
[46] Philip Kennedy's translation with some amendment to convey the idea of "almost," which I discuss in what follows. (*Abu Nuwas: A Genius of Poetry* (Oxford: Oneworld, 2005), 86.)
[47] al-Qāḍī al-Jurjānī, *al-Wasāṭa*, 61.

image, despite its absurdity, as more acceptable than similar ones by earlier classical poets, precisely because Abū Nuwās qualified it with the article "*la-*."[48] Interpreting it as implying *la-takādu* (it almost . . .), they argued that this sufficiently rendered the idea of the fear already instilled in the unborn children of unbelievers a *near* possibility, without claiming that it is actually the case. Although many did not find this argument convincing, Qudāma explains that it clearly renders the idea a comparison (*mathal*) intended for exaggerating the power of the addressee.[49] Thus, even proponents of *muḥdath* poetry defended hyperbolic statements, such as this one by Abū Nuwās, by claiming their closeness to literal truth.

The Limits of Figurative Imagery

The old school of criticism also emphasized the need to keep figurative language as close as possible to being literally accurate. Al-Āmidī states, for example, "the closer a (figurative)[50] meaning is to literal truths (*ḥaqā'iq*), the more appealing it is to the soul and the more pleasing it is to the ear, and thus the more deserving it would be of admiration."[51] Ibn Ṭabāṭabā (d. 322/934) in his *'Iyār al-shi'r* (*The Standard of Poetry*) similarly underscores the fact that "the mind finds pleasure in speech that is correct, accurate, and true, that is possible, known, and familiar [. . .] and finds ugly speech that deviates from the right course, is wrong, false, groundless, absurd, unknown, and disproved."[52] He warns his readers that "a poet should avoid far-fetched allusions, obscure representations, and difficult signs, and instead seek the opposite, and use figurative language that is close to the literal truth and does not veer far from it [. . .]."[53] As an example of such far-fetched imagery a poet should avoid, Ibn Ṭabāṭabā cites a pair of verses in which the poet has his camel speaking:

تَقولُ إذا دَرأْتُ لَها وَضِينِي   أَهٰذا دينُهُ أَبَداً ودينِى
أَكُلَّ الدَّهرِ حَلٌّ وَٱرْتِحالٌ   أَمَا يُبْقِي عَلَيَّ وما يَقينِى

48 al-Āmidī, *al-Muwāzana*, 1:40; Qudāma ibn Ja'far, *Naqd al-shi'r*, 95.

49 Qudāma ibn Ja'far, *Naqd al-shi'r*, 95.

50 Manuscript variant has "*majāzāt*" instead of "*ma'ānī*" (al-Āmidī, *al-Muwāzana*, 1:157n3).

51 Ibid.

52 Abū al-Ḥasan Ibn Ṭabāṭabā, *'Iyār al-shi'r*, ed. 'Abd al-'Azīz ibn Nāṣir al-Māni' (Riyad: Dār al-'Ulūm, 1985), 20.

53 Ibid., 199–200.

It says when I spread my saddle on it:
    Is this forever his way and mine?
Is all of Time about staying and leaving?
    Doesn't he have mercy on me and protect me?
               ~ al-Muthaqqab al-ʿAbdī (pre-Islamic)

He explains, "This representation of his camel is of the [type of] figurative speech that pushes literal truth far away (mubāʿid li-l-ḥaqīqa)."[54] What the poet actually meant to say, Ibn Ṭabāṭabā goes on to explain, is that *were the camel able to speak*, it would have expressed its complaints with such a statement."[55] However, the poet makes it seem as if the camel actually spoke. This was to be avoided according to Ibn Ṭabāṭabā's recommendation.

As an example of a representation of "speaking" animals that is closer to the literal truth (ḥaqīqa), he cites the following verse by Bashshār ibn Burd (d. 167/783):

غَدَتْ عَانَةٌ تَشْكُو بِأَبْصَارِها الصَّدَى   إِلَى الجَأْبِ إِلَّا أَنَّها لا تُخاطِبُهُ

A herd came complaining with their eyes of thirst
    to the zebra, except they did not speak to it

The implication is that despite suggesting that the animals articulate complaint like humans, the poet limited their "speech" to the look in their eyes and explicitly stated that they expressed their grievance without actually speaking. Ibn Ṭabāṭabā seems to find this verse more acceptable than the previous ones because it qualifies the human-like qualities attributed figuratively to animals and explicitly removes any possibility of them actually speaking, thus keeping the language close to being literally accurate.

***

In a similar vein, Qudāma shows how metaphorical leniency can lead to self-contradiction, something he considers a flaw, unless their figurative status is explicitly pointed out.[56] In the following verse by Ibrāhīm ibn Harma (fl. second/eighth century), for example, the poet's figurative attribution of speech to a dog while proclaiming its inability to speak at one and the same time creates an apparent inconsistency:

تَراهُ إِذا ما أَبْصَرَ الضَيفَ مُقْبِلاً   يُكَلِّمُهُ مِن حُبِّهِ وَهُوَ أَعْجَمُ

---

[54] Ibid., 200.   [55] Ibid.   [56] Qudāma ibn Jaʿfar, *Naqd al-shiʿr*, 195–201.

You find it (the dog) whenever it sees a guest coming
speaking to him out of love while mute

Qudāma explains that the contradiction lies in the fact that the poet attributed speech to the dog, then rendered it inexistent by describing it as mute, "without adding to the discourse any indication that what he mentioned was meant metaphorically."[57]

In later criticism, this very verse, among other similar ones, is praised for the meaning it implies about the dog's owner's generosity: the dog is so friendly with the guests because he is so accustomed to seeing visitors given his owner's hospitality.[58] Such far-fetched allusions that require multistep reasoning was the opposite of "figurative language that is close to the literal truth," and therefore discouraged in the old school of criticism, as we have seen Ibn Ṭabāṭabā do. Qudāma also cautions that implied meaning, which he calls *irdāf* (making a meaning come as a consequence), should not require too many steps of reasoning.[59] (The opposite becomes desirable in the new school of criticism: the more steps a listener has to go through to reach the intended implied meaning, the better.)[60] Explicitness and closeness to literal accuracy were important, therefore, in the old school of criticism, but also the straightforwardness of the meaning.

Truthfulness of Ideas

Nevertheless, al-Qāḍī al-Jurjānī does warn against holding up poetry to the standards of pure verification. After discussing metaphors that are illogical and taken to an extreme, he states:

These matters when held up to verification (*taḥqīq*) and when pure exactitude (*taqwīm*) is sought in them, they are taken beyond of the ways of poetry. When [the path of poetic] licenses is followed and they are put forth with [too much] flexibility, [on the other hand] this leads to corruption in the language and

[57] Ibid., 199.

[58] Abū Yaʿqūb al-Sakkākī, *Miftāḥ al-ʿulūm*, ed. ʿAbd al-Ḥamīd Hindāwī (Beirut: Dār al-Kutub al-ʿIlmiyya, 2000), 516; Jalāl al-Dīn (al-Khaṭīb) al-Qazwīnī, *al-Īḍāḥ fī ʿulūm al-balāgha*, ed. Muḥammad ʿAbd al-Munʿim Khafājī, 3rd ed. (Beirut: Dār al-Kitāb al-Lubnānī, 1971), 460–1.

[59] Qudāma ibn Jaʿfar, *Naqd al-shiʿr*, 159.

[60] See my discussion of *kināya* in Chapter 4. Note that this is not because the aesthetic sensibility shifted to one that is more tolerant of indirect and allusive language for its own sake. Rather, because the aesthetic framework changed completely to one that values the ability of speech to make the listener go through an experience of discovery and hence wonder. Having to work toward grasping the meaning enhances this experience, as we will see.

convolutedness of speech. Rather, the goal is moderation and contenting [oneself] with what is close and known, limiting [oneself] to what is apparent and clear.[61]

Old-school critics, therefore, did allow for some figurative expansion. However, even in these cases, being close to the truth remains important. Al-Āmidī, for example, finds the following verses by Abū Tammām acceptable despite being intricate and subtle in their meaning (*daqīq al-maʿnā*), a quality he generally dislikes because it renders poetry more philosophical than poetic.[62] Addressing, in the traditional way, the remnants of the beloved's tribe's deserted encampment, Abū Tammām says:

مِنْ سَجايَا الطُّلولِ ألاَّ تُجيبَا   فصَوابٌ مِن مُقْلَة أَنْ تَصُوبَا

فاسأَلَنْها واجْعَلْ بُكَاكَ جَوَاباً   تَجِدِ الشَّوْقَ سائِلاً ومُجيبَا

It is natural for ruined encampments not to respond,
  And it is correct for an eye to shed tears[63]
So ask them, and make your weeping the answer
  You will find that yearning [both] asks and answers

The poet concludes with an apparent contradiction: yearning both asks and answers. Al-Āmidī, however, finds this idea plausible, though only after some explanation. He clarifies that since the ruins will not respond, you might as well have your tears be the answer. This is "because if they did respond, they would with what would cause you to weep, or because when they did not respond you realized that he who could have responded has deserted them, which would also lead to your weeping" (because either way the abandoned ruins symbolize the beloved's absence).[64] This logic leads to the contradictory conclusion that yearning for the beloved leads to both the question (posed to the ruins) and the answer (tears). However, al-Āmidī permits its plausibility since "you stood at the remnants of the encampment and addressed them with a question out of longing for him who used to be there. Then you cried as a result of longing as well. As such, longing is the cause of the question and the cause of the weeping [which is the answer]."[65] Al-Āmidī says this is "beautiful logic (*falsafa ḥasana*)," despite being intricate and crafty.[66] Even though the image requires some

[61] al-Qāḍī al-Jurjānī, *al-Wasāṭa*, 359.

[62] Julia Ashtiany, "The Muwāzana of al-Āmidī" (DPhil Dissertation, University of Oxford, 1983), 52n66 and 72n47; and al-Āmidī, *al-Muwāzana*, 1:423–5.

[63] I have used Beatrice Gruendler's translation of the first verse, which appears in al-Ṣūlī's biography of Abū Tammām (Muḥammad ibn Yaḥyā al-Ṣūlī, *The Life and Times of Abū Tammām*, trans. Beatrice Gruendler, Library of Arabic Literature (New York: New York University Press, 2015), 257).

[64] al-Āmidī, *al-Muwāzana*, 1:499. [65] Ibid. [66] Ibid., 1:499–500.

interpretation and abstraction, therefore, it is acceptable to al-Āmidī because it is ultimately plausible and verifiable on a literal level.[67]

Innovation

The ideas represented in poetry were not only judged in terms of their literal accuracy, but also in terms of their adherence to convention and norms. Among the flaws in poetic ideas, for example, Qudāma lists "contradicting convention, and bringing forth what is against custom and natural inclination."[68] Within this system, strange and novel ideas (*maʿānī al-istighrāb wa-l-ṭarāfa*) in and of themselves were not encouraged for their own sake. Qudāma explains that novelty and strangeness are irrelevant for the quality of poetry; poetry is either good or not, regardless of its newness.[69] (The opposite becomes true in later criticism, where strangeness and novelty become central aspects of poetic quality, as we will see.) Previous occurrences of ideas in the poetic heritage were regularly cited by early critics in order to give legitimacy to similar modern usages.[70] Divergence from the standard repository of poetic imagery was generally regarded with disapproval, even if the image was realistic.

Discussing flaws in al-Buḥturī's poetry, for example, al-Āmidī criticizes the description in one of his verses of a horse's tail as "trailing [behind him] like a garment."[71] The description is wrong, he explains, because a horse's tail that touches the ground is considered a flaw in horses, not to mention having it trail behind it. Better is the description by Imruʾ al-Qays, the celebrated pre-Islamic poet, in his *muʿallaqa*, in which he describes the horse's tail as "just above the ground."[72] As Julia (Ashtiany) Bray has argued, truthfulness according to al-Āmidī does not necessarily entail a representation of the poet's own authentic experience of an external reality. Rather, it is an adherence to a conventional set of traditional representations of an external reality.[73] Since this precedence-based

[67] Another example of "fine logic" that al-Āmidī approves of is in a verse by Abū Tammām that attributes the cause of gray hair to the heart. Al-Āmidī finds this acceptable even though many have found fault in it. This is because the real cause of gray hair is the worries of the heart. So attributing it to the heart metaphorically is close enough to the truth (ibid., 2:213). See also Ashtiany, "The Muwāzana of al-Āmidī," 72n47.

[68] Qudāma ibn Jaʿfar, *Naqd al-shiʿr*, 203. [69] Ibid., 152.

[70] Ashtiany, "The Muwāzana of al-Āmidī," 76. [71] al-Āmidī, *al-Muwāzana*, 1:371.

[72] Ibid.

[73] Julia (Ashtiany) Bray has pointed out that, while al-Āmidī's aesthetic in his *Muwāzana* is "essentially an aesthetic of truth," she notes that "we find no true polarity between *ṣidq* and

"truth" depends on a stock repertory of ideas and conventional imagery, Bray fairly concludes that this renders al-Āmidī's "definition of poetry subject to historical contingency rather than to constant laws."[74] Thus, truthfulness according to the old school of criticism also entailed what the cultural context at the time considered correct poetic representations.

***

What all these examples show is that the notion of truthfulness, variously expressed as *ṣidq* or *ḥaqīqa*, had to do with the accurateness and correctness of the language on a literal level, the plausibility of the ideas, and adherence to conventional imagery.[75] Even critics who espoused the idea that "the best poetry is the most untruthful," defended falsehoods (i.e., hyperbole and figurative language) by arguing that they were nonetheless accurate on a literal level. Whether one leaned toward one extreme or the other, in other words, the critical apparatus of the old school of criticism remained one of truth.

Early Defenses of the New Style

Early attempts to defend the new style of poetry were largely restricted to the framework established by the old school of criticism. As Suzanne Stetkevych has shown, early critics did not succeed in articulating what was novel about *muḥdath* poetry.[76] Abū Bakr al-Ṣūlī, in his defense of Abū Tammām, for example, criticized those who disliked his kind of poetry simply for not making enough effort to understand it;[77] therefore, not

kadhib (truth and falsehood)" in his work (Ashtiany, "The Muwāzana of al-Āmidī," 72 and 77, respectively). Rather, there are two kinds of truth, neither of which is based on an accurate representation of an external reality: "those embodied in the stock repertory of *ma'ānī*, and those which can be assimilated to them by analogy" (ibid., 76). I owe much of my thinking about and analysis of the question of truth and falsehood here to Julia Ashtiany's work in her unpublished dissertation on al-Āmidī.

74 Ibid., 76–7.

75 Key's recommendation to think of *ḥaqīqa* as "accuracy" instead of denoting "truth" per se would therefore hold very well here (*Language between God and the Poets*).

76 Stetkevych, "Toward a Redefinition"; Stetkevych, *Abū Tammām*, ch. 1.

77 See al-Ṣūlī's defense of Abū Tammām in his letter to Abū al-Layth Muzāḥim ibn Fātik published in: Abū Bakr al-Ṣūlī, *Akhbār Abī Tammām*, ed. Muḥammad 'Abduh 'Azzām, Khalīl Maḥmūd 'Asākir, and Naẓīr al-Islām al-Hindī, 3rd ed. (Beirut: Dār al-Āfāq al-Jadīda, 1980), 1–56. See translation in al-Ṣūlī, *Life and Times*, 1–63. For a discussion of the work, see Beatrice Gruendler, "Modernity in the Ninth Century: The Controversy around Abū Tammām," *Studia Islamica* 112, no. 1 (2017).

really articulating what precisely was aesthetically pleasing about the new style. Al-Qāḍī al-Jurjānī attempts to give some legitimacy to al-Mutanabbī's modern-style use of *badīʿ* by suggesting the possibility of employing rhetorical figures in a natural, inartificial way.[78] The championing of falsehood, though within limits, as discussed above, was also an attempt to give legitimacy to the tendency in the new style to embrace hyperbole and figurative imagery. However, they did so by showing how close they were to truthfulness, as we have seen. All these attempts, therefore, remained boxed in the dichotomies of "natural vs. artificial" and "truth vs. falsehood," which assumed an ideal in the effortless truthful aesthetic of the old classical style.

One of the most significant attempts to articulate the aesthetics of the new style was forged by Ibn al-Muʿtazz in his *Kitāb al-badīʿ* (*The Book of Innovation*), written in 274/887.[79] This was the first attempt in classical Arabic literary criticism to identify and classify rhetorical figures, i.e., the innovations (*badīʿ*) of *muḥdath* poetry. This in itself was a groundbreaking achievement, as Kamal Abu Deeb reminds us, as he was the first to identify and classify rhetorical figures in the Arabic critical tradition.[80] Nevertheless, Ibn al-Muʿtazz's approach was to argue that there was nothing so new about these innovations after all. A *muḥdath* poet himself, he cites the employment of *badīʿ* in pre-Islamic poetry, the Quran, and *ḥadīth* as evidence that its use by the modern poets was not a deviation from the classical tradition.[81] While the very notion of *badīʿ*, which links rhetorical figures with innovativeness, implies wonder, as Thomas Bauer has suggested,[82] Ibn al-Muʿtazz's project was still couched in an old-school framework, justifying *badīʿ* through classical precedence rather than articulating what was poetic about rhetorical figures in themselves. This changes with the rise of the new school of criticism, which develops a completely new aesthetic paradigm that eventually replaces the paradigm of truth that dominated the old school of criticism.

78 See Ajami's discussion of al-Qāḍī al-Jurjānī's treatment of the question of naturalness and artificiality in *Neckveins*, 31–8.

79 Ibn al-Muʿtazz, *Kitāb al-badīʿ*, 58. On Ibn al-Muʿtazz's treatise on *badīʿ*, see Bonebakker, "Reflections on the *Kitāb al-badīʿ* of Ibn al-Muʿtazz."

80 Kamal Abu Deeb, "Literary Criticism," in *ʿAbbasid belles-lettres*, ed. Julia Ashtiany, et al., the Cambridge History of Arabic Literature (Cambridge: Cambridge University Press, 1990), 348.

81 Ibn al-Muʿtazz, *Kitāb al-badīʿ*, 1–3.

82 Thomas Bauer, "Rhetorik, außereuropäische: V. Arabische Kultur," in *Historisches Wörterbuch der Rhetorik*, ed. Gert Ueding (Tübingen: Max Niemeyer Verlag, 2007), 115.

II THE NEW SCHOOL OF CRITICISM

As the old school of criticism was cementing itself in a few more works of criticism in the fifth/eleventh century,[83] a new way of thinking about poetic beauty was percolating.[84] One of the spearheads of this new school of criticism was the famous grammarian and literary theorist ʿAbd al-Qāhir al-Jurjānī. The importance of al-Jurjānī's works for the development of medieval Arabic literary theory as well as his contribution to the appreciation of *muḥdath* poetry has been repeatedly acknowledged by modern scholars. They have particularly noted his advancement of theories of imaginative speech with his discussion of "*takhyīl*" (make-believe imagery)[85] and have attributed to him the depolarization of the naturalness/artificiality and truth/falsehood debates.[86] However, they tend to attribute this to an increased leniency toward falsehood and artifice. As we will see, instead of transforming a negative attitude toward artificiality and falsehood to a positive one, the new school of criticism goes beyond these binaries altogether and articulates a new aesthetic – one that is defined by a poetic statement's ability to move the listener and evoke wonder.[87] This enables the articulation of

[83] Al-Marzūqī and Ibn Rashīq are some of the last representatives of the old school of criticism in the fifth/eleventh century.

[84] Ajami points out that after the fifth/eleventh century, "*ʿamūd al-shiʿr* was no longer a force for unifying poetic expression and critical judgement, and so lapsed into a state of occultation" ("ʿAmūd al-shiʿr': Legitimization of a Tradition," 48). Among the reasons he cites for this decline is the appearance of "major treatises on rhetorics and related fields," including ʿAbd al-Qāhir al-Jurjānī's works (ibid., 47).

[85] Renate Jacobi, for example, states: "Es ist das grosse Verdienst Ǧurǧānīs, in der [...] Charakterisierung der "phantastischen" Dichtung und in der anschliessenden Beschreibung ihrer Techniken und Stilmittel eine Würdigung des spätʿabbasidischen Stils gegeben zu haben [...]" ("Dichtung und Lüge," 97).

[86] On al-Jurjānī's depolarization of the artificiality and naturalness dichotomy, see Ajami, *Neckveins*, 51–66. On the question of falsehood and truthfulness, see Ajami, *Alchemy*; and Bürgel, "Die beste Dichtung," 67–76.

[87] While modern scholarship has noted the role of "wonder" in *muḥdath* poetry, they do not discuss its presence as an aesthetic theory in literary criticism. Reinert has discussed the wonder-effect of the new style and compared it to the "acutezza" device in baroque literature, which relies on producing a surprise effect in the audience ("Der Concetto-Stil in den islamischen Literaturen"). Von Grunebaum has argued that the wonder-effect offered an outlet for the medieval Arab poet (not the critic) to express originality within a tradition-oriented literature ("Aesthetic Foundation," 328). They rely, however, on Western theory and on their own interpretations of medieval Arabic poetry in coming to these conclusions, overlooking the medieval Arabic discussions of precisely this effect. Nevertheless, Jacobi and Bürgel have suggested a link between al-Jurjānī's discussion of

what was intrinsically beautiful about *badīʿ*, and hence by extension *muḥdath* poetry.

In the remainder of this chapter, I will first discuss how ʿAbd al-Qāhir al-Jurjānī changes the conception and scope of truth and falsehood with his new category of make-believe (*takhyīl*). I will then focus on his treatment of a variety of literary figures that were widely used in *muḥdath* poetry, which he classifies as make-believe imagery. I will highlight how their poeticity did not depend on their falsehood, but on intrinsic linguistic structures that allow for the production of an unexpected meaning. I will then show how the same logic governs al-Jurjānī and his successors' treatment of hyperbole, the other source of untruthfulness in poetry. Finally, I argue that the same principles underlie the beauty of *badīʿ* figures in general, including paronomasia (*tajnīs*), "padding" (*ḥashw*), and disguising (*tawriya*), among others. As we will see, the very structures of *badīʿ* figures often inherently entail mechanisms of hiding and obscuring meaning, and misleading and tricking the listener, allowing for the discovery of an unexpected meaning. These structures betray an aesthetic, which I am summarily characterizing as "wonder." Poetic beauty, therefore, comes to depend on mechanisms of conveying meaning in such a way that allows the listener to go through an experience of discovery and the ensuing wonder. *Badīʿ* figures are one way of achieving this aesthetic experience.

Make-Believe (Takhyīl)

Al-Jurjānī discusses a variety of *badīʿ* figures typical of *muḥdath* poetry under a rubric he calls "*takhyīl*" (make-believe).[88] These entail figurative imagery that is presented as if it were literally true – something the old school of criticism disapproved of, as we have seen. These include literary

takhyīl (make-believe) and "wonder" and "magic," respectively (Jacobi, "Dichtung und Lüge," 95; Bürgel, "Die beste Dichtung," 75; and *The Feather of Simurgh: The "Licit Magic" of the Arts in Medieval Islam* (New York: New York University Press, 1988), 65–9). Kamal Abu Deeb and Muḥammad Khalafallah have also noted and investigated the psychological approach of al-Jurjānī in his *Asrār al-balāgha* (Abu Deeb, *Poetic Imagery*; Muḥammad Khalafallah, "Naẓariyyat ʿAbd al-Qāhir fī Asrār al-balāgha," *Majallat kulliyyat al-ādāb, Alexandria* 2 (1944)). However, they do not link this "psychological approach" to the concept of wonder.

[88] A translation of the entire section on *takhyīl* in *Asrār al-balāgha* can be found in van Gelder and Hammond, *Takhyīl*, 29–69. Unless noted, all translations in this section are my own.

devices known as "fantastic etiology" (*al-taʿlīl al-takhyīlī*) or "beautiful etiology" (*ḥusn al-taʿlīl*), amazement (*taʿajjub*), and feigned ignorance (*tajāhul al-ʿārif*), among others.[89] Al-Jurjānī's use of the term *takhyīl* to describe this set of literary devices is idiosyncratic to a certain degree for it is never employed by later authors in the same way as a category of figures.[90] As a technical term, the word "*takhyīl*," which literally denotes "making one imagine something [as something else]," has different connotations in different disciplines, as Wolfhart Heinrichs has nicely laid out.[91] Al-Jurjānī's category of *takhyīl* refers to the kind of make-believe logic common to the various metaphorical constructions, which he classifies under it. It is in his identification of this logical mechanism that he is able to change the discourse from a surface assessment of literal accuracy of a statement to an assessment of the intrinsic merit of an image's construction. This make-believe logic continues to be adduced in later criticism as a poetic mechanism that enhances poeticity.

Truth and Falsehood according to al-Jurjānī

The question of poetic truth and falsehood, al-Jurjānī clarifies, is not a matter of whether or not a poet is honest in his depiction of something or someone.[92] Nor is it a matter of simply using metaphoric language. Rather, it has to do with

[89] Many of these figures are discussed in later medieval works as reinforcements of metaphor (see my discussion of "The Aesthetics of Make-Believe" below, as well as Chapter 4, section on "Variation in *Bayān*"). For discussions of al-Jurjānī's notion of *takhyīl*, see Suʿād al-Mānīʿ, "Mafhūm muṣṭalaḥ 'al-majāz' ʿind al-Sijilmāsī fī ʿalāqatihi bi-muṣṭalaḥ 'al-takhyīl,'" *Majallat Abḥāth al-Yarmūk, Silsilat al-Ādāb wa-l-Lughawiyyāt* 17, no. 1 (1999); Abu Deeb, *Poetic Imagery*, 157–64, for a discussion of some types of al-Jurjānī's *takhyīl* devices; and Larkin, *Theology of Meaning*, ch. 6.

[90] The literary devices al-Jurjānī groups under "*takhyīl*" continue to be discussed as *badīʿ* figures independently under their more specific titles, including *taʿajjub*, *tajāhul al-ʿārif*, and *ḥusn al-taʿlīl*, as well as under metaphor. The grouping of these figures under the rubric "*takhyīl*" starts and ends with al-Jurjānī, however. The term *takhyīl* is used in the science of eloquence in combination with "*istiʿāra*," to describe a particular kind of analogy-based metaphor that would not fall under al-Jurjānī's definition of the term (Wolfhart Heinrichs, "Takhyīl: Make-Believe and Image Creation in Arabic Literary Theory," in *Takhyīl: The Imaginary in Classical Arabic Poetics*, ed. Geert Jan van Gelder and Marlé Hammond (Cambridge, UK: Gibb Memorial Trust, 2008), 12–13).

[91] See ibid., and Wolfhart Heinrichs, "Die antike Verknüpfung von Phantasia und Dichtung bei den Arabern," *Zeitschrift der Deutschen Morgenländischen Gesellschaft* 128 (1978). Most notably for our purposes, *takhyīl* in the Aristotelian critical tradition denotes the kind of make-believe acknowledgment of the truth of a poetic statement/syllogism. I will discuss the philosophical notion of *takhyīl* in Chapter 2.

[92] See al-Jurjānī, *Asrār*, 250–1.

the nature of the logicality of the image a poet constructs and whether it presents a metaphor as if it were literally true. Therefore, instead of dividing poetic ideas into truthful and false ones, al-Jurjānī divides them into two new categories he calls: rational meanings (*maʿānī ʿaqliyya*) and make-believe meanings (*maʿānī takhyīliyya*).[93] The difference is that the truth/falsehood binary depends on extrinsic values, while the rational/make-believe binary depends on the intrinsic logic of an image. The truthfulness or falsehood of a representation, according to al-Jurjānī, depends on whether or not it requires the listener to accept fantastic ideas as truth. As a result, he explains that he who says "the best poetry is the most untruthful" embraces the kind of poetry in which "figurative expansion (*ittisāʿ*) and make-believe (*takhyīl*) are relied upon, truth is claimed for that which is merely an approximation or analogy, subtlety (*talaṭṭuf*) and interpretation (*taʾwīl*) are aimed for, and hyperbole and exaggeration are adopted."[94] He who prefers truthfulness, on the other hand, "abandons exaggeration, hyperbole, and figural flexibility (*tajawwuz*) for verification and proof."[95] He recognizes that the first attitude expands artistic possibility and allows "the poet [to] find the way to innovate and add [to the old], to contrive new imagery [. . .] and have at his disposal an endless source of material."[96] The adherent of truthfulness, on the other hand, is limited in material and artistic possibility, and "usually narrates to the listeners known ideas and widespread images."[97]

At the same time, in defense of truthfulness in poetry, he argues that the material at the disposal of the poet within the realm of truth is not as limited and fixed as one might think. New truthful ideas can still be discovered, as the poet Abū Firās al-Ḥamdānī (d. 357/968), a rival of al-Mutanabbī, is able to realize in the following verse in praise of Sayf al-Dawla, the patron they both shared:

[93] Al-Jurjānī introduces this division on p. 241 (ibid.). Note that al-Jurjānī also uses the term "ʿ*aqlī*" in juxtaposition to "*ḥissī*" (perceptible through the senses) in his discussion of the various kinds of points of similarity on which a comparison/metaphor may be based. In this case *ʿaqlī* stands for matters that need to be derived through intellectual reasoning. Larkin translates the term as "noetic" or "intellectual" (Larkin, *Theology of Meaning*, ch. 3 on *majāz*, particularly p. 81). The term in that context could summarily be understood as referring to "abstract" matters that cannot be perceived through the senses. In this case, therefore, one should not associate *ʿaqlī* with "truth" since the question of truth and falsehood is irrelevant when the term is used in juxtaposition with meanings that are perceptible through the senses (*maʿānī ḥissiyya*), which can also be true or real.

[94] al-Jurjānī, *Asrār*, 250.

[95] Ibid. This opinion is also expressed by Ibn Rashīq. He says that someone who is anti-*mubālagha* (hyperbole), i.e., anti-falsehood in poetry, would by default not tolerate metaphor, simile, and other rhetorical figures (*al-ʿUmda*, 2:55).

[96] al-Jurjānī, *Asrār*, 250–1. [97] Ibid., 251.

وكُنَّا كَالسَّهامِ إِذا أَصابَتْ   مَرامِيَها فَرامِيها أَصابا

We were like arrows; if they hit
   their targets, [it is thanks to] the shooter's good aim

Praising the ruler of the Ḥamdānid state in Syria and his achievements in war, the poet compares his soldiers to arrows, crediting their success in battle to the shooter's good aim (i.e., Sayf al-Dawla's good leadership). This idea, al-Jurjānī explains, is accurate on a literal level (because the analogy is made explicit) and passes logical rigor, yet Abū Firās was the first to have discovered it and "uncovered its secret," apparently.[98] In other words, there are some truths still out there for poets to discover and reveal, even though they might be small in number and difficult to find.[99] Novel truthful ideas are therefore not impossible to find. It is worth noting that the criterion that guides al-Jurjānī's assessment of the quality of the verse is novelty. The reason truthful imagery is *limiting* is that it often *lacks* novelty. However, this does not mean that it is necessarily devoid of it.

Furthermore, in defense of the expansiveness of truthfulness, al-Jurjānī argues that metaphor, in and of itself, does not fall under the rubric of make-believe (*takhyīl*) and hence falsehood. That is because the intention in metaphor is "not to affirm the meaning of the borrowed utterance [as literally true]; rather it intends to affirm a similarity there. The wording is therefore not in conflict with the message."[100] In other words, a word used metaphorically does not purport to claim its literal meaning as truth. That is, a basic metaphor does not require the listener to "make believe" that it is literally true. By calling something with another name, it merely suggests a similarity between the two things.[101] Elsewhere he further clarifies that:

metaphor (*istiʿāra*) amounts to [nothing more than] omission in that if you returned to its origin, you would find that the person saying it is affirming a rational and correct matter and is making a claim that is rooted in logic.[102]

---

[98] Ibid.

[99] The idea that truths are limited is found elsewhere, most notably in Ibn Sīnā's commentary on the *Poetics*, where he states that we are oblivious of the truths that are not known to us and that they are therefore inaccessible (*al-Shifāʾ, al-Manṭiq 9: al-Shiʿr*, ed. ʿAbd al-Raḥmān Badawī (Cairo: al-Dār al-Miṣriyya li-l-Taʾlīf wa-l-Tarjama, 1966), 24). Ibn Ṭabāṭabā also acknowledges that the challenge facing modern Abbasid poets is greater, since the ancients have already said everything there is to be said (*ʿIyār al-shiʿr*, 13).

[100] al-Jurjānī, *Asrār*, 252, "لا يكون مَخبَرُه على خلاف خبره".

[101] See Chapter 4 on metaphor. Cf. Key's discussion of lexical accuracy in al-Jurjānī's works in *Language between God and the Poets*, 220–8.

[102] al-Jurjānī, *Asrār*, 253.

In other words, the similarity that the use of metaphor implies remains in the realm of rational thinking and does not entail any acceptance of fantastic ideas as literally true. As a result, since metaphor is in the realm of rational ideas and not make-believe, the field of truthfulness in poetry is more expansive than the proponents of falsehood and hyperbole admitted.[103]

Al-Jurjānī acknowledges the merits of both *takhyīlī* and *ʿaqlī* ideas and does not take sides. Modern scholars have attributed this ambivalence in his position to external religious and societal constraints. Heinrichs, for example, says that "ʿAbd al-Qāhir al-Jurjānī [. . .] leaves no doubt – considering his elaborate and loving descriptions of *takhyīlī* poetry – that he prefers this kind [. . .]."[104] He goes on to state that the fact that untruthful meanings cannot possibly occur in the Quran, "forces our author to assign greater value to the *maʿānī ʿaqliyya* (rational meanings)."[105] Larkin similarly attributes this ambivalence in al-Jurjānī's work to his being both a theologian and literary critic. She believes that al-Jurjānī ultimately grants precedence to truthful statements arguing that: "[he] was constrained to grant precedence, albeit somewhat grudgingly, to the *maʿānī ʿaqliyya* because, by definition, the Qur'an is *ʿaqlī*."[106]

Given the dominance of the truth–falsehood framework in the old school of criticism, it is not surprising to want to pin down the side on which al-Jurjānī stands and to justify why he does not wholeheartedly endorse make-believe imagery while discussing it so positively. However, unlike the old school of criticism, which bases the appreciation of poetry on one's preference for either truthfulness or falsehood, al-Jurjānī does not treat the two qualities as mutually exclusive. He simply presents both arguments and explains what each view encompasses or excludes. He does not agree or disagree with either extreme as there is good poetry that is *ʿaqlī* and good poetry that is *takhyīlī*. What concerned him rather is debunking the assumption that creativity and innovation can only take place in make-believe imagery.[107] As Abu Deeb correctly explains:

103 Ibid., 252.
104 Heinrichs, "*Istiʿāra* and *Badīʿ*," 209. See also his discussion of truth and falsehood in al-Jurjānī's concept of *takhyīl* in Heinrichs, *Arabische Dichtung*, 61–5.
105 van Gelder and Hammond, *Takhyīl*, 12. 106 Larkin, *Theology of Meaning*, 141.
107 It seems that al-Jurjānī is arguing against an assumed reader who espouses the idea that "the best poetry is the most untruthful." This suggests that by his time this view was dominant. Indeed, al-Marzūqī, who lived around the same time as al-Jurjānī, states that most critics were adherents of this view (*Sharḥ Dīwān al-Ḥamāsa*, 11–12). It is possible

It is to be noted that in distinguishing these two types of meaning [*ʿaqlī* and *takhyīlī*], al-Jurjānī is not rejecting one and accepting the other; he considers them both proper modes of poetic creation. His concern is to assert that, although it may be thought that the *takhyīlī* type allows a greater freedom and creativity, the *ʿaqlī* type allows such creativity also.[108]

Ironically, this assumption that truthful and rational ideas cannot be creative or poetic seems to exist even in modern scholarship. The above-cited opinions, for example, assume that being a proponent of truthfulness in poetry can only be motivated by religious concerns and that poetic beauty can only take place in the imaginary fantastic realm.[109] However, there are aesthetic reasons to condone truthfulness as well. In fact, most of al-Jurjānī's treatise on eloquence concerns literary devices that he considers within the realm of rational (*ʿaqlī*) imagery and not *takhyīl*, including simile and metaphor, the latter of which he explicitly excludes from the realm of make-believe, as we have seen.

Furthermore, rational ideas do not necessarily exclude the imaginary. The notions of the "imaginary" and "falsehood" are sometimes conflated in modern scholarship, leading to an equation between the falsehood which al-Jurjānī talks about under the rubric of *takhyīl* with "the imaginary" that remains in the realm of literal truth. This is not exactly accurate. There is a distinction between *takhyīl*, which is an active production of an image, and *khayāl*, which is the imaginary. Al-Jurjānī is quite comfortable with *khayāl* or unrealistic imagined representations in general as long as their imaginary status remains clear. Thus, the imaginary can also exist within the realm of truthfulness.

For example, in his discussion of composite comparisons (i.e., comparisons that are made up of a combination of matters),[110] al-Jurjānī explains that they are divided into two types: one in which the poet imagines the combination of two things which *do not exist* in reality and one that is made up of a combination of things that *do exist* in reality.[111] An example of the first is a verse by al-Ṣanawbarī (d. 334/945–6) comparing anemones to:[112]

that by the fifth/eleventh century, the debate had shifted so far to the other side (i.e., pro-falsehood) that it was the poeticity of truthfulness that needed to be defended.

108 Abu Deeb, "Literary Criticism," 385.

109 Adonis also misunderstands al-Jurjānī's juxtaposition of *ʿaqlī* and *takhyīlī*. See *al-Thābit wa-l-mutaḥawwil*, 3:287. He assumes *ʿaqlī* is nonpoetic and *takhyīlī* is.

110 See Chapter 3 for a description of "composite comparisons" under the section "Simile and the Science of *Bayān*."

111 al-Jurjānī, *Asrār*, 154–7.

112 Verse cited earlier; ibid., 146.

أعلامُ ياقوتٍ نُشِرْ * نَ على رِماحٍ من زَبَرجَدْ

Banners of ruby unfurled
on lances of peridot

An example of the second is the following verse by Ibn al-Muʿtazz:[113]

غدا والصُّبحُ تحتَ اللّيلِ بادٍ كطِرْفٍ أَشهَبٍ مُلْقَى الجِلالِ

He departed as the morning appeared under the night
like a pale steed whose [dark] horsecloth was slipping off

Speaking of the latter, al-Jurjānī explains that this image is one that:

exists and is known, for a pale horse that is letting its blanket slide off is not inexistent so that one could say it is limited to the hypothetical and the imagination. As for the former, it does not go beyond the [realm of] the imagination and the hypothetical.[114]

He goes on to say that the anemones comparison is particularly far from existence given that the poet describes the banners as "unfurling" and the "unfurling of rubies, which are stones, cannot be imagined to exist [in reality.]"[115]

Hellmut Ritter in his edition of al-Jurjānī's *Asrār al-balāgha* titles this section as "make-believe composite comparisons (*al-tashbīh al-murakkab al-takhyīlī*),"[116] even though the text itself never mentions the term "*takhyīl*" in this section. In the same manner, von Grunebaum links this imaginary type of comparison to *takhyīl*.[117] Heinrichs rightly warns against conflating the two "kinds of *takhyīl*," without elaborating on the difference, however.[118] The imaginary in the case of such composite comparisons, however, does not function as "make-believe" (*takhyīl*) in al-Jurjānī's sense, i.e., it does not claim something untrue to be true. Rather, it is simply "*khayāl*" (imaginary). This is attested in later renditions of this category in simile, which al-Sakkākī and al-Khaṭīb al-Qazwīnī designate as "*murakkab khayālī*" (imaginary composite [comparisons]), not "*takhyīlī*" (make-believe).[119]

What is at stake in this distinction is that imaginary unrealistic images can exist in poetry without rendering it "false." As long as it remains a statement of comparison and does not claim something unrealistic as

113 Ibid., 155. 114 Ibid. 115 Ibid. 116 Ibid., 154.
117 G. E. von Grunebaum, *Kritik und Dichtkunst* (Wiesbaden: Harrassowitz, 1955), 47–50; cited in Heinrichs, "Takhyīl," 12.
118 van Gelder and Hammond, *Takhyīl*, 12.
119 See my discussion of the *murakkab khayālī* kind of comparison in Chapter 3.

literally true, it remains in the realm of "rational ideas." In this case, al-Jurjānī has no problem with comparing something to an imaginary and completely made-up image. On the contrary, as we will see in Chapter 3, invented imaginary comparisons, such as al-Ṣanawbarī's anemones example, are even preferred for their rarity. The imagery that the old school considered "false," therefore, becomes part of al-Jurjānī's category of "rational meanings," which he designates as truthful. Literal truthfulness and the imaginary, therefore, are not mutually exclusive and being an adherent of truthfulness in poetry does not eliminate the imaginary in the general sense of "*khayāl*."

Takhyīl, on the other hand, is a particular kind of fantastic figure: one that – as the Arabic word denotes – *makes* the listener imagine something as something else. Unreal, made-up images like the anemones comparison remain in the realm of "truthfulness" because, being a comparison, they merely beckon the listener to imagine something inexistent, but they do not require him to accept it as truth. *Takhyīl*, on the other hand, is a kind of poetic construction that *tricks* one into accepting a false claim. Indeed, al-Jurjānī's definition of *takhyīl* involves some "trickery of the mind (*khidāʿ li-l-ʿaql*)." He explains that it is a process in which "the poet asserts as a proven fact a matter which is not proven at all, makes a claim that is impossible to realize, and says something in a way that tricks the mind and allows it to see what cannot be seen."[120]

Al-Jurjānī therefore modifies the understanding of truth and falsehood in poetry by shifting the discourse to the internal logic of an image and dividing representations based on whether they are rationally viable or require the listener to suspend belief. What was previously treated as untruthful in the old school of criticism, such as figurative language and imaginary comparisons, becomes part of the realm of truthfulness because they do not require their acceptance as an actual truth and remain accurate on the literal level. The realm of falsehood, in turn, is expanded to incorporate fantastic imagery that makes a false poetic claim. The imaginary can exist in both realms and any apparent approval of *takhyīl*-based imagery is not due to al-Jurjānī's tolerance of falsehood, as some scholars have suggested. Rather, as we will see in the following section, it is due to a new understanding of poetic beauty, one that is based on the ability of a poetic representation to evoke wonder in the listener.

[120] al-Jurjānī, *Asrār*, 253.

The Aesthetics of Make-Believe

Make-believe imagery allows for an experience of wonder in the listener because it is able to produce unexpected novel ideas by "tricking" the listener into accepting false premises as truth. Al-Jurjānī explains that those who say that "the best poetry is the most untruthful" do not have in mind an artless and reckless fabrication of lies, "such as describing a guard with the attributes of a caliph or saying of a destitute wretch: 'You are the prince of both Iraqs [i.e., Baṣra and Kūfa].'"[121] Rather, what is intended with falsehood in poetry is "craftsmanship in its art and a kind of meticulousness in its meanings that requires cunning intelligence, penetrating understanding, and great insight."[122] One of the examples al-Jurjānī gives to illustrate this kind of crafty fantastic imagery is the following verse:

الشَّيبُ كُرهٌ وكُرهٌ أنْ يُفارِقَني   أَعجِبْ بشيءٍ على البَغْضاءِ مَوْدودُ

Gray hair is hateful; yet [more] hateful is for it to leave me
How strange it is to love something despite despising it!
~ Ibn al-Mu'tazz[123]

He explains that on the surface the meaning of the verse appears to be literally accurate: While the appearance of gray hair is not desirable, its loss is also undesirable (because it implies death).[124] However, if one examines the verse, al-Jurjānī explains, one realizes that "while the hatred for the gray hair is based in reality, the love of it is imagined and does not truly exist in reality. Rather the [real] object of love and desire is life and immortality."[125] In other words, while the object of the poet's hatred in the first instance is the hair's actual physical appearance, the object of his desire in the second is what its continued presence implies and not the hair itself. Therefore, the claim that the actual gray hair is the poet's object of desire is technically "false," yet the listener accepts it.[126]

121 Ibid. ("both Iraqs" refers to Kūfa and Baṣra. See van Gelder and Hammond, *Takhyīl*, 38; and Edward William Lane and Stanley Lane-Poole, *An Arabic-English Lexicon* (Beirut: Librairie du Liban, 1968), s.v. *'-r-q*).

122 al-Jurjānī, *Asrār*, 253.

123 The verse is also attributed to Muslim ibn al-Walīd and Bashshār ibn Burd, both *muḥdath* poets as well. See ibid., 246n300.

124 Ibid., 246. 125 Ibid.

126 For a discussion of this verse, see Larkin, *Theology of Meaning*, 136–7. She states that "the basis for considering hoariness desirable is a *takhyīlī* one, i.e., its coincidental association with something that is in truth dear to a person, namely life." The mere existence of some relationship between two things that allows for the one to

In order for the poet's resulting amazement at gray hair being at once loved and hated to be "bought," one *has to* accept his "false premise" that the disappearance of the *actual* gray hair is what is detested. Al-Jurjānī explains this as follows:

> The substance of poetry and oratory (*khaṭāba*) is to render the concurrence of a characteristic in two things[127] the basis for a judgment they [the poet and the orator] wish to make, even if it is irrational and goes against reason. The poet is not expected to verify what he has established as a basis and cause for his claim as something to be proved or disproved in a proposition, and [he is not required] to provide rational evidence for what he has established as a basis and foundation. Rather the premise he adopts is accepted without evidence.[128]

If a listener is to accept the poet's observation above, which claims that something so hated can be so loved at one and the same time, he has to grant the poet the false premise that the object of his love is the actual gray hair and not what it is initially meant to symbolize, i.e., life and immortality.[129]

This idea becomes clearer with another example al-Jurjānī gives for *takhyīl*. In this case, a fantastic explanation is given for something real, a literary figure known as fantastic etiology (*al-taʿlīl al-takhyīlī*):[130]

الرّيحُ تَحسُدني عليـ * ـك ولم اخَلْها في العِدا
لَمّا هَمَمْتُ بِقُبْلةٍ رَدَّتْ على الوَجْهِ الرِّدا

> The wind is jealous of me over you and I had not imagined it an enemy
> When I meant to give a kiss, it blew the cloak over the face
>
> ~ al-Ṣūlī (d. 335/946)

represent the other is not *takhyīl* in and of itself, however. Depending on the nature of this relationship – whether it is a similarity or a part of a whole, for example – the substituting word would simply be a metaphor (*istiʿāra*), figurative speech more generally (*majāz*), or metonymy (*kināya*) (al-Jurjānī discusses this in great detail in chapter 24 of the *Asrār*). It is not simply the fact that the poet uses the loss of gray hair as a symbol for death that renders the image "*takhyīlī*." Rather, it is the fact that he takes this symbol literally and arrives at a conclusion (that the actual gray hair is both hated and loved) on the basis of a false premise.

127 That is, *majāz*/figurative language. The existence of a relationship between two things is the basis on which figurative language is constructed. See al-Jurjānī's discussion of *majāz* from chapter 21 onward in his *Asrār*.

128 al-Jurjānī, *Asrār*, 248. As several scholars have noted, this description sounds curiously similar to the philosopher's description of poetic syllogisms (see, for example, Larkin, *Theology of Meaning*, 138).

129 This resulting contradictory statement is similar to the one Qudāma criticizes about the dog who "speaks" and yet is mute, discussed earlier.

130 al-Jurjānī, *Asrār*, 257–8.

The poet describes a real event (the wind blowing the cloak over the face) and claims for it an imaginary cause (the jealousy of the wind). The image works only if we accept the premise that the wind is jealous, a false premise. The listener is thus "tricked" into buying into the illusion that an inanimate object has human qualities that motivate its behavior.

In another example, al-Jurjānī discusses the construction of speech around a metaphor as if it were literally true. He cites the following verses by al-Buḥturī in praise of the Abbasid caliph al-Mutawakkil (r. 232/847–247/861), in which he employs the common metaphor of the sun literally:[131]

طَلَعْتَ لَهُم وَقْتَ الشُّروقِ فعايَنُوا　　سَنَا الشّمْسِ من أُفْقٍ ووَجْهَك من أُفْقِ
وما عايَنوا شَمْسَينِ قَبْلَهُما ٱلْتَقَى　　ضِياؤُهُما وَفْقاً من الغَرْبِ والشَّرْقِ

You appeared to them at sunrise so that they saw
  the sun's splendor from one horizon and your face from another
Never before had they seen two suns, meeting
  with equal radiance from west and east

Al-Jurjānī explains: "It is known that the intention is to bring the listeners to a state of wonder for seeing that which they have never seen before and which is out of the ordinary."[132] But then he goes on to explain that this wonder would not work were it not for the listener's acceptance of an apparent lie, "forcing the mind, willingly or not, to imagine a second sun that has risen from where the sun [normally] sets."[133] The poet therefore "tricks" the listener into accepting the illusion that the caliph is a *real* sun. It is not merely the fact that it is fantasy that makes it wonder-evoking, therefore. Rather, it is the fact that the listener is, willingly or not, "forced" to "buy into" an illusion and see something never seen before based on accepting this false premise.

In another example by none other than the old-school critic, Ibn Ṭabāṭabā, the mechanism of make-believe imagery is explained even more explicitly:[134]

لا تَعْجَبوا من بِلَى غِلالَتِهِ　　قَدْ زُرَّ أَزْرارَهُ على القَمَرِ

Do not be surprised at the wearing out of his undergarment:
  Its buttons are buttoned on the moon

[131] Ibid., 281. See complete poem in al-Buḥturī, *Dīwān al-Buḥturī*, ed. Ḥasan Kāmil al-Ṣayrafī (Cairo: Dār al-Maʿārif, 1963–4), 1546–7.
[132] Ibid. [133] Ibid. [134] Ibid., 282.

It was believed among the Arabs that the moon had the effect of wearing out clothes, especially linen.[135] The poet, in this case, takes the common metaphor of the moon literally in reference to a beautiful person and ascribes to that person the supposed tendency of the moon to spoil fabric. Al-Jurjānī explains:

The intention with all this is to make it known that there is no doubt or suspicion that [we are] dealing with the moon itself and that the talk is about the moon proper and nothing else. The comparison is forgotten and is made to be forgotten.[136]

It is in this concealment and erasure of the status of the image as a metaphor where the beauty of *takhyīl* lies. Al-Jurjānī asks us to consider what would happen if we were to spell out the comparison and say: "do not be surprised at the wearing out of his undergarment for its buttons are buttoned on someone as beautiful as the moon." He goes on to ask rhetorically: "would you see anything but mediocre speech and a common idea? [...] would you experience the same kind of pleasure you had before, [...] would you see [in the eyes of the listeners] the kind of expression of happiness and sign of admiration that you had seen before?"[137] He proceeds to point out that it is impossible to have the same experience of pleasure, since exposing the similarity negates the whole point of the verse. There would be nothing for the poet to declare "not to be amazed about."

In the standardized science of eloquence (*ʿilm al-balāgha*) the category of make-believe as a rubric for classifying a set of poetic devices is not maintained.[138] However, as we will see in Chapter 4, treating a metaphor as literally true and building an image on it is one way

[135] This is also noted by al-Thaʿālibī in *Yatīmat al-dahr fī maḥāsin ahl al-ʿaṣr*, ed. Mufīd Muḥammad Qumayḥa, vol. 5, *Tatimmat al-Yatīma* (Beirut: Dār al-Kutub al-ʿIlmiyya, 1983), 10. The alleged effect of the moon on linen is also mentioned by al-Jāḥiẓ in "*Risālat al-tarbīʿ wa-l-tadwīr*" (*Rasāʾil al-Jāḥiẓ*, ed. ʿAbd al-Salām Hārūn, 4 vols. (Beirut: Dār al-Jīl, 1991), 3:90–1).

[136] al-Jurjānī, *Asrār*, 283. [137] Ibid.

[138] Nevertheless, they do use the term to describe the mechanism of make-believe in various contexts, as we will see below, for example, in al-Khaṭīb al-Qazwīnī's discussion of reinvigorating overused similes. Note that al-Sakkākī and his school also start applying the idea of *takhyīl* to describe metaphors that "borrow something for something else." One of the typical examples they cite for this kind of metaphor is the description of death as having claws in a famous verse by the pre-Islamic/early Islamic poet Abū Dhuʾayb al-Hudhalī, or the description by the famous pre-Islamic poet Labīd of the north wind as having hands that are holding on to reigns (al-Khaṭīb al-Qazwīnī, *al-Īḍāḥ*, 444–5). Heinrichs has described these as the old kind of metaphor. This is in contrast with the new metaphors, which are based on a similarity between the tenor and the vehicle, not on "borrowing," which is what the word for metaphor in Arabic (*istiʿāra*) literally means (*The*

of intensifying the illusion that the metaphor and the matter it intends to stand in for are one and the same thing. This process, which they call *tarshīḥ* (fostering or development), enhances the beauty of metaphor because it reinforces the equation between the two things compared. This helps obscure the intended meaning in a way that makes its subsequent discovery more pleasing.[139] As such, make-believe, including in the form of the *badīʿ* figure of "amazement," serves as reinforcement to the metaphor. The aesthetic logic continues to be one of wonder and its value lies in its ability to enhance this experience.

It is not a change in attitude about falsehood, therefore, that allows al-Jurjānī and his successors to appreciate the beauty of make-believe imagery. Rather, it is the ability of such imagery to trick the listener into accepting an illusion and to discover meaning where it is not expected. It is not the falsehood of the image that renders it beautiful, in other words; rather the aesthetic experience that its make-believe mechanism is able to produce.[140] In fact, al-Jurjānī credits make-believe imagery with the ability to breathe new life into old ideas. It is precisely the ability of make-believe imagery to trick one into discovering a new meaning that allows a poet to produce new and unique images. As an example, al-Jurjani cites the following verse by Abū Nuwās, which puts a new twist on the standard comparison of generosity to rain or dew:

إنَّ السَّحابَ لَتَسْتَحي إذا نَظَرَتْ   إلى نَداك فقاسَتْهُ بما فيها

The clouds would be truly ashamed if they looked
at your rain [i.e., generosity] and measured it against their own

He explains that the verse is in essence a mere comparison. However, "it has been expressed indirectly, [in such a way] that you are tricked (*khūdiʿt*) and enchanted by way of magic and in the manner of *takhyīl*."[141] Elsewhere he adds more specifically that the poet "gives you the illusion

Hand of the Northwind: Opinions on Metaphor and the Early Meaning of Istiʿāra in Arabic Poetics, Abhandlungen für die Kunde des Morgenlandes (Wiesbaden: Kommissionsverlag Franz Steiner, 1977)). The old kind of metaphor is not discussed under the rubric of *takhyīl* by al-Jurjānī. Al-Sakkākī and al-Khaṭīb al-Qazwīnī, however, suggest that these kinds of metaphor require one to "make believe" that the north wind has hands, for example, which are holding onto reigns, for the metaphor to work. (Note that there is some discrepancy in the scope each of the authors delimits for these kinds of "make-believe" metaphors. It is, however, tangential to our discussion here.)

139 See Chapter 4, discussion of metaphor under "Variation in *Bayān*."

140 Moreover, Key has stressed the importance of lexical accuracy for al-Jurjānī even in his treatment of make-believe imagery in *Language between God and the Poets*, 226–8.

141 al-Jurjānī, *Asrār*, 316.

(*yūhimuka*) with the statement 'the clouds are ashamed' that the clouds are living [beings], conscious and able to reason, and that they measure their bounty against that of the hand of the eulogized person so that they become ashamed."[142] While the basis of the image is the likening of the rain of the clouds to a person's generosity, a common simile, the poet builds on this comparison using the false premise that the clouds are animate, giving them the human emotion of shame, and thus indirectly exaggerating the addressee's generosity.

Make-believe as a mechanism is also adduced as a way of reinvigorating overused similes in the science of eloquence. Al-Khaṭīb al-Qazwīnī discusses the following verse by al-Mutanabbī, for example, which adds novelty to the hackneyed comparison of a radiant face to the sun through personification:[143]

لم تَلْقَ هَذا الوَجْهَ شَمسُ نَهارِنَا إلّا بوَجْهٍ لَيسَ فيهِ حَيَاءُ

The sun of our daytime has not met this face
except with a face that has no shame

In other words, the (real) sun has the gall to appear in front of the eulogized person's face only "out of insolence; otherwise there is no need for it in the presence of [the addressee's] face," as al-Wāḥidī (d. 468/1076) explains in his commentary on al-Mutanabbī's *Dīwān*.[144] The poet, therefore, not only reverses the typical simile and makes the addressee more deserving of being called the sun than the sun itself, but he does so indirectly by giving the sun the human emotion of shamelessness. This idea of the sun's shame, al-Khaṭīb al-Qazwīnī explains, takes the cliché simile "out of commonplaceness to strangeness."[145] Thus, make-believe imagery with its ability to produce new meanings in indirect ways is valued precisely for its ability to defamiliarize familiar similes, producing unexpected new imagery.

Hyperbole

These last two examples of make-believe fall under the category of falsehood not only because they give human qualities to inanimate objects, but also because they entail hyperbole. Abū Nuwās exaggerates the addressee's

[142] Ibid., 317. [143] al-Khaṭīb al-Qazwīnī, *al-Īḍāḥ*, 385.
[144] al-Mutanabbī and al-Wāḥidī, *Dīwān Abī al-Ṭayyib al-Mutanabbī wa-fī athnāʾ matnih sharḥ al-Imām al-ʿAllāma al-Wāḥidī*, ed. Fridericus Dieterici (Berlin: 1861), 201.
[145] al-Khaṭīb al-Qazwīnī, *al-Īḍāḥ*, 385.

generosity by making him more generous than the standard symbol of generosity, the cloud. Al-Mutanabbī exaggerates his addressee's splendor by making his face brighter than the sun. The beauty of such hyperbolic meaning, as we will see, does not depend on hyperbole for its own sake. Instead, the reasons al-Jurjānī and his successors give for the success of hyperbole are very similar to the aesthetic logic that underlies their discussions of make-believe.

Hyperbole comes up in al-Jurjānī's extensive treatment of "reversed similes," a literary figure typical in *muḥdath* poetry.[146] Some reversed similes simply give an old comparison a new twist, such as taking the standard comparison of the eye to the narcissus, for example, and reversing it so that the narcissus is likened to the eye, as in the following verse by Abū Nuwās:[147]

لدى نَرْجِسٍ غَضِّ القِطافِ كأَنّه   إذا ما مَنَحْناه العُيونَ عُيونُ

(Next to)[148] freshly picked narcissus, which resemble
– if we grant them our eyes – eyes

Reversed similes, however, often serve to exaggerate the quality being compared by making the secondary matter the principal object of comparison. Al-Jurjānī's explanation of the beauty of such reversed similes goes beyond its truth or falsehood. Instead, he explains that such a reversed simile is particularly "magical" because "it conveys a hyperbole in a manner that is not felt (or noticed) and without exposing [that the poet is making a false] allegation. This is because he based his speech, as one who compares does, on a [seemingly] agreed upon and accepted principle."[149]

In other words, by reversing the simile, the poet takes something secondary and renders it the principal matter to which other things should be compared, thus emphasizing or exaggerating what would otherwise be the inferior part of the comparison. However, the exaggeration is an implicit secondary meaning one arrives at indirectly. Thus, the aesthetic mechanism al-Jurjānī identifies that renders hyperbole beautiful is based on the production of unexpected meaning, the discovery of which is

146 Al-Jurjānī dedicates a whole chapter to reversed simile (al-Jurjānī, *Asrār*, ch. 13, pp. 187–219).
147 Ibid., 188.
148 This is in reference to wine described in the preceding lines of the poem not cited here. See complete poem in Abū Nuwās, *Dīwān*, ed. Ewald Wagner and Gregor Schoeler, 5 vols. (Wiesbaden: Franz Steiner Verlag, 1958–2003), 3:305–8.
149 al-Jurjānī, *Asrār*, 206.

obscured and delayed in this case through "turning the primary [matter being compared] into the secondary and vice versa."[150] That is, al-Jurjānī explains, "the poet intends in the manner of *takhyīl* to give the illusion that something that is lacking in a quality with respect to its counterpart, [actually] exceeds it [...] by making it the principal [part of the comparison]."[151] For example, in the following verse:

وبَدا الصَّباحُ كأنّ غُرّتَه وَجْهُ الخَليفَة حين يُمتدَحُ

And the morning appeared as if its brightness
were the countenance of the caliph while being praised
~ Muḥammad ibn Wuhayb (fl. third/ninth century)

reversing the comparison made it seem as if what is typically the *primum comparandum* (*al-mushabbah*) is more known for a particular characteristic than what typically inhabits the *secundum comparatum* (*al-mushabbah bihi*). In this case, the caliph's face, it is implied, is more known for brightness than is the rise of dawn.

Al-Jurjānī states that meanings conveyed in this manner evoke "a special kind of pleasure and marvelous kind of joy, like a good deed not tarnished by the feeling of obligation and a favor not spoiled by keeping count."[152] He proceeds to explain that reversed similes allow you to gain an added meaning where you do not expect it and "in sum, you discover existence from where you imagined non-existence."[153] Like make-believe imagery, reversed similes create an illusion and make you imagine something as something else, allowing you to discover an unexpected meaning. Indeed, al-Khaṭīb al-Qazwīnī later calls these kinds of reversed similes "*takhyīlī*," even though al-Jurjānī himself does not classify them under his rubric of make-believe imagery.[154]

In distinguishing regular similes from reversed ones, al-Sakkākī and al-Khaṭīb al-Qazwīnī explain that normally similes serve to expose something about the original matter being compared (*al-mushabbah*) by likening it to something else. However, when the purpose is to reveal something about the *secundum comparatum* (*al-mushabbah bihi*), such as in reversed similes, then the point is to "give the illusion that it is more complete than the *primum comparandum* (*mushabbah*) in the aspect of the similarity."[155] In other words, going back to the last example, by rendering the "countenance of the caliph" the *secundum*

[150] Ibid., 187. [151] Ibid., 205. [152] Ibid., 206.
[153] Ibid. "تجد على الجملة الوجود من حيث توهمت العدم".
[154] al-Khaṭīb al-Qazwīnī, *al-Īḍāḥ*, 336ff. See also 361ff. [155] al-Sakkākī, *al-Miftāḥ*, 450.

comparatum and making it the thing to which the morning's brightness is likened, the poet "gives the illusion" that the countenance of the caliph is "more complete" in its brightness than the morning. The examples could also be more abstract, such as in the following verse, quoted by al-Sakkākī:

ولقد ذكرتُكِ والظَّلامُ كأنّهُ　　يومُ النَّوى وفُؤادُ مَنْ لَمْ يَعْشَقِ

I remembered you in a darkness that resembled
 the day of separation and the heart of one who has never loved
~ Abū Ṭālib al-Raqqī (likely fl. late third/ninth, early fourth/tenth century)

Al-Sakkākī explains that usually tragedy is compared to darkness. However, the poet reverses the simile and compares darkness to tragedy, by likening it to the day of separation (from the beloved) and a heart that has not loved, as if separation and lack of love are blacker than blackness.[156] Al-Khaṭīb al-Qazwīnī, quoting al-Jurjānī, states that this kind of reversal serves hyperbole in a subtle unnoticeable way. Conveying meanings in such a way, he goes on to say, "has a kind of pleasure that is marvelous (*ʿajīb*)."[157]

Hyperbole (*mubālagha*) is itself treated as a rhetorical figure in the branch of the science of eloquence focused on *badīʿ*. Plausibility remains a necessary criterion for the acceptability of exaggerated meanings. However, implausible ideas can also be made acceptable either through qualifying an idea as a "near possibility" of the kind we saw in the old school of criticism or through make-believe imagery.[158] Thus make-believe becomes a legitimate way of creating an acceptable kind of hyperbole. To illustrate this, al-Khaṭīb al-Qazwīnī cites the following verse by al-Mutanabbī, which exaggerates the intensity of the dust of battle:

عَقَدَتْ سَنابِكُها عَلَيْها عِثْيَراً　　لوْ تَبْتَغي عَنَقاً عَلَيْهِ لأمْكَنا

Their hooves set over them a [layer of] dust
 If they wished to [walk] on it fast-paced, they could have

The poet claims that dust from the hooves of the horses collected over their heads so densely that it became a ground on which horses could walk. Al-Taftāzānī, in his supercommentary on al-Sakkākī's *al-Miftāḥ*, states that this is an impossible image in terms of "logic and custom, but is a good kind of make-believe."[159]

[156] al-Sakkākī, *al-Miftāḥ*, 451. [157] al-Khaṭīb al-Qazwīnī, *al-Īḍāḥ*, 361. [158] Ibid., 515–16.
[159] Saʿd al-Dīn al-Taftāzānī, *al-Muṭawwal: Sharḥ Talkhīṣ Miftāḥ al-ʿulūm*, ed. ʿAbd al-Ḥamīd Hindāwī, 3rd ed. (Beirut: Dār al-Kutub al-ʿIlmiyya, 2013), 666.

Similarly, in his discussion of fantastic etiology, al-Khaṭīb al-Qazwīnī also acknowledges the benefits of make-believe for producing beautiful hyperbole.[160] One of the examples he presents is another verse by al-Mutanabbī in which he praises the prince Badr ibn ʿAmmār (al-Kharshānī), who was the governor of the district (*Jund*) of Jordan for a short while during 329/940, when he patronized the poet. In a short poem he purportedly improvised on the spot, he said of him:[161]

ما بِهِ قَتْلُ أعاديهِ ولكِنْ   يَتّقي إخلافَ ما ترْجو الذّئابُ

He does not have it in him to kill his enemies. However,
he does not want to disappoint the wolves

The idea behind the verse is that the wolves have become so accustomed to feeding on the battle's casualties, that the governor kills his enemies out of loyalty to the wolves' expectations. Al-Khaṭīb al-Qazwīnī explains that this is:

. . . an exaggeration in the description of his generosity. It also entails an exaggeration in the description of his bravery in a make-believe way. That is, his bravery reached such an extent that it was apparent even to speechless animals, so that when he left for war, the wolves [waited] in hope of reaping some of his enemies' flesh.[162]

By giving a fantastic cause to the addressee's gallantry, therefore, al-Mutanabbī not only exaggerates his supposed generosity toward the wolves, but also, indirectly, his reputation in battle (which is apparent even to the wolves).

While the old school of criticism evaluated the figure based on how much it remains close to the truth despite exaggerating, as we have seen, the new school emphasized the ability to exaggerate indirectly, conveying hyperbolic meaning in subtle and unexpected ways. This does not mean that they condoned limitless and reckless exaggeration. However, the reasons they gave for the acceptability of implausible hyperbole were based on its expression in indirect ways. This can be achieved through reversing a simile or through make-believe imagery. In both cases, the

[160] On the figure of fantastic etiology and its development, see Geert Jan van Gelder, "'A Good Cause': Fantastic Etiology (*Ḥusn al-Taʿlīl*) in Arabic Poetics," in *Takhyīl: The Imaginary in Classical Arabic Poetics*, ed. Geert Jan van Gelder and Marlé Hammond (Cambridge, UK: Gibb Memorial Trust, 2008).

[161] al-Mutanabbī, *Dīwān Abī al-Ṭayyib al-Mutanabbī*, ed. ʿAbd al-Wahhāb ʿAzzām (Cairo: Lajnat al-Taʾlīf wa-l-Tarjama wa-l-Nashr, 1944), 131–2. On the patron, see also *Badr al-Kharshanī*, in *EI*^{2}.

[162] al-Khaṭīb al-Qazwīnī, *al-Īḍāḥ*, 520.

reasoning they provide for the beauty of hyperbole is the fact that these figures give the illusion of something, which implicitly conveys a secondary exaggerated meaning. The logic underlying the beauty of such fantastic hyperbole, therefore, remains one of wonder.

The Aesthetics of Badīʿ

A single aesthetic theory, which I am summarily describing as one of wonder, begins to become apparent in the new school of criticism's treatment of make-believe figures and hyperbole. This theory also explains the aesthetics of *badīʿ* in general. Instead of regarding *badīʿ* as mere embellishment whose excessive use renders poetry artificial and untruthful, as the old school of criticism would have it, al-Jurjānī grants it an integral role in poetry's ability to produce an emotional effect in the listener. As such, for the first time in Arabic criticism, a theory that explains the beauty of *badīʿ* is forged.

While al-Jurjānī limits his direct discussion of *badīʿ* to only a few figures, he suggests that this aesthetic is universal across rhetorical figures. We will see how this is the case in relation to paronomasia (*tajnīs*) and a figure called "padding" (*ḥashw*). In addition, looking at the kinds of constructions the Arabic critical tradition identifies as rhetorical figures in the first place (many of which do not have counterparts in English), one can identify in many of them a pattern of obscuring, misleading, and trickery for the sake of producing an unexpected and surprising meaning.[163] In other words, many rhetorical figures inherently entail structures that allow for an experience of discovery and wonder in the listener.

Paronomasia (*Tajnīs*) and Padding (*Ḥashw*)

Al-Jurjānī explicitly likens the aesthetic mechanism of reversed similes (discussed above) to that of paronomasia (*tajnīs*).[164] Even though paronomasia, which entails the repetition of similar-sounding words in a verse, can easily be regarded merely as an acoustic ornament, al-Jurjānī

[163] For a list and overview of many of the figures featured in the science of *badīʿ*, see Heinrichs, "Rhetorical Figures," in *Encyclopedia of Arabic Literature*. For a discussion of *badīʿ* figures in general as delineated in medieval Arabic critical texts, see Geert Jan van Gelder, *Badīʿ*, in *EI*^{3}; and Pierre J. Cachia, *The Arch Rhetorician or the Schemer's Skimmer: A Handbook of Late Arabic badīʿ Drawn from ʿAbd al-Ghanī an-Nābulsī's Nafaḥāt al-azhār ʿalā nasamāt al-asḥār* (Wiesbaden: Harrassowitz, 1998).

[164] al-Jurjānī, *Asrār*, 206.

emphasizes that its beauty lies in how the figure affects the conveying and reception of meaning, not in its sound. More specifically, it is due to some additional meaning (*fā'ida*) it communicates despite appearing not to.

One of the examples al-Jurjānī cites for a good paronomasia is the following old Arabian hemistich describing an arrow penetrating the prey:[165]

حتَّى نَجا من جَوفِه وما نَجا

So that it escaped from its belly and it did not escape

~ Anonymous

The word "*najā*," meaning escaped or survived, is repeated in the verse but with different subjects: the arrow and the prey. In other words, the arrow penetrated and went through the belly of the prey, escaping from it, while the prey did not escape death.[166] In another example of good paronomasia, he quotes a verse, which he specifies is by a *muḥdath* poet:[167]

ناظِراهُ فيما جَنَى ناظِراهُ   أو دَعاني أَمُتْ بما أودعاني

Dispute [*nāẓirāh*] what his eyes [*nāẓirāh*] have committed
Or let me [*aw da'ānī*] die from what they have caused me [*awda'ānī*]

Two pairs of similar-sounding utterances are repeated with different meanings. *Nāẓirāh*, a verb in the imperative dual form meaning "dispute" in the first instance, and a noun meaning "his two eyes" in the second. And *aw-da'ānī*, which in the first instance is constructed of two words, *aw* meaning "or" and *da'ānī* meaning "let me" in the imperative dual form, and in the second instance is one word, a past tense verb in the dual form, meaning "caused" or "produced." Al-Jurjānī explains that the beauty of paronomasia in these examples lies in the meaning that the repeated words add and not simply in the repeated utterances themselves. More specifically, he says, the poet:

165 Ibid., 7n3. Also mentioned in 'Abd al-Qāhir al-Jurjānī, *Dalā'il al-i'jāz*, ed. Maḥmūd Muḥammad Shākir, 5th ed. (Cairo: Maktabat al-Khānjī, 2004), 523. One variation has it *khawf* (fear) instead of *jawf* (belly), which might be a typographical mistake given the similarity in the shapes of the letters "*kh*" and "*j*" in Arabic. I am following al-Jāḥiẓ's reading of it as *jawf* in *Kitāb al-ḥayawān*, ed. 'Abd al-Salām Hārūn, 8 vols. (Beirut: Dār al-Jīl, 1996), 3:75. Interestingly, unlike 'Abd al-Qāhir al-Jurjānī, the author of *al-Wasāṭa*, al-Qaḍī al-Jurjānī, regards it an ugly verse for the contradiction it entails (*al-Wasāṭa*, 392), though he perhaps read the variant *khawf*, which does make the verse less clear.

166 al-Jurjānī, *Asrār*, 7.

167 Ibid. The verse is variously attributed to Shamsawayh al-Baṣrī (Abbasid), al-Ṭāhir al-Jazarī (d. 401/1011), and Abū al-Fatḥ al-Bustī (d. 354/965) (see ibid., n4).

repeats an utterance as if he is tricking you (*yakhdaʿuka*) into [believing] that there is no additional meaning (*fāʾida*) while providing you with one, and as if he is giving you the illusion (*yūhimuka*) that he is not adding anything [to the meaning] while adding [to it] and completing it.[168]

In another instance, he elaborates, discussing an example of an imperfect paronomasia, in which two words sound the same, save for one letter. Citing the following verse by Abū Tammām,[169]

يَمُدّونَ مِن أَيدٍ عَواصٍ[170] عواصمٍ   تصولُ بأسْيافٍ قَواضٍ قَواضِبِ

They stretch arms, striking (*ʿawāṣ-in*) and protective (*ʿawāṣim*),
which attack with swords, deadly (*qawāḍ-in*) and sharp (*qawāḍib*)

al-Jurjānī states:

You imagine, before you hear the end of the word, the "m" in *ʿawāṣim* and the "b" in *qawāḍib*, that they are the same as those preceding them, only repeated for emphasis, until your mind becomes aware of their conclusions and you hear their endings, and you let go of your initial expectation and step away from what you had first imagined. This is what I mean by an added meaning (*fāʾida*) arising after [you almost] give up, and by gaining profit after you misjudge it so you see that it is the [very source] of wealth.[171]

The recurrence of a word in paronomasia, in other words, makes one assume it is a mere repetition, but then a small change in a vowel or a final sound makes one realize that it is something else. Elsewhere, he sums up the beauty of paronomasia being in the "added meaning (*ḥusn al-ifāda*) despite the appearance of repetition."[172]

In a similar vein, al-Jurjānī discusses another rhetorical figure, known as "padding" (*ḥashw*), which entails apparent redundancies and irrelevant parentheses, often added only for the sake of the rhyme or meter. Al-Jurjānī explains that *ḥashw* (lit. stuffing) is by definition "padding," which does not add anything to the meaning; if it were to have meaning, it would

168 Ibid., 8.
169 Ibid., 18. The verse either has an omitted object or an added preposition, which medieval grammarians debated, as al-Tibrīzī (d. 502/1109) explains in his commentary on Abū Tammām's *Dīwān* (Abū Tammām, *Dīwān Abī Tammām bi-sharḥ al-Khaṭīb al-Tibrīzī*, ed. Muḥammad ʿAbduh ʿAzzām, 4 vols. (Cairo: Dār al-Maʿārif, 1957–65), 1:206–7).
170 From the root ʿ-ṣ-w, meaning to strike with a stick or sword.
171 al-Jurjānī, *Asrār*, 18.
172 Ibid., 17. This applies also to *sajʿ* (rhymed prose). The same argument is repeated by al-Jurjānī in *Dalāʾil*, 523–4. In his discussion of paronomasia under the science of *badīʿ*, al-Khaṭīb al-Qazwīnī also states that it is not the sound in and of itself that makes it beautiful. Rather, it is the effect the repeated sound has on our expectation of meaning (or lack thereof), giving us the illusion of redundancy while adding meaning (*al-Īḍāḥ*, 537 & 539).

not be called *ḥashw*. Nevertheless, some of the best passages, he explains, are those that appear to be mere padding, but then turn out to have a meaningful point. This is particularly beautiful because:

It provides an added meaning (*ifāda*) in a place that one is not accustomed to expect it [. . .]. It is like receiving a good deed from where you do not foresee it or a benefit from where you do not anticipate it.[173]

Al-Jurjānī goes on to state that all types of *badīʿ* figures, including metaphor and antithesis, depend on the meaning they convey: "There is no doubt that beauty and ugliness [are matters that] do not manifest themselves in speech except specifically from the aspect of meaning, without the utterances playing any role in this."[174] While sound does have a place in Arabic poetry and was certainly a concern to critics, its discussion was generally relegated to specialized works on poetic meters and rhyme.[175] From the perspective of eloquence and linguistic beauty, poetic value depended on the ways in which meaning is conveyed. As al-Sakkākī and his commentators remind the reader at the end of their discussion of utterance-based *badīʿ* figures (*al-badīʿ al-lafẓī*), "the source of beauty in all this is that words be in the service of meaning and not the meaning in the service of [words]."[176]

If we keep in mind the logic al-Jurjānī provided for explaining the beauty of paronomasia and padding, however, it is not simply the conveying of meaning in and of itself that is moving or pleasurable, rather it is its conveyance in a particular way. Both paronomasia and padding are figures

[173] al-Jurjānī, *Asrār*, 19–20. Al-Jurjānī does not give examples of padding. However, one can see examples of good and bad "padding" in a later work by al-Muẓaffar al-Ḥusaynī (d. 656/1258) entitled *Naḍrat al-ighrīḍ fī nuṣrat al-qarīḍ*, ed. Nuhā ʿĀrif al-Ḥasan (Damascus: Majmaʿ al-Lugha al-ʿArabiyya, 1976), 180–3. The term *ḥashw al-lawzīnaj* ("almond paste stuffing") was used by several writers for felicitous padding; see van Gelder, *Sound and Sense in Classical Arabic Poetry*, 168.

[174] al-Jurjānī, *Asrār*, 20. Al-Jurjānī addresses the question of utterance vs. meaning (*lafẓ* vs. *maʿnā*) at length in his *Dalāʾil al-iʿjāz*, where he also places eloquence in the realm of meaning, not in the acoustics of utterances. For a discussion of *lafẓ* and *maʿnā* in al-Jurjānī's works, see Harb, "Form, Content, and Inimitability."

[175] Al-Sakkākī has a section on poetic meters in his *Miftāḥ*. While it complements the science of eloquence, it is not part of it. Ibn Sīnā, as we will see in Chapter 2, relegates the discussion of rhyme and meter to the musician and the prosodist (as opposed to the logician) (Ibn Sīnā, *al-Shiʿr*, 23–4). See van Gelder, *Sound and Sense in Classical Arabic Poetry*, for a discussion of the role sound plays in Arabic poetry.

[176] al-Sakkākī, *al-Miftāḥ*, 542; al-Khaṭīb al-Qazwīnī, *al-Īḍāḥ*, 554–5. Rhetorical figures are divided in the science of *badīʿ* in the Sakkākī-Qazwīnī school of eloquence into two kinds: those based on meaning (*maʿnā*) and those based on utterance (*lafẓ*). Paronomasia and padding are among the latter.

that build up a certain expectation of repetition and meaninglessness in the listener. It is the breaking of this expectation and the discovery of an added meaning despite its unlikelihood that moves the listener. In other words, the beauty of these devices is a result of the discovery of meaning where it is not anticipated, thus resulting in amazement and pleasure. If even the beauty of acoustic-based figures such as paronomasia and apparently meaningless padding depends on the production of unexpected meaning, one could expect other figures, which are structured around meaning, to be even more capable of producing such an effect. This is indeed the case, as we will see in the following.

Tawriya and Other Figures of Disguise

Unexpected meaning can be produced through a variety of *badīʿ* figures, whose function by definition depends on disguising meaning and misleading the listener. These include such figures as double entendre (*tawjīh*),[177] a figure itself called "disguising" (*tawriya*) or giving the illusion (*īhām*), and *istikhdām* (the employment [of a word in two senses]), which is a type of double entendre, which depends on employing a word in one sense then referring back to it in its other sense.[178] These figures were identified as *badīʿ* devices only after the time of al-Jurjānī, as Bonebakker has argued.[179] The specific meanings and definitions of these figures varied considerably across critical texts and changed over time. However, the general mechanism common to all of them is one of disguise, whose source of aesthetic pleasure results from the discovery of an unexpected meaning.

While al-Jurjānī does not give it a name, he discusses an example of wordplay in which the poet plays on the ambiguity of the agreement

[177] al-Sakkākī, *al-Miftāḥ*, 537. For a discussion of *tawjīh*, see Seeger Adrianus Bonebakker, *Some Early Definitions of the Tawriya and Ṣafadī's Faḍḍ al-Xitām ʿan al-Tawriya wa-'l-istixdām* (The Hague and Paris: Mouton & Co., 1966), 20–2.

[178] al-Khaṭīb al-Qazwīnī, *al-Īḍāḥ*, 502. Al-Sayyid al-Sharīf al-Jurjānī, in his glosses on al-Taftāzānī's supercommentary on al-Sakkākī's *al-Miftāḥ*, interestingly argues for reading it *istikhdhām*, with the letter "*dh*" instead of the similar looking letter "*d*," which literally means "cutting," to refer to the cutting away of one meaning through the referring back of a pronoun to its other meaning (*al-Ḥāshiya ʿalā al-Muṭawwal*, ed. Rashīd Aʿraḍī (Beirut: Dār al-Kutub al-ʿIlmiyya, 2007), 412–13). Ṣalāḥ al-Dīn al-Ṣafadī (d. 764/1363) dedicated a treatise to precisely the two figures of *tawriya* and *istikhdām* in his *Faḍḍ al-khitām ʿan al-tawriya wa-l-istikhdām* (*Lifting the Seal off* Tawriya *and* Istikhdām). On this work, see Bonebakker, *Some Early Definitions*.

[179] The first author to deal with these figures seems to have been Usāma ibn al-Munqidh (d. 584/1188) in his *Kitāb al-badīʿ* (Bonebakker, *Some Early Definitions*, 28 and 30).

in sound of the single word *kallamatnī* (she spoke to me) and the combination of the two separate words, *kalla matnī* (my back became weak):[180]

مَرَرْتُ بِبابِ هندَ فكَلَّ مَتْنِي   فَلا واللهِ ما نَطَقَتْ بِحَرفِ

When I passed by Hind's door, she spoke to me (*kallamatnī*)/
my back became weak (*kalla matnī*)
And no, by God, she did not utter a word

~ Unknown

The listener is misled and made to assume that the poet intended the first, more expected meaning of "she spoke to me," but is then surprised by the poet's declaration that "she did not utter a word." One realizes at this point that the actual intended meaning is quite different from our initial understanding. This kind of wordplay would have been considered by later critics a type of *tawriya* (disguising) or *īhām* (giving the illusion of something), which al-Sakkākī describes as "when an utterance has two uses: one more obvious and one less so and it is mentioned in order to give the illusion that the intention is the more obvious meaning until it becomes apparent that it is the less obvious one."[181]

Al-Jurjānī cites the above example of wordplay, along with other figures, as a way of reinvigorating common ideas and making them unique. He attributes originality in this verse and the others he cites to the fact that the intended meaning is expressed "through another matter that is not apparent and known, but oblique and obscure, which the poet deliberately employs for the sake of hiding the intention, so that what is [normally] known effortlessly, is learned [only after] examination and analysis."[182] Therefore, hiding and misleading are desirable attributes in poetic language because they make one discover meaning only after examination and analysis.

The figure that the science of *badī'* later identifies as *istikhdām* also tries to obfuscate meaning in ways that force the listener to reexamine his initial understanding of a word. In the following verse by al-Buḥturī two different meanings of the word *ghaḍā* are employed in different instances:

180 al-Jurjānī, *Asrār*, 316.

181 al-Sakkākī, *al-Miftāḥ*, 537; al-Khaṭīb al-Qazwīnī, *al-Īḍāḥ*, 499. See Bonebakker, *Some Early Definitions*, 9–18.

182 al-Jurjānī, *Asrār*, 316.

فسَقَى الغَضَا والسَّاكِنِيهِ وإنْ هُمُ   شَبُّوهُ بينَ جَوانِحِي وضُلُوعِي

May it rain on Ghaḍā/*ghaḍā* and its inhabitants, even though they set it ablaze between my front and back ribs

Ghaḍā is both a name of a place and a kind of desert tree known as Euphorbia.[183] In the first instance, when one reaches the words "its inhabitants" in reference to Ghaḍā, one understands that the poet intended the place. However, as one goes on and hears the poet say that the inhabitants had "set it ablaze" in his heart, one understands that he intends the wood of the *ghaḍā* tree (known for being good firewood)[184] and that he means that the fire of love was set ablaze in him (by his beloved, who is from Ghaḍā).[185] His wish for it to rain applies equally well to Ghaḍā the place and *ghaḍā* the firewood ablaze in his heart.

While *tawriya* intends the less obvious of two possible meanings, *istikhdām* is a device that makes use of *both* meanings of a word.[186] However, the word's employment in one sense in the first instance in *istikhdām* creates an expectation that is then broken when it is referred to the second time in its second sense. This produces an unexpected surprising meaning. The aesthetic mechanism at play therefore in all these figures of disguise involves a breaking of expectation by adducing or allowing for a second less obvious meaning that is grasped only after examination.

Other *Badīʿ* Figures

Another set of rhetorical figures described under the science of *badīʿ* also entails speech that appears at first to be something other than it is. These do not quite have an equivalent in English, but their names in and of themselves reveal some form of disguise or deception. These include figures known as "affirming praise with what looks like rebuke" (*taʾkīd al-madḥ bimā yushbih al-dhamm*) and vice versa;[187] "jest intended as seriousness" (*hazl yurād bihi jidd*);[188] speaking in the affirmative (*al-qawl bi-l-mūjib*), which entails affirming someone else's speech in a way

[183] Ghaḍā was a name used in reference to Najd in central Arabia "because of the abundance of [the trees called] *ghaḍā* there" (Lane, s.v. *gh-ḍ-w*).
[184] Ibn Manẓūr, *Lisān al-ʿArab*, s.v. *gh-ḍ-w*. [185] al-Khaṭīb al-Qazwīnī, *al-Īḍāḥ*, 502.
[186] Ibn Abī al-Iṣbaʿ, *Taḥrīr al-taḥbīr*, 275.
[187] al-Sakkākī, *al-Miftāḥ*, 537; al-Khaṭīb al-Qazwīnī, *al-Īḍāḥ*, 524–5.
[188] al-Khaṭīb al-Qazwīnī, *al-Īḍāḥ*, 530.

that is clearly not how it was intended;[189] and "producing a consequence" (*istitbāʿ*) by making a compliment indirectly imply a second compliment (unexpectedly).[190] Related to the last figure, but more general than it, is a figure called fusion (*idmāj*).[191] It involves "the incorporation of some other [second] meaning in speech composed for a [certain primary] meaning,"[192] as Ibn al-Muʿtazz does in the following verse, describing the yellowness of the *Khīrī* flower (Latin name: *Cheiranthus cheiri*):[193]

قَد نَفَضَ العاشِقُون ما صَنَعَ الـ * ـهَجْرُ بألوانِهِمْ على وَرَقِهْ

Lovers shook off what separation did
to the color [of their complexion] onto its leaves

Lovers were often described in classical Arabic poetry as being yellowish in color in their pining for their beloved. However, the point of the verse is to describe the yellowness of the *Khīrī* flower. The poet does so circuitously by comparing its color to the yellowness of lovers. In this way, the poet slips a description of love into a description of the flower, fusing two ideas.[194] This verse is additionally beautiful, al-Khaṭīb al-Qazwīnī explains, because it gives the illusion of prolixity while being at once concise: it is wordy for the main intended meaning (describing the yellowness of the flower), but concise in that it combines two ideas (the flower and a description of love).[195]

Besides rhetorical devices that add meaning in unexpected ways, one can identify a set of figures that depend on distribution and balance. These figures are structured in such a way that produces symmetry and proportion. Nevertheless, such structures also present information in a way that is either surprising or less obvious. Antithesis (*muṭābaqa*), for example, often

[189] Ibid., 532ff. The figure is similar to what is discussed under the science of meanings as "the shrewd way" (*al-uslūb al-ḥakīm*) (see my discussion of this device in Chapter 5). Al-Ṣafadī (d. 764/1363) dedicates an entire book to this figure entitled *al-Hawl al-muʿjib fī al-qawl bi-l-mūjib*, ed. Muḥammad ʿAbd al-Majīd Lāshīn (Cairo: Dār al-Āfāq al-ʿArabiyya, 2005). For a discussion of al-Ṣafadī's book and the differences between these similar figures, see Bassām al-ʿAfw al-Qawāsimī, "al-Hawl al-muʿjib fī al-qawl bi-l-mūjib li-Ṣalāḥ al-dīn al-Ṣafadī (d. 764AH): Dirāsa naqdiyya taḥlīliyya," *Majallat al-jāmiʿa al-islāmiyya (Silsilat al-dirāsāt al-insāniyya)* 19, no. 1 (Jan 2011).

[190] al-Sakkākī, *al-Miftāḥ*, 539; al-Khaṭīb al-Qazwīnī, *al-Īḍāḥ*, 526. [191] Ibid., 526–8

[192] Ibid., 526.

[193] Ibn Abī al-Iṣbaʿ, *Taḥrīr al-taḥbīr*, 548; see editor's footnote on the flower.

[194] al-Khaṭīb al-Qazwīnī, *al-Īḍāḥ*, 527.

[195] Ibid. In fact, Ibn Abī al-Iṣbaʿ uses this verse as an example of a figure he calls spreading or stretching (*basṭ*), which he defines as conveying a meaning with more words than necessary in order to incorporate another meaning that adds beauty to speech (*Taḥrīr al-taḥbīr*, 544–8).

amounts to a paradox, requiring one to examine how one matter can be something and its opposite at once.[196] Related to antithesis is a figure called reversal and switching (*ʿaks wa-tabdīl*), which exposes the closely-knit yet ironic relationship between matters, such as al-Mutanabbī's verse in which he states that:

فَلا مَجْدَ في الدّنْيَا لمَنْ قَلّ مَالُهُ   وَلا مالَ في الدّنيا لمَنْ قَلّ مَجدُهُ

There is no glory on earth for him whose wealth is little
And there is no wealth on earth for him whose glory is little[197]

Both of these figures involve the presentation of ideas in ways that are surprising and require examination.

Otherwise, several figures entail various ways of arranging information, such as heeding correspondence between items (*murāʿāt al-naẓīr*); having two conditional phrases correspond to two consequences (*muzāwaja*), and respective listing (*laff wa-nashr*, lit. rolling up and unrolling), where the listener has to figure out which element corresponds to which,[198] such as in the following verse:[199]

كَيْفَ أَسْلُو وأَنْتِ حِقْفٌ وَغُصْنٌ   وغَزَالٌ لَحْظاً وَقَدّاً وَرِدْفاً

How can I find solace and you are a sand dune, a [tender] branch,
And a gazelle, in [your] eyes, waist, and hips
~ Ibn Ḥayyūs (d. 473/1081)

In this case, the poet adds an extra twist by reversing the list: the beloved's glance is compared to a gazelle's, her waist to a branch, and her hips to a sand dune. All these comparisons are standard representations of feminine beauty in classical Arabic poetry. However, the poet's listing one set first and their corresponding significances second requires one to examine momentarily which one belongs to which. Even figures of distribution, such as these, therefore, seem to deal with listing and dividing items in non-straightforward ways that force the listener to figure out what belongs to what. This allows for an experience of discovery that would otherwise not be possible in a more straightforward listing of items.

***

Classical Arabic treatises on *badīʿ* are often focused on classifying rhetorical figures, without delving in depth into the aesthetics of *badīʿ* per se.

[196] al-Sakkākī, *al-Miftāḥ*, 533; al-Khaṭīb al-Qazwīnī, *al-Īḍāḥ*, 477ff. [197] Ibid., 498.
[198] al-Sakkākī, *al-Miftāḥ*, 534. [199] al-Khaṭīb al-Qazwīnī, *al-Īḍāḥ*, 504.

Nevertheless, as I have tried to show in this section, the kinds of figures that are identified as *badīʿ* often entail intrinsic structures that either mislead or obscure. In the case of paronomasia, padding, and figures of disguise such as *tawriya* and *istikhdām*, certain expectations are created just to be broken through the repetition of similar-sounding words, apparent meaninglessness, and a play on double meaning.[200] Other figures such as the one called "fusion" (*idmāj*) also produce meaning where it is not expected. Even figures that depend on symmetry and balance, I have argued, entail the distribution of information in non-straightforward ways that require examination. All this allows in the listener an experience of "discovery," which hence explains the pleasure and wonder one feels as a result of *badīʿ*.

This sketch is not a comprehensive account of all the rhetorical figures discussed in classical Arabic criticism. I have limited my discussion to a selection taken from those figures identified by al-Sakkākī and al-Khaṭīb al-Qazwīnī, in the branch of the science of eloquence that comes to be defined as the science of *badīʿ*. This catalog, however, was not all-inclusive. The list of figures in works dedicated exclusively to *badīʿ* expands over the centuries to encompass ever-more specific variations in addition to new figures. While Ibn al-Muʿtazz, in his *Kitāb al-badīʿ*, for example, identifies around 17 figures, Ibn Abī al-Iṣbaʿ (d. 654/1256), a few centuries later, identifies around 125 figures in his *Taḥrīr al-taḥbīr* (*Explaining Embellishment*).[201] In comparison, al-Khaṭīb al-Qazwīnī identifies thirty-seven figures and al-Sakkākī even less. Nevertheless, what I am suggesting here is that the aesthetic logic underlying *badīʿ* figures in general is one that summarily can described as wonder. The very structures that Arabic criticism identifies as *badīʿ* are by definition ones that make the discovery of meaning less straightforward, more surprising, and unexpected.[202]

200 It is worth noting that this is different from the concept of "horizons of expectation" put forth by Hans Robert Jauss's reception theory, which is context dependent and contingent on expectations created by social and historical literary knowledge. The expectations produced through *badīʿ* are intrinsic to the structure of the language of the text.

201 Even though Ibn al-Muʿtazz presents only five of these figures as *badīʿ* and the remainder as "embellishments" (*maḥāsin*), thus making a distinction between the two, Bonebakker has shown how later authors, namely, Ibn Abī al-Iṣbaʿ, believed Ibn al-Muʿtazz intended the term *badīʿ* for all the figures in the book (Bonebakker, "Ibn Abi'l-Iṣbaʿ's Text of the Kitāb al-badīʿ of Ibn al-Muʿtazz," 89).

202 This would suggest that an aesthetic of wonder is already implicit in works as early as Ibn al-Muʿtazz's *Kitāb al-badīʿ*, who was the first to attempt to classify rhetorical figures. This might very well be the case. However, as discussed earlier in the chapter, Ibn al-Muʿtazz

Moreover, while it is standard for works dedicated to cataloging rhetorical figures to incorporate metaphor, simile, and metonymy (*kināya*) under *badīʿ*, these figures are treated separately within the formalized science of eloquence developed by al-Sakkākī and al-Khaṭīb al-Qazwīnī, under the science of *bayān* (elucidation). As we will see in Chapters 3 on simile and 4 on metaphor and metonymy, the theory behind those figures is developed very elaborately and is consistent with an aesthetic of wonder as well.

CONCLUSION

Al-Jurjānī states that variation in literary merit does not exist in that which is "general, common to all, [...] straightforward, apparent, untouched by craft, simple, and unembellished."[203] It *does* exist, however, in that which "has a [secondary] meaning built upon it, is coupled with a fine subtlety, contains elements of *kināya* (metonymy), suggestion, symbols, and allusion."[204] Quite contrary to the old school of criticism, which valued straightforwardness, naturalness, and truthfulness, poetic quality in the new school depended on indirect meaning and craft. This was not because the new school had a greater tolerance for affectedness, *badīʿ*, and falsehood. Rather, it was the result of a major paradigm shift in their assessment of poetic quality. This new aesthetic framework depended on the ability of poetic language to produce unexpected and surprising meanings. This can be achieved both through speech that is literally accurate and through make-believe imagery. The question of truth and falsehood, which was so central to the old school of criticism, therefore, became irrelevant for the new-school aesthetic. The beauty of *badīʿ* instead was the result of its ability to obscure, mislead, and produce unexpected meanings.

These linguistic maneuvers that are identified as *badīʿ* produce an emotional impact on the listener that is characterized by wonder. Al-Jurjānī describes the poet's artfulness as lying in "images that please the listeners and astound them (*turwiʿuhum*) and illusions (*takhyīlāt*) that excite the praised addressees and move them."[205] He likens the experience of the listener to that of the viewer of an amazing painting or sculpture:

> Just as [an excellent painting or sculpture] amazes and enchants, pleases and delights, and brings into the soul a strange state (*ḥāla gharība*) upon seeing it that

was still bound by the discourse of his contemporaries and defended the employment of rhetorical figures by citing precedence in pre-Islamic poetry and the Quran.

[203] al-Jurjānī, *Asrār*, 315. [204] Ibid. [205] Ibid., 317.

> did not exist before, that is characterized by a kind of seductive appeal that cannot be denied or concealed [. . .] so does poetry with the images it creates, the artifices it shapes, and the meanings it conjures up in the soul which give the illusion that a speechless inanimate object is alive and able to speak [. . . etc.][206]

He goes on to compare the seductiveness of poetry to that of idols for their worshipers, and compares the magical ability of the poet to alter substances and change qualities to that of alchemy and elixir, "except that it is psychological in nature, employing the imagination and intellect instead of earthly and heavenly bodies."[207] This description of the experience poetry produces in the listener coupled with the attribution of poetic beauty to mechanisms that allow for the discovery of unexpected meanings lead me to describe the aesthetic of the new school of criticism as an aesthetic of wonder.

We have focused in this chapter on poetic devices that were at the center of the debate surrounding *muḥdath* poetry, namely, fantastic imagery, hyperbole, and *badīʿ*. Nevertheless, this new framework of wonder articulates the aesthetics of other fundamental poetic figures as well, namely, simile and metaphor, which come to be treated separately from *badīʿ*, as we will see in Chapters 3 and 4. It also underlies their explanations of the aesthetics of the Quran, as we will see in Chapter 5. As such, the new school of criticism is not only able to legitimize the new style of *muḥdath* poetry, but, more importantly, it also provides a comprehensive theory of what renders language beautiful, including that of the Quran. This shift in paradigm to an aesthetic of wonder is not limited to al-Jurjānī and the science of eloquence, as developed by al-Sakkākī and al-Khaṭīb al-Qazwīnī. It is also visible in Arabic philosophy's interpretation of Aristotle's *Poetics*, which we turn to next.

206 Ibid. Note that the Arabic text in the Ritter edition starts a new paragraph mid-sentence. Hellmut Ritter corrects this misplacement of the new section in his German translation (*Die Geheimnisse der Wortkunst (Asrār al-balāgha) des ʿAbdalqāhir al-Jurjānī* [Asrār al-balāgha], trans. Hellmut Ritter (Wiesbaden: In Kommission bei Franz Steiner, 1959), 369n1).

207 al-Jurjānī, *Asrār*, 318.

2

Wonder in Aristotelian Arabic Poetics

The early Abbasid period witnessed a vibrant translation movement, from the cultures of the regions to which Islam had spread at the time, of literary and scientific texts, as well as Greek philosophy.[1] Aristotle, in particular, known as "the first teacher" to the Arabs, had an enormous influence on the development of philosophy in Arabic. Building on the Greek and Syriac commentarial tradition of late antiquity, philosophers of the Islamicate world writing in Arabic saw the Aristotelian corpus as providing the model for reaching true and universal knowledge.[2] In particular, Aristotle's logical teachings in the *Organon* provided the scientific tools for gaining knowledge. "All knowledge," Ibn Sīnā (better known as Avicenna in the Latin West) states, "is either [the result of] forming concepts (conception) or acknowledging the truth of a proposition (assent)."[3] The former results from definition and the latter from syllogistic reasoning, the two pillars of the logical sciences. It is a part of these logical sciences that Aristotle's *Poetics* came into the picture in the Arabic context.

Arabic philosophy inherited an extended version of the *Organon* from the Alexandrian philosophical tradition of late antiquity that included Aristotle's works on *Rhetoric* and *Poetics.*[4] As a result, in addition to the

[1] The Abbasid caliph al-Maʾmūn (r. 198/813–218/833) was one of the main promoters of the translation of Greek philosophy into Arabic. (On the translation movement in the early Abbasid period, see Dimitri Gutas, *Greek Thought, Arabic Culture: The Graeco-Arabic Translation Movement in Baghdad and Early ʿAbbāsid Society (2nd–4th/8th–10th Centuries)* (London: Routledge, 1998).)

[2] Cristina D'Ancona, "Aristotle and Aristotelianism," in *Encyclopedia of Islam, THREE* (2008).

[3] Ibn Sīnā, *Kitāb al-najāt*, ed. Mājid Fakhrī (Beirut: Dār al-Āfāq, 1982), 97.

[4] The classification of the *Poetics* and *Rhetoric* as parts of the *Organon* has been termed "context theory" by O. B. Hardison. He, however, uses the term in a derogatory way, as he

six core books on logic (the *Categories*, the *De Interpretatione*, the *Prior and Posterior Analytics*, the *Topics*, and the *Sophistical Refutations*), Arabic philosophy understood *Rhetoric* and *Poetics* as descriptions of means of arriving at and gaining knowledge. Arabic philosophers were therefore interested in Aristotle's *Poetics* insofar as it relates to logic. Like their Alexandrian predecessors, they were faced with the task of making sense of poetic language as a form of syllogistic logic.

In late antiquity, initial attempts by Alexandrian philosophers based the classification of poetic speech on a truth-scale, as Deborah Black has shown, differentiating poetic syllogisms from demonstrative ones, for example, by arguing that the latter are absolutely true and the former absolutely false. In the Arabic context, a new concept of "*takhyīl*" (make-believe) emerges as a solution, which gave poetry a unique status in the logical sciences – one that is eventually delinked from truth and falsehood.[5] This concept of *takhyīl*, which describes the kind of truth that one acknowledges in a poetic syllogism as "make-believe," is marked by its ability to produce an emotional impact on the listener, and especially wonder.[6]

believes that the logical construal of the *Poetics* is a "warping" of the Aristotelian text (see Deborah Black, *Logic and Aristotle's "Rhetoric" and "Poetics" in Medieval Arabic Philosophy* (Leiden: E.J. Brill, 1990), 1). In fact, the classification of Aristotle's works was much debated throughout the history of Aristotelianism up to the sixth century CE. One cannot claim that the conclusions of the philosophers of late antiquity were less legitimate than later classifications. For an overview of early debates about Aristotle's works, see Paul Moraux, *Les listes anciennes des ouvrages d'Aristote* (Louvain: Éditions Universitaires de Louvain, 1951), especially 172–83 with regard to the *Rhetoric* and the *Poetics*. See Dimitri Gutas's analysis of the transmission of this classification from Elias (sixth century CE) to Paul the Persian (sixth century CE), as preserved in Arabic by Miskawayh (fourth/tenth century), and to al-Fārābī in "Paul the Persian on the Classification of the Parts of Aristotle's Philosophy: A Milestone between Alexandria and Bagdâd," *Der Islam* 60 (1983). Deborah Black analyzes and evaluates the various attempts at understanding *Rhetoric* and *Poetics* as parts of the logical sciences in both the Alexandrian and Arabic traditions in *Logic*.

5 The connection between poetry and image-evocation in the logical sciences goes back to late antiquity. The most concrete evidence we have for this is in a text by Paul the Persian (sixth century CE), which nevertheless has only survived in a later Arabic transmission by Miskawayh (d. 421/1030). In it, poetic syllogisms are described as "inducing imaginary impressions [*muḫayyila*]." However, they are also immediately qualified as "false in all respects" (see translation in Gutas, "Paul the Persian," 234). See also Heinrichs, "Takhyīl," 4–5, where he wonders whether "the fascinating combination of 'all false' and 'inducing imaginary impressions' to characterize poetic statements and syllogisms can safely be attributed to Paul's original text" (p. 5). What is significant and new about the development of the concept of *takhyīl* in Arabic, however, is its decoupling from falsehood, namely, in Ibn Sīnā's works.

6 Note that, while there is much overlap with ʿAbd al-Qāhir al-Jurjānī's concept of *takhyīl* discussed in Chapter 1, the term has a technical meaning in the philosophical context

While al-Fārābī (d. 339/950) begins to talk about *takhyīl*, traces of the truth-scale-based classification of the *Poetics* from late antiquity are still evident in his work. The concept truly replaces the old truth-scale-based taxonomy with Ibn Sīnā (d. 428/1037). As a result, we see a shift in philosophical works similar to that found in literary criticism (from a truth-based judgment of poetry to one based on its ability to evoke wonder in the listener) taking place around the same time (i.e., turn of the fifth/eleventh century). While the immediate disciplinary context of these two shifts were different (ʿAbd al-Qāhir al-Jurjānī was not concerned with understanding poetics as a branch of logic), they were both guided by the view that poetic beauty is based on a statement's ability to evoke wonder. This aesthetic outlook allowed both traditions to go beyond the truth–falsehood dichotomy and provided a new framework for articulating the poetic. This new framework continues to form the underlying aesthetic in Ibn Rushd's (Averroes, d. 595/1198) treatment of the *Poetics*, though in slightly different ways. It is also apparent in later works of literary criticism influenced by philosophy, namely, those authored by Ḥāzim al-Qarṭājannī (d. 684/1285) and al-Sijilmāsī (d. after 704/1304). This idiosyncratic strand of "Aristotelian" literary theory, as a result, has more in common with the mainstream strand of literary theory spurred by al-Jurjānī than previously acknowledged.

In this chapter, we will delve into the philosophical concept of *takhyīl* and show how wonder shapes the philosophers' aesthetic outlook when defining the poetic. Intertwined with the concept of *takhyīl* is the Arabic understanding of the Aristotelian notion of mimesis (*muḥākāt*). While for Aristotle in his *Poetics* mimesis mainly describes the imitative nature of the dramatic genres of tragedy and comedy, Arabic philosophy equates *muḥākāt* in poetry primarily with simile and metaphor. This not only reflects an adaptation of Aristotle's poetics to two fundamental literary figures in Arabic poetry and criticism, but it also allows for the interpretation of poetic language as syllogism.

The Arabic *Poetics*, therefore, ends up looking quite different from Aristotle's Greek *Poetics*. For some, this has been reason enough to dismiss it altogether as a misinterpretation. Given the concern with logic rather than poetry per se, there is also a tendency in modern scholarship to dismiss the philosophers' remarks about the *Poetics* as irrelevant for

denoting the kind of acknowledgment of the truth of a syllogism one reaches in poetic syllogisms, as we will see in this chapter. For an overview of the meanings of *takhyīl* in different disciplines, see Heinrichs, "Takhyīl."

literary criticism or at best an exception. However, as we will see, the philosophers' interpretation of the *Poetics* in Arabic is rich with clues about their cultural context and aesthetic assumptions, precisely because they were faced with the task of fitting it into logic. The philosophical interest in the *Poetics* required them to articulate more explicitly certain views on aesthetics that were taken for granted in literary criticism proper. Thus, while philosophers might have been interested in the *Poetics* from the point of view of the logical sciences, their interpretations of Aristotle's work reflect their contemporary culture's attitudes toward the poetic and the presumed conception of the literary. In fact, while constituting distinct disciplines, we will see much resonance across philosophy and literary criticism.

BACKGROUND

Translations of the *Poetics* began to appear in Arabic in the early third/ninth century.[7] In the fourth/tenth century, the *Poetics* was translated into Arabic from a Syriac translation of the Greek by two famous translators in Baghdad: Abū Bishr Mattā ibn Yūnus (d. 328/940), whose translation still exists, and Yaḥyā ibn ʿAdī (d. 363/974), whose translation is now lost.[8] Al-Kindī (d. after 256/870), one of the earliest philosophers writing in Arabic, is said to have already written a commentary on the work, but it has not survived.[9] Three short treatises written about a century later by al-Fārābī (dubbed the "second teacher" after Aristotle) have survived. The two more extensive surviving treatises by philosophers are those by Ibn Sīnā and Ibn Rushd. Nevertheless, given that the *Poetics* was understood as part of logic, statements about poetic language can be found throughout their discussions of the logical sciences and are not limited to their commentaries on the *Poetics* proper.

Later, some literary critics wrote works on poetry that were particularly influenced by the philosophers' understanding of the *Poetics* and their

[7] These early translations are all lost. See O. J. Schrier, "The Syriac and Arabic Versions of Aristotle's 'Poetics'," in *The Ancient Tradition in Christian and Islamic Hellenism*, ed. G. Endress and R. Kruk (Leiden: Research School CNWS, 1997).

[8] Abū Bishr's medieval translation, along with the Syriac translation on which it was based, is published in D. S. Margoliouth, *Analecta orientalia ad poeticam aristoteleam* (Hildesheim; New York: G. Olms, 2000), 1–76.

[9] Ibn al-Nadīm, *Kitāb al-fihrist*, 310. See also Shukrī Muḥammad ʿAyyād, *Kitāb Arisṭūṭālis fī al-shiʿr* (Cairo: Dār al-Kātib al-ʿArabī, 1967), 193–5, for a description of the earliest commentaries on Aristotle's *Poetics*.

language. These include the Andalusian scholar from Cartagena, Ḥāzim al-Qarṭājannī, in his *Minhāj al-bulaghā' wa-sirāj al-udabā'* (*The Path of the Eloquent and the Light of the Lettered*) and the Moroccan from Sijilmāsa, Abū Muḥammad al-Qāsim al-Sijilmāsī, in his *al-Manzaʿ al-badīʿ fī tajnīs asālīb al-badīʿ* (*The Novel Trend in Classifying the Techniques of Literary Figures*).[10] These represent a unique strand in Arabic literary criticism for their adoption of philosophical terminology. However, as we will see, they were also not writing in a vacuum. While their methodology and explanations differ from the more traditional literary criticism, they share a common aesthetic outlook.

The story of the transmission of Aristotle's *Poetics* into Arabic is long and complex, starting with problems in the translations themselves from Greek to Syriac and then to Arabic,[11] as well as questions of interpretation, including the treatment (namely, by Ibn Rushd) of the Greek genres of tragedy and comedy as the (very different) Arabic genres of panegyric and invective poetry.[12] However, the most significant factor that shaped the interpretation of the *Poetics* in Arabic was perhaps its treatment, along with *Rhetoric*, as a branch of the logical sciences. In addition to

[10] Other philosophically oriented works of literary criticism include Ibn ʿAmīra's (d. 656/1258 or 658/1260) *al-Tanbīhāt ʿalā mā fī al-tibyān min al-tamwīhāt* and Ibn al-Bannā' al-Marrākushī's (d. c. 721/1321) *al-Rawḍ al-marīʿ fī ṣināʿat al-badīʿ*.

[11] See Aristotle, *Poetics: Editio Maior of the Greek Text with Historical Introductions and Philological Commentaries*, ed. Leonardo Tarán and Dimitri Gutas (Leiden: Brill, 2012), for a detailed discussion of the translations.

[12] The Arab (mis)interpretation of the Greek genres has been subject to much fantasy, including Jorge Luis Borges's short story entitled "Averroes's Search," in which he imagines the philosopher's struggle to make sense of Aristotle's text. However, it should be noted that Ibn Rushd is unique among the commentators on Aristotle's *Poetics* in interpreting the terms as such and applying them to the Arabic genres. This could have been due to his reliance on Abū Bishr Mattā's translation, which renders them as such, or because he intentionally made an effort to apply Aristotelian poetics to Arabic poetry. His predecessor, Ibn Sīna, recognizes the genres as unique to Greek literature and maintains them in transliterated form in his commentary. Moreover, the Arabs and the translators of the *Poetics* were not as oblivious of Greek genres as some might assume. See Iḥsān ʿAbbās, *Malāmiḥ yūnāniyya fī al-adab al-ʿArabī* (Beirut: al-Muʾassasa al-ʿArabiyya li-l-Dirāsāt wa-l-Nashr, 1977), 29, who relates the surviving anecdotes about Ḥunayn ibn Isḥāq reciting Homer in Baghdad. Maria Mavroudi has also shown that Greek literary works, including Homer's *Odyssey*, were available in Syriac translations and hence likely known to the Arabic-speaking world in the third/ninth century ("Greek Language and Education Under Early Islam," in *Islamic Cultures, Islamic Contexts: Essays in Honor of Professor Patricia Crone*, ed. Behnam Sadeghi, et al. (Leiden: Brill, 2015)). Even if the work itself might not have been easily accessible in Arabic, there was an awareness of Homer as a poet and of the Homeric epic, as Barbara Graziosi has shown in "On Seeing the Poet: Arabic, Italian and Byzantine Portraits of Homer," *Scandinavian Journal of Byzantine and Modern Greek Studies* 1 (2015): 28–36.

demonstrative, dialectical, and sophistical syllogisms, the standard three types of syllogisms discussed by Aristotle, Arabic logic also included rhetorical and poetic syllogisms. Like their predecessors in late antiquity, philosophers of the Islamicate world were faced with the challenge of explaining rhetorical and poetic speech as types of syllogisms and differentiating them from the other types.

One of the ways in which their predecessors in late antiquity incorporated rhetorical and poetic syllogisms into logic was by evaluating the various kinds of syllogisms based on the degree of true knowledge that results from them. In such a system, syllogisms ranged from being able to produce absolutely true knowledge, achieved through demonstrative or apodictic logic, to absolutely false knowledge, which results from poetic logic.[13] Traces of this understanding can still be seen in al-Fārābī's thought. However, this truth-based view of logic begins to change with al-Fārābī himself and is completely rejected by Ibn Sīnā. Instead, they differentiate the various types of syllogisms based on the kind of assent (*taṣdīq*) they elicit. That is, syllogisms differ in the nature of the conclusion that their premises lead us to accept, i.e., the nature of the "acknowledgment of the truth (*ṣidq*) of the proposition" (lit. *taṣdīq*).[14] Demonstrative syllogisms, for example, lead to certain and complete acknowledgment of the truth of their propositions, while dialectical and sophistical ones lead to speculative and deceptive kinds of acknowledgments, respectively. The acknowledgment of the truth of rhetorical syllogisms, in turn, is described as "conviction," while poetic syllogisms are described as producing a "make-believe" kind of acceptance of the conclusion called "*takhyīl*" (lit. making one imagine something [as something else]/giving the illusion), sometimes translated as "imaginative assent."[15] That is, poetic syllogisms make one imagine something as if it were true.

13 See Black, *Logic*. See the useful chart of the various types of syllogisms, their truth-values, and their "mental result" in Heinrichs, "Takhyīl," 5.

14 *Taṣdīq* is often translated as "assent." A more literal translation is "the acknowledgment of the truth (*ṣidq*) of the proposition" (i.e., the conclusion one reaches after considering the premises of a syllogism). For a description of Ibn Sīnā's terminology and epistemological system, see Dimitri Gutas, "The Empiricism of Avicenna," *Oriens* 40 (2012): 394ff.

15 "Imaginative assent" is the rendering adopted by many scholars writing about the topic in English, including Ismail Dahiyat in his translation of Ibn Sīnā's commentary on the *Poetics*. This rendering, however, lacks the active sense of "making one imagine" that the term "*takhyīl*" connotes. The term is also often translated as "image-evocation." This is more accurate. However, since the syllogistic process of *takhyīl* entails, as we will see, a process of making one imagine something as something else, and not merely the evocation of an image, I prefer to translate it as "make-believe" in most cases.

Takhyīl is therefore a kind of "make-believe" acknowledgment of the truth of a syllogism's proposition.[16] This make-believe kind of conclusion is emotive in character. It is in the philosophers' discussion of this process of *takhyīl* where we can glean the role of aesthetic experience in poetry.

AL-FĀRĀBĪ: THE BEGINNINGS

Only three short treatises by the Central Asian philosopher Abū Naṣr al-Fārābī have survived that deal directly with poetry and poetics: *Risāla fī qawānīn ṣināʿat al-shuʿarāʾ* (*Treatise on the Rules of the Craft of the Poets*),[17] *Kitāb al-shiʿr* (*The Book of Poetry*), also known as *Jawāmiʿ al-shiʿr* (*The Short Compendium on Poetry*),[18] and *Qawl al-Fārābī fī al-tanāsub wa-l-taʾlīf* (*al-Fārābī's View on Harmony and Composition*).[19] Our knowledge of what he said and thought about poetry is, therefore, comparatively sketchy. Nevertheless, we do know from these and other works of his that he considered poetic speech a type of syllogism[20] and assigned to it the process of image-evocation (*takhyīl*):

[16] As we have seen in Chapter 1, the term *takhyīl* in ʿAbd al-Qāhir al-Jurjānī's discussion of poetic imagery refers to a specific kind of make-believe imagery. In the philosophical context, however, the concept of make-believe applies more broadly to poetic language in general. Nevertheless, in both contexts *takhyīl* entails accepting a false premise as truth for the sake of a poetic conclusion. There is more overlap between the different contexts than current research allows for, as Wolfhart Heinrichs also speculates ("Takhyīl," 1).

[17] Published with a translation in al-Fārābī and Arberry, "Fārābī's Canons of Poetry." Also published in ʿAbd al-Raḥmān Badawī, *Fann al-shiʿr* (Cairo: Maktabat al-Nahḍa al-Miṣriyya, 1953), 149–58; and Abū Naṣr al-Fārābī, *al-Manṭiqiyyāt li-l-Fārābī*, ed. Muḥammad Taqī Dānish Pazhūh (Qum: Manshūrāt Maktabat Āyatullah al-ʿUẓmā al-Marʿashī al-Najafī, 1987), 1:493–9.

[18] Abū Naṣr al-Fārābī, "Jawāmiʿ al-shiʿr (Kitāb al-shiʿr)," in *Talkhīs kitāb Arisṭuṭālis fī al-shiʿr*, ed. Muḥammad Salīm Sālim (Cairo: Maṭābiʿ al-Ahrām al-Tijāriyya, 1971). Also published in Abū Naṣr al-Fārābī and Muḥsin Mahdī, "Kitāb al-shiʿr," *Shiʿr* 12 (1959); al-Fārābī, *al-Manṭiqiyyāt*, 1:500–3. For a translation, see van Gelder and Hammond, *Takhyīl*, 15–18.

[19] Abū Naṣr al-Fārābī, "Qawl al-Fārābi fī al-tanāsub wa-l-taʾlīf," in *al-Manṭiqiyyāt li-l-Fārābī*, ed. Muḥammad Taqī Dānish Pazhūh (Qum: Manshūrāt Maktabat Āyatullah al-ʿUẓmā al-Marʿashī al-Najafī, 1987).

[20] In *Iḥṣāʾ al-ʿulūm*, where al-Fārābī gives an overview of the various sciences, he explains that there are five types of syllogism: demonstrative (*burhāniyya*), dialectic (*jadaliyya*), sophistic (*sūfisṭāʾiyya*), rhetorical (*khuṭbiyya*), and poetic (*shiʿriyya*) (*Iḥṣāʾ al-ʿulūm*, ed. ʿUthmān Amīn, 3rd ed. (Cairo: Maktabat al-Anglū al-Miṣriyya, 1968), 79).

Poetic speech is made up of things the purpose of which is to make one imagine in the subject matter some state of being or something better or worse: that is, in terms of beauty or ugliness, loftiness or lowliness, and the like.[21]

In fact, this process of *takhyīl* becomes the defining feature of poetic language, trumping its truth or falsehood, as he explains in his *Qawl fī al-tanāsub wa-l-ta'līf* :

It is a mistake to say [. . .] that poetry is pure lies, because the goal of poetry is not to be false or not false. Rather, its goal and purpose is to move the imagination (*taḥrīk al-khayāl*) and excite the soul (*infi'āl al-nafs*). This is clear from its definition, which is the following: poetry is composed speech that makes one imagine [something as something else] (*kalām mu'allaf mukhayyil*), which is kept in a concordant rhythm with sentences of equal rhythms and repeated similar letter-endings.[22]

In *Kitāb al-shi'r*, he reiterates the importance of *takhyīl* regardless of the truth and falsehood of the poetic speech producing it, stating:

The intended purpose of make-believe speech is to move the listener to do that which he was made to imagine about a given matter, either in search for it, or in escape from it, in yearning for it or in hatred of it, or other actions that result from a worsening or bettering [of the subject matter], *whether the image that was evoked is true or not*, and *whether the matter in reality is as it was represented or not*.[23]

Nevertheless, in *Qawānīn al-shi'r* al-Fārābī classifies poetic speech as completely false.[24] He thus continues to retain from late antiquity the truth-scale-based definition of the various types of syllogism. However, we also start seeing in al-Fārābī's writings the prioritization of poetry's affective aspects over its truth or falsehood – an attitude that is later cemented by Ibn Sīnā.

The main way of producing such an effect on the listener is through *muḥākāt*, the Arabic term for "mimesis." In *Kitāb al-shi'r*, al-Fārābī makes the point that, while poetry is made up of "mimetic" speech and meter, "the more important of these two [aspects] in the constitution of poetry is *muḥākāt* and knowledge of the things with which *muḥākāt* is produced; the less important is meter."[25] Because of the central role given to *muḥākāt*

21 Ibid., 83.

22 In other words, meter and rhyme (*qāfiya*) (al-Fārābī, "Qawl al-Fārābi fī al-tanāsub wa-l-ta'līf," 506).

23 al-Fārābī, "Kitāb al-shi'r," 175 (emphasis added).

24 al-Fārābī and Arberry, "Fārābī's Canons of Poetry," 267–8. This has led scholars to conclude that it was not until Ibn Sīnā that poetry's association with falsehood was categorically rejected (see, for example, Bürgel, "Die beste Dichtung"). It is clear, however, that Ibn Sīnā's ideas were already dwelling in al-Fārābī's statements.

25 al-Fārābī, "Kitāb al-shi'r," 173.

in poetic speech, it comes to be employed in the Arabic commentaries almost synonymously with *takhyīl*. The distinction between the two terms therefore is often vague.

The two terms, however, refer to different aspects of the poetic process: *takhyīl* is the resulting effect of a poetic statement in the listener, while *muḥākāt* is the means through which this effect is produced. Al-Fārābī explains: "speech composed of that which imitates (*yuḥākī*) something seeks to make one imagine (*takhyīl*) that thing."[26] In other words, *muḥākāt* is the poetic process through which *takhyīl* is achieved, or, as Walid Hamarneh has put it, *takhyīl* revolves around the "reception" of poetry and *muḥākāt* is the "poetic text" itself through which a certain "reception" is achieved.[27]

Mimesis came to mean something very different in Arabic philosophy from its Greek counterpart. While in Aristotle's text it refers mainly to the representation/imitation "of actions and of life"[28] (in a tragic drama, for example), in Arabic philosophy it was primarily applied to figures of comparison and similitude: that is, simile and its related figure, metaphor.[29] Indeed, Abū Bishr Mattā, in his translation of the *Poetics* into Arabic, renders the term mimesis using the pair "*muḥākāt* and *tashbīh*" (imitation and simile), in most cases. Thus, mimesis in Arabic had more the sense of "likening" one matter to another or comparison, rather than imitating and producing a faithful copy.[30] Considering the centrality of simile (*tashbīh*) for Arabic poetry, as a figure in its own right but also as the foundation

[26] Ibid., 174.

[27] Walid Hamarneh describes "*takhyīl*" and "*muḥākāt*" as such in the context of al-Qartājannī's use of the terms. The description, however, applies equally well to the philosophers' employment of the same terms, on whose ideas al-Qarṭājannī bases his analysis ("Arabic Theory and Criticism," in *The Johns Hopkins Guide to Literary Theory and Criticism*, ed. Michael Gorden, Martin Kreiswirth, and Imre Szeman (Baltimore and London: The Johns Hopkins University Press, 2004), 60).

[28] Aristotle, *Poetics*, trans. James Hutton (New York: Norton and Company, 1982, 51 (1450a).

[29] Traces of such an interpretation of mimesis are already visible in late antiquity. Aristotle himself also discusses metaphor in terms of mimesis (Gregor Schoeler, "The 'Poetic Syllogism' Revisited," *Oriens* 41 (2013): 17–18).

[30] I will therefore usually render the translation of *muḥākāt* as "comparison," in this chapter, or simply keep the Arabic form of the word in transliteration. This is not to say that the word *muḥākāt* cannot be understood as "imitation." However, the imitation that they have in mind is the likening of one matter to another in simile or metaphor, not a representation of an external world as in the Greek context. I hope to detail the understanding of the concept of mimesis in medieval Arabic literature in future research.

of metaphor,[31] another much-discussed figure in literary criticism, it was fitting for the philosophers to single it out as the fundamental aspect of poetic speech. Moreover, simile or comparison lends itself more easily to being described as a syllogism than the Greek conception of mimesis. As Hamarneh has pointed out, the Greek concept of mimesis in the sense of producing copies "would have been [...] of little help in poetry as a syllogism. The concept of '*tashbīh*,' which was persistently added by the logician Matta [in his translation of the *Poetics*], tended to emphasize the devices of mimetic activity particular to poetry namely comparison and image making."[32] Thus, both the literary backdrop and the classification of the *Poetics* as part of logic likely contributed to the understanding of mimesis as comparison in the Arabic context.

Although the application of syllogistic logic to poetry becomes much more explicit in Ibn Sīnā's works, al-Fārābī begins to formulate what a poetic syllogism looks like. He explains:

> the poetic syllogism makes one imagine what "is not" as "is," i.e., that which does not exist as existing, like seeing [the reflection of] the crescent moon or a person in water, or imagining something in one's dreams and judging that it exists due to its existence in our imagination.[33]

[31] Heinrichs has argued that the word *istiʿāra* originally only referred to the kinds of metaphor in which a word is borrowed from one thing for something else, such as saying "the claws of death." Only gradually, did the term start incorporating metaphors that are based on similarity, such as saying "narcissus" in reference to the eye. He locates the ultimate acceptance of this "new type" of "*tashbīh*-based" metaphor in al-Jurjānī's works, which then becomes the standard definition of metaphor (Heinrichs, *Hand of the Northwind*, 55). The "old type" of *istiʿāra* also becomes redefined by al-Jurjānī in terms of similarity, as one based on analogy (see Kamal Abu Deeb, "al-Jurjānī's Classification of *Istiʿāra* with Special Reference to Aristotle's Classification of Metaphor," *Journal of Arabic Literature* 2 (1971): especially 73–4). While Heinrichs looks at the poetic and Quranic critical traditions, he does not incorporate philosophical works in his study. It seems, however, that the philosophers were already thinking of metaphor as being based on similarity. Al-Fārābī, for example, explains that metaphors and figurative speech entail naming something with a word other than the one coined for it based on some relationship between the two words, including a relationship of similarity (Abū Naṣr al-Fārābī, *Kitāb al-ḥurūf*, ed. Muḥsin Mahdī (Beirut: Dār al-Mashriq, 1986), 141). In later works, starting with al-Jurjānī, metaphor comes to be defined exclusively as a type of figurative speech based on similarity. Figurative speech based on other relationships, such as association, is not strictly a metaphor. This comes to be known in the science of eloquence as "unrestricted figurative speech" (*majāz mursal*) (see Chapter 4).

[32] Walid Hamarneh, "The Reception of Aristotle's Theory of Poetry in Arab-Islamic Medieval Thought," in *Poetics East and West*, ed. Milena Doleželová-Velingerová (Toronto: Toronto Semiotic Circle, Victoria College in the University of Toronto, 1989), 189.

[33] al-Fārābī, "Qawl al-Fārābi fī al-tanāsub wa-l-taʾlīf," 505.

He goes on to say that:

> we obtain the syllogism[34] through correspondents and similarities, such as [saying that] man is beautiful, and the sun is beautiful, therefore man is the sun. Or: fire is fast-acting, the sword is fast-killing, therefore the sword is fire.[35]

We begin to get a sense from these statements of how al-Fārābī understands the functioning of poetic statements as syllogisms. Moreover, it is clear that the poetic speech he has in mind is a simile or metaphor.

The quality of *muḥākāt* varies. The components that affect the effectiveness of a comparison, al-Fārābī informs us, depend on whether it is a direct or indirect likeness/*muḥākāt*. Al-Fārābī explains that "mimetic speech is of two kinds: one makes one imagine the thing itself, the other makes one imagine the existence of the thing in something else."[36] He goes on to say: "The one defines the thing in itself, like definition. The other defines the existence of the thing in something else, like demonstration (i.e., syllogistically)," definition and syllogism being the two pillars of the logical sciences.[37] To illustrate these two types of *muḥākāt*, al-Fārābī offers an analogy to sculpting:

> We may not know Zayd [in person], but see a sculpture of him, and know him through that which imitates him for us, not through Zayd in his own form. And perhaps we do not see the sculpture itself; rather we see its reflection in a mirror. In this way, we know Zayd through that which imitates the imitation of him, and thus we become twice removed from his real [form].[38]

Unfortunately, al-Fārābī does not provide us with examples to illustrate what these different forms of expression would look like in poetry. Gregor Schoeler, with evidence from a work by a later philosopher, Ibn Ṭulmūs (d. 620/1223), argues that the first type of *muḥākāt*, the direct

[34] I adopt Aouad and Schoeler's reading of "*qiyāsiyya*" as "*qiyāsuhu*" ("Le syllogisme poétique selon al-Fārābī: un syllogisme incorrect de la deuxième figure," *Arabic Sciences and Philosophy* 12 (2002): 191).

[35] al-Fārābī, "Qawl al-Fārābi fī al-tanāsub wa-l-taʾlīf," 505. See Gregor Schoeler's analysis of al-Fārābī's syllogisms in Schoeler, "The 'Poetic Syllogism' Revisited," especially 7.

[36] al-Fārābī, "Kitāb al-shiʿr," 174.

[37] Ibid. The establishment of a correspondence between poetic speech and definition seems unique to al-Fārābī as later philosophers, namely, Ibn Sīnā, tend to describe poetic speech only in terms of syllogism. An exception is a work by Ibn Ṭumlūs, which Gregor Schoeler discusses in "The 'Poetic Syllogism' Revisited."

[38] al-Fārābī, "Kitāb al-shiʿr," 175. The editor suggests that al-Fārābī is taking this from Plato's *Republic* (Bk10) (ibid., 175n1). However, Plato talks about two kinds of copies of an idea (form), the first copy is produced by the maker, the second, produced by the artist, is a copy of the maker's copy. Al-Fārābī here is talking about two types of poetic mimesis, however, both produced by the artist/poet.

one that corresponds to "definition," amounts to metaphor.[39] The indirect type of *muḥākāt*, which corresponds to "syllogism," seems to amount to a simile/*tashbīh*. Deborah Black has pointed out the difficulties al-Fārābī's analogy poses in terms of identifying how the two types of *muḥākāt* apply to actual poetic examples.[40] There remain problems in making metaphor and simile correspond to copies of an original once and twice removed respectively, especially since metaphor itself is based on simile. Furthermore, al-Fārābī goes on to explain that one could create further copies of copies and the distance of the imitation from the original matter could be several degrees.[41] Understanding direct and indirect *muḥākāt* as metaphor and simile, respectively, remains an unsatisfying explanation.

I am tempted to understand indirect *muḥākāt* as an extended metaphor akin to the types cataloged by al-Jurjānī under the rubric of *takhyīl*, such as the rhetorical figure known as amazement *(taʿajjub)* or feigned ignorance (*tajāhul al-ʿārif*). If we consider, for example, the verse by Ibn Ṭabāṭabā discussed in Chapter 1, in which the poet tells us not to marvel at the wearing out of clothes worn by the moon (i.e., the beautiful person):[42]

لا تَعْجَبوا من بِلَى غِلالَتِهِ　　　قَدْ زُرَّ أَزْرارَهُ على القَمَرِ

Do not be surprised at the wearing out of his undergarment:
Its buttons are buttoned on the moon

The first level of representation (copy 1) would involve the identification of the beautiful person with the moon. This would be like definition: the beautiful person and the real moon belong to the same category of "moon."[43] The second level of representation (copy 2) builds an image based on copy 1 (i.e., the moon), not the original. In our example, this would be akin to a syllogism in the following way: So-and-so is a moon, everyone who is a moon wears out clothes, therefore so-and-so wears out clothes.[44] This description is twice removed from the original person being

39 Schoeler, "The 'Poetic Syllogism' Revisited," 12–16 and 16n66.

40 Black, *Logic*, 220–3. 41 al-Fārābī, "Kitāb al-shiʿr," 175.

42 See my discussion of the verse under "Aesthetics of Make-Believe" in Chapter 1.

43 Al-Sakkākī and al-Khaṭīb al-Qazwīnī betray a similar way of thinking about metaphor, in the sense that they describe metaphor as making the claim that the tenor and the vehicle belong to the same species. See my discussion of metaphor in Chapter 4 under "Variation in *Bayān*."

44 This is, of course, a make-believe poetic syllogism. Ibn Sīnā spells these out more explicitly, as we will see.

described: a copy of a copy. One can also imagine the poet building further on this twice-removed image.[45]

Whether these kinds of metaphors were what al-Fārābī had in mind remains a matter of speculation. However, he explains that "many people consider representing (*muḥākāt*) something through a distant matter better than representing it through something close. They consider him who composes words in this way to be more entitled to [the employment of] *muḥākāt* and more in tune with the craft and its ways."[46] This attitude goes against the mainstream ideas of his contemporaries in literary criticism, who, as we have seen in Chapter 1, preferred figurative speech that is close to reality. In his *Qawānīn al-shiʿr*, al-Fārābī similarly states that the quality of simile varies depending on its closeness or farfetchedness:

The quality of simile (*tashbīh*) varies: that which is in terms of the matter itself lies in the similitude being close and appropriate; Or it may lie in the attention to artifice (*ṣanʿa*)[47] that brings two different elements together in a corresponding way in an image.[48]

He goes on to say:

this includes comparing A with B and B with C. Because there exists a close, fitting, and known similarity between A and B, as well as between B and C, the poets may make the speech flow in such a way as to bring to the mind of the listeners and audience a similarity between A and C, even though it may have been originally farfetched.[49]

Thus, we begin to see how similes (and metaphors) can vary in terms of their closeness and farfetchedness. While close comparisons simply depend on the poet exposing a similarity between closely related matters, far-fetched similes depend on the skill of the poet to expose a similarity between distant matters.[50]

45 Al-Qarṭājannī also divides *muḥākāt* into direct and indirect and uses the same analogy of al-Fārābī's of the statue and the mirror to describe the two levels of representation. See my discussion of "*Muḥākāt* and Wonder" in the section on al-Qarṭājannī.

46 al-Fārābī, "Kitāb al-shiʿr," 175.

47 I follow the Qum edition (al-Fārābī, *al-Manṭiqiyyāt*, 1:299), which has *ṣanʿa* (craft/artifice) instead of *ṣīgha* (form) in Sālim's edition (al-Fārābī, "Kitāb al-shiʿr," 175).

48 al-Fārābī and Arberry, "Fārābī's Canons of Poetry," 272. 49 Ibid.

50 If we accept my speculation above about such far-fetched imagery and take the example of the garments being worn out because they are buttoned on a person who is like the moon, the likening of A to B would entail the metaphor of the moon for the beautiful person; the likening of B to C entails the similarity between the moon and the action of wearing out fabric. The resulting image concludes that the real person (A) has the quality of wearing out fabric (C).

He attributes the effect of *muḥākāt* on the listener to its ability to bring something to one's mind (*al-ikhṭār bi-l-bāl*). He says that this possesses "great wealth" and an "amazing splendor" (*rawnaq ʿajīb*).[51] Bringing to mind an image of something distant (and as a result unexpected) through a far-fetched simile or make-believe imagery, one can speculate from his statements quoted above, is particularly amazing. While al-Fārābī does not explicitly talk about wonder, he does begin to lay down some basic principles of poetics that foreshadow the new school of criticism. These principles and their connection to aesthetic experience are greatly developed by his successors, as we will see. Nevertheless, he was ahead of his time compared to his contemporary literary critics who were still cementing the principles of the old-school aesthetic at the time.

IBN SĪNĀ: A NEW CONCEPTION OF THE POETIC

The next to tackle the *Poetics* was Abū ʿAlī Ibn Sīnā (Avicenna). Born towards the end of the fourth/tenth century in the outskirts of Būkhāra (modern-day Uzbekistan) and dubbed "The Preeminent Master" (*al-Shaykh al-Raʾīs*), Ibn Sīnā develops al-Fārābī's ideas about *takhyīl* and *muḥākāt* and connects them more explicitly to aesthetic experience.[52] He clearly distinguishes poetic speech from other kinds of speech by highlighting the emotional impact that it produces, which he describes as make-believe (*takhyīl*). It is not the falsehood of poetic speech that defines its poeticity, however. Rather, it is its ability to evoke wonder in the listener. This can happen through an actual process of "make-believe," in which something is likened to something else (simile) or taken as something else (metaphor) based on make-believe premises. These figures grouped under the concept of *muḥākāt* constitute the main form of achieving *takhyīl*. However, the term "*takhyīl*" also seems to refer more generally

[51] Ibid.

[52] Ibn Sīnā's main discussion of poetic speech takes place in his commentary on the *Poetics*, published in Ibn Sīnā, *al-Shiʿr*, and translated by Ismail M. Dahiyat as *Avicenna's Commentary on the Poetics of Aristotle: A Critical Study with an Annotated Translation of the Text*. His short treatise known as *Kitāb al-majmūʿ* or *al-Ḥikma al-ʿArūḍiyya* includes many of the ideas presented in *Kitāb al-shiʿr*, some of which are stated even more explicitly and with more detail. Important statements about poetry can also be found in his commentary on the *Prior Analytics*, *Kitāb al-qiyās*, and his commentary on the *Rhetoric*, which, along with his commentary on the *Poetics*, are parts of a larger work known as *Kitāb al-shifāʾ* (*The Book of Healing*). Finally, the first volume of his *al-Ishārāt wa-l-tanbīhāt* (*Remarks and Admonitions*), which also deals with logic, contains important details about poetics.

in Ibn Sīnā's works to the wondrous effect poetic speech may have, even when the process of producing it is not the result of actual "make-believe."

Takhyīl

From the outset in his commentary on the *Prior Analytics* (*Kitāb al-qiyās*), Ibn Sīnā declares that the division of premises based on their possibility or impossibility is to be done away with and should not be considered in any aspect.[53] Poetic premises are to be looked at instead from the aspect of their image-evocation, "regardless of whether they are true or false in their totality or not."[54] He goes on to explain that this is because "the soul is moved as a result of [poetic speech] towards rejecting or embracing something, not because it is true, but because of a make-believe movement (*ḥaraka takhyīliyya*) it experiences from it."[55]

In his commentary on the *Poetics*, he clarifies the nature of *takhyīl* explaining that it constitutes an emotional rather than a rational reaction:

> [Speech] which makes you imagine something [as something else] (*al-mukhayyil*) is speech to which the soul yields, becoming attracted to matters and repulsed from them, without examination, thought, or choice. In sum, [the soul] reacts to it in a way that is psychological, not rational.[56]

He goes on to specify that this emotional response involves feelings of wonder and pleasure:

> Imagining (*takhayyul*)[57] [something as something else] is a compliance [to the proposition]. The acknowledgment of the truth of a proposition [i.e., *taṣdīq*] is a compliance [as well]. Imagining, however, is a compliance due to the wonder (*taʿajjub*) and the pleasure that are caused by the [poetic] speech itself, while the acknowledgment of the truth of a proposition is a compliance due to the realization that the thing is what it is said to be.[58]

To understand this pivotal statement in Ibn Sīnā's treatise on the *Poetics*, which links the poetic with the receiver's experience of wonder, we must

[53] Ibn Sīnā, *al-Shifāʾ, al-Manṭiq 4: al-Qiyās*, ed. Ibrāhīm Madkūr and Saʿīd Zāyid (Cairo: al-Hayʾa al-ʿĀmma li-Shuʾūn al-Maṭābiʿ al-Amīriyya, 1964), 4.

[54] Ibid., 5. [55] Ibid. [56] Ibn Sīnā, *al-Shiʿr*, 24 "تنفعل له انفعالا نفسانيا غير فكري".

[57] *Takhayyul* is the listener's own process of imagining something as something else, while *takhyīl* is the statement's ability to make the listener imagine [something as something else].

[58] Ibn Sīnā, *al-Shiʿr*, 24.

first analyze what exactly he means by *takhyīl* and how in practice it can be produced through poetic speech.

Like al-Fārābī, Ibn Sīnā considers poetic speech to be part of logic and hence syllogistic in nature and – like al-Fārābī – he defines poetry as "make-believe speech"[59] (*kalām mukhayyil*).[60] Ibn Sīnā, however, elaborates more on the syllogistic nature of poetic statements and the mechanisms by which they result in make-believe (*takhyīl*). In *Kitāb al-qiyās*, he explains that, while a poetic syllogism does not attempt to result in a "real" acceptance of the truth of a proposition, it does follow the rules of demonstrative syllogisms as if its premises were true: "so far as it is poetry, it is not said to be false, when the premises are used as if they were accepted."[61] He gives the example of comparing a fair-faced person to the moon and explains:

> If one says "so-and-so is a moon" because he is fair of face, then one reasons as follows: so-and-so is fair of face; everyone who is fair of face is a moon; therefore so-and-so is a moon. If one accepts what is in this statement, then the conclusion must follow. The poet, however, does not really want this conclusion to be believed, even if he seems to, insofar as he is a poet; rather, his aim is to make one imagine the necessary conclusion as a result of the soul's appreciation of the object of praise.[62]

A poetic syllogism is therefore based on premises that are not necessarily true. The poet does not want the audience to believe that so-and-so is really a moon. But if one accepts the premises that so-and-so is fair of face and that everyone who is fair of face is a moon, one must accept the conclusion that "he is a moon." Therefore, even though a poetic syllogism may be untruthful, it follows correct syllogistic reasoning, as long as the poetic

59 Dahiyat, in his translation of Ibn Sīnā's *Poetics*, translates the term "*kalām mukhayyil*" as "imaginative speech." The active sense of speech's production of an image in the listener is lost, however, with such a rendering and it gives the impression that Ibn Sīnā is talking about any imagined or creative speech, which is not the case. A more exact translation would be "image-evoking speech" such as Schoeler's German translation of *mukhayyil* as "vorstellungsevozierend" (Gregor Schoeler, *Der poetische Syllogismus: Ein Beitrag zum Verständnis der "logischen" Poetik der Araber*, in *Zeitschrift der Deutschen Morgenländischen Gesellschaft* (1983)). Because the evocation of the image is one that is then taken as truth, even though it is not, I prefer translating the term as "make-believe."

60 In addition to being "image-evoking speech," Ibn Sīnā also defines poetry as being "composed of utterances that are metered (*mawzūna*), commensurate (*mutasāwiya*), and, in Arabic, rhymed" (Ibn Sīnā, *al-Shiʿr*, 23). He goes on to say, however, that the logician's concern with poetry is only insofar as it is image-evoking speech. The other two aspects of poetry are relegated to the musician and prosodist.

61 Ibn Sīnā, *al-Qiyās*, 57. 62 Ibid.

premises are accepted insofar as they are poetry.[63] As a result, what distinguishes a poetic syllogism from other kinds of syllogisms is not the logical method of reasoning; rather the *type of premises* it uses and the *kind of acceptance* of the conclusion it produces.

In the "Ninth Method" of his *Remarks and Admonitions* (*al-Ishārāt wa-l-tanbīhāt*), Ibn Sīnā discusses the various types of premises employed by the different kinds of syllogisms. For example, demonstrative syllogisms are composed of conceded premises, which he calls "admitted premises"; dialectical syllogisms are composed of "widely known or 'endoxic' premises"; and rhetorical ones are composed of "suppositional premises."[64] Poetic syllogisms (*al-qiyāsāt al-shiʿriyya*), on the other hand, are composed of "make-believe premises" (*muqaddimāt mukhayyila*).[65] The defining aspect of these make-believe premises, in turn, is their ability to produce an emotional reaction in the listener.

In the "Sixth Method" of the same book, where Ibn Sīnā discusses "propositions from the aspect of what [allows] the acknowledgment of their truth and the like," he explains that "make-believe propositions are such that, when they are stated, they leave in the soul a marvelous effect (*taʾthīr ʿajīb*) [resulting in] repulsion or attraction."[66] This "marvelous effect" can result from a variety of aspects, including even the truthfulness of a statement. In a poetic syllogism, however, it is the result of *muḥākāt* (comparison). In *Remarks and Admonitions*, Ibn Sīnā states:

> [Emotionally] moving make-believe speech depends on the wonder (*taʿajjub*) [it produces] either by [1] the quality of its form,[67] [2] the force of its truth, [3] how widely held [of an opinion] it is (*shuhra*), or [4] the goodness of its comparison (*muḥākāt*).[68]

He goes on to say that:

[63] For the most up-to-date analysis of the poetic syllogism and the scholarship surrounding it, see Schoeler, "The 'Poetic Syllogism' Revisited." See also Schoeler, *Der poetische Syllogismus*; and Black, *Logic*.

[64] For an overview of Ibn Sīnā's syllogism-related terminology, see Gutas, "The Empiricism of Avicenna," 394–8.

[65] Ibn Sīnā, *al-Ishārāt wa-l-tanbīhāt, with the Commentary of Naṣīr al-Dīn al-Ṭūsī*, ed. Sulaymān Dunyā, 3 vols. (Cairo: Dār al-Maʿārif, 1960), 1:511.

[66] Ibid., 1:412.

[67] The philosopher Naṣīr al-Dīn al-Ṭūsī (d. 672/1274), in his margins to the same passage, explains that what is meant by "form" (*hayʾa*) here is the quality of the wording or speech itself (ibid.).

[68] Ibid., 1:413.

We reserve the name "make-believe propositions" for those which leave an effect [on the soul] through comparison (*muḥākāt*).[69]

With regard to the true and widely held/endoxic propositions, Ibn Sīnā clarifies that although their primary purpose is to produce a [real] acknowledgment of their truth (*taṣdīq*), they could also result in a make-believe acknowledgment of their truth (*takhyīl*).[70] He explains that "they are primary (i.e., true) and endoxic from one aspect, and make-believe from another."[71] For, as we have seen, *takhyīl* is an acceptance resulting from an emotional response to a statement, whereas *taṣdīq* is a result of the rational soundness of a proposition. Therefore, if a true or endoxic statement produces *takhyīl*, its production is the result of something in the statement that provokes an emotional reaction alongside the rational acknowledgment of its truth. In fact, Ibn Sīnā explains that:

A truthful utterance, when deflected from the usual and when something that is congenial to the soul is imparted to it, may result in both an acknowledgment of its truth (*taṣdīq*) and make-believe (*takhyīl*).[72]

He goes on to say that the "make-believe [aspect] may be so distracting that the acknowledgment of its truth is neither recognized nor felt."[73] In other words, true and endoxic propositions may also produce *takhyīl*. This, however, is not a result of their "truth" or "wide acceptance." Instead, *takhyīl* results from speech that is composed in such a way that produces an emotional effect. This leaves us with two elements (out of the four quoted above) that lead to *takhyīl*: "the form of the statement" and "*muḥākāt*." In other words, the truth or falsehood of a statement in itself is not what makes it poetic. Rather, it is its "form" and the "*muḥākāt*" it contains.

Muḥākāt

On the most general level, Ibn Sīnā regards all arts as mimetic. He frequently compares poetic mimesis to painting and sculpting. In poetry,

[69] Ibid.

[70] I follow Gutas's translation of "*mashhūrāt*" as "endoxic." See his definition with examples in Gutas, "The Empiricism of Avicenna," 397–8.

[71] Ibn Sīnā, *al-Ishārāt*, 1:413. It is not clear what kinds of statements Ibn Sīnā has in mind here. However, philosophers, including Ibn Sīnā and al-Fārābī, do see the potential of poetry and rhetoric to instruct a more general public with truths that specialists arrive at through demonstrative proofs (see, for example, Ibn Sīnā, *al-Shiʿr*, 25; al-Fārābī, *Kitāb al-ḥurūf*, 152).

[72] Ibn Sīnā, *al-Shiʿr*, 24. [73] Ibid.

more specifically, mimesis is found in three aspects: meter, melody, and speech.[74] Ibn Sīnā, however, relegates the discussion of the first two to the prosodist and the musician.[75] He is concerned with poetry, instead, from a logician's perspective and therefore focuses on poetic speech itself and its syllogistic nature, not its rhyme and meter.

As already noted, Ibn Sīnā states that a poetic syllogism seeks to make one imagine something as something else based on a likeness between them (*muḥākāt*). In *Kitāb al-najāt*, he again emphasizes the function of *muḥākāt* in the poetic syllogism: "Make-believe [premises] (*mukhayyilāt*) are premises that are not said for [the sake of] acknowledging their truth (*taṣdīq*), rather for one to imagine that something is something else through *muḥākāt*."[76] As discussed above, a poetic syllogism amounts to a comparison of some sort, and Ibn Sīnā states explicitly that *muḥākāt* in poetic speech is of three types: "simile (*tashbīh*), metaphor (*isti'āra*), and a combination of the two."[77] So we can safely conclude that when Ibn Sīnā talks about *muḥākāt* in poetic speech, he means simile or metaphor.[78]

Muḥākāt *and Wonder*

Given that Ibn Sīnā singles out *muḥākāt* as the main path to *takhyīl* in poetic syllogisms and given that *takhyīl* depends on the production of wonder in the listener, let us investigate what about *muḥākāt* makes it wonder-evoking. Salim Kemal argues that an imitation or a mimetic statement is by definition wonder-evoking. He says "its nature as an imitation prevents it from becoming a 'recognized truth ... devoid of novelty' because it is always something other than an original. [...] And this tantalizing position is the source of our wonder or awe, for the imitation

[74] Ibid., 32. [75] Ibid., 23–4.

[76] Ibn Sīnā, *Kitāb al-najāt*, 101. See also Ibn Sīnā, *al-Ishārāt*, 1:413.

[77] Ibn Sīnā, *al-Shi'r*, 36. In *al-Ḥikma al-'Arūḍiyya*, Ibn Sīnā lists the three types of mimesis as being: simile, metaphor, and overly used comparisons (Ibn Sīnā, *Kitāb al-majmū' aw al-Ḥikma al-'Arūḍiyya fī ma'ānī al-shi'r*, ed. Muḥammad Salīm Sālim (Cairo: Maṭba'at Dār al-Kutub, 1969), 18).

[78] Black and Schoeler also conclude that the poetic syllogism amounts to simile or metaphor. For more detail on the syllogistic nature of a poetic statement, see their respective discussions in *Logic*, ch. 7; and *Der poetische Syllogismus*. Salim Kemal understands *muḥākāt* to also mean description (*waṣf*). This understanding, however, is never explicitly stated in Ibn Sīnā's texts and is more influenced, I suspect, by a modern, Greek-based understanding of mimesis (Salim Kemal, *The Poetics of Alfarabi and Avicenna* (Leiden: E.J. Brill, 1991), 155).

'is and is not' the recognized truth."[79] While this is an interesting and plausible explanation for the source of wonder in *muḥākāt*, I would like to point out two more specific explanations that Ibn Sīnā gives for *muḥākāt*'s ability to produce wonder. The first has to do with the process of discovering the resemblance that a comparison presents and the second with its novelty and strangeness.

Discovery

In both his commentaries on the *Poetics* and *Rhetoric*, Ibn Sīnā compares *muḥākāt* to learning and teaching. Like *muḥākāt*, he explains, "teaching consists of a certain depiction of a matter on the 'page of the soul.'"[80] Just as *muḥākāt* evokes an image in one's mind, in other words, learning also creates an image in our minds and souls. This process is pleasurable in both cases because of the wonder it evokes:

> Just as learning is pleasurable because of the wonder (*ta'ajjub*) it evokes, imitations in all their forms, like painting and sculpting, among others, are pleasurable.[81]

In his commentary on the *Rhetoric* he goes on to explain:

> Even an image that is found ugly in itself could be pleasurable if it achieves the intended likeness of something else, which is also ugly. The pleasure would thus not arise from its beauty, but from the excellence of its resemblance of the [original] when comparing the two.[82]

The cognitive process of comparing the likeness with the original matter to which it is compared and discovering the resemblance between the two is, therefore, the source of wonder and pleasure in the observer/listener. In fact, if a person is unfamiliar with the original, and hence cannot assess the similarity between the copy and the original, the pleasure will not be complete. It would exist only insofar as the manner of the speech and the composition itself is pleasing:

[79] Kemal, *The Poetics*, 155.

[80] Ibn Sīnā, *al-Shi'r*, 37. Ibn Sīnā metaphorically compares the representation of a matter in the soul to its depiction on a piece of paper with the phrase "page of the soul (رقعة النفس)." See Dahiyat's footnote on the phrase, Ismail M. Dahiyat, *Avicenna's Commentary on the Poetics of Aristotle: A Critical Study with an Annotated Translation of the Text* (Leiden: E.J. Brill, 1974), 78.

[81] Ibn Sīnā, *al-Khaṭāba*, 103. [82] Ibid., 103–4.

Men, therefore, find great delight in portrayed forms if they can well relate these to their originals. If they have not perceived them before, their pleasure would not be complete, but approximate; in this case, they delight in the form itself – its manner, composition, and so forth.[83]

We can come to two conclusions from this discussion: wonder in *muḥākāt* is a result of the discovery of the similarity between the likeness and the original, i.e., between the two things compared. When this process of discovery is not possible (because the original is unknown to the observer/listener), the wonder and pleasure resulting from it is incomplete. Ibn Sīnā therefore attributes wonder resulting from *muḥākāt* to a process of learning and discovery that the comparison enables in the receiver.

Aristotle also states that the pleasure one experiences from mimesis is rooted in its capacity to produce an experience of learning.[84] Stephen Halliwell describes the aesthetic pleasure of mimesis, as treated by Aristotle in the *Poetics*, as an "essentially cognitive experience."[85] However, when it comes to the application of this experience to the poetic arts, the main genre Aristotle discusses is tragedy. The mimetic components that lead to this experience are based on features related primarily to plot. As we have seen in the Arabic context, the core components the philosophers are interested in amount to simile and metaphor. This leads to a different conceptualization of poeticity despite both (simile and plot) being "essentially cognitive experiences." [86]

Strangeness

What makes the wonder experienced from *muḥākāt* different from that experienced from the discovery of actual truths? Discovery resulting from

[83] Ibn Sīnā, *al-Shi'r*, 37–8; Dahiyat, *Avicenna's Commentary*, 78.

[84] Aristotle, *Poetics*, 1448b.

[85] See Stephen Halliwell's overview of Aristotle's treatment of pleasure in the *Poetics* where he describes the aesthetic pleasure of mimesis as an "essentially cognitive experience" (Stephen Halliwell and Aristotle, *Aristotle's Poetics* (Chicago: University of Chicago Press, 1998), 81).

[86] The discussions about simile and metaphor in Arabic philosophy are nevertheless influenced by Aristotle, who talks about metaphor in both the *Poetics* (1457b2–1458a7, 1458b13) and the *Rhetoric* (1404b32–1405b20, 1406b5–27, 1407a11–16, 1410b13, 1411a1–1413b2). (For a discussion of Aristotle's treatment of metaphor, see John T. Kirby, "Aristotle on Metaphor," The American Journal of Philology 118, no. 4 (1997).) Aristotle, however, treats metaphor as a type of word that can enhance style. It remains secondary to plot in the *Poetics* and is not the main aspect that renders the literary arts mimetic. In the Arabic context, however, metaphor and simile are the central aspects of literary mimesis.

regular learning is wonder-evoking because we acknowledge the truth of something. Make-believe "learning" is wonder-evoking because we pretend to acknowledge the truth of something imagined insofar as it is poetry. *Muḥākāt* is wonder-evoking, therefore, because it simulates the experience of truthful discoveries. The discovery of actual truths, however, are rarely experienced. As a result, Ibn Sīnā attributes to *muḥākāt* a greater degree of wonder, declaring: "*muḥākāt* has an element of wonder-evocation (*taʿjīb*) that truth lacks."[87] He goes on to explain that this is "because a known truth is like [something] done with, which has no novelty to it. An unknown truth, [in turn,] is not noticed."[88] It is not that truths can never evoke wonder in and of themselves. It is merely the fact that we are oblivious to the unknown ones that would. Otherwise, known truths are too familiar to stir our emotions.[89] In fact, he suggests, as we have seen, truthful speech can have an emotional effect if it is manipulated in a way as to make it less "usual."[90] In other words, wonder can be injected into truth by rendering its familiarity strange.

In practical terms, familiar truths can be rendered strange through "mimetic" devices such as metaphor and figurative speech. In his commentary on the *Rhetoric*, Ibn Sīnā describes the estranging effect of metaphor, stating:

> The splendor (*rawnaq*) associated with metaphor and substitution[91] results from amazement (*istighrāb*) and wonderment (*taʿajjub*), and the feelings of respect, veneration, and awe that follow. This is similar to what a person feels when seeing foreign people, for he is confounded and stupefied by them in a way that he is not by familiar people.[92]

By likening the kind of awe one feels when faced with a metaphor to the feeling one has when confronted with a foreign and unfamiliar people, Ibn

87 Ibn Sīnā, *al-Shiʿr*, 24. 88 Ibid.

89 This resonates with Zakariyyā al-Qazwīnī (d. 682/1283), who argues that everything in the world is wonder-evoking. It is only our familiarity with the world that strips away its wonder. See his *ʿAjāʾib al-makhlūqāt*, 31–5.

90 Ibn Sīnā, *al-Shiʿr*, 24.

91 Substitution (*tabdīl*) is a term Ibn Sīnā uses for the process of metaphorization. See Dahiyat, *Avicenna's Commentary*, 100n4.

92 Ibn Sīnā, *al-Khaṭāba*, 203. Ibn Sīnā discusses metaphor in the *Rhetoric*, as it constitutes one of the "aids" (*aʿwān*) that enhance the effectiveness of rhetorical speech. Its uses in rhetoric are different from those in poetry. In the former, it is merely an aid and should be used sparingly, while in the latter it has a fundamental function. For a detailed discussion of the difference between rhetorical and poetic language, see Ulfat Kamāl al-Rūbī, *Naẓariyyat al-shiʿr ʿind al-falāsifa al-muslimīn: Min al-Kindī ḥattā Ibn Rushd* (Beirut: Dār al-Tanwīr, 1983), ch. 4. More generally on the Arab reception of Aristotle's *Rhetoric*, see Uwe Vagelpohl, *Aristotle's Rhetoric in the East: The Syriac and Arabic Translation and Commentary Tradition* (Leiden: Brill, 2008).

Sīnā links wonder produced by figurative speech to strangeness. Besides the process of discovery that *muḥākāt* enables through simile, therefore, it also has an estranging effect through the use of metaphor and figurative speech.

The Ways of Producing Takhyīl: Muḥākāt *and* Badīʿ

Speaking of make-believe premises, Ibn Sīnā states in *al-Ḥikma al-ʿArūḍiyya* that "most of them are comparisons (*muḥākayāt*) of things with [other] things that are intended for the purpose of achieving these make-believe [images]. So the brave person is likened to a lion, the beautiful person to the moon, and the generous to the sea."[93] He goes on to say, however, "not all [make-believe premises] are comparisons (*muḥākayāt*). Rather, many of them are premises devoid of imitation (*ḥikāya*) altogether, except that the manner of their speech is geared towards make-believe (*takhyīl*)."[94]

What other elements can contribute to making a statement make-believe? In his commentary on the *Poetics*, Ibn Sīnā explains:

> The elements that make speech make-believe include (i) those having to do the temporal measures of speech and their quantity, which is its meter; (ii) those having to do with what is *heard* of speech; (iii) those related to what is *understood* of speech; and (iv) those vacillating between the heard and the understood.[95]

He does not elaborate on meter's ability to produce *takhyīl*, as he relegates that discussion, as we have seen, to the prosodist. He simply states that it is also mimetic and that it enhances the poetic statement by facilitating its effect on the soul.[96] As for "the heard" and "the understood," they correspond to the conventional division of poetic language in medieval Arabic criticism into wording/form (*lafẓ*) and meaning/content (*maʿnā*). Ibn Sīnā goes on to explain that what is heard and what is understood, i.e., wording and meaning, can be wonder-evoking (*muʿajjib*) either with or without artifice.[97]

[93] Ibn Sīnā, *al-Ḥikma al-ʿArūḍiyya*, 16. [94] Ibid., 16–17.

[95] Ibn Sīnā, *al-Shiʿr*, 25 (emphasis added).

[96] Ibn Sīnā, *al-Ḥikma al-ʿArūḍiyya*, 20; Ibn Sīnā, *al-Ishārāt*, 1:512.

[97] Ibn Sīnā, *al-Shiʿr*, 25; Ibn Sīnā, *al-Ḥikma al-ʿArūḍiyya*, 21–2. In his commentary on the *Poetics*, Ibn Sīnā uses the term "*ṣanʿa*" for "artifice" and in *al-Ḥikma al-ʿArūḍiyya*, he calls it "*ḥīla*" (trick or artifice). Cf. Schoeler's discussion of this passage, *Einige Grundprobleme der autochthonen und der aristotelischen arabischen Literaturtheorie: Ḥāzim al-Qarṭāğannīs Kapitel über die Zielsetzungen der Dichtung und die Vorgeschichte der ihm*

From his discussion in *al-Ḥikma al-ʿArūḍiyya*, it becomes clear that Ibn Sīnā considers simile (*tashbīh*) and metaphor (*istiʿāra*) the kinds of make-believe speech that do *not* employ "artifice."[98] It also becomes clear that he understands simile as belonging to the realm of meaning and content (*maʿnā*), while metaphor belongs to wording (*lafẓ*).[99] While both are types of *muḥākāt*, he distinguishes between simile and metaphor as follows:

> *Tashbīh*-based *muḥākāt* is of two types: one that compares one thing to another with an indication that the comparison is indeed a comparison, through the inclusion of an article of comparison, such as "like," "as," "as if," or "as is"; the other does not point to the comparison, but [equates] the imitation with the original. As for metaphor (*istiʿāra*): it is close to simile (*tashbīh*), except for one difference, which is that metaphor exists only as added to a state or essence and it does not contain an indication of the comparison through the use of an article of comparison.[100]

That is, simile involves making a statement of comparison, whether explicitly through the use of an article of comparison or implicitly without using one. A metaphor, on the other hand, replaces or "substitutes" the original completely and is used as a word in a statement that is added to other words conveying some meaning about its "state or essence." Black explains the difference between simile and metaphor as "consist[ing] in whether one says: 'A is B' or 'A is like B,' both of which are examples of *tashbīh*; or whether, in a metaphorical statement about A, A itself is not mentioned, but instead one says, 'B X-ed.'"[101] Since metaphor replaces the original word indicating the object, it is considered to function at the level of utterance (*lafẓ*). The simile, instead, because it is a statement about the resemblance of two things, remains in the realm of meaning or content (i.e., *maʿnā*).[102]

dargelegten Gedanken (Wiesbaden: Kommissionsverlag Franz Steiner GMBH, 1975), 58ff.

98 Ibn Sīnā, *al-Ḥikma al-ʿArūḍiyya*, 21–3.

99 This is also affirmed in his treatment of metaphor as one of the types of signifying utterances (*al-alfāẓ al-dālla*): In chapter 7 of the *Poetics*, Ibn Sīnā lists them as such: "every signifying word is either common and standard, or foreign, [or transferred,] or ornamental, or invented, or separated, or altered (*mutaghayyar*)" (Ibn Sīnā, *al-Shiʿr*, 66). "Altered" words, as he elaborates in his commentary on the *Rhetoric*, amount to metaphor (Ibn Sīnā, *al-Khaṭāba*, 202–5).

100 Ibn Sīnā, *al-Ḥikma al-ʿArūḍiyya*, 19–20. Cf. Aristotle, *Rhetoric*, 1406b20–7.

101 Black, *Logic*, 245.

102 ʿAbd al-Qāhir al-Jurjānī makes the same distinction between *istiʿāra* and *tashbīh* in terms of their correspondence to wording and content respectively (see Harb, "Form, Content, and Inimitability").

In a rare instance in which Ibn Sīnā provides poetic examples, he cites the following verse from Imruʾ al-Qays's *muʿallaqa* as an illustration of make-believe speech that employs "artifice-free wording (*lafẓ*)":

وَمَا ذَرَفَتْ عَيْنَاكِ إلاَّ لِتَضْرِبِي   بِسَهْمَيْكِ فِي أَعْشَارِ قَلْبٍ مُقَتَّلِ

Your eyes have shed tears only for you to strike
with your two arrows (*sahmayki*) the pieces of my slain heart[103]

The word "*sahmayki*" (your two arrows) is a metaphor referring to the beloved's eyes. It is a metaphor and not a simile because the word is used as a *substitute* for eyes. As for meaning (*maʿnā*), Ibn Sīnā offers another oft-cited verse by Imruʾ al-Qays, in which he compares the moistness and dryness of the food (birds' hearts) an eagle brings back to its young ones in their nest to fresh jujube fruits and old dry dates:

كَأَنَّ قُلُوبَ الطَّيرِ رَطْباً وَيَابِساً   لَدَى وَكْرِهَا العُنَّابُ والحَشْفُ البَالِي

As if the birds' hearts both moist and dry
upon [the eagle's landing] in its nest are jujubes and withered dates[104]

This example is a simile because both parts of the comparison are mentioned and the article of comparison, "as if" (*kaʾanna*), is also stated.

Muḥākāt (i.e., simile and metaphor), therefore, forms the basic structure of artifice-free poetic language, both in terms of wording and meaning. By separating simile and metaphor from artifice, Ibn Sīnā distinguishes them from other literary figures, adding to their importance in poetry.[105] Furthermore, the central role *muḥākāt* plays in his definitions of *takhyīl* elevates the status of simile and metaphor to constituting the fundamental components of poetic speech.

As for speech that evokes wonder *with* artifice, Ibn Sīnā states: "Wonder (*al-taʿajjub*) may originate in simple or composite artifice in either wording

[103] Ibn Sīnā, *al-Ḥikma al-ʿArūḍiyya*, 22.

[104] Ibid., 23. For a discussion of medieval critics' fascination with this verse, see Jābir ʿUṣfūr, *al-Ṣūra al-fanniyya fī al-turāth al-naqdī wa-l-balāghī ʿind al-ʿArab*, 3rd ed. (Beirut: al-Markiz al-Thaqāfī al-ʿArabī, 1992), 178–81.

[105] Up to that point and beyond, metaphor and simile were simply listed among other literary figures in the critical tradition as in Ibn al-Muʿtazz's *Kitāb al-badīʿ*. They slowly gain prominence with the development of *ʿilm al-bayān* (science of elucidation), whose foundational ideas begin to be expressed by ʿAbd al-Qāhir al-Jurjānī in the fifth/eleventh century (see Chapters 3 and 4).

or meaning.[106] Examples of a composite artifice in wording include internal rhyme (*tasjīʿ*), metrical correspondence (*mushākala fī al-wazn*), internal correspondence in rhyme and word forms (*tarṣīʿ*), and inversion (*qalb*)."[107] Ibn Sīnā goes on to describe five types of artifices based on proportion and contrast, completeness and incompleteness, and *lafẓ* and *maʿnā*.[108] As Schoeler has shown, these artifices correspond to rhetorical figures (*badīʿ*) as set forth by literary critics, including paronomasia, *sajʿ*, antithesis, and parallelism.[109] In fact, Schoeler attributes the provenance of Ibn Sīnā's idea of wonder-evocation through artifice, something he adds to Aristotle's treatise, to the *badīʿ* style of the *muḥdath* poets.[110] Poetic speech, therefore, evokes wonder not only through *muḥākāt* (simile and metaphor), but also through poetic devices (*badīʿ*) that are not necessarily comparative/imitative in nature.[111]

To sum up, I will quote Ibn Sīnā's passage on what makes speech wonder-evoking in full:

> The wonder-evoking (*al-muʿajjib*) in sound or sense is each of two types: Either (i) it is without artifice (*ḥīla*). Rather, the wording is eloquent in itself without craftiness (*ṣanʿa*) or the meaning is unusual in itself, without craftiness, for nothing but the strangeness of its comparison (*muḥākāt*) and the image it evokes. Or (ii) the wonder (*al-taʿajjub*) may be the result of artifice in the wording or meaning, either in accordance with its simplicity or compositeness.[112]

As we have seen, "artifice-free sound and sense" amount to metaphor and simile respectively and represent the "mimetic" aspect of poetic speech (i.e., *muḥākāt*). "Sound and sense *with* artifice," on the other hand, amount to poetic devices, which Ibn Sīnā considers distinct from metaphor and simile.

Ibn Sīnā's attribution of wonder in speech in his *Remarks and Admonitions* to "[1] the quality of its form, [2] the force of its truth, [3] how widely held [of an opinion] it is (*shuhra*), or [4] the goodness of its

[106] Rhetorical figures in the scholastic science of *badīʿ*, which becomes formalized in the seventh/thirteenth century as we have seen in Chapter 1, are also divided into meaning-based figures and utterance-based ones.
[107] Ibn Sīnā, *al-Shiʿr*, 25–6. [108] Ibid., 26; Dahiyat, *Avicenna's Commentary*, 64.
[109] Schoeler nicely lays out Avicenna's artifices as described both in the *Poetics* and the *Rhetoric*. See *Grundprobleme*, ch. 3, and especially 67–70, for the artifices described in Ibn Sīnā's *Poetics*.
[110] Ibid., 71.
[111] Dahiyat's assertion that the artifices Ibn Sīnā talks about include metaphor is unfounded (Dahiyat, *Avicenna's Commentary*, 64n2).
[112] Ibn Sīnā, *al-Shiʿr*, 25.

comparison (*muḥākāt*),"[113] which we encountered earlier, starts becoming clear. We have already established that "true" statements [2] and "widely held opinions" [3] can produce wonder if they are novel or altered in such a way as to make them less usual. *Muḥākāt* [4], in turn, in the form of simile or metaphor, produces wonder through strangeness and the process of discovering the similarity between the two things compared. Finally, wonder can be the result of artifice, which amounts to the various ways in which a statement can be adorned using *badīʿ* figures. This last element is likely what he means by "the quality of the form/state (*hayʾa*)" of a statement [1] in the list above. These various ways through which wonder is produced in poetry help make the listener comply and submit to a statement. Ultimately, however, *muḥākāt* is the main way through which poetic statements are rendered "make-believe," as we have seen.

IBN RUSHD AND THE POETICS OF ALTERATION

While the Cordovan philosopher Abū al-Walīd Ibn Rushd (Averroes) shares much with Ibn Sīnā, his approach to the *Poetics* is distinct. He is much less concerned with forcing syllogistic logic onto poetic speech and he makes a greater effort to apply Aristotelian poetics to Arabic poetry, providing plenty of poetic examples. Nevertheless, wonder remains the assumed desired effect of poetry on the listener for Ibn Rushd. His explanation of the same effect, however, is different. While he is still concerned with *muḥākāt* and *takhyīl* as defining aspects of poetic speech, he also develops the concept of "*taghyīr*" (alteration), whose importance his predecessors did not stress. For Ibn Rushd, alteration, which entails the use of metaphor and any uncommon use of language, constitutes a defining aspect of poetic speech. It renders speech poetic because it makes it strange and unfamiliar, and hence wonder-evoking. Nevertheless, he also cites the process of discovery that metaphor and simile permit in the listener as a reason for their pleasing effect and, like Ibn Sīnā, compares it to learning through syllogistic reasoning.

*Alteration (*Taghyīr*)*

In his discussion of the various types of utterance that are at the disposal of the poet in the seventh chapter of his commentary on the *Poetics*, Ibn Rushd explains:

[113] Ibn Sīnā, *al-Ishārāt*, 1:413.

> When the poet aims at clarification, he employs standard, established nouns (*asmā' mustawliya*); and when he aims at producing wonder and pleasure (*al-ta'jīb wa-l-ildhādh*), he employs the other sorts of nouns.[114]

These "other sorts of nouns" include "the strange and transferred, the altered, and the foreign."[115] He states:

> Therefore someone would be laughed at if he wants clarity but employs ambiguous (*asmā' mushtaraka*), strange (*gharība*) [words], foreign loanwords (*al-alsun*), or invented utterances (*ma'mūlāt*). Similarly, someone would be laughed at if he aims at producing wonder and pleasure (*al-ta'jīb wa-l-ildhādh*) but employs common/overused words (*asmā' mubtadhala*).[116]

We can conclude two matters from these statements: First, that poetry has two purposes according to Ibn Rushd: clarification and/or the production of wonder and pleasure; second, that wonder and pleasure are associated with a certain degree of strangeness and ambiguity.

Ibn Rushd discusses the various kinds of utterances in both his commentaries on the *Poetics* and the *Rhetoric*.[117] He explains that the noun can either be "literal, a foreign/loanword, transferred and employed in a rare way, ornamented, invented, intellected and separated, or altered."[118] He goes on to inform us that the "intellected and separated" type as well as the

[114] Ibn Rushd, *Kitāb al-shi'r*, 116. For an English translation of the work, see Ibn Rushd, *Averroes' Middle Commentary on Aristotle's Poetics*, trans. Charles E. Butterworth (Princeton, NJ: Princeton University Press, 1986).

[115] Ibn Rushd, *Kitāb al-shi'r*, 116. The Arabic edition I am citing and Butterworth's translation both understand the term "الأسماء اللغوية" as "*laghwiyya*," meaning "nonsensical" (see Ibn Rushd, *Averroes' Middle Commentary*, 124). I believe it makes more sense to understand it as "*lughawiyya*," referring – in this context – to foreign loanwords. Such a reading fits better with the types of words Ibn Rushd lists earlier in the chapter (see my discussion of these types below). Furthermore, Ibn Rushd uses the noun "*lugha*," from which the adjective *lughawiyya* is derived, for foreign-/loanwords in his commentary on the *Rhetoric* (see Ibn Rushd, *Talkhīṣ al-Khaṭāba*, ed. Muḥammad Salīm Sālim (Cairo: al-Majlis al-A'lā li-l-Shu'ūn al-Islāmiyya, 1967), 535–6).

[116] Ibn Rushd, *Kitāb al-shi'r*, 116. Butterworth translates the term "*alsun*" as "eloquent [nouns]" (Ibn Rushd, *Averroes' Middle Commentary*, 124). I have opted to interpret it as loanwords, as I believe it is in reference to "*al-dakhīl fī al-lisān*" (i.e., loanwords), which Ibn Rushd lists as one of the types of nouns (see my discussion below).

[117] The two lists do not correspond perfectly. In *al-Khaṭāba*, Ibn Rushd has categories for "error-making" words (*mughalliṭa*), "strange" and "compound" words (which are part of "altered words") and he does not have a category for "transferred" words. These differences do not seem to be significant, however, at least not for our purposes here.

[118] Ibn Rushd, *Kitāb al-shi'r*, 113.

"ornamented" are unique to Greek and do not exist in Arabic.[119] This leaves us with five types:

(1) *Literal words* (*al-ḥaqīqī*) are those words that belong to a particular language and are common to it. These are often called "*mustawliya*" (established).[120]
(2) *Loanwords* (*al-dakhīl*), also known as "*lugha*" (dialectical or jargon), are those that have entered a language from a foreign tongue or dialect.[121]
(3) The *rare transferred* use of a word (*al-manqūl al-nādir al-istiʿmāl*) is the use of a word in a context other than that in which it is normally used, such as referring to "old age as the evening of life."[122] These and the other examples Ibn Rushd gives amount to various kinds of figurative speech. Indeed, he explicitly relates "transfer" to metaphor when citing the following verse by al-Mutanabbī in which he uses technical grammatical terms to express a nongrammatical idea:

إذا كانَ ما تَنْوِيهِ فِعْلاً مُضارِعاً مَضَى قَبْلَ أَنْ تُلقَى عَلَيْهِ الجَوازِمُ

If your intention is an action in the present tense
It is past [tense] before it can be made jussive[123]

[119] Ibid., 115; and Ibn Rushd, *al-Khaṭāba*, 536. Aristotle's discussion of the types of nouns can be found in the *Poetics*, 1457b1ff.

[120] Butterworth's translation of the term "*ḥaqīqī*" as "authentic" is inaccurate. (Dahiyat does the same in his translation of Ibn Sīnā's commentary on the *Poetics*, *Avicenna's Commentary*, 113.) It is clear from the context that what Ibn Rushd (as well as Ibn Sīnā) intends with the term "*ḥaqīqī*" is the literal usage of words. In fact, as Heinrichs has shown, the term "*ḥaqīqa*" comes to stand in opposition to "*majāz*" (i.e., figurative or tropical language) in literary criticism, taking on the meaning not of truth vs. falsehood, but rather of nonfigurative vs. figurative. Heinrichs explains: "Since *majāz* had been used as a term describing the idiomatic use of certain words and constructions, it was all but natural that *ḥaqīqa*, when coupled with *majāz*, should gradually be wrested from its ontological moorings and acquire a secondary, linguistic, meaning – that of the non-idiomatic, literal use of a word or a construction" (Heinrichs, "The ḥaqîqa-majâz Dichotomy," 137–8). The understanding of "*ḥaqīqa*," in this context, as "authentic" places it in opposition to "false," instead of "figurative," which makes less sense. Here again, Alexander Key's argument for treating *ḥaqīqa* as a stable concept across disciplines denoting "accuracy" (in this case lexical accuracy) holds true. (See his discussion of *ḥaqīqa* in philosophy, especially Ibn Sīnā, in *Language between God and the Poets*, 189–95.)

[121] Ibn Rushd, *Kitāb al-shiʿr*, 113; and Ibn Rushd, *al-Khaṭāba*, 535–6.

[122] Ibn Rushd, *Kitāb al-shiʿr*, 113–14. *Manqūl*, meaning "transferred," is a literal translation of what Aristotle calls "metaphor." The example Ibn Rushd gives here is the same as Aristotle's (*Poetics*, 1457b24).

[123] Ibid., 114. The verse is from al-Mutanabbī's famous panegyric about the recapture of the Ḥadath (Gr. Adata) fortress from the Byzantines in 343/954, which opens with: "على قدر أهل العزم تأتي العزائم." The general idea of the verse is that what the Aleppine prince Sayf al-Dawla (al-Mutanabbī's patron) is about to do (in this case wage a battle against the Byzantines to recapture the fortress of Ḥadath) is already done or predetermined, i.e., his victory is certain. See full translations of the poem in Geert Jan van Gelder, *Classical*

A verb in the present tense in Arabic can be made jussive through the use of the negative imperative *lā* (do not!), the past tense negation *lam* (did not), or the affirmative imperative *li-* (let [it happen]). The idea al-Mutanabbī is expressing about the patron he is praising is that his intention is an accomplished fact before anyone would have time to prohibit, negate, or order it to happen.[124] Here technical grammatical terms are "transferred" to express something nontechnical in an unusual context.

Nevertheless, "transfer" is not limited to metaphor. It also includes other transformations such as the use of new kinds of verbal inflection. To illustrate this, Ibn Rushd cites a hemistich also by al-Mutanabbī, in which he uses the sixth form "*tafāwaḥa*" of the verb "*fāḥa*," which was unprecedented:[125]

تفاوح مِسْكُ الغانياتِ ورَنْدُهُ

The musk of the beautiful women and the [valley's] laurel wafted (*tafāwaḥa*) to and fro[126]

(4) *Invented words (maʿmūl mukhtaraʿ)*, also called *mawḍūʿ* (coined), are neologisms. He explains, however, that these exist in the new sciences and do not exist in the poetry of the Arabs. Interestingly, he goes on to assert that most neologisms, even in the sciences, tend to be transferred rather than newly invented.[127]

Arabic Literature: A Library of Arabic Literature Anthology (New York: New York University Press, 2013), 61–1; Arthur John Arberry, *Arabic Poetry: A Primer for Students* (Cambridge: Cambridge University Press, 1965), 84–90.

124 See Abū al-ʿAlāʾ al-Maʿarrī's (d. 449/1057) commentary on al-Mutannabbī's *Dīwān* for an explanation of the various possible grammatical interpretations (*Muʿjiz Aḥmad: Sharḥ Dīwān Abī al-Ṭayyib al-Mutanabbī*, ed. ʿAbd al-Majīd Diyāb (Cairo: Dār al-Maʿārif, 1988), 3:424–5).

125 See Butterworth's footnote on the verse in Ibn Rushd, *Averroes' Middle Commentary*, 123.

126 The pronoun in *randuhu* refers to the valley mentioned in the preceding verse not quoted here. See full poem in al-Mutanabbī, *Dīwān*, 450–4.

127 See Ibn Rushd, *Kitāb al-shiʿr*, 114; and Ibn Rushd, *al-Khaṭāba*, 538. Techniques of incorporating new words into Arabic were developed and standardized by the translation movement that thrived in Baghdad in the fourth/tenth century. While some words were simply transliterated or arabicized, others were created from existing roots, such as, for example, the derivation of new words like *ṣufār* for jaundice and *duwār* for dizziness from the already existing Arabic roots of *ṣ-f-r* and *d-w-r* (see Kees Versteegh, *The Arabic Language* (New York: Columbia University Press, 1997), 62). Ibn Rushd does not give an example of "invented" words. It is strange, however, that he states that they do not exist in poetry and yet lists them among the wonder-producing words. One possible explanation is that by stating that it does not exist in "the poetry of the Arabs" he only means in old Arabic poetry, for he often juxtaposes "Arab poets" and the "*muḥdathun*" (see *Kitāb al-shiʿr*, 96 and 97, for example).

(5) Finally, *altered* words (*al-mughayyar*), also referred to as "*ibdāl*" (substitution), are borrowed utterances (*asmāʾ mustaʿāra*), i.e., metaphors.[128] Ibn Rushd divides metaphor into three types: (a) those derived from *likeness*, like referring to a star as an eagle, (b) those derived from the *opposite*, like referring to the sun as darkness, and (c) those derived from an *association*, like referring to rain as sky. In his commentary on the *Rhetoric*, Ibn Rushd includes simile in his definition of "altered" words.[129]

Our philosopher emphasizes the necessity of maintaining a certain amount of common and familiar words in a poetic statement. This is because if it were devoid of such clear words it would become "an enigma and a riddle."[130] He says: "The virtue of the dignified poetical statement is that it is made up of both standard nouns (*asmāʾ mustawliya*) and those other kinds."[131] Explaining further, he states: "It is as though the poet must not so indulge in his use of unfamiliar nouns to the extent of producing a riddle or so indulge in familiar nouns that he diverges from the path of poetry to common discourse."[132]

Although Ibn Rushd emphasizes the importance of maintaining comprehensibility, it is the unfamiliarity and strangeness of speech that renders it poetic. He summarily divides speech into "altered" and "literal" and says that "poetic speech *is* altered [speech]."[133] The evidence, he states, lies in the fact that "if literal/standard speech is altered, it is called poetry or poetic speech and it is found to have the function of poetry."[134] By "the function of poetic speech," he means "the moving of the soul (*taḥrīk al-nafs*)."[135] Likewise, in his commentary on the *Rhetoric*, he states: "the virtue of rhetorical and poetic speech and its beauty lie in *alteration*. And what I mean here with 'alteration' is the use of all the [various] types of nouns and words except for the standard type. For each one of them, except for that one, constitutes some sort of alteration."[136]

[128] There is clearly an overlap between "altered" and "transferred" words. Interestingly, the "transferred" type is not discussed in Ibn Rushd's commentary on the *Rhetoric*.

[129] See Ibn Rushd, *al-Khaṭāba*, 532. I will discuss this further when I talk about *muḥākāt* below.

[130] Ibn Rushd, *Kitāb al-shiʿr*, 116. Here too I differ from Butterworth's translation (*Averroes' Middle Commentary*, 124) and the editor's choice of the Arabic edition of the word "*laghw*" (nonsensical) instead of "*lughz*" (riddle), both of which appear in the extant manuscripts according to footnote 3 in the Arabic edition. "Riddle" makes sense in light of its juxtaposition with "clarity" in the context. Moreover, the pair of words "*ramz wa-lughz*" are repeated in the plural (*rumūz wa-alghāz*) in the sentence that follows, giving further evidence that the intended word is "*lughz*," not "*laghw*" (nonsensical).

[131] Ibn Rushd, *Kitāb al-shiʿr*, 116. [132] Ibid., 116–17. [133] Ibid., 121 (emphasis added).

[134] Ibid. [135] Ibid., 125. [136] Ibn Rushd, *al-Khaṭāba*, 538–9 (emphasis added).

Besides the use of nonstandard words, Ibn Rushd explains, normal speech can be altered through the use of "words that are in harmony with each other in terms of balance and amount."[137] By "harmony between words," he means agreement in sound. This constitutes the various types of paronomasia (*mujānasa*).[138] As for balance (*muwāzana*), he means the pairing of words that belong together either due to some similarity (e.g., the sun and the moon), as opposites (e.g., night and day), in terms of use (e.g., bow and arrow), or for being commensurate (e.g., king and God).[139] Speech can also be taken out of the ordinary through alterations to the sentence structure such as "reversal, omission, addition, subtraction, pre- and post-positioning (*taqdīm wa-ta'khīr*), and moving from affirmation to negation or vice versa, [...] in sum, through all of the types that we call *majāz* (figurative speech/ permissible transgression)."[140]

Alteration becomes a defining aspect of poetry's poeticity for Ibn Rushd. He states: "If you contemplate poems that are moving, you will find them all to be such. Those that have been stripped of such alterations possess nothing of the meaning of poeticity (*ma'nā al-shi'riyya*) other than meter alone."[141] A poem that contains little alteration can be good, but more for the truth it possesses than its poeticity.[142] In sum, what makes a statement poetic is the alteration of normal speech through the use of nonstandard words, production of balance and harmony, and/or the manipulation of standard sentence structures.

137 Ibn Rushd, *Kitāb al-shi'r*, 121.

138 See his discussion of the various types of agreement of utterances with each other, with many examples, in article 92 of his commentary on the *Poetics* (ibid., 117–20).

139 See his discussion on balance in article 93 of his commentary on the *Poetics* (ibid., 120–1).

140 Ibid., 123; and see also Ibn Rushd, *al-Khaṭāba*, 623. These are all matters relating to sentence construction, which al-Jurjānī discusses under what he calls "*naẓm*" (sentence structure), and which becomes standardized by al-Sakkākī as *'ilm al-ma'ānī* (the science of meanings) in the scholastic study of eloquence (see Chapter 5). Ibn Rushd's description of such manipulations of sentence structure as *majāz*, a word typically reserved for figurative speech, is unusual but not inexistent. *Majāz* can refer to any allowable transgression of ordinary rules.

141 Ibn Rushd, *Kitāb al-shi'r*, 122. Interestingly, in the same article, Ibn Rushd goes on to give examples of such alterations from the Quran. As we will see in Chapter 5, the debate about the inimitability of the Quran is ultimately settled as lying primarily in its composition (*naẓm*). Ibn Rushd's explicit statement here that the different techniques of composition and sentence structures serve to "alter" a more straightforward and standard way of presenting ideas agrees with what I argue is the underlying aesthetic of 'Abd al-Qāhir al-Jurjānī's theory of *naẓm*.

142 Ibid., 131.

Ibn Rushd gives three examples for such altered speech. In the first, he cites Kuthayyir ʿAzza's (d. 105/723) verse, with which I opened this book, for figuratively stating what would normally be simply expressed as "we talked and we walked":[143]

أَخَذْنا بِأطرافِ الأحاديثِ بَيْنَنا وسالتْ بأَعْناقِ المَطِيِّ الأَباطِحُ

We took to the choicest of speech between us
as the broad valleys flowed with the necks of camels[144]

He also cites an image from a verse by ʿUmar ibn Abī Rabīʿa (d. 93/712) for describing the length of a woman's neck in an unusual way:[145]

بَعيدَةُ مَهْوَى القُرْطِ

[Having a] long-dropping earring

Finally, he cites the following verse by Ibn al-Muʿtazz (d. 296/908), which combines several alterations of standard speech, which render it poetic:

يا دارُ أيْنَ ظِباؤُكِ اللَّعَسُ قدْ كانَ لي في إِنْسِها أُنُسُ

O Abode! Where are your dark-lipped gazelles?
For I found in its people (*ins*) companionship (*uns*)

The last verse is made poetic, Ibn Rushd explains, first, by addressing the abode as if it were a speaking person; second, through the employment of the term "gazelles" instead of "women" (i.e., metaphor); and finally,

143 Ibid., 122. This verse is often cited as an example of banal meaning expressed with beautiful wording (e.g., Ibn Qutayba, *al-Shiʿr wa-l-shuʿarāʾ*, 1:66; al-ʿAskarī, *Kitāb al ṣināʿatayn*, 59. See also Ibn Ṭabāṭabā, *ʿIyār al-shiʿr*, 138). Van Gelder discusses the verses in *Beyond the Line*, 45 and 135–6. Al-Jurjānī more specifically attributes its beauty to the way the sentence in the second hemistich is constructed (see my discussion of the verse in Chapter 4, under "What Makes One Metaphor Better than Another?").

144 The idea of the "choicest of speech" is implied through the expression "fringes of speech" (*aṭrāf al-aḥādīth*) in the Arabic, as Ibn Manẓūr explains in his seventh-/thirteenth-century lexicon *Lisān al-ʿArab* (*The Tongue of the Arabs*). Discussing this very verse, he explains that "the fringes of speech" is the kind of speech that "lovers exchange and that those yearning and captivated [by love] negotiate [which entails] hints, allusions, and insinuations, without explicit [statement]. This is sweeter, lighter, more flirtatious, and more appropriate than being direct, exposed, explicit, and overt" (*Lisān*, s.v. *ṭ-r-f*).

145 Ibn Rushd, *Kitāb al-shiʿr*, 122. Other poets have employed this same image as well (see ʿUmar ibn Abī Rabīʿa, *Sharḥ Dīwān ʿUmar ibn Abī Rabīʿa al-Makhzūmī*, ed. Muḥammad Muḥyī al-Dīn ʿAbd al-Ḥamīd (Cairo: Maṭbaʿat al-Saʿāda, 1952), 200n3). The image was often discussed in the critical tradition as an example of metonymy (*kināya*).

through the agreement between *ins* and *uns* as utterances – the last point being an example of paronomasia.[146]

Why Is Alteration Poetic?

In his commentary on Aristotle's *Rhetoric*, Ibn Rushd explains that overused terms "do not evoke in the listener any sense beyond the meaning [they denote]."[147] Altered words, on the other hand, "give the meaning an additional sense because of the strangeness they comprise."[148] Adopting Ibn Sīnā's analogy, he explains:

> Just as the inhabitants of a town experience awe and reverence when seeing foreigners come upon them, so is the case with strange words when they happen upon the ears of the listener. Therefore, he who desires to succeed in these two arts [i.e., rhetoric and poetry] must make their speech strange. The beauty of altered words [. . .] depends on the degree of their strangeness.[149]

In conclusion, a statement is poetic when it can produce a sense of awe and wonder in the listener. Wonder, in turn, is produced by altering ordinary speech and rendering it strange and unfamiliar.

What about Muḥākāt?

Poetry for Ibn Rushd is "mimetic," as it is for Ibn Sīnā. *Muḥākāt* in poetry can come in the form of melody, meter, and/or mimetic speech. Like Ibn Sīnā, Ibn Rushd is also concerned with poetic mimesis insofar as it is produced through speech, for that is the logical aspect of poetry: "The make-believe arts or that which produces *takhyīl* are three: the art of melody, the art of meter, and the art of creating mimetic utterances, and [the last] is the logical science that we look at in this book."[150] As his predecessor also argues, the conclusion of a poetic statement for Ibn Rushd is make-believe (*takhyīl*), which he even refers to on one occasion as "poetic *taṣdīq* (*taṣdīq shiʿrī*)," i.e., poetic acknowledgment of the truth of a proposition.[151] This suggests that Ibn Rushd did indeed think of

146 Ibn Rushd, *Kitāb al-shiʿr*, 122; Ibn al-Muʿtazz, *Dīwan Ibn al-Muʿtazz* (Beirut: Dār Ṣādir, 1961), 268. Ibn al-Muʿtazz cites this verse in his *Kitāb al-badīʿ* as an example of paronomasia (*tajnīs*) (p. 32).

147 Ibn Rushd, *al-Khaṭāba*, 540. 148 Ibid., 541. 149 Ibid.

150 Ibn Rushd, *Kitāb al-shiʿr*, 57–8. 151 Ibid., 78.

the poetic statement and hence *muḥākāt* as a type of syllogism. As Black has argued, however, the connection between poetics and syllogistic logic in Ibn Rushd's writings is not as clear as in Ibn Sīnā's: the former shies away from describing a poetic statement explicitly as a poetic syllogism.[152] In his "Short Commentary on the *Poetics*," he describes poetic statements as "not really employing syllogistic reasoning," despite having "syllogistic characteristics."[153] Although Ibn Rushd continues the convention in Arabic philosophy of regarding poetic speech as part of logic, he does not insist on its syllogistic nature the way Ibn Sīnā does.

Nevertheless, simile and its derivatives continue to constitute the basic paradigm that makes speech "mimetic" and hence poetic. Throughout his commentary on the *Poetics*, Ibn Rushd uses the terms *takhyīl*, *muḥākāt*, and *tashbīh* interchangeably. Moreover, from the outset, he lists the types of *takhyīl* as various types of simile. He explains that there are three categories of *takhyīl* and *tashbīh*. The first encompasses simile (*tashbīh*), metaphor (*istiʿāra*/*ibdāl*), and metonymy (*kināya*).[154] The second is a reversed simile, where one says "the sun is like so-and-so [in beauty]" instead of saying "so-and-so is like the sun," a figure associated with hyperbole as we have seen in Chapter 1.[155] The third, he simply says, is a combination of the first two without elaborating.[156] In his "Short

[152] Black, *Logic*, 184.

[153] Ibn Rushd, *Averroes' Three Short Commentaries on Aristotle's "Topics," "Rhetoric," and "Poetics" (Jawāmiʿ li-kutub Arisṭūṭālīs fī al-jadal wa-l-khaṭāba wa-l-shiʿr)*, ed. and trans. Charles E. Butterworth (Albany: State University of New York Press, 1977), 205. Cf. al-Fārābī and Arberry, "Fārābī's Canons of Poetry," 268, where al-Fārābī also describes the poetic syllogism as potentially syllogistic (*bi-l-quwwa*) and not in actuality (*bi-l-fiʿl*).

[154] Simile, figurative speech (including metaphor), and metonymy become the standard figures of what becomes formalized as "the science of elucidation" (*ʿilm al-bayān*) (see Chapters 3 and 4).

[155] See Ibn Rushd's discussion of the types of *muḥākāt* with examples in *Kitāb al-shiʿr*, 54–6.

[156] Ibid., 56. This seems to be an attempt to make *muḥākāt* correspond to Aristotle's plot-based concepts of recognition (*anagnorisis*) and reversal (*peripeteia*), which he does explicitly later in the commentary (ibid., 80–2). Unlike Ibn Sīnā, who understands "tragedy" and "comedy" as genres unique to the Greeks, Ibn Rushd interprets them as genres of Arabic poetry: panegyric (*madīḥ*) and invective (*hijāʾ*), as Abū Bishr Mattā does in his translation of Aristotle's *Poetics*. As a result, he tries to make sense of Aristotle's discussion of plot elements in tragedy in terms of Arabic praise poetry. He understands reversal, which he terms "*idāra*" (turning around), and recognition, which he terms "*istidlāl*" (deduction), therefore, as two types of simile. The type that is categorized under recognition amounts to a normal straightforward comparison. This is not surprising if a poetic comparison is seen as a kind of syllogism whose conclusion needs to be discovered and "recognized."

Commentary on the *Poetics*," on the other hand, he simply divides *muḥākāt* into simile and metaphor, in agreement with Ibn Sīnā's division. It is not clear how these divergent classifications fit with each other. However, what is important to note here is that Ibn Rushd consistently thinks of *muḥākāt* and *takhyīl* as simile or some sort of comparison, including metaphor.

The Relationship between Muḥākāt *and* Taghyīr *(Alteration)*

There is an overlap between the concepts of *muḥākāt* and *taghyīr* (alteration) in the figure of metaphor. As we have seen above, besides generally denoting any change to ordinary language, alteration more specifically denotes the use of metaphor. Given that *muḥākāt* also encompasses metaphor, *muḥākāt* and alteration are ultimately different ways of describing the same thing. When discussing metaphor as an alteration, however, Ibn Rushd focuses on the difference between it and ordinary speech. When discussing it as *muḥākāt*, on the other hand, he focuses on the comparative aspect, a characteristic contained in both metaphor and simile. These two different ways of describing metaphor, in turn, lead to different explanations of the pleasure and wonder it produces. As an alteration, a metaphor is pleasurable and wonder-evoking because it presents something in a novel and strange way that is different from ordinary speech. As *muḥākāt*, on the other hand, a metaphor (and simile) is pleasurable and wonder-evoking because, functioning on the basis of a similarity between two matters, it reveals something hidden.[157]

Like Ibn Sīnā, Ibn Rushd compares the pleasure resulting from *muḥākāt* to that resulting from learning. He elaborates:

> If learning is pleasurable [. . .], then *takhyīl* and *muḥākāt* are also pleasurable for their similarity to learning. [. . .] The pleasure in that with which existing matters are likened to one another (*tuḥākā bihā*) does not lie in the beauty or ugliness of the compared images, rather in that it constitutes a kind of syllogistic reasoning (*muqāyasa*). Describing the hidden, which is the absent matter being compared (*mushabbah*), with something more apparent, which is the likeness (*mithāl*) that takes its place, constitutes, in a way, one of the kinds of learning that happens through syllogism. In other words, the image (*khayāl*) of the thing plays the role

[157] Ibid., 63. That is, besides the fact that humans by nature find "imitation" pleasurable. Ibid., 63ff.

of the "premise," and what one is made to imagine (*takhyīl*) and understand plays the role of the "conclusion." Because of this similarity that exists between *takhyīl* and learning, *takhyīl* is pleasurable.[158]

Ibn Rushd, therefore, also attributes the pleasure that results from comparison to a process of discovery. Similar to learning and syllogistic reasoning, *muḥākāt* also causes something hidden to become apparent. Just as this process of "discovery" is pleasurable in learning, so it is in *muḥākāt*, whether in the form of simile or metaphor.

***

In sum, Ibn Rushd introduces the concept of "alteration" as a defining aspect of poetic speech. Alteration entails the use of metaphor, but more generally describes any nonstandard use of language. Speech is rendered poetic in this way because it is made strange and unfamiliar through alteration, and hence wonder-evoking. Metaphor, as well as simile, are also pleasurable because they involve a process of syllogistic discovery. This process of discovery, like learning, is also pleasurable and wonder-evoking.[159] Nevertheless, as José Miguel Puerta Vílchez has pointed out, Ibn Rushd criticizes comparisons that are too far-fetched and prefers greater realism and adherence to poetic convention.[160] This is a question al-Qarṭājannī develops further in terms of poetic reception, as we will see in the following section.

AL-QARṬĀJANNĪ: STRANGE-MAKING AND RECEPTION

We remain in al-Andalus with our next scholar, Ḥāzim al-Qarṭājannī, who in the seventh/thirteenth century writes a unique work of literary criticism entitled *Minhāj al-bulaghāʾ wa-sirāj al-udabāʾ* (*The Path of the Eloquent and the Light of the Lettered*). Its uniqueness stems from the fact that al-Qarṭājannī follows the philosophers' view of poetry as syllogistic in nature and adopts their terminology, including *muḥākāt*, which is rarely used in non-Aristotelian works of literary criticism.[161] At the same time, he is

[158] Ibn Rushd, *al-Khaṭāba*, 187.

[159] Cf. Puerta Vílchez, *Aesthetics*, 323–60, where he highlights Ibn Rushd's emphasis on the ethical and pedagogical purposes of poetry.

[160] Ibid., 339–43. See Ibn Rushd's discussion of the different types of *muḥākāt*/simile in *Kitāb al-shiʿr*, 90–100.

[161] He states, for example: "That which of syllogistic speech is built on *takhyīl* and contains *muḥākāt* is considered poetic speech, whether its premises are demonstrative, dialectical, or rhetorical" (Abū al-Ḥasan Ḥāzim al-Qarṭājannī, *Minhāj al-bulaghāʾ wa-sirāj al-udabāʾ*,

motivated by literary concerns rather than philosophical ones. For him, like for the philosophers preceding him, *takhyīl* and *muḥākāt* are the defining aspects of poetry. Al-Qarṭājannī formalizes the centrality of *muḥākāt* for the poetic process by identifying two types of *takhyīl*. The primary form of *takhyīl* results from *muḥākāt* (i.e., simile/metaphor). Secondary *takhyīl* results from all the other features of poetry, including word choice, structure, and style, that serve as aids to the primary *takhyīl*. The effect of poetic speech, also for al-Qarṭājannī, is one of pleasure and wonder.[162] He offers a new explanation for *muḥākāt*'s ability to evoke wonder, however, one that is based on its inherent rarity. Otherwise, strangeness is an important enhancer of the wonder effect, which can be produced through uncovering something hidden and combining disparate matters in contradictory and paradoxical ways. All this exposes the listener to something new and unexpected and hence produces a sense of awe and wonder. Al-Qarṭājannī, however, also considers the limits of strangeness and wonder in poetry and discusses the role of the listener's disposition and readiness to be affected by poetry. The believability of a statement, therefore, as well as the listener's personal inclinations, and his recognition of the medium of expression, affect the effectiveness of poetic speech on the receiver.

Primary and Secondary Takhyīl

Al-Qarṭājannī's treatise on poetry is divided into four parts focusing on the following aspects of poetry: (1) utterances (*alfāẓ*), (2) meanings (*maʿānī*), (3) structures (*mabānī*), which includes a discussion of sentence construction (*naẓm*) and meter, and (4) style (*uslūb*).[163] These four aspects

ed. M. al-Ḥabīb Ibn al-Khawja (Beirut: Dār al-Gharb al-Islāmī, 1981), 67). For important studies of al-Qarṭājannī's *Minhāj*, see Heinrichs, *Arabische Dichtung*; Schoeler, *Grundprobleme*; and Saʿd Maṣlūḥ, *Ḥāzim al-Qarṭājannī wa-naẓariyyat al-muḥākāt wa-l-takhyīl fī al-shiʿr* (Cairo: ʿĀlam al-Kutub, 1980).

162 Heinrichs concludes that wonder does not play a fundamental role in al-Qarṭājannī's poetic theory (Heinrichs, *Arabische Dichtung*, 159–60). Schoeler is careful not to conflate wonder with pleasure in al-Qarṭājannī's treatment of artifice and warns against interpreting it as valid for Arabic poetry in general (Schoeler, *Grundprobleme*, 84). While al-Qarṭājannī might employ different adjectives to describe the aesthetic effect of poetry, I hope to show that the explanations he (and others) give for this effect (in whichever way it is described) constitute characteristics that lead to an experience of wonder. In other words, an aesthetic of wonder is implied in his discussions, even when not explicitly identified as such (see my discussion of wonder in the Introduction).

163 Unfortunately, the first part on "utterances" is lost. Al-Qarṭājannī explains the relationship between these various aspects of poetry as follows: "Style is to meaning what

constitute the various ways through which *takhyīl* is produced.[164] There is, however, a "necessary" type of *takhyīl* and an "unnecessary" one, which, nevertheless, strengthens and aids the necessary type. The former consists of "making one imagine (*takhyīl*) a meaning through utterances," while the latter results from: "the utterance itself, the style, the meter and sentence construction."[165]

Elsewhere, al-Qarṭājannī divides *takhyīl* in a similar vein based on the kinds of sources it may result from:

(a) imagining the [object of description] through the speech [describing it], and (b) imagining things [that result from both] the object of description and the speech [itself] in its utterances, meanings, composition/meter, and style. The first *takhyīl* is like delineating and shaping a painting. The second *takhyīl* is like decoration in paintings, ornamentation in clothing, and the arrangement of pearls and [precious] stones in necklaces.[166]

He adds: "A lot of speech that is not poetic in the first sense of *takhyīl*, is poetry in the second sense, even though many people fail to notice this [difference]."[167] The first and "necessary" type of *takhyīl* amounts to *muḥākāt*, which al-Qarṭājannī discusses extensively in part II of his treatise (on meanings). The second and "unnecessary" type of *takhyīl* includes the remaining components of poetry: utterances, structure and composition (of the verse and poem as a whole), and style.[168]

Both of these types of *takhyīl* seek to evoke an emotional reaction in the soul. Al-Qarṭājannī explains:

Takhyīl is the representation of an image (*ṣūra*) and its placement in the imagination of the listener through the poet's image-evoking utterances, meanings, style, and composition. The listener in turn feels excitement, as a result of imagining this

composition (*naẓm*) is to utterances." This is because style results from the way in which descriptions flow from one aspect to another and composition (*naẓm*) constitutes the way in which utterances and expressions flow and connect to each other (al-Qarṭājannī, *Minhāj*, 363).

164 Ibid., 89.

165 Ibid. When al-Qarṭājannī talks about "the utterance itself," he means its sound independent of its meaning. This is distinct from the use of utterances as signifiers of meaning (i.e., signs) that form the components of the necessary type of *takhyīl*.

166 Ibid., 93. 167 Ibid., 94.

168 This explains why *takhyīl* and *muḥākāt* are often used interchangeably in discussions of what makes a statement poetic in Aristotelian Arabic poetics. While utterances, sentence structures, meter, and style all contribute to the evocation of an image in the mind, the primary way through which poetry makes one imagine something is *muḥākāt*. This prioritization of *muḥākāt* in poetry is already visible in the works of the philosophers discussed above. Al-Qarṭājannī, however, formalizes it.

image or picturing other images associated with it, in such a way that moves him unconsciously towards pleasure or distress.[169]

Furthermore, he repeatedly states that wonder enhances this process of *takhyīl* and strengthens its effect: "Amazement (*istighrāb*) and wonderment (*taʿajjub*) are movements of the soul, which, if they link up with its imaginative movement, strengthen its excitement and its being affected by it."[170] Elsewhere he states: "The more strangeness (*gharāba*) and wonder-evocation (*taʿjīb*) are associated with image-evocation (*takhyīl*), the more excellent [it is]."[171] Therefore, while the poet's intention might be to make something appear more beautiful (causing pleasure) or uglier (causing distress), the experience of strangeness and wonder and the excitement that it arouses should always be present.

Muḥākāt *and Wonder*

The concept of *muḥākāt* in al-Qarṭājannī's work, as in the philosophical works discussed above, has yet to be thoroughly analyzed. The scholarship on the topic is not conclusive. I will not attempt to give a definitive account of what *muḥākāt* entails for al-Qarṭājannī here. Generally, however, we can safely conclude that it includes simile and metaphor, and perhaps more generally any figurative use of language.[172] In fact, reading *muḥākāt* directly as meaning figurative speech or metaphor sheds light on many passages in which al-Qarṭājannī discusses poetry, which are otherwise obscure if the concept is understood as "imitation." Nevertheless, the idea of imitation plays a fundamental role in his articulation of the causes of pleasure, even in figurative speech.

Al-Qarṭājannī cites Ibn Sīnā when explaining why we find pleasure in poetry, arguing first that it is human nature to find *muḥākāt* pleasurable.

[169] al-Qarṭājannī, *Minhāj*, 89. Note that the pleasure or distress resulting from a moving image refers to the listener's resulting attitude to the matter described, not the aesthetic experience. That is, the poet might describe something horrific that nevertheless produces a sense of wonder in the listener as a result of the way in which this image is brought to his mind.

[170] Ibid., 71. [171] Ibid., 91.

[172] Some have argued that *muḥākāt* consists of *tasbhīh* and *istiʿāra* (Maṣlūḥ, *Ḥāzim al-Qarṭājannī*, 88). Others have suggested that it includes the general concept of *waṣf* (description) as well (Heinrichs, *Arabische Dichtung*, 168). Interestingly, al-Qarṭājannī also mentions "narrative mimesis" (*muḥākāt al-qiṣaṣ*), indicating that he had a broader understanding of *muḥākāt* (*Minhāj*, 97).

The proof of this, he explains, lies in the fact that people are fascinated by a painting of ugly and disgusting animals, which if they saw directly would repel them. "What is delightful," in this case, "is not the image itself, nor its embellishments, but the fact that it is an imitation (*muḥākāt*) of something else if done well."[173] The second reason people find poetic speech pleasing is their love of "harmonious composition and melody."[174] He goes on to explain that what Ibn Sīnā meant with "harmonious composition" is "its combination with compositional beauties and eloquent pleasing forms."[175] In other words, poetry is beautiful because of primary and secondary *takhyīl.* He argues that a meaning or an idea could come to one's mind in a number of ways and *not* have an effect on the soul. Yet when the same meaning is presented in a beautiful way, it moves the soul. He compares this to placing a drink in a glass or crystal bowl as opposed to opaque pottery. The soul delights in the glimmer of the liquid that shines through the transparent glass in a way that it cannot in the other case, even though it is the same liquid.[176]

Does this mean that presenting something through *muḥākāt* is more moving than the thing itself being presented? Or in poetry: Does this mean that presenting something metaphorically is more moving than expressing it literally? As we have seen, Ibn Sīnā certainly implies this when he states that "*muḥākāt* has an element of wonder that truth lacks," attributing the disparity to the latter's commonness and lack of novelty.[177] Al-Qarṭājannī makes the same claim, giving a number of explanations and analogies. First, he attributes the wonder we may feel upon seeing something real as opposed to seeing an imitation of it to different sources. To illustrate this, he provides an analogy of a statue's representation of a person:

> The movement of the soul caused by the statue and the person in whose form it is made should be considered to differ in kind. The statue moves through causing amazement (*taʿjīb*) by the beautiful imitation and the striking craftsmanship such that it implies the thing it imitates. The person of whom it is a model, however, moves the soul – if he is deemed beautiful – on account of the ardent love of his beauty and other ambitions one may have in this connection, for instance if the statue portrays a girl.[178]

[173] al-Qarṭājannī, *Minhāj*, 117. [174] Ibid. [175] Ibid., 118. [176] Ibid.
[177] Ibn Sīnā, *al-Shiʿr*, 24.
[178] Translation from van Gelder and Hammond, *Takhyīl*, 111. al-Qarṭājannī, *Minhāj*, 127. Some sections of al-Qarṭājannī's *Minhāj* are translated in van Gelder and Hammond, *Takhyīl*, 85–113. Where available I will use their translation.

Similarly,

> Amazement (*ta'jīb*) caused by image-evoking speech (*al-qawl al-mukhayyil*) is either on account of the striking imitation of something and its making one imagine [something as something else] (*takhyīl*), as was the case with the statue, or on account of the fact that the imitated thing belongs to the class of curious and rare matters.[179]

He further explains that the imitation is usually more wonder-evoking than the thing imitated:

> It happens that the movement caused by the statue, in the manner of causing amazement, is greater than the movement caused by that of which it is a likeness, in the other manner. In fact, this is what happens in most cases.[180]

In other words, image-evoking speech causes wonder through the *muḥākāt* (i.e., metaphor) itself and the poetic skill exhibited in it, whereas wonder caused by the thing that is imitated is the result of it belonging to "the class of curious and rare matters."[181] Aesthetic pleasure, therefore, can be the result of the poetic representation itself, or the subject matter it is representing. Al-Qarṭājannī argues that the degree of skill in a *muḥākāt* is quite often higher than the degree of "rarity and curiosity" of the thing represented. As a result, the degree of wonder resulting from the representation is "in most cases" more than that resulting from the real object being represented. In poetry, this would translate into the idea that expressing something through metaphor is rarer and more curious than expressing it literally, unless the matter represented is itself rare and strange.[182]

Like al-Fārābī, al-Qarṭājannī divides *muḥākāt* into two types: direct (without an intermediary), which brings to mind the matter itself, and indirect (with an intermediary), which makes one imagine the thing in something else.[183] In other words, "it leaves the idea that evokes the thing, and [instead] evokes an image through that which is a likeness of the idea."[184] Like al-Fārābī, he correlates direct *muḥākāt* with "the

179 van Gelder and Hammond, *Takhyīl*, 111; al-Qarṭājannī, *Minhāj*, 127 (translation slightly modified).

180 Ibid. 181 Ibid.

182 The idea that figurative speech is more beautiful than literal speech is a common statement expressed and theorized in classical Arabic literary criticism (see Chapter 4). Al-Qarṭājannī, however, comes at it from a different angle through the concept of *muḥākāt*.

183 al-Qarṭājannī, *Minhāj*, 94.

184 Ibid., 126. Using al-Fārābī's example discussed above, direct *muḥākāt* would be the evocation of A through B. Indirect *muḥākāt* would entail the evocation of A not through B, but through some other idea, C, which is a likeness of B. It is thus twice removed from A.

statue" in the analogy discussed above and indirect with its reflection in a mirror.[185] While the beauty of direct *muḥākāt* lies in the fact that a metaphoric expression is by definition rarer and more unusual than expressing something literally, building on the metaphor and making it correspond with something else that is similar to it is even more beautiful. To illustrate this, he considers the beauty of seeing the reflection of trees in clear water together with the real trees:

> The conjunction of the two lines of foliage of a brook lined with trees, with their likeness (*mithāl*) appearing in the clear water, is one of the most wonderful things and the most delightful scenes.[186]

Al-Qarṭājannī attributes this feeling of wonder and delight to the rarity of the conjunction of the two conditions:

> The circumstance of beholding the shapes of these things in water occurs less frequently to a person than observing the realities of these forms; therefore they are more strongly experienced as something rare.[187]

He goes on to liken the wonder-evoking conjunction of the trees and their reflection in the water to the conjunction between a metaphor and literal speech that resembles the metaphor:

> Its counterpart in *muḥākāt* of a beautiful conjunction is found when a literal thing (*al-shay' al-ḥaqīqī*) in speech is joined with something that is a likeness of it and which resembles it, by way of figurative speech, either analogously or metaphorically.[188]

In other words, indirect *muḥākāt* moves the soul because of the rarity of the conjunction it presents between a literal expression and a metaphorical one that resembles it.

As an example, he cites a verse by Abū Tammām, in which raindrops on the remnants of the beloved's encampment coincide with lovers' tears:[189]

دِمَنٌ طَالَما التَقَتْ أدْمُعُ المُزْ * نِ عَلَيْها وأدْمُعُ العُشّاقِ

Vestiges [of a deserted campsite], where the clouds' tears
have so often met with lovers' tears

185 Ibid., 94.
186 Ibid., 127–8; van Gelder and Hammond, *Takhyīl*, 111 (translation slightly modified).
187 van Gelder and Hammond, *Takhyīl*, 112; al-Qarṭājannī, *Minhāj*, 128.
188 van Gelder and Hammond, *Takhyīl*, 111–12 (translation slightly modified); al-Qarṭājannī, *Minhāj*, 128.
189 van Gelder and Hammond, *Takhyīl*, 112; al-Qarṭājannī, *Minhāj*, 128.

The lovers' literal tears are made to coincide with the clouds' metaphorical tears. We are made to imagine a correspondence between the real tears and the illusory tears. The second example he gives is a verse by Ibn al-Tanūkhī (d. 384/994),[190] in which the poet describes what he tells his beloved the moment her tribesmen discover them together and he had no hope of escape:[191]

لَمَا ساءَنِي أَنْ وَشَّحَتْنِي سُيُوفُهُمْ وَأَنَّكِ لِي دُونَ الوِشَاحِ وِشَاحُ

It did not concern me that their swords were encircling me,
While you, more closely than the sword (*wishāḥ*), were [like]
a sash (*wishāḥ*) to me[192]

In this case, the resemblance is linguistic resulting from the paronomasia created by the repeated word *wishāḥ*, once intended literally and once metaphorically. Al-Qarṭājannī explains:

The beautiful conjunction of the lovers' tears, which are literally true (*ḥaqīqa*),[193] with the tears of the clouds, which are not literally true, and the conjunction of *wishāḥ* (sword), which is literally true, with the non-literal *wishāḥ* (sash) by which the clinging of someone who embraces is intended: all this has the same beautiful impact on the ear and the soul as the conjunction of real tree-tops with their non-real image in the brook has on the eye.[194]

Comparing raindrops to tears is not an unusual metaphor in itself. What makes the image striking is the similarity the poet proposes between the metaphorical "tears" of the rain and the real tears of the beloved. Ibn

[190] The poet Ibn al-Tanūkhī is the well-known prose writer and author of *al-Faraj ba'da al-shidda* and *Nishwār al-muḥāḍara*, who is known as "al-Tanūkhī" (see van Gelder and Hammond, *Takhyīl*, 112).

[191] This is expressed in the preceding verse, not quoted by al-Qarṭājannī, but is quoted in Abū Manṣūr al-Tha'ālibī, *Yatīmat al-dahr fī maḥāsin ahl al-'aṣr*, ed. Muḥammad Muḥyī al-Dīn 'Abd al-Ḥamīd, 4 vols. (Cairo: al-Maktaba al-Tijāriyya, 1956), 2:346.

[192] I have opted for the interpretation of the word *wishāḥ* (lit. sash or belt) as meaning "sword" in the first instance, which is also one of the possible meanings of the word (see *Lisān*, Lane, and *Tāj al-'arūs*, s.v. *w-sh-ḥ*), as opposed to "encirclement like a sash" as interpreted by van Gelder (see van Gelder and Hammond, *Takhyīl*, 112 and 266). As van Gelder, himself, rightly points out, speaking of his understanding of *wishāḥ* as "sash" in both cases, both uses of the word would be figurative, not one literal and one figurative as al-Qarṭājannī proceeds to claim (Geert Jan van Gelder, "The Lamp and Its Mirror," in *Takhyīl: The Imaginary in Classical Arabic Poetics*, ed. Geert Jan van Gelder and Marlé Hammond (Cambridge, UK: Gibb Memorial Trust, 2008), 266n5). As a result, I believe we must read it as literally meaning "sword" in the first instance and "sash" in the second to metaphorically describe the beloved's embrace.

[193] I am reading *ḥaqīqa* when in reference to language as meaning "literal," rather than "real." Cf. van Gelder, "The Lamp and Its Mirror," 266.

[194] Ibid., 266 (with some modification); al-Qarṭājannī, *Minhāj*, 128.

al-Tanūkhī's verse functions similarly in that the poet establishes a conjunction between a literal *wishāḥ* (sword) and a metaphorical *wishāḥ* (sash). The metaphorical raindrop tears "reflect" the literal tears of the beloved and the metaphorical *wishāḥ* (sash) "reflects" the literal *wishāḥ* (sword) just as the clear water reflects the trees.[195] Just as the last is a less frequently observed occurrence and therefore a more moving image, the verses similarly present a conjunction of events or words that is more unusual and is therefore more striking.

The Arts of "Strange-Making"

According to al-Qarṭājannī, we can conclude, *muḥākāt* in its very essence is wonder-evoking. This is because, by definition, it is (usually) less common than the real matter being represented literally as is. In fact, generally speaking, rarity, strangeness, and unusualness are what determine the production of wonder in poetry:

> The production of wonder (*al-taʿjīb*) arises from finding novel (*istibdāʿ*) the subtleties in a poet's speech the likes of which are seldom achieved. Their occurrence is therefore seen as rare and unusual: like encountering something that is seldom encountered such as a hidden cause, aim, evidence, a similarity or difference; or like combining two disparate things in a way in which they can be related to each other, and other aspects that the soul would find strange.[196]

While al-Qarṭājannī declares that "the arts of strange-making (*ighrāb*) and wonder-evocation (*taʿjīb*) in *muḥākāt* are many,"[197] he does not tell us much about what they are. From the above statement, however, we can glean at least two ways through which strangeness can be produced: first, through exposing something hidden (like a cause, a similarity, a difference, etc.); second, by combining disparate things. While the text is devoid of any examples of the former,[198] al-Qarṭājannī gives us some examples that illustrate what he probably had in mind for the latter.

[195] These examples that al-Qarṭājannī provides for direct and indirect mimesis are different from the make-believe example I proposed above in my discussion of al-Fārābī. Al-Qarṭājannī seems to be emphasizing the linguistic "reflection" of words repeated once literally and once figuratively. I cannot see, however, how al-Fārābī's equation of direct mimesis with definition and indirect with syllogism can be applied to al-Qarṭājannī's examples.

[196] al-Qarṭājannī, *Minhāj*, 90 (cf. translation van Gelder and Hammond, *Takhyīl*, 94).

[197] al-Qarṭājannī, *Minhāj*, 96.

[198] Heinrichs suggests that exposing a hidden cause is the *badīʿ* figure "*ḥusn al-taʿlīl*" (fantastic etiology) where something is explained through fantastic reasoning. See Heinrichs, *Arabische Dichtung*, 210n1.

In one passage, al-Qarṭājannī divides *muḥākāt* into types based on strangeness and familiarity,[199] stating that:

> Strange comparisons (*muḥākayāt mustaghraba*) have a strong impact on the soul. This is because if the mind is made to imagine in something an amazing and unusual matter, it experiences an amazement [. . .] similar to that experienced by one who marvels at that which he has never seen before.[200]

To illustrate this "strange" or "unfamiliar" type of *muḥākāt*, al-Qarṭājannī cites the following verse by Abū ʿUmar Ibn Darrāj al-Qasṭallī (d. 421/1030):[201]

وسُلافةُ الأَعْنابِ تُشعَلُ نارُها   تُهدَى إلَيّ بيانِعِ العُنّابِ[202]

> The purest wine of grapes whose fire ablaze
> is presented to me by ripe jujube fruits (i.e., henna-dyed fingers)[203]

The scene the poet is describing is of the wine-pourer's beautiful henna-dyed fingers offering the glowing fine wine to the poet. By describing the wine as a blazing fire and the red-stained fingers holding it as ripe jujube fruits (on slender branches/fingers, as the metaphor implies), the poet succeeds in combining two things that do not normally go together. Al-Qarṭājannī explains: "the norm is for tender plants to wither in proximity of fire, not to ripen. As a result, [the poet] rendered the *muḥākāt* strange (*aghraba fī hādhihi al-muḥākāt*), as you see."[204] Thus, through referring to

[199] See al-Qarṭājannī, *Minhāj*, 94–6. There are six types of *muḥākāt*, as a result: "(1) imitation of a familiar situation; (2) imitation of a strange situation; (3) imitating familiar through familiar; (4) strange through strange; (5) familiar through strange; (6) strange through familiar" (ibid., 95).

[200] Ibid., 96. Based on the same logic, he also concludes that invented (*mukhtaraʿ*) comparisons are more moving to the soul because they are not as familiar as commonly used ones (see ibid., and his discussion of "invented meanings" on pp. 192–6. See also Heinrichs' overview of the treatment of convention and originality in Arabic poetics in Heinrichs, *Arabische Dichtung*, 82–99).

[201] al-Qarṭājannī, *Minhāj*, 95.

[202] I follow the verse as it appears in Ibn Darrāj's *Dīwān* which has *tushʿal* (to be set on fire) and *tuhdā* (to be presented) in the passive tense, unlike the published edition of the *Minhāj*, which has both as active verbs (Ibn Darrāj al-Qasṭallī, *Dīwān*, ed. Maḥmūd ʿAlī Makkī (Damascus: Manshūrāt al-Maktab al-Islāmī, 1961), 183). The former reading makes more sense in the context and agrees with the variant that has *tūqad* (to be set on fire, a synonym of *tushʿal*) in the passive form (see al-Thaʿālibī, *Yatīmat al-dahr*, 2:115).

[203] Henna-dyed fingers are often compared to jujube fruits hanging at the ends of slender branches as a description of beauty. See discussion of the same metaphor in a verse by Ibn al-Muʿtazz in Chapter 4, under "What Makes One Metaphor Better than Another?"

[204] al-Qarṭājannī, *Minhāj*, 95.

the hand and the wine metaphorically, the poet ends up combining two aspects that do not normally coexist, creating an unfamiliar image.[205]

In another instance, al-Qarṭājannī seems to link paradox to wonder. He first explains that a comparison intending to attract the listener to or repel him from the object being described does so by comparing beauty with beauty and ugliness with ugliness. Comparing something that is meant to attract to something repellent, or vice versa, is "wrong" and "contradictory."[206] However, *muḥākāt* can also simply aspire to match the two parts of a comparison, without intending to attract or repel the listener.[207] This is also best done by comparing good with good and bad with bad. However, it is also possible, in this case, for "something that is beautiful in one context and with regard to one purpose to be likened to that which is ugly in another context and with regard to another purpose."[208] This is because "the *muḥākāt* of both [contradictory] aspects is only meant insofar as they match [each other]."[209] He goes on to say that "it could also be intended as a type of strange-making (*ighrāb*), rendering more acceptable the representation of something to which the soul inclines with something that repels it."[210]

He gives, as an example, a verse by Ibn al-Rūmī (d. 283/896) describing food (bread and muttonheads) coming out of the oven:[211]

هَامٌ وَأَرْغِفَةٌ وِضَاءٌ فَخْمَةٌ   قَدْ أُخْرِجَتْ مِنْ جَاحِمٍ فَوَّارِ
كَوُجوهِ أَهْلِ الجَنَّةِ ٱبْتَسَمَتْ لَنا   مَقْرونَةٌ بِوُجوهِ أَهْلِ النَّارِ

[Mutton]heads[212] and white thick [round] bread loaves
taken out of the blaze and flame
Smiled at us like faces from paradise
joined with faces from hell

These verses present a paradox by comparing the grilled animal heads and freshly baked white bread to hellish and heavenly faces, respectively. The

205 Of course, the strangeness of the combination only results if one suspends belief and imagines real fire at proximity to fresh ripening fruits.

206 See al-Qarṭājannī, *Minhāj*, 113. Al-Qarṭājannī cites a verse by Abū Tammām in which the poet conveys the intensity of the wine's flavor (something positive) by having the taster react by frowning (something negative). This, according to al-Qarṭājannī, is a bad *muḥākāt*.

207 Ibn Sīnā also states that poetry can be composed for the purpose of inclining the listener towards or away from something (which amounts to what he calls "civil purposes") or it can be composed for wonder alone (see Ibn Sīnā, *al-Shi'r*, 25; Dahiyat, *Avicenna's Commentary*, 63, paragraph 5).

208 al-Qarṭājannī, *Minhāj*, 113. 209 Ibid. 210 Ibid. 211 Ibid., 114.

212 Heinrichs believes that "heads" here refer to muttonheads, which seems right. See Heinrichs, *Arabische Dichtung*, 242n3.

comparison is not intended to move the listener towards or away from the subject matter being described; rather it aspires merely to inspire awe (*ighrāb*). One can conclude that paradox, which a poet can produce through likening things to contradictory matters, is a strange-making technique. That is, even though a poet would usually compare something to something more beautiful to present it in a better light or vice versa, he could also compare something to both matters that are beautiful and ugly. In this case, the unusual coincidence of good and bad side-by-side serves to evoke strangeness and wonder.

In sum, wonder can be produced through the unusual combination of metaphors that do not normally go together, like fire and ripening fruit, or by likening connected things to contradictory matters, creating a paradox through the similes. So while *muḥākāt* is – to begin with – rarer than the real object being described, its wondrous effect can be enhanced through such strange-making techniques as choosing metaphors and similes that combine unusual matters and contradictory attributes.[213] It is worth recalling that such contradictions that are produced through figurative speech, which al-Qarṭājannī is praising here, were criticized in the old school of criticism.[214]

Believability and Reception

Al-Qarṭājannī famously defends poetry against the accusation that it is all lies, prevalent in the pre-Avicennan categorization of poetic syllogisms and in the old school of criticism, by arguing that truthfulness and untruthfulness are irrelevant in poetry:

> It is not considered poetry based on whether it is true or false, but rather on the basis of its being image-evoking speech (*kalām mukhayyil*).[215]

[213] Hoda El Sadda astutely observes: "It is tempting to compare Hazim [al-Qarṭājannī]'s definition of 'estrangement' with the modern concept of defamiliarization, especially if we bear in mind that he is predominantly interested in a philosophical exploration of the impact and function of poetry . . ." ("Figurative Discourse in Medieval Arabic Criticism," *Alif: Journal of Comparative Poetics* 12, "Metaphor and Allegory in the Middle Ages" (1992): 98). There are certainly rich parallels to be drawn. I would attribute this view of "estrangement" in al-Qarṭājannī's work more to a predominant aesthetic of wonder in late classical (i.e., post-fourth-/tenth-century) Arabic culture rather than specifically to his philosophical tilt.

[214] See my discussion of truthfulness in the old school of criticism in Chapter 1.

[215] al-Qarṭājannī, *Minhāj*, 63. For a discussion of the question of truth and falsehood in al-Qarṭājannī's thinking, see Bürgel, "Die beste Dichtung," 77–87.

Nevertheless, he argues that blatant untruthfulness is ugly in poetry. Just as bad *muḥākāt*, bad form, and ugly utterances diminish the effectiveness of a poetic statement, "obvious untruthfulness inhibits [the soul] from being moved."[216]

Just as the poet has to eliminate any matters that can obstruct the effect of poetic speech on the listener, the listener also has to be open to being affected by poetic speech. Al-Qarṭājannī explains that poetry moves the soul to varying degrees, depending on "the disposition (or readiness) one finds in the soul to be receptive to the poetic representation (*muḥākāt*) and to be influenced by it."[217] He goes on to explain that there are two kinds of disposition:

In one of these the soul has a state and an inclination by which it is conditioned to be moved by a certain utterance in proportion to the strength of its correspondence to this state and this inclination. As al-Mutanabbī says:

إنّما تَنْفَعُ المقالةُ في المرْ * ءِ إذَا وافَقَتْ هَوىً في الفُؤادِ

Words benefit a man only
when they match his heart's desire

The second kind of disposition is that souls firmly give credence to the idea that poetry is an arbiter and creditor that demands from noble souls that they respond to its claims, through the pleasurable thrill it gives, because of the beautiful comparison. Thus was the firm belief of the Arabs regarding poetry.[218]

Al-Qarṭājannī acknowledges here the subjectivity of poetry's impact on the soul. The various inclinations of different people affect the degree to which one might be moved by a line of poetry. This is something the philosophers before him do not seem to consider. Moreover, he points out the importance of accepting and believing in the medium of expression to begin with. If one does not believe in the legitimacy of poetry as a mode of expression, one cannot be moved by it. He affirms that Arabs did have a firm belief in poetry, more so than other nations.[219]

Besides resulting from the quality of the poetic comparison and form, therefore, the effectiveness of poetic speech depends on (a) its believability (even if it is not truthful), (b) the listener's individual inclinations, and (c) the credibility of the medium of expression in the audience's eyes.

216 al-Qarṭājannī, *Minhāj*, 72. 217 Ibid., 121; van Gelder and Hammond, *Takhyīl*, 106.

218 al-Qarṭājannī, *Minhāj*, 121–2; translation of prose passage from van Gelder and Hammond, *Takhyīl*, 107, with modification of "imitation" as "comparison."

219 See the rest of al-Qarṭājannī's discussion of Arabs' belief in poetry: al-Qarṭājannī, *Minhāj*, 122; van Gelder and Hammond, *Takhyīl*, 107.

A statement's apparent truthfulness and the speaker's readiness to accept it, therefore, help make the listener "buy into" the poetic image, whether it is true or not. This is a necessary condition for it to be able to move the listener and evoke wonder.

AL-SIJILMĀSĪ: TRUTH–FALSEHOOD REVISITED

In his *al-Manzaʿ al-badīʿ fī tajnīs asālīb al-badīʿ* (*The Innovative Trend in Classifying the Forms of Literary Figures*), the eighth-/fourteenth-century Maghrebi literary theorist Abū Muḥammad al-Qāsim al-Sijilmāsī takes another unique approach to literary theory, adapting Aristotelian/Avicennan ideas in a very different way from al-Qarṭājannī. Nonetheless, he confirms the place of aesthetic experience as a defining characteristic of poetic speech. Like his predecessors, he characterizes the experience as one of wonder and attributes it to human nature's instinctual desire to search for and discover meaning. The stranger and more unusual this process of discovery is, the better. He places value in the fantastic and revisits the debate about truth and falsehood in poetry. Nevertheless, he defends falsehood not for its own sake, but for its ability to evoke an experience of wonder due to its strangeness and novelty.

Al-Sijilmāsī continues the philosophical tradition of understanding poetic speech as moving "make-believe" speech, generally speaking. More specifically, he classifies "*takhyīl*" as one of ten "higher genera" into which he divides poetics.[220] He defines it as "speech composed of a relation or relations between one thing and another."[221] These amount to four types of literary figures: (a) simile (*tashbīh*), (b) metaphor (*istiʿāra*), (c) analogy (*mumāthala/tamthīl*), and (d) *majāz* (figurative speech, broadly speaking).[222] In other words, *takhyīl* for al-Sijilmāsī comes to replace the term "*muḥākāt*."

As we have seen, *takhyīl* and *muḥākāt* for the authors discussed above signify two distinct processes: *takhyīl* is the effect a poetic statement has on

[220] Besides *takhyīl*, the ten genera include: brevity (*ījāz*), allusion (*ishāra*), emphasis (*mubālagha*), word arrangement and combination (*raṣf*), coupling (*muẓāhara*), clarification (*tawḍīḥ*), ambiguity (*ittisāʿ*), digression (*inthināʾ*), and repetition (*takrīr*) (see Wolfhart Heinrichs, *al-Sidjilmāsī*, in *EI*²).

[221] al-Sijilmāsī, *al-Manzaʿ al-badīʿ fī tajnīs asālīb al-badīʿ*, ed. ʿAllāl al-Ghāzī (Rabat: Maktabat al-Maʿārif, 1980), 219.

[222] *Majāz* for al-Sijilmāsī, as Suʿād al-Mānīʿ has argue, and as we will see further in my discussion, refers to the kind of make-believe imagery that al-Jurjānī categorizes under "*takhyīl*" (see al-Mānīʿ, "Mafhūm muṣṭalaḥ 'al-majāz'").

the soul and *muḥākāt* is one of the ways – be it the main way – through which *takhyīl* is produced. We have also seen that *muḥākāt* for the most part refers to various types of comparison, namely metaphor and simile. The importance of comparison for the production of *takhyīl* is evident in the writings of all three philosophers discussed above. Al-Qarṭājannī proceeds to formally associate *muḥākāt* with the primary "necessary" type of *takhyīl*. When we get to al-Sijilmāsī, we see that the link between *muḥākāt* and *takhyīl* must have been so firmly established that he directly categorizes the various modes of comparison as *takhyīl*.[223] In other words, he equates the means of production (*muḥākāt*) with the effect (*takhyīl*). In fact, by doing so, he is the most explicit about what "*muḥākāt*" is, despite his avoidance of the term.

While al-Sijilmāsī equates *takhyīl* with what others have called *muḥākāt*, practically eliminating the latter term altogether,[224] he retains the general meaning of *takhyīl* as an effect on the soul. He affirms that make-believe speech that is "composed of a relation or relations between one thing and another" is composed in such a way that (quoting Ibn Sīnā) "the soul submits to it accepting and rejecting matters without reflection or thought."[225] Moreover, he states, more explicitly than anyone before him, that this movement of the soul is the essence and foundation of poetry. He declares that (what he calls) the "genus" of *takhyīl* is "the subject of the poetic craft" and its "essence."[226] Elsewhere, more generally, he says: "The subject of the poetic craft is *takhyīl* and excitement (*istifzāz*),"[227] and that *takhyīl* "is the pillar of poetry, as it holds in it the essence, nature, and true existence of poetic speech."[228] In fact, al-Sijilmāsī talks about the production of *takhyīl* in other "genera" as well.[229] While al-Sijilmāsī uses the term "*takhyīl*" in a specific sense to refer to the figures of simile, metaphor, analogy, and *majāz*, therefore, he also uses the term in a general sense to describe poetry's effect of exciting the soul. This movement of the soul, nevertheless, is primarily produced

223 Heinrichs, in his article on al-Sijilmāsī in EI^2, translates *takhyīl* as "imagery" and suggests that this is an unusual use of the term (see Heinrichs, *al-Sidjilmāsī*). It is not a complete anomaly, however, given that al-Sijilmāsī's understanding of *takhyīl* is in complete agreement with his philosophical predecessors who closely link *takhyīl* with comparison.

224 Al-Sijilmāsī does use the term *muḥākāt* in another section in his book where he defines "*takhyīl*" as "*muḥākāt* and analogy" (al-Sijilmāsī, *al-Manzaʿ*, 407). He was therefore aware of the term even though he does not employ it in the chapter on *takhyīl*.

225 Ibid., 219. 226 Ibid., 218. 227 Ibid., 274. 228 Ibid., 407.

229 See, for example, in "exaggeration," ibid., 274; in "coupling," 407; and in "repetition," 501.

through simile and its affiliates, although it can also be produced by other literary figures and techniques.[230]

Takhyīl *and Discovery*

The centrality of comparison for *takhyīl* can also be gleaned from al-Sijilmāsī's explanation of how and why *takhyīl* is moving to the soul. He says:

> The reason for compliance and pleasure [arising from an image-evoking statement] is the delight that arises in the human soul from becoming aware of the relations, commonalities, and connections between things.[231]

He goes on to say:

> The subject of the poetic craft lies in the strangeness of the commonality and the nongeneric relation that is [found] in one thing in relation to another, as if it were through comparing and representing one of the two sides with the other. For it is the nature of the human soul to become aware of the presence of something in something else to which it has a relation or in which it contains an allusion or a similarity and for there to ensue a sense of psychological relaxation (*inbisāṭ rūḥānī*) and delight (*ṭarab*).[232]

Al-Sijilmāsī, therefore, emphasizes the process of discovering the connection between things, attributing to it the source of pleasure we feel from poetry. Furthermore, he points out that "the subject of the poetic craft" (i.e., *takhyīl* and the ability to move the soul) lies in the "strangeness" of the similarity that is discovered between two things.[233]

230 Because of al-Sijilmāsī's use of *takhyīl* in two senses, there might be confusion as to whether he means that simile and its derivatives are the essence of poetry or whether it is the movement of the soul generally speaking, in whichever way it is produced, that forms the essence of poetry. ʿAllāl al-Ghāzī, the editor of *al-Manzaʿ*, points out and discusses this question of specificity and generality in the concept of *takhyīl* as treated by al-Sijilmāsī. He wonders whether *takhyīl* forms the essence of poetry as a genus or whether it applies to all genera (see ʿAllāl al-Ghāzī, "Taṭawwur muṣṭalaḥ 'al-takhyīl' fī naẓariyyat al-naqd al-adabī ʿind al-Sijilmāsī," *Majallat kulliyyat al-ādāb wa-l-ʿulūm al-insāniyya bi-Fās* 4 (1988): 317–18). In other words, are comparisons (including simile, metaphor, analogy, and *majāz*) the essence of poetry? Or is the movement of the soul resulting from poetry generally speaking the essence? While I agree with his conclusion that both are true (the essence of poetry is its ability to move the soul and comparison just happens to be the best way of achieving this), this confusion only arises when al-Sijilmāsī is taken out of context. Looking at his use of the term in relation to his philosophical predecessors, it becomes clear why he categorizes comparisons under the heading of "*takhyīl*," given that they constitute the primary form of producing *takhyīl* for the philosophers.

231 al-Sijilmāsī, *al-Manzaʿ*, 219. 232 Ibid. 233 Ibid.

Al-Sijilmāsī reasons in a similar fashion when explaining the effect of allusion (*ishāra*) on the soul, the third of the ten "higher genera" he discusses in his book. In his description of one of its types, "*iqtiḍāb*" (cutting off/concision), which for al-Sijilmāsī means the use of an unusual or indirect signifier and includes such figures as metonymy (*kināya*), the author attributes the resulting pleasure and delight to the strangeness and unexpectedness that this type of signification entails. He further explains that "the reason for all this is the natural disposition of the soul to seek and become aware of relations, connections, and commonalities between things, and what consequently follows this and is experienced of psychological relaxation and delight."[234] Among the examples he cites is a verse from Imru᾽ al-Qays's *mu῾allaqa*, often cited as an example of metonymy (*kināya*). In it, the poet conveys the aristocratic status of a woman by mentioning the fact that she sleeps in:

ويُضْحِي فَتِيتُ المِسْكِ فَوْقَ فِرَاشِهَا   نَؤُومُ الضُّحَى لم تَنْتَطِقْ عن تَفَضُّلِ

In the morning crumbled musk lies on her bed,
as she sleeps into the late morning, not wearing a belt
nor having put on her dress (*mifḍal*)[235]

Thus, the beauty of the verse lies in the fact that the listener experiences pleasure from discovering the connotations that this description of the woman imply. A woman who sleeps in late in the morning and does not have to bother to get dressed by an early hour implies that she is well-off and does not have to do chores. The process of discovering the meaning of the verse, in other words, which the soul seeks instinctually, is pleasurable and delightful.[236]

Under the same "genus of allusion," as al-Sijilmāsī describes it, he discusses another literary figure, which he calls "obscuration" (*ibhām*), of which one subtype is "glorification" (*tanwīh*). He explains that glorification and exaltation through obscuration makes the soul aspire to grasp the meaning. An example of this can be found in the Quran when the unknown is exclaimed: "The Calamity! What is the Calamity? (القارعة ما القارعة)" (Q101:1–2) or "The Reality! What is the Reality? (الحاقّة ما الحاقّة)" (Q69:1–2). Leaving such statements as such without providing an

[234] Ibid., 263.
[235] Alan Jones's translation with a slight modification (*Early Arabic Poetry: Selected Poems*, 2nd ed. (Reading, UK: Ithaca Press, 2011), 1:69). *Mifḍal* is a woman's dress (see Jones's note on the word on p. 65).
[236] See my discussion of *kināya* in Chapter 4.

explanation makes the listener yearn to understand them. When this attempt at understanding fails, "the soul is awestruck (*hālahā al-amr*) and strives obsessively to decipher it in whatever way possible."[237]

It is clear, therefore, that al-Sijilmāsī links the emotional effect that poetic language has on the soul to the process of searching for and discovering meaning. When it comes to comparison, the soul seeks to find the connection between its various parts. In allusion, when the link between the signifier and the signified is hidden either through an unusual expression of a meaning or through obscuration, the human soul, by instinct, has the urge to search for and discover the meaning. The more mysterious the meaning, the more striking and awe-inspiring is the poetic speech.

Return to the Truth–Falsehood Debate?

Al-Sijilmāsī argues that *majāz* is the most moving of the four types of *takhyīl* he lists. His logic goes as follows: Poetry is judged based on its ability to move the soul. False and invented speech has a greater impact on the soul. *Majāz* is by definition untruthful, invented speech. Therefore, *majāz* is the most moving kind of poetic speech:

> *Majāz* is speech that is exciting to the soul and whose falsehood is certain. It is made up of invented false premises that evoke matters in the imagination and imitate states.[238] Since the poetic premise is [judged] solely with respect to its ability to evoke an image and excite, as we have seen before, and invented speech that is certainly false is more image-evoking, exciting, and pleasurable to the soul (since the more untruthful a poetic premise, the greater the make-believe and excitement for the reason mentioned at the beginning of this genus and especially in this type [i.e., *majāz*] given the additional strangeness resulting from its unexpectedness and the soul's fondness of this), this [type of *takhyīl*] is best in its meaning and the firmest of the types of this genus in its ability to evoke the imagination and excite.[239]

Majāz is therefore particularly moving because it contains more strangeness and novelty than the other types of comparisons. This is due to the fact that it is more false and inventive than other comparisons, according to al-Sijilmāsī.

[237] al-Sijilmāsī, *al-Manzaʿ*, 267.
[238] I prefer the variation *aḥwāl* (states), which is found in one of the surviving manuscripts according to the editor's footnote, to his choice of *aqwāl* (utterances or speech) (ibid., 252n126).
[239] Ibid., 252.

The exact meaning of *majāz* fluctuates throughout the history of Arabic literary theory. Generally speaking, it means the figurative, nonliteral use of language, and it came to be juxtaposed with *ḥaqīqa*, which generally means "truth" or "reality," but paired with *majāz* denotes literal speech.[240] Furthermore, *majāz* is typically a broader category than metaphor and incorporates it rather than constituting a separate category. Al-Sijilmāsī's division of comparisons into simile, analogy, metaphor, and *majāz* is unusual and the distinction between *majāz* and the other types is not standard or obvious. He gives no explanation beyond its blatant association with falsehood, leaving us only with a set of poetic examples to decipher its definition.

By looking at these poetic examples, Suʿād al-Mānīʿ has argued that al-Sijilmāsī's concept of *majāz* is comparable to what ʿAbd al-Qāhir al-Jurjānī calls *takhyīl*.[241] *Takhyīl* in al-Jurjānī's treatise on eloquence, as we have seen in Chapter 1, refers to various kinds of make-believe imagery and not to a general effect of poetry, as the term implies in philosophy. The figures al-Jurjānī discusses under make-believe are characterized by the use of fantastic imagery, such as personification and fantastic etiology, which often build an image based on taking a metaphor literally. This kind of imagery, as we have seen, became particularly popular in *muḥdath* poetry. As al-Mānīʿ shows, the examples that al-Sijilmāsī provides for what he calls "*majāz*" are very similar to al-Jurjānī's "*takhyīl*" examples in that they abound with personifications and fantastic etiologies and all come from later *muḥdath* poetry.

For example, in the following verse by Abū al-ʿAlāʾ al-Maʿarrī (d. 449/1058), which al-Sijilmāsī cites as an example of "*majāz*," the arrow is animated by being given the attribute of thirst:

تَوَهَّمَ كلَّ سابِغَةٍ غَديراً   فرَنَّقَ يَشرَبُ الحَلَقَ الدِّخالا

[The arrow] fancied every armor a pool of water,
so it hovered drinking its intertwined metal rings[242]

In another example, also by al-Maʿarrī, the moon and the stars are given fictive purposes to express the night's fear of the eulogized person's powerful horses:

كأنّ اللّيلَ حارَبَها فَفِيهِ   هِلالٌ مِثلُ ما آنْعَطَفَ السِّنَانُ
ومِنْ أُمِّ النُّجُومِ عَلَيهِ دِرْعٌ   يُحاذِرُ أَنْ يُمَزِّقَها الطِّعانُ

[240] See Heinrichs, "The ḥaqîqa-majâz Dichotomy."
[241] al-Mānīʿ, "Mafhūm muṣṭalaḥ 'al-majāz.'" [242] al-Sijilmāsī, *al-Manzaʿ*, 252.

As if the night was fighting [the horses]
with its crescent drawn like a spearhead
And its milky way an armor
guarding against being ripped by stabs[243]

Al-Sijilmāsī does not explicitly associate personification or fantastic etiology with *majāz*. The examples he gives do reveal, however, that he has fantastic imagery in mind like those al-Jurjānī classifies under "*takhyīl*." This explains why *majāz*, according to him, is by definition linked with absolute untruthfulness and perhaps why its untruthfulness is the source of the excitement it produces. However, it is not the fact that it is fantastic in and of itself that makes al-Sijilmāsī's *majāz* particularly moving. Rather, it is the "additional strangeness resulting from [the] unexpectedness"[244] of the fantastic images, as he explains, that makes it moving to the soul.

In the section on hyperbole (*ghuluww*), al-Sijilmāsī revisits the old truth–falsehood debate that thrived in the fourth/tenth century.[245] He explains the division in opinion about the palatability of falsehood in poetry and presents the diverging tastes, as we have seen explained by the old school of criticism, saying that some favor the use of false and invented speech, while the others prefer moderation and the avoidance of invention and falsehood:

There are two opinions [with regard to the use of hyperbole (i.e., falsehood)]: one group – and they are the majority – sees that its condition and foundation is that it exceeds the state of both types of existence, intellectual and sensual, and reaches the unreal, untrue, and invented. And another group sees moderation as preferable, more praiseworthy, and better in the craft out of concern and fear of invention and lies.

He goes on to argue in favor of the former opinion, by first explaining that truthfulness and falsehood are irrelevant for evaluating the poeticity of poetry:

We say: he who wishes to understand which of these two opinions is preferable and more appropriate for the craft cannot but examine the subject of the poetic craft. So we say: what the first philosophers settled on in their treatment of logic is that the subject of the poetic craft constitutes make-believe [imagery] and the excitement [of the emotions . . .] so that a poetic proposition is approached in terms of make-believe and excitement alone without looking at its truth or lack thereof. Another group sees that a poetic proposition should be treated in terms of its unrealizability

243 Ibid., 256. 244 Ibid., 252.
245 See my discussion of the question as it relates to *muḥdath* poetry in Chapter 1.

or fantasticness (*imtināʿ*).[246] The subject of the poetic craft for them constitutes that which does not exist. This view is disliked and rejected by the first philosophers. Abū ʿAlī Ibn Sīnā stated his disapproval [of this view] at the beginning of his book on *Analytics* of his book [*al-Shifāʾ*].[247]

Al-Sijilmāsī here lays out plainly the old pre-Avicennan way of classifying poetic speech within the logical sciences as completely false speech and Ibn Sīnā's rejection of this with the concept of make-believe (*takhyīl*). Nevertheless, al-Sijilmāsī says that it does not hurt to expose which of the two opinions about falsehood in poetry is better. He explains:

[. . .] it is clear therefore that the first opinion (i.e., pro-falsehood) is preferable and sounder in matters of the craft whether we consider poetry make-believe (*mukhayyil*) or unrealizable [false] speech (*mumtaniʿ*). The second group's fear of engaging with pure falsehood and invented impossible speech is [altogether] outside of the [concern of the] craft. The right opinion lies with the first [group].[248]

Thus, al-Sijilmāsī affirms that poetic speech is to be defined based on its make-believe nature and its ability to excite the soul and not based on its truth or falsehood. The poetic effect on the soul, as we have seen earlier, is the pleasure one feels as a result of process of discovery that simile, metaphor, and fantastic *majāz* allow in the listener. Thus, the defining aspect of poetry is the aesthetic experience it makes possible, not its falsehood or unrealizable imagery. Nevertheless, if one had to choose between the two opinions about poetry, the one that supports falsehood and the one that advocates for moderation, al-Sijilmāsī states that the former has more validity. Based on his earlier reasoning, one can conjecture that this is because the fantastic is more moving than realism because it is less known, more novel, and stranger. These are all qualities that would

[246] Al-Ghāzī understands this group that sees poetry as composed of fantastic premises as a third opinion, separate from those who define poetry based on its truth or falsehood. He argues that al-Sijilmāsī is aligned with earlier theorists (Qudāma ibn Jaʿfar and Ibn Sinān al-Khafājī) who set a limit to what is permissible in hyperbole and exclude the fantastic (see al-Ghāzī, "Taṭawwur muṣṭalaḥ 'al-takhyīl,'" 296–8). I disagree with this interpretation. The proponents of poetry as fantastic speech are those who judge poetry based on its truth and falsehood. In fact, what he cites in Ibn Sīnā is his rejection of exactly this truth-scale-based view of poetry (see following note). Al-Sijilmāsī does not put limits on the degree of fiction and fantasy permissible in hyperbole. On the contrary, his whole point is that poetry is judged by its ability to excite, whether it is invented and fantastic or not.

[247] al-Sijilmāsī, *al-Manzaʿ*, 274–5. Ibn Sīnā states that the view of ordering the various types of syllogism based on a truth–falsehood scale, in which poetic speech is viewed as being made up of unrealizable or fantastic premises (*muqaddimāt mumtanaʿa*), is wrong (Ibn Sīnā, *al-Qiyās*, 4).

[248] al-Sijilmāsī, *al-Manzaʿ*, 275.

allow for the aesthetic experience of wonder to take place. The opinion of those who advocate for moderation, on the other hand, is born out of a fear of veering too far away from truthfulness. This concern, he states, has nothing to do with poetry as a craft in the first place.

CONCLUSION

With the evocation of wonder as the assumed goal of poetry, our Aristotelian-influenced authors have formulated theories that explain the aesthetic function of poetic language. While their individual explanations for the production of wonder may differ, they complement each other, offering collectively a theory of aesthetic experience. This experience of wonder, as we have seen, results from: (1) a process of discovering something hidden (be it the similarity between two things compared or the meaning of an indirect or obscure signifier); (2) the rarity of metaphor compared to expressing something literally, as well as the rarity of an image in its bringing together the literal and the metaphorical in a relationship of correspondence; and (3) the strangeness of poetic speech, whether produced through altering normal speech, paradox, or fantastic imagery.

Aristotle also speaks of wonder as an effect of tragic drama in his *Poetics*.[249] His analysis of the term as a literary effect largely depends, however, on the narrative nature of the Greek genres. He attributes, for example, the arousal of wonder to three different components of plot, summarized by Kirsti Minsaas as: "(1) an unexpected reversal (*peripeteia*) in the flow of events, (2) a character's recognition (*anagnorisis*) [of something previously unknown to him], and (3) events that occur contrary to reason (*alogon*)."[250] Such a theory of wonder would not be applicable to classical Arabic poetry, with its focus on verbal expression rather than plot.[251] As a result, the concept of wonder as a literary effect takes a very different shape in the Arab philosophers' commentaries on the *Poetics*. Nevertheless, the general principles that explain the causes of wonder,

[249] The passages in Aristotle's *Poetics* dealing with wonder include: 1452a 1–10, 1454a 2–4, 1455a 16–21, 1456a 19–25, 1459a 7–8, and 1460a 11–18.

[250] Kirsti Minsaas, "Poetic Marvels: Aristotelian Wonder in Renaissance Poetics and Poetry," in *Making Sense of Aristotle: Essays in Poetics*, ed. Øivind Andersen and Jon Haarberg (London: Duckworth & Co., 2001), 147–52.

[251] In fact, the Arab philosophers' development of the concept of wonder does not take place in their discussion of these plot-based elements. Their treatment of these plot elements has yet to be fully analyzed in the Arabic context.

whether resulting from plot-based elements or simile and metaphor, remain the same. Though achieved through different means, wonder in both cases results from the unusual, the unobvious, and the experience of discovery.

The focus on aesthetic experience in Aristotelian Arabic poetics paves the way for the formulation of a definition of the poetic that is divorced from its truth or falsehood. While pre-Avicennan attempts in late antiquity to explain the *Poetics* and *Rhetoric* as parts of the logical sciences were based on a truth-scale, the concept of *takhyīl* shifts the focus to the emotional impact a poetic statement has, regardless of its truth status. This understanding is then adopted by al-Qarṭājannī and al-Sijilmāsī, who justify the fantastic in poetry by citing its wonder-evoking character and not its fictiveness. This outlook, as we have seen, is not unique to Aristotelian Arabic poetics and provides an alternative to the binary thinking of the old school of criticism. Is it then the philosophers who shape the new school of criticism represented by ʿAbd al-Qāhir al-Jurjānī?

The question of the influence of Aristotelian Arabic philosophy on al-Jurjānī has been debated.[252] The concept of *takhyīl* in philosophy matures with Ibn Sīnā slightly prior to al-Jurjānī's work in the early fifth/eleventh century. While there are clear parallels between the two, one must keep in mind some important matters when claiming such influence. First, the theory of *takhyīl* that al-Fārābī introduces and Ibn Sīnā develops has little to do with Aristotle.[253] Even though it is a response to a certain understanding of his work, *takhyīl* as a way of distinguishing poetic speech is something specific to Arabic philosophy, not Aristotle, developed in order to make sense of the *Poetics* in the context of the *Organon*. We must keep in mind, therefore, if we want to talk about influence on al-Jurjānī, that it is Avicennan,[254] not

[252] See Taha Hussein, "al-Bayān al-ʿArabī min al-Jāḥiẓ ilā ʿAbd al-Qāhir," in *Naqd al-nathr*, ed. Taha Hussein and A. H. al-ʿAbbādī (Cairo: al-Maṭbaʿa al-Amīriyya, 1941); Larkin, *Theology of Meaning*, 144ff; Abu Deeb, *Poetic Imagery*, 303–22; Abu Deeb, "al-Jurjānī's Classification of *Istiʿāra*"; and Key, *Language between God and the Poets*, chs. 6 and 7.

[253] Anne Sheppard in the preface of *Takhyīl* (ed. van Gelder and Hammond) speculates on the possible Greek origins of *takhyīl*. Her focus is on the Aristotelian concept of *phantasia* as visualization, however, which does not correspond with the make-believe aspect of *takhyīl* and its emotional impact on the listener.

[254] As discussed earlier in the chapter, while al-Fārābī begins to formulate some basic ideas of *takhyīl*, it is Ibn Sīnā who greatly develops the concept and categorically divorces it from truth and falsehood. While this might be an assessment biased by the dearth of material on poetics that has survived from al-Fārābī, al-Sijilmāsī, as we have seen, also credits Ibn Sīnā with delinking the poetic from falsehood.

Aristotelian per se.[255] Second, it is hard to imagine that Ibn Sīnā developed his view of poetic speech in isolation, detached from the literary norms that surrounded him. While he makes use of it to solve the philosophical question of classifying poetry as part of the logical sciences, the assumption that poetic speech is supposed to move the listener into wonder through make-believe imagery is something that is more likely coming out of the cultural sensibility of the time. Rather than their ideas originating from a single exceptional source, I believe that al-Jurjānī and Ibn Sīnā are drawing from a common cultural well. As we will see in Chapter 3, other disciplinary paths led to similar conclusions about what makes speech – including simile and metaphor – poetic.

[255] This distinction is why I believe Abu Deeb and Taha Hussein arrive at divergent conclusions about the influence of philosophy on al-Jurjānī. The former means Aristotelian philosophy and the latter has Avicennan in mind. In this case, their opinions do not clash at all.

3

Discovery in *Bayān*

إنّ مِن البَيانِ لَسِحْرا

Some of eloquence (*bayān*) is indeed magic

~ *Prophet Muhammad*

One of the earliest statements in Arabic about the effect of eloquent speech on the listener comes in the above-quoted tradition in which the Prophet Muhammad associates eloquence (*bayān*) with magic.[1] Opinions differed about the interpretation of this oft-cited pronouncement of the Prophet. Some viewed it as a condemnation of the power of speech to distort truth.[2] Most saw it as a positive acknowledgment of the ability of poetic speech to enchant and move the listener.[3] What concerns us here, however, is not so much the debates about whether it was a negative or positive judgment of eloquence as the association between *bayān* and magic in the first place.

Bayān is one of the main words used in Arabic to refer to eloquence or beautiful speech, along with *balāgha* and *faṣāḥa*.[4] As the infinitive noun of

[1] Transmitted in al-Bukhārī, *Ṣaḥīḥ al-Bukhārī* (Damascus, Beirut: Dār Ibn Kathīr, 2002), *Kitāb al-ṭibb* 51, *Bāb inna min al-bayān siḥran* (no. 5767); and *Kitāb al-nikāḥ* 47, *Bāb al-khuṭba* (no. 5146).

[2] Ibn Ḥajar al-ʿAsqalānī (d. 852/1449) cites both positive and negative interpretations of the tradition in *Fatḥ al-bārī bi-sharḥ Ṣaḥīḥ al-Bukhārī*, ed. ʿAbd al-ʿAzīz ibn ʿAbd Allāh ibn Bāz, Muḥammad Fuʾād ʿAbd al-Bāqī, and Muḥibb al-Dīn al-Khaṭīb, 13 vols. (Cairo: al-Maktaba al-Salafiyya, 1979), 10:237, *Kitāb al-ṭibb* 51, *Bāb inna min al-bayān siḥran* (no. 5767).

[3] See, for example, Ibn Rashīq's discussion of the *ḥadīth* in *al-ʿUmda*, 1:27 and 248–9.

[4] Each of these terms develops to have slightly different connotations, as we will discover throughout the rest of this book. See Epilogue for the culminating account.

bāna (to be distinct and clear), *bayān* has the meaning of "perspicuity, clearness, distinctness [. . .] in speech or language."[5] As a substantive from *bayyana* (to make apparent), it also denotes "the *means* by which one makes a thing [distinct,] apparent, manifest [. . .]."[6] More specifically, it is "that through which a thing is made apparent, such as signification (*dalāla*) and other [means]."[7] *Bayān*, therefore, possesses both the sense of clarity and the *process* of clarification.[8] It is the latter meaning, i.e., the *process* of clarifying or conveying meaning, that is important for *bayān* as eloquence, not clarity in and of itself.

However, *bayān* as eloquence does not involve any kind of clarifying or conveying of meaning. Rather, it involves the conveying of meaning in a way that moves the soul. According to al-Khaṭṭābī (d. 386/996 or 388/998), as quoted in Ibn Ḥajar's *ḥadīth* commentary, there are two types of *bayān*:

> One entails conveying what is intended in whichever way. The other encompasses craft (*ṣanʿa*) in such a way that it pleases the listeners and attracts their hearts. This is what is likened to magic, as it captures the heart and overcomes the soul so that it transforms the reality of something and distracts one from it such that it appears to the onlooker as something else.[9]

Bayān in the sense of eloquence, therefore, is the kind of speech that conveys meaning in a way that enchants the listener. What is it about the way in which a meaning is revealed that makes it magical? *Bayān* is magical because it entails the conveying of meaning in such a way that allows the listener to go through an experience of discovery. Ironically, for this to happen, meaning has to be conveyed in indirect and inexplicit ways, as we will see.

Early discussions of *bayān* encompassed all sorts of matters that have the capacity to "make something apparent" or to "signify," including nonverbal ones. For al-Jāḥiẓ (d. 255/868–9), for example, in his foundational work on eloquence, *al-Bayān wa-l-tabyīn* (*Elucidation and Exposition*), speech is just one of five ways through which meaning can be revealed. Writing is another linguistic form of conveying meaning. Meaning can also be conveyed through nonverbal signs, such as physical

5 Lane, *Lexicon*, 1:288 (s.v. *b-y-n*). 6 Ibid. (emphasis added).
7 Ibn Manẓūr, *Lisān*, s.v. *b-y-n*.
8 For an overview of the word *bayān*, see Noy, "The Emergence of *ʿIlm al-Bayān*," 95–135.
9 Ibn Ḥajar al-ʿAsqalānī, *Fatḥ al-bārī*, 10:237, *Kitāb al-ṭibb* 51, *Bāb inna min al-bayān siḥran* (no. 5767).

gestures (*ishāra*) and calculation (*ʿuqad* or *ḥisāb*). Ultimately, everything in the world is a sign pregnant with meaning (*niṣba*), for al-Jāḥiẓ.[10]

Over the centuries, the scope of *bayān* became increasingly specific and discussions of it eventually narrowed down to speech alone. By the seventh/thirteenth century, the study of linguistic expressions became formalized as a "science of *bayān*" that incorporated a specific set of literary devices: simile (*tashbīh*), figurative speech (*majāz*), which includes metaphor (*istiʿāra*), and metonymy (*kināya*).[11] These figures all presented modes of conveying meaning in a way that could have a magical effect on the soul. In this chapter, I will focus on the first of these figures, simile. Approaching simile from the perspective of *bayān*, i.e., its power to reveal or elucidate, allowed our medieval authors to articulate an aesthetic of discovery, to which they attributed the "magical" quality of poetic speech. This, in turn, formed the basis of the aesthetics of metaphor and metonymy, which I will discuss in Chapter 4.

Simile is beautiful because it allows for an experience of discovery to take place in the listener. This is because it has the capacity to reveal something otherwise hidden or to shed light on what is less known through likening it to what is more or better known. The more effort is required to

[10] al-Jāḥiẓ, *al-Bayān wa-l-tabyīn*, 76; and al-Jāḥiẓ, *al-Ḥayawān*, 1:33–5. For an overview of al-Jāḥiẓ's understanding of *bayān*, see Badawī Ṭabāna, *al-Bayān al-ʿArabī: Dirāsa fī taṭawwur al-fikra al-balāghiyya ʿind al-ʿArab wa-manāhijihā wa-maṣādirihā al-kubrā* (Cairo: Maktabat al-Anjlū al-Miṣriyya, 1958), 54–62. See also Yasir Suleiman, "*Bayān* as a Principle of Taxonomy. Linguistic Elements in Jāḥiẓ's Thinking," in *Studies on Arabia in Honour of Professor G. Rex Smith*, ed. J. F. Healey and V. Porter (Oxford: Oxford University Press, 2002) 273–95; and von Grunebaum, *Bayān*. Several scholars have discussed the term "*niṣba*." See Carlo A. Nallino, "Del Vocabolo Arabo '*Niṣbah*' (con '*ṣād*')," *Rivista degli Studi Orientali* 8, no. 1/4 (1919/1920); Jeannie Miller, "*Bayan*, Gesture, and Genre: Self-Positioning in al-Jurjānī's Introductions," in "ʿAbd al-Qāhir al-Jurjānī," ed. Alexander Key, special issue, *Journal of Abbasid Studies* 5 (2018): 83. James Montgomery translates it as "locatedness" in *Al-Jāḥiẓ: In Praise of Books*. Elsewhere, translating it as "location," he sees in it a translation of the seventh of the ten Aristotelian categories (*waḍʿ* in Ibn Sīnā, *mawḍūʿ* in Isḥāq ibn Ḥunayn). See his article "Al-Jāḥiẓ's *Kitāb al-Bayān wa-l-Tabyīn*," in *Writing and Representation in Medieval Islam*, ed. Julia Bray (London; New York: Routledge, 2006), 128–9. It is briefly discussed by Josef van Ess, who connects it with the Muʿtazilite concept of *naṣb al-adilla*, and by Ramzi Baalbaki, who translates it as "posture," in Arnim Heinemann et al., eds., *Al-Jāḥiẓ: A Muslim Humanist for Our Time* (Würzburg: Ergon Verlag, 2009), 12 and 108, respectively. See also Lale Behzadi, *Sprache und Verstehen: al-Ǧāḥiẓ über die Vollkommenheit des Ausdrucks* (Wiesbaden: Harrassowitz, 2009), 63, 76–7. Thomas Bauer translates *niṣba* as "milestone" (*Rhetorik, außereuropäische*, 130). In all these cases, it is an object that serves as a sign.

[11] The exact definitions of these literary figures in medieval Arabic criticism do not always correspond perfectly with the modern Western definitions of simile, metaphor, metonymy, and figurative speech. See this chapter and Chapter 4 for their definitions in the Arabic context.

discover the similarity presented, the more rewarding the result. Strangeness and rarity, consequently, become commendable aspects of simile precisely because of their capacity to delay discovery, enhancing the pleasure of the listener once the meaning is grasped.

SIMILE AS *BAYĀN*

Before *bayān* became a formalized science in the seventh/thirteenth century, *bayān* in speech encompassed a variety of aspects of language and was not limited to simile, figurative speech, and metonymy. Nevertheless, these literary figures did feature prominently in early works as modes of expression. Al-Jāḥiẓ, for example, discusses metaphor and metonymy, among the elements that contribute to *bayān* in speech.[12] Isḥāq ibn Wahb (d. after 335/946–7), in his *Kitāb al-burhān fī wujūh al-bayān* (*The Book of the Demonstration of the Aspects of Bayān*), also includes simile (*tashbīh*) and metaphor (*istiʿāra*) in the list of ways in which meaning is conveyed through speech.[13] At the same time, simile and metaphor are being defined by other fourth-/tenth-century authors in terms of their ability to elucidate or convey meaning, in other words, in a "*bayānī*" way. Abū Hilāl al-ʿAskarī (d. after 395/1005), for example, who sees himself as building on al-Jāḥiẓ's book on *bayān* in his *Kitāb al-ṣināʿatayn* (*The Book of the Two Arts*),[14] discusses simile in terms of its ability to elucidate. He divides it into types based on how it moves the listener from a less knowledgeable state to a more knowledgeable one.[15] A comparison that does the opposite, "making the apparent hidden and the visible concealed," is a bad one.[16] Al-Rummānī (d. 384/994), although he lists "good *bayān*" as a topic separate from simile in his treatise on the inimitability of the Quran, defines a good simile as one that "moves from obscurity to clarity" and states that "eloquence in simile lies in the fact that it combines two things through a meaning that unites them and grants clarity (*bayān*) to both of them."[17] His definition of metaphor is also based on its elucidating

[12] See Ṭabāna, *al-Bayān al-ʿArabī*, 59–60, for a list of the various rhetorical figures discussed by al-Jāḥiẓ.

[13] Other elements include techniques such as omission (*ḥadhf*) and pre- and post-positioning (*taqdīm wa-taʾkhīr*), which later become part of the "science of meanings" (*ʿilm al-maʿānī*), in addition to suggestion (*ramz*), enigma (*lughz*), and parables (*amthāl*), among others (Ibn Wahb, *al-Burhān*, 122ff).

[14] See al-ʿAskarī, *Kitāb al-ṣināʿatayn*, 5. [15] Ibid., 230–2. [16] Ibid., 257.

[17] al-Rummānī, *al-Nukat fī iʿjāz al-Qurʾān*, in *Thalāth rasāʾil fī iʿjāz al-Qurʾān*, ed. Muḥammad Khalafallāh and Muḥammad Zaghlūl Sallām (Cairo: Dār al-Maʿārif, 1976), 81. Von Grunebaum suggests that al-Rummānī's classification of the elements of rhetoric

properties: "[It is] the attribution of a phrase to what it is not conventionally meant for by way of transfer for the sake of elucidation (*ibāna*)."[18] As a result, while simile and metaphor in the third/ninth and fourth/tenth centuries were usually discussed as literary (*badīʿ*) figures,[19] they start being given particular attention as means of elucidation. In other words, rather than treating simile and metaphor as mere ornaments to speech, they begin to be conceived of as fundamental components of the expression of meaning.

In the fifth/eleventh century, ʿAbd al-Qāhir al-Jurjānī dedicates much of his *Asrār al-balāgha* (*The Secrets of Eloquence*) to the study of simile and metaphor. While *bayān* at this point had not yet been established as a defined field of study, al-Jurjānī's approach is "*bayānī*" in that he is concerned with how different forms of speech convey meaning differently and what makes one way more eloquent than another. He is firmly of the belief that eloquence has nothing to do with the utterances themselves as sound units, rather with their capacity to convey meaning.[20] He asks at the outset of his *Asrār*: "how is one to judge variations in speech if he wants to distinguish between them in terms of their beauty?"[21] The main topics on which al-Jurjānī focuses in response to this question are simile (*tashbīh*), analogy (*tamthīl*), which he considers a type of simile, metaphor (*istiʿāra*), which is a kind of figurative speech (*majāz*), and metonymy (*kināya*).[22] Although al-Jurjānī does not define this focus as *bayān*, he establishes the foundation on which later authors develop a more defined science.

The study of these figures subsequently becomes the focus of the "science of *bayān*," one of the three branches of the "science of eloquence," as established by al-Sakkākī in the seventh/thirteenth century. As we will see in more detail in Chapter 4, the science of *bayān* investigates

and his listing of *ḥusn al-bayān* as a separate category indicates a "completely different strain of thought," compared to those of al-Jāḥiẓ and Iṣḥāq ibn Wahb (von Grunebaum, *Bayān*). While the taxonomy might be different, his definition of figures like simile and metaphor as "elucidating" is in agreement with the other approaches to *bayān*.

18 al-Rummānī, *al-Nukat*, 85.

19 Ibn al-Muʿtazz (d. 296/908), in his foundational book on *badīʿ*, for example, includes *istiʿāra* as one of its core figures and *tashbīh* as one of the "beautifying" figures of language.

20 See my article on the relationship between utterance and meaning in al-Jurjānī's work, "Form, Content, and Inimitability." For an analysis of al-Jurjānī's view of meaning and its theological implications, see Larkin, *Theology of Meaning*.

21 al-Jurjānī, *Asrār*, 3.

22 al-Jurjānī discusses *tashbīh*, *tamthīl*, and *istiʿāra* in both *Asrār al-balāgha* and his other important work, *Dalāʾil al-iʿjāz*, although they are much more the focus in the former. *Kināya* is discussed only in the *Dalāʾil*.

the poeticity of the ways in which words refer to their intended meaning. Simile is incorporated in this "science of elucidation," mainly for its being the foundation of metaphor.[23] Nevertheless, despite its relegation to being in the service of metaphor, simile remains a central figure and is considered one of the "pillars" of *bayān*. In fact, al-Sakkākī declares: "he who perfects [simile] holds the reins of practicing the art of elucidating magic (*al-siḥr al-bayānī*)."[24]

The inclusion of simile in *bayān*, on the one hand, distinguishes it from other literary figures as a mode of conveying meaning, instead of being relegated to mere "ornamentation" under a separate science (*ʿilm al-badīʿ*). On the other hand, approaching simile from the perspective of *bayān* allowed our authors to articulate its aesthetic mechanism and, through it, the aesthetic mechanism of other *bayān* figures. The way in which simile "reveals meaning" allows the listener to experience aesthetic pleasure. This experience is the result of simile's inherent structure that permits the listener to go through a process of discovery as well as its ability to make something appear novel or strange. Their analyses of the beauty of simile constitute some of the most elaborate articulations of the literary mechanisms of wonder-evocation.

AL-JURJĀNĪ AND THE WONDERS OF DISCOVERY

Al-Jurjānī's approach to eloquence is "*bayānī*" in the sense that poetic beauty for him lies in the way speech conveys meaning and elucidates it. He considers the pillars on which the beauty of language is built to be simile (*tashbīh*), analogy (*tamthīl*), and metaphor (*istiʿāra*).[25] Among those, simile is the basic building block of the other two "pillars": Analogy is defined as a kind of simile[26] and metaphor is built on simile.[27] Given the centrality of simile, al-Jurjānī provides his most

[23] Both al-Sakkākī and al-Khaṭīb al-Qazwīnī emphasize the importance of *tashbīh* as the basis on which *istiʿāra* is built (al-Sakkākī, *al-Miftāḥ*, 439; al-Khaṭīb al-Qazwīnī, *al-Īḍāḥ*, 327). However, they do not consider it a *bayān* figure in and of itself (see my discussion of "Simile as Indirect Signification?" in Chapter 4).

[24] al-Sakkākī, *al-Miftāḥ*, 439. [25] al-Jurjānī, *Asrār*, 26.

[26] Al-Jurjānī defines analogy as a kind of simile in which the similarity requires interpretation (see ibid., 80–8).

[27] al-Jurjānī, *Asrār*, 28. The definition of *istiʿāra* as based on a relationship of similarity was already established in philosophy, as we have seen in Chapter 2. Earlier definitions of *istiʿāra* in literary criticism, however, were based on the idea of "borrowing" something for something else, as Heinrichs has shown, not a relationship of similarity. Al-Jurjānī

detailed analysis of the impact of poetic speech on the listener in his discussion of simile. This impact is attributed primarily to two factors, discovery and strangeness, which are nonetheless intertwined.

Discovery

Before presenting his theory of aesthetic experience in simile, al-Jurjānī presents two general principles about human nature that provide the foundation for his theory. First, he makes an observation about the source of pleasure:

> The pleasure of the soul is based on being lifted from the hidden to the visible, being presented with the plain after the enigmatic, being moved from the known to the better and more intimately known.[28]

I will call this principle "discovery." Although al-Jurjānī does not explicitly use this term, it succinctly describes the experience the listener goes through when "being lifted from the hidden to the visible." Discovery is the listener's aesthetic experience of *bayān*.

The second principle al-Jurjānī lays out involves human susceptibility to different ways of gaining knowledge:

> It is known that initial knowledge comes to the soul first and foremost through the senses and then through contemplation and intellect. [. . .] If you moved it through a comparison from something perceived through pure intellect or thought to that which is perceived through the senses and known intuitively [. . .] you would be like him who appeals for it to a stranger through a close friend, and for a new friendship through an old love.[29]

Information received through the senses or intuitively, therefore, is more easily perceived than that derived through contemplation and reasoning. This principle is relevant for achieving an experience of discovery through simile, as we will see.

Al-Jurjānī goes on to explain that there are two types of comparison: (i) one in which the original meaning is obscure or improbable, and (ii) another in which the original meaning is not obscure and is possible. In the first type, the simile serves to clarify and show the possibility

introduces the simile-based definition to literary criticism, which is then adopted by his successors (see Heinrichs, *Hand of the North Wind*).

[28] al-Jurjānī, *Asrār*, 108. [29] Ibid., 109.

of the existence of an improbable meaning. The second type of comparison serves to reveal something additional about the original meaning, even if it is known and possible, such as affirming it or showing its degree.[30]

To illustrate the first, al-Jurjānī cites a verse by al-Mutanabbī (d. 354/965), in which he describes the superiority of the eulogized addressee over mankind:

فَإِنْ تَفُقِ الأنامَ وأنت مِنهُم   فَإِنَّ المِسْكَ بَعْضُ دَمِ الغَزَالِ

You exceed mankind even though you are one of them
for indeed musk is of gazelle's blood[31]

Al-Jurjānī explains that the idea in the first hemistich is strange and improbable: How can one belong to a species but then exceed it such that he ceases to belong to it? The comparison with musk clarifies this strange suggestion and allows one to see how it can be possible, since, in a similar fashion, something as good as musk is indeed extracted from something as unattractive as gazelle's blood. The analogy, therefore, allows the listener to discover how this improbable proposition of being human yet exceeding humanity is possible.

However, al-Jurjānī points out that we are also moved when an analogy illustrates a meaning that is known to be true (i.e., a meaning that does not require clarification or justification), through something more known, more visible, and easier to perceive.[32] This is also pleasing because, as we have seen in the second principle presented above, the same information can be known to varying degrees of intimacy. Thus, comparing something we know intellectually to something we know through the senses or intuitively also allows for an experience of discovery to take place, since our degree of knowledge of the thing increases.

To illustrate this type of simile, al-Jurjānī discusses the following verse, in which the poet expresses his disappointment at not being able to attain his beloved Laylā:[33]

فَأَصْبَحْتُ مِن لَيْلَى الغَدَاةَ كَقَابِضٍ   عَلَى المَاءِ خَانَتْهُ فُرُوجُ الأَصَابِعِ

[30] Ibid., 111. [31] Ibid., 109. [32] Ibid., 112.

[33] Ibid., 110. The poet is most likely Qays ibn al-Mulawwaḥ al-ʿAmirī (fl. mid-first/seventh century), also known as Majnūn Laylā (Laylā's madman), although the verse seems to be an amalgamation of two hemistichs of two different verses (see ibid., 110n100).

By the morning, I became [in relation] to Laylā as one whose fist
is betrayed by the gaps between his fingers as he tries to grasp water

The idea expressed in this verse (i.e., the impossibility of attaining the beloved) is not unusual or hard to imagine. The comparison, therefore, does not clarify something obscure or improbable. It does, however, make the idea more apparent. Al-Jurjānī argues that through illustrating the idea *visually*, the analogy brings the meaning closer to the heart and makes it more moving to the soul. Seeing (*mushāhada*) is what moves the soul in this case and reinforces the meaning in the heart. The discovery that takes place therefore entails the gaining of a new awareness of an otherwise mundane matter.

To further illustrate the effect such a presentation has on the soul, al-Jurjānī asks us to imagine someone putting his hand in water and physically enacting the idea of "seeking the unattainable." This, he says, "has an impact additional to that of just saying and uttering the words without doing."[34] Analogy in poetry functions in a similar way. It illustrates an abstract idea by comparing it to a visible and tangible image. As a result, even though it might not serve to reveal a hidden meaning, the listener still goes through an experience of discovery because it presents the idea using types of knowledge to which the soul is more receptive. In this case, "analogy (*tamthīl*) through seeing (*mushāhada*) adds to one's pleasure even if it does not serve to correct a meaning."[35] Fittingly, the word *tamthīl* means both actual enactment and poetic analogy in Arabic. *Tamthīl* in the sense of enacting or performing an idea physically has an added emotional impact on the soul as result of visibly showing the matter at hand. Likewise, *tamthīl* in the sense of "poetic analogy" makes one "see" a meaning by "enacting" it and making it visible through imagery in a way that deepens one's knowledge of it.

In both types of comparison, some degree of elucidation takes place, whether from obscurity to knowledge or from less knowledge to more. In the first case, the original meaning being described has to be "strange and novel, such that it can be disagreed with or its existence can be claimed as impossible or unthinkable."[36] In the second case, the original idea is known, but can nevertheless be better known through comparing it to something closer to the senses. In both cases, the listener goes through a process of discovery, which explains the source of pleasure in simile.

[34] Ibid., 113. [35] Ibid. [36] Ibid., 109.

Effort

Later in the *Asrār*, al-Jurjānī presents us with a third observation about human nature. He argues that the more effort is required by the listener to discover the meaning, the more pleasurable it is:

> It is human nature that if something is gained after searching, effort, and yearning, its attainment is more beautiful and pleasurable.[37]

He compares this to the effort required to break a shell in order to reach its pearl.[38] The longer it takes and the more effort is required, the more enjoyable the reward.

This does not mean, however, that complication (*taʿqīd*) and obscuration (*taʿmiya*) are desirable qualities in poetry.[39] Al-Jurjānī reminds us that effort, which does not yield a commensurate return, is bad. Complication that tires and frustrates without any gain is most deserving of censure.[40] He thus distinguishes between two kinds of complexity: what he calls "*muʿaqqad*" (convoluted), which is speech that puts obstacles in the way of one's understanding, and, conversely, "*mulakhkhaṣ*" (condensed), which is a kind of complexity that nevertheless helps light the way to the meaning.[41] What is worthy of scorn in the former, he explains, is not that it requires you to think and contemplate, but that it hinders your thinking and obstructs your search for meaning without bearing any fruit. Beauty in speech is, therefore, the result of what induces thought and contemplation, but without unnecessary complication. Thus, conveying an idea in a way that requires effort to grasp it enhances the experience of discovery and the pleasure resulting from it.

The Distance Formula

One of the best ways to stimulate contemplation and thought in simile and thus increase the effort to discover its meaning is revealing a similarity between matters that are different: "[Comparing] things that share the same genus or are of the same type does not require the kind of work and contemplation to discover the similarity [that comparing different genera requires]."[42] In fact, the further apart the two items compared, the more striking the image: "if you inspect similes, you will find that the greater the distance between the two things [compared], the more wonder-evoking it

[37] Ibid., 126. [38] Ibid., 128. [39] Ibid., 127. [40] Ibid., 130. [41] Ibid., 135.
[42] Ibid., 136.

is to the soul."[43] To illustrate this – what we may call – "distance formula," he gives an example of a simile that likens violets drooping in front of red hyacinths to flames:[44]

وَلازَوَرْديَّةٌ تَزْهُو بِزُرْقَتِها   بَيْنَ الرِّياضِ على حُمْرِ اليَواقِيْتِ
كَأَنَّها فَوْقَ قَامَاتٍ ضَعُفْنَ بِها   أوائِلُ النَّارِ في أَطْرافِ كِبْرِيْتِ

> And violets radiate with their blueness
> in the meadows against the redness of the hyacinths
> As if, over stems, weakened, they were
> the beginnings of fire at the edges of sulfur

Al-Jurjānī explains that this comparison is "stranger (*aghrab*), more wonderful (*aʿjab*), and more deserving of admiration than comparing a narcissus to 'pearl vials filled with carnelian (*ʿaqīq*),'" a verse he discusses earlier.[45] He goes on to explain that this is because the violet simile compares fresh and moist flowers to flames of fire, alluding to the remoteness between the two parts of the comparison.[46] He adds that if the poet "had compared the violet to some other plant, or had found some similarity between it and some colorful item, one would not find this degree of strangeness and it would not be this beautiful."[47] The reason for this, as he explains, lies in human nature, giving us a fourth general observation about the source of pleasure in human beings:

> It is human nature and his instinct that when something appears from an unexpected place and emerges from an unusual source, the soul feels greater fondness and excitement for it. It is equally as evoking of wonder (*taʿajjub*) and producing of the splendor of amazement (*rawʿat al-mustaghrib*) to discover something in a place in which it does not belong, as it is to discover the existence of something that does not exist or is not known.[48]

The strangeness of the above comparison, therefore, lies in the fact that red hot flames have little to do with the tender blue flowers. The two things are not normally associated with each other and do not normally come to mind in conjunction with each other. As a result, the comparison is unexpected and novel. Whereas the comparison of the narcissus flower to "pearl vials filled with carnelian" is a more obvious simile that matches

[43] Ibid., 116.
[44] Ibid., 117. The verses are usually attributed to Ibn al-Muʿtazz, although they have also been attributed to Ibn al-Rūmī, among others (see ibid., 117n107).
[45] Ibid., 117. The carnelian verse is also attributed to Ibn al-Muʿtazz. Al-Jurjānī discusses it on p. 85.
[46] Ibid., 117. [47] Ibid., 118. [48] Ibid.

the white and orange colors of the narcissus to the colors of pearls and carnelian. It is not as unexpected as the violets example.

Similarity in Opposites

If the further apart the two things compared are, the better, then the most extreme case would be exposing a similarity in opposites. It is particularly beautiful, therefore, al-Jurjānī explains, to combine life and death, for example, as in comparing a person to life and death at once (to his friends and to his enemies respectively), or combining water and fire as in the following example:[49]

أَنا نارٌ في مُرتَقَى نَظَرِ الحَا * سِدِ ماءٌ جارٍ مع الإِخْوانِ

I am fire in the eyes of him who envies;
running water with my companions

~ Ibn Muqla (d. 328/940)[50]

Another beautiful example he cites unites presence and absence:

أَيا غائِباً حاضِراً في الفؤادِ سَلامٌ عَلى الحَاضِرِ الغائِبِ

O absent presence in my heart
greetings to the present absentee[51]

~ Unknown

Speaking of the powerful impact such comparisons have on the soul, al-Jurjānī asks rhetorically:

Do you doubt that [comparison] does the work of magic when it finds harmony in opposites, truncating the distance between east and west, uniting him who is Syria-bound and him who is Iraq-bound (*al-mush'im wa-l-mu'riq*), showing you in imagined meanings a similarity with actual people and real bodies, making the mute utter, the incomprehensible elucidating, showing you life in the inanimate, compatibility in the mutually exclusive, unifying life and death, water and fire.[52]

[49] Ibid., 119.

[50] For the attribution of the verse to Ibn Muqla, see al-Tha'ālibī, *Yatīmat al-dahr*, 3:101; Ibn Khallikān, *Wafayāt al-a'yān*, ed. Iḥsān 'Abbās (Beirut: Dār Ṣādir, 1968), 5:116; and Ibn al-Ṭiqṭaqā, *al-Fakhrī*, ed. Hartwig Derenbourg (Paris: Bouillon, 1895), 370. The citations of the verse in these sources read "*murtaqā nafas al-ḥāsid*" instead of "*murtaqā naẓar al-ḥāsid*," making the speaker "fire in the breath of the envier" instead of merely in his eyes. The variation in the *Asrār* could very well be a mistake, since the two readings could be easily confused in writing.

[51] al-Jurjānī, *Asrār*, 119. [52] Ibid., 118.

He goes on to argue that the comparison is most amazing when something is *made into* its opposite. Speaking of the life–death opposition, he says: "another fine point in this meaning, which if you look closely is more amazing and more deserving of wonder, is making death itself a recommenced life, so that one would say 'in death, he fulfilled his life,' as in the expression 'so-and-so lived when he died' [as a result of his fame and remembrance],"[53] or as in the following verses:[54]

بأَبِي وأُمِّي كُلُّ ذِي نَفْسٍ تَعافُ الضَّيْمَ مُرَّهْ
تَرْضَى بأَنْ تَرِدَ الرَّدَى فَيُميتُها ويُعيشُ ذِكْرَهْ

[I would ransom with the life of] my father and mother him whose
  resolute soul abhors injustice
and willingly welcomes death
  thus killing [his soul] and keeping alive his name
~ Ibn Nubāta al-Saʿdī (d. 405/1014)

Al-Jurjānī reminds us, however, that wonder is not merely the result of the extremeness of the difference between the two things compared. It is rather the result of finding a similarity *despite* the extreme difference.[55] It is the unexpectedness of finding "intense agreement with intense difference"[56] that is beautiful and pleasing. The similarity, therefore, has to be a real and believable one. The skill of the poet lies in finding such hidden similarities between matters that appear on the surface to be unconnected.[57]

Strangeness

Besides the distance formula, comparisons can necessitate more pondering and effort to grasp their meanings through strangeness (*gharāba*). In fact, al-Jurjānī defines strangeness by linking it to the *speed* with which an image is comprehended, giving us a fifth observation about human nature:

> The general cause of strangeness (*gharāba*) lies in the intended similarity being one that the mind does not reach quickly and which does not occur to the imagination immediately, but rather only after the soul's analysis, recollection, and scrutiny of the images it knows and the activation of imagination in order to bring forth what has been hidden from it.[58]

53 Ibid., 121.
54 Ibid., 122. See whole poem in Ibn Nubāta al-Saʿdī, *Dīwān*, ed. ʿAbd al-Amīr Mahdī Ḥabīb al-Ṭāʾī (Baghdad: Dār al-Ḥurriyya, 1977), 2:41–2.
55 al-Jurjānī, *Asrār*, 140. 56 Ibid. 57 Ibid., 138–9. 58 Ibid., 144.

Al-Jurjānī describes two factors that can make an image less familiar and hence "slow down" the process of grasping it: (1) details, and (2) rarity.[59]

(1) Details

With regard to details, he gives us a sixth general observation, explaining that:

> [It is human nature for] the totality to be more familiar to the soul than particulars. [...] The more deeply [an image] goes into details, the more one needs to stop, remember, contemplate, and slow down.[60]

To illustrate this, he compares the following two lines of poetry by two of the most celebrated pre-Islamic poets, in which they both compare the sword or spear to fire:[61]

يُتَابِعُ لا يَبْتَغِي غَيْرَهُ بِأَبْيَضَ كَالقَبَسِ المُلْتَهِبْ

He persists, seeking no one but him
with a white [sword] like a blazing flame
~ ʿAntara ibn Shaddād (pre-Islamic)

And,

جَمَعْتُ رُدَيْنِيّاً كَأَنَّ سِنَانَهُ سَنَا لَهَبٍ لم يَتَّصِلْ بِدُخَانِ

I grabbed a Rudaynī[62] [spear], whose arrowhead was like
the blaze of a flame untouched by smoke
~ Imruʾ al-Qays (d. c. 550 CE)

Al-Jurjānī explains that despite the fact that the simile in both verses revolves around a flame, the two images are not equally as praiseworthy. The difference lies in that "the second [image] aimed at a fine detail, while the first passed as a whole."[63] He goes on to clarify that the added detail of the flames being "untouched by smoke" in the second verse

[59] Abu Deeb has discussed these as "factors which contribute to the need for *taʾawwul*" (interpretation) in "al-Jurjānī's Classification of *Istiʿāra*," 63–8. His point is to show that al-Jurjānī's classification of metaphor is based on the point of similarity and not on the domains of the terms involved in the simile in order to highlight the difference between al-Jurjānī's approach and Aristotle's. In the process, he also notes the importance of remoteness and strangeness in al-Jurjānī's evaluation of metaphor and its emotional impact (ibid., 61, especially n2).

[60] al-Jurjānī, *Asrār*, 147. [61] Ibid., 149–50. [62] A "*Rudaynī*" is a well-straightened spear.

[63] al-Jurjānī, *Asrār*, 150.

forces one to stop and investigate how and why the simile is limited to the flames alone and to imagine them without smoke. This is a detail that does not come to one's imagination at first glance. The simile in the first verse, on the other hand, which adheres to the image of the flame as a whole without breaking it up into its particulars, is more easily (and quickly) imaginable. Hence, it is less "strange" and therefore less praiseworthy.

Furthermore, al-Jurjānī argues, the *more* detail an image incorporates, the better. If we were to compare two images, one incorporating detail from two aspects and the other from three, the latter would be superior. To illustrate this, he compares three verses that portray flashing swords in the dust of battle:[64]

يَزورُ الأَعادِي في سَمَاءِ عَجَاجَةٍ   أَسِنَّتُهُ في جَانِبَيْها الكَوَاكِبُ

He visits the enemy in the dust-filled sky
his spears stars in its midst
~ al-Mutanabbī (d. 354/965)

تَبْنِي سَنابِكُها مِن فَوْقِ أَرْؤُسِهِمْ   سَقْفاً كَوَاكِبُهُ البِيْضُ المَبَاتِيرُ

The hooves [of the horses] build over their heads
a ceiling [of dust]; its stars white sharp [swords]
~ ʿAmr ibn Kulthūm (pre-Islamic)

كَأَنَّ مُثارَ النَّقْعِ فَوْقَ رُؤُوسِنا   وأَسْيافَنا لَيْلٌ تَهاوى كَوَاكِبُهْ

The dust, stirred up over our heads,
and our swords [in its midst] were like a night with shooting stars
~ Bashshār ibn Burd (d. c. 167/784)

Al-Jurjānī explains:

The detail in all three verses is practically the same, since each one of them compares the shining of the swords in the dust to the stars in the night, except that you find in Bashshār's verse a considerable and undeniable degree of superiority, graciousness, and subtlety in its effect on the soul. This is because he took into consideration what the others did not in that he made the stars "shooting/falling." As such, he perfected the comparison and expressed the state of the swords [...] as they rise and drop and come and go, and did not limit [the image] to their brightness in the midst of the dust, as the others did. It is this addition that increased its precision and rendered it "details upon details."[65]

[64] Ibid., 159–60. [65] Ibid., 160.

Through specifying that the stars are "shooting stars," Bashshār is more able to capture the chaotic movement of the swords in battle, since shooting stars move in a similar chaotic way, crossing each other's paths. Moreover, al-Jurjānī explains, the added detail more accurately represents the shapes of the swords, since shooting stars look rectangular in shape as opposed to circular when they were still.[66] While all three verses contain detail, Bashshār managed to give his an additional subtlety that made it unquestionably superior to the others. This is not simply because of its detailed accuracy, but because such subtlety requires more thought and contemplation to fully grasp it.

(2) Rarity

The other factor to which al-Jurjānī attributes the "slowing down" of the grasping of an image is rarity. He explains with a seventh observation about human nature:

> What makes something immediately accessible in the memory and its image secure in the soul is that it is frequently seen [. . .] and is sensed all or most of the time. Conversely, the reason something is far from thought and the imagination is the infrequency with which it is seen and that it is sensed only occasionally and rarely.[67]

Rarity, therefore, causes one to pause, contemplate, and search in one's memory and imagination. The rarer the comparison, the stranger it is, and hence the more time and effort it takes to grasp it.

To illustrate this, al-Jurjānī compares the following two similes:[68]

(كَحْلاءُ في بَرَجٍ صَفْراءُ في نَعَجٍ) كَأَنَّهَا فِضَّةٌ قد مَسَّهَا ذَهَبُ

([She has] kohled wide eyes, a complexion white [with a hint of] yellow)
like silver with a touch of gold[69]

~ Dhū al-Rumma (d. 117/735)

And,

وَكَأَنَّ أَجْرامَ النُّجُومِ لَوامِعاً دُرَرٌ نُثِرْنَ على بِسَاطٍ أَزْرَقِ

[66] Ibid., 160–1. [67] Ibid., 151. [68] Ibid., 157.

[69] This verse is from Dhū al-Rumma's famous *bā'iyya* (poem rhyming in "b"). The first hemistich is not quoted in the *Asrār*. See full verse in Dhū al-Rumma, *Dīwān Dhī al-Rumma: Sharḥ Abī Naṣr al-Bāhilī*, ed. 'Abd al-Quddūs Abū Ṣāliḥ, 3 vols. (Beirut: Mu'assasat al-Īmān, 1982), 1:33–4.

The shining bodies of the stars were like
pearls strewn on a blue carpet

~ Abū Ṭālib al-Raqqī (d. unknown)[70]

Al-Jurjānī argues that the second verse is better than the first because the image is rarer, "for people always see works of silver decorated or painted with gold, while it might never come about that [they see] pearls strewn on a blue carpet."[71] Comparisons, therefore, differ in quality based on their commonness or rarity. The rarer the comparison, the more deserving it is of being described as "strange" and the loftier and more excellent it is.[72]

The rarest kind of comparison is one that finds a similarity with something fantastic or unattainable (*mumtaniʿ*). That is, it does not exist in reality, but is conceivable: "Something cannot be further away from sight than when its existence is improbable so that it cannot be pictured except in the imagination."[73] To illustrate this he cites the following verse by al-Ṣanawbarī (d. 334/945–6) describing anemones as:[74]

أَعْلامُ يَاقُوتٍ نُشِرْ * نَ على رِمَاحٍ مِن زَبَرْجَدْ

Banners of ruby unfurled
on lances of peridot[75]

If we were to compare this verse to the image of "pearls strewn on a blue carpet," he explains, we see that the pearls comparison is not as powerful from the aspect of rarity. This is "because if it belongs to what is known to exist, even if it is not widespread, but rare and infrequent, it does not evade entering the mind and memory to the extent that something inexistent, which is never seen and is unlikely to be imagined, is able to evade."[76]

70 Full verse quoted earlier in the *Asrār* on p. 146. Abū Ṭālib al-Raqqī is an obscure poet who likely lived around the late third/ninth, early fourth/tenth century (see ibid., 146n155).

71 al-Jurjānī, *Asrār*, 157. 72 Ibid., 151.

73 Ibid., 158. See my discussion of *imtināʿ* (unrealizability or the fantastic) and *istiḥāla* (impossibility) in Chapter 1, under "Hyperbole" in the section on the "Old School of Literary Criticism."

74 Ibid., 146 and 158. See my discussion of this verse in Chapter 1 under "Truth and Falsehood according to al-Jurjānī" in the section on "Make-Believe (*Takhyīl*)."

75 Peridot is a greenish gemstone.

76 al-Jurjānī, *Asrār*, 158. Al-Ṣanawbarī's anemone comparison is adopted by al-Jurjānī's successors as an example of an imaginary composite comparison (*murakkab khayālī*). See my discussion below.

Although rarity is something that might be more dependent on the cultural context or individual experience, al-Jurjānī presents us with some concrete characteristics that make its evaluation accessible to us centuries later. He concludes, "With this information, you can know how similes differ in their degree of strangeness, why they vary in their [ability] to bring forth what is wondrous (*ʿajīb*), and the causes of finding one statement moving and another not."[77]

***

Although al-Jurjānī does not employ the term "*bayān*" per se to describe the mechanisms of simile, his approach is "*bayānī*" in the sense that he understands simile as involving a process of revelation of meaning, which in turn produces an experience of discovery in the listener. This is an outcome inherent in its structure, which, through likening something to something else, can reveal something hidden or make something more intimately known. The more effort is required to discover the meaning, the more rewarding the result. The less obvious and the stranger the comparison, in other words, the more delightful the experience of discovering the meaning.

SIMILE AND THE SCIENCE OF *BAYĀN*

Al-Jurjānī's ideas about simile were subsequently reorganized by his successors, starting with Fakhr al-Dīn al-Rāzī, and followed by al-Sakkākī and al-Khaṭīb al-Qazwīnī. The last two establish *bayān* as a science. Many of the ideas they present about simile in the science of *bayān* were already expressed by al-Jurjānī. Many of the examples they employ are identical to his. Their selections, however, highlight what they found relevant in his works. The way they organize and distill his ideas helps clarify al-Jurjānī's complex theories.

Al-Sakkākī organizes al-Jurjānī's ideas about simile, clearly basing them on a concept of *bayān* as elucidation: how a simile moves one from obscurity to clarity or from what is less known to what is more intimately known. Al-Khaṭīb al-Qazwīnī, furthermore, clearly associates the pleasure that arises from simile as resulting from the experience of discovery that this process of *bayān* produces in the listener. Moreover, both al-Sakkākī and al-Khaṭīb al-Qazwīnī consider strangeness an enhancement to eloquence and systematically identify the different categories of estranging factors in more specific and defined ways than al-Jurjānī.

[77] Ibid., 159.

Their "obsession with taxonomy," as some scholars derogatively describe it, results in a clear identification and classification of the causes of strangeness in poetic speech. Furthermore, their statements about these estranging factors affirm their purpose as slowing down and increasing the effort to discovery. Thus, taxonomy serves an underlying aesthetic theory that is founded on wonder.

The Purpose of Simile: Discovery and Novelty

Everyone agrees that simile enhances eloquence, al-Khaṭīb al-Qazwīnī declares, and that it is a way of conveying meaning that is more beautiful than simply stating the intended meaning as is.[78] He goes on to explain that "following up an idea with a [simile] increases its power to move the soul towards its intention, whether it be praise, satire, self-pride, or otherwise."[79] To illustrate this, he asks the reader to consider the following two verses:[80]

وَطُولُ مُقَامِ الْمَرْءِ فِي الْحَيِّ مُخْلِقٌ　　لِدِيبَاجَتَيْهِ فَاغْتَرِبْ تَتَجَدَّدِ
فَإِنِّي رَأَيْتُ الشَّمْسَ زِيدَتْ مَحَبَّةً　　إِلَى النَّاسِ إِذْ لَيْسَتْ عَلَيْهِمْ بِسَرْمَدِ

Staying long in a place wears out
　one's appearance. So be a stranger, and you'll renew
For I have noticed that the sun enjoys greater adoration
　from people since it is not continuously in their presence
~ Abū Tammām (d. c. 232/845)

Al-Khaṭīb al-Qazwīnī asks us to compare our state upon reading the first verse (before going on to the second) to our state after completing and understanding the second verse. He writes: "you know how different the two states are in [terms of] securing the meaning in you,"[81] indicating how likening popularity to the adoration people have for the sun cements the poet's argument that it is due to not being continuously present.

Another example he discusses is a saying attributed to the Prophet Muhammad. Al-Khaṭīb al-Qazwīnī says:

> Witness the difference between saying "the world is not lasting" and stopping [there], and following it up with what has been attributed to the Prophet as having said: "whoever is in this world is a guest and what is in his hand is a loan. A guest [must] leave, and a loan [must] be returned."[82]

[78] al-Khaṭīb al-Qazwīnī, *al-Īḍāḥ*, 328–9. [79] Ibid. [80] Ibid., 330. [81] Ibid. [82] Ibid.

In each of these examples, he goes on to exclaim, the meaning is nobler and more excellent in the second case, after incorporating a simile, than the first. This difference, according to al-Khaṭīb al-Qazwīnī, is due either to: (1) "the pleasure the soul experiences as a result of [a] being lifted from the hidden to the visible, [. . .] [b] being moved from what it finds unfamiliar to what it finds familiar, [. . .] or [c] from what it knows to what it knows better"; or (2) the ability of simile to make something appear strange or novel (*istiṭrāf*).[83] In other words, the pleasure one experiences from simile is either the result of a process of discovery or of strangeness. These depend on the author's intention in his employment of simile.

The success of a simile, in turn, depends on its specific intent.[84] The goals of simile as they define them entail revealing something about the matter being compared in a way that:[85]

(1) shows that it is possible;
(2) shows its state;
(3) shows its degree;
(4) affirms and emphasizes it;
(5) presents it in a more beautiful light in order to make it more desirable or disfigures it in order to make it reprehensible; and
(6) makes it seem new and striking (*istiṭrāf*).

The first five goals involve a process of discovery, while the last seeks to evoke a sense of novelty and strangeness.

The nature of the thing to which something is compared (the *secundum comparatum*) in each process differs. If the goal is to elucidate some aspect of the original subject being described, including beautifying or uglifying it (goals 1–5), then the matter to which our subject is likened should be more familiar and more securely known.[86] In other words, the *secundum comparatum* has to have a greater degree of familiarity and must be more securely known in relation to the thing compared (*primum comparandum*). This allows for a process of elucidation to take place, such as moving the mind "from what occurs to it through thought to what it knows through instinct," and "from what is [perceived] through the intellect to

[83] Ibid., 331–2. [84] al-Sakkākī, *al-Miftāḥ*, 462–3; al-Khaṭīb al-Qazwīnī, *al-Īḍāḥ*, 389.

[85] I paraphrase. al-Sakkākī, *al-Miftāḥ*, 448–9; al-Khaṭīb al-Qazwīnī, *al-Īḍāḥ*, 356–9.

[86] al-Sakkākī, *al-Miftāḥ*, 462–3. See al-Taftāzānī's criticism of al-Sakkākī's discussion of the necessary characteristics of the *secundum comparatum* (*al-mushabbah bihi*) in *al-Muṭawwal*, 544–5. Compare to al-Sayyid al-Sharīf's resolution of the disagreement in his glosses on al-Taftāzānī's *al-Muṭawwal* (*al-Ḥāshiya*, 345–6).

what is perceptible through the senses."[87] The *primum comparandum*, in turn, has to be less known and less familiar in some way (goals 2–5), or improbable, in the case of goal 1 (to show that it is possible). If the purpose of simile, on the other hand, is to make something seem strange or novel (*istiṭrāf*) (goal 6), then the comparison itself or the *secundum comparatum* should be strange.[88]

When discussing the first goal of simile (showing that the *primum comparandum* is possible), al-Khaṭīb al-Qazwīnī adds "this happens with any strange matter, on which opinions can differ or whose existence can be challenged."[89] Citing the same musk comparison by al-Mutanabbī that al-Jurjānī cites,[90] al-Khaṭīb al-Qazwīnī explains that the idea of the eulogized person exceeding mankind to the degree that he ceases to be part of it is "a strange matter, such that he who claims it fails to prove the possibility of its existence."[91] Comparing the proposition to musk, which is in actuality something beautiful that surpasses its origin and ceases to belong to it, "reveals that [the poet's] claim has a basis in reality in general."[92]

Similarly, when discussing the ability of simile to show the state of something (goal 2), al-Khaṭīb al-Qazwīnī quotes from the Quranic verse:

وَإِذْ نَتَقْنَا الْجَبَلَ فَوْقَهُمْ كَأَنَّهُ ظُلَّةٌ

And when we raised the mountain over them as if it were a dark cloud
~ Q7:171

He explains that in this comparison "that which is out of the ordinary is revealed through something more ordinary."[93] In other words, the state of mountains raised above people, which is difficult to imagine, is made more imaginable by being likened to the ordinary sight of clouds.

Simile can also serve to show the degree of something in terms of its strength, weakness, abundance, or lack (goal 3). In this case, the *primum comparandum* is not strange or improbable, rather something known, which is then compared to a matter that is more known for a certain aspect in order to highlight its intensity or abundance. To illustrate this point, al-Khaṭīb al-

[87] al-Khaṭīb al-Qazwīnī, *al-Īḍāḥ*, 331.
[88] al-Sakkākī, *al-Miftāḥ*, 462–3; al-Khaṭīb al-Qazwīnī, *al-Īḍāḥ*, 389. For a discussion of al-Sakkākī's linking the evaluation of a comparison to its intent, see William Smyth, "Some Quick Rules Ut Pictura Poesis: The Rules for Simile in *Miftāḥ al-'Ulūm*," *Oriens* 33 (1992). Smyth argues that through al-Sakkākī's introduction of the concept of "*istiṭrāf*" or "making something striking," he reconciles between *tashbīh qarīb* (close similes) and *ba'īd* (far-fetched), by giving each a different purpose (ibid., 228).
[89] al-Khaṭīb al-Qazwīnī, *al-Īḍāḥ*, 356.
[90] See my discussion of al-Jurjānī's treatment of discovery above.
[91] al-Khaṭīb al-Qazwīnī, *al-Īḍāḥ*, 357. [92] Ibid. [93] Ibid., 358.

Qazwīnī contrasts the following two verses by the third-/ninth-century poets al-Buḥturī and Ibn al-Rūmī, in which they compare the night and ink:

على بابِ قِنَّسْرِينَ واللَّيْلُ لاطِخٌ جَوانِبَهُ من ظُلْمَةٍ بِمِدادِ

At the gate of Qinnasrīn as the night
  out of darkness smears its walls with ink

~ al-Buḥturī (d. 284/897)

حِبْرُ أَبِي حَفْصٍ لُعَابُ اللَّيْلِ ...

Abū Ḥafṣ's ink is the saliva of the night
  ...

~ Ibn al-Rūmī (d. 283/896)

Following the principle that one's knowledge should move from what is known to what is more known, he argues that al-Buḥturī's is weaker because he compares the blackness of the night, which is a known characteristic of the night, to that of ink, which is less intensely associated with blackness.[94] Ibn al-Rūmī's simile, on the other hand, compares ink to the blackness of the night. It is, therefore, more powerful because he conveys the intensity of the blackness of ink through what is more known for that characteristic, thus moving the listener from what is less known to what is more known and not the other way around. Otherwise, a revelation does not take place and the listener does not go through an experience of discovery.[95]

The goal of simile could also be to produce a novel and strange image for its own sake. This kind of simile does not move the listener from the hidden to the visible or the impossible to the possible. Quite the opposite, it compares something possible with the impossible, such as likening lit embers to "a sea of musk with golden waves."[96] Alternatively, the simile could be strange due to the novelty and rarity of the combination of the two things it compares. This is like the violet–fire comparison that al-Jurjānī uses to illustrate his "distance formula" discussed above.[97]

Strangeness

While strangeness could be the purpose of simile in and of itself, it is also a commendable quality in simile in general, even when the goal is

[94] Ibid., 385.

[95] Of course, similes can be purposely reversed, as we have seen in Chapter 1, in order to give the illusion that the *primum comparandum* more perfectly represents a certain characteristic for the sake of hyperbole.

[96] al-Khaṭīb al-Qazwīnī, *al-Īḍāḥ*, 359. [97] Ibid., 359–60.

elucidation. This is because "when something is attained after a search and a struggle, its attainment is sweeter and its place in the soul is more pleasing and more deserving of joy," al-Khaṭīb al-Qazwīnī explains, following what we have seen in al-Jurjānī.[98] As a result, the strangeness of a simile becomes a central criterion for evaluating its beauty regardless of its specific goal.

Al-Sakkākī and al-Khaṭīb al-Qazwīnī divide similes based on their familiarity and strangeness.[99] "Familiar overused" similes (*al-qarīb al-mubtadhal*) are those in which "the movement from the *primum comparandum* to the *secundum comparatum* takes place without scrutiny because of the obviousness of the similarity from first sight."[100] These should be avoided. "Far-fetched, strange" similes (*al-baʿīd al-gharīb*) are those "in which the move from the *primum comparandum* to the *secundum comparatum* takes place only after contemplation because of the unapparentness of the similarity at first sight."[101] These are the eloquent type.[102]

This does not mean that convolutedness and intentional obscuration is desirable in poetry.[103] Rather, strangeness depends on general tendencies in human nature in their susceptibility to knowledge. Al-Sakkākī distills these tendencies into principles, which summarize as follows:[104]

(1) Grasping the whole is easier than grasping details.
(2) The conjuring of an image that the senses experience frequently is faster than that of one to which the senses are exposed infrequently.

98 Ibid., 383–4.
99 Although al-Jurjānī certainly discusses elements that add to a comparison's strangeness, he does not explicitly divide *tashbīh* into "close" and "far-fetched." Before al-Sakkakī and al-Khaṭīb al-Qazwīnī, Fakhr al-Dīn al-Rāzī had already consolidated al-Jurjānī's discussion of "strange-making" under the heading of "*tashbīh qarīb* and *gharīb*" (*Nihāyat al-īјāz*, 118–21). Discussions of "far-fetched similes" also existed in the old school of criticism. However, they were generally treated negatively. Al-Mubarrad (d. c. 285/898 or 286/899), for example, also defined it as a simile "that requires explanation and does not stand on its own." However, he immediately follows this statement with "this is crude speech" (*al-Kāmil*, ed. Muḥammad Aḥmad al-Dālī, 3rd ed., 4 vols. (Beirut: Muʾassassat al-Risāla, 1997), 1032). Note that the fact that al-Mubarrad in the section on simile in his *al-Kāmil* introduces several examples as "wondrous similes" does not indicate an aesthetic of wonder, but merely an expression of approval (ibid., 922ff.). His preference remains for those meanings that are familiar and close to convention.
100 al-Khaṭīb al-Qazwīnī, *al-Īḍāḥ*, 376. Al-Sakkakī also describes familiarity and "closeness" in simile as being of a "lower rank" (al-Sakkākī, *al-Miftāḥ*, 460).
101 al-Khaṭīb al-Qazwīnī, *al-Īḍāḥ*, 377.
102 Al-Khaṭīb al-Qazwīnī says so explicitly: "the eloquent among similes is of this type, I mean the far-fetched, for its strangeness . . ." (ibid., 383–4).
103 Ibid., 384. 104 al-Sakkākī, *al-Miftāḥ*, 459–60.

(3) Items that fit with each other or go together (like bathroom and bucket, al-Sakkākī suggests) come to mind more easily than those that do not.
(4) Bringing to mind one thing is easier than conjuring the memory of several things.
(5) The soul leans more to things perceived through the senses than those perceived through the intellect.
(6) The soul is more welcoming of what it knows than what it does not know.[105]
(7) A new image is more desirable and pleasing than a repeated one.

These are all ideas we encounter to various degrees of explicitness in al-Jurjānī's *Asrār al-balāgha*. Al-Sakkākī, however, collects and boils them down to a list, clarifying more explicitly the causes of familiarity and strangeness in simile, developing what al-Jurjānī had started. Based on these principles, he defines the factors that contribute to familiarity as follows:[106]

(1) The point of similarity is of a single aspect (like a color). [principle 4]
(2) The two things compared fit with each other (like comparing a jar to a jug). [principle 3]
(3) The thing to which the original object of description is compared is frequently present in our "store of images" (like comparing the beautiful face the full moon). [principle 2][107]

[105] Smyth conflates the fifth and sixth principles (the soul being more receptive to what it perceives through the senses and to what it knows) in his analysis and argues that they are basically the same point ("Rules for Simile," 221). Perception through the senses, however, includes al-Jurjānī's theory of "*mushāhada*" (seeing) discussed above. It involves a particular way of gaining and ascertaining knowledge. This is a different idea from the soul being more open to what it knows than to what it does not know.

[106] al-Sakkākī, *al-Miftāḥ*, 460.

[107] It is surprising that al-Sakkākī is not exhaustive in his list, given that he is so careful and systematic with the rest of his discussion. Based on his general principles, he seems to be excluding principle 1 (the whole being easier to perceive than the details), principle 5 (the greater receptiveness of the soul to matters learned through the senses than the intellect), and principle 6 (the soul being more welcoming to what it knows than what it does not know). What is known (principle 6) and what is perceived through the senses (principle 5) could arguably be subsumed under the more general familiarity rule of close similes (principle 2). The grasping of the whole as opposed to details (principle 1) could be subsumed under the single aspect rule (principle 4). The latter is in fact what al-Sayyid al-Sharīf suggests in his commentary on the *Miftah* entitled *al-Miṣbāḥ*. He also connects each factor to the general principles al-Sakkākī lays out and points out the connection between principles 4 and 1 (ʿAlī ibn Muḥammad al-Sayyid al-Sharīf al-Jurjānī, *al-Miṣbāḥ fī sharḥ al-Miftāḥ*, ed. Yüksel Çelik (PhD Dissertation, Marmara University, Istanbul, 2009), 555).

As for far-fetched comparisons, al-Sakkākī lists the following elements as factors contributing to strangeness:[108]

(1) The point of similarity is composed of several aspects (i.e., detail).
(2) The two things compared are far from being associated with each other, yet share a similarity (i.e., the distance formula).
(3) The thing to which the original object of description is compared rarely crosses our minds (i.e., rarity). This is due to its being:
   (a) estimative (*wahmī*),
   (b) an imaginary composite (*murakkab khayālī*),
   (c) an intellected composite (*murakkab ʿaqlī*).

These factors build on what al-Jurjānī had already established as strangeness-enhancing elements. The first corresponds to his discussion of "details." The second is what we are calling the "distance formula." The third revolves around rarity. Al-Khaṭīb al-Qazwīnī provides the same list of strange-making factors as al-Sakkākī, except that he more explicitly describes the first factor as involving "details," and under the third factor, he includes a fourth element, the "perceptible yet rarely experienced," along with the estimative, imaginary, and intellected matters, among the aspects that render an image unusual.[109]

(1) Detail

Adding detail is one of the ways in which a simile can be made less obvious. Al-Khaṭīb Qazwīnī explains:

> He who seeks details is like he who seeks a thing amidst the whole and tries to distinguish it from what is mixed in with it. [Whereas] he who seeks to generalize is like he who wants to take a matter in bulk (without scrutiny).[110]

According to al-Khaṭīb al-Qazwīnī, the incorporation of details entails "the inspection of multiple characteristics of one thing or more."[111] This can take place in many ways, but the most common are: (a) taking some aspects and leaving others, and (b) considering all aspects. An example of the first is Imruʾ al-Qays's comparison of a spear to smokeless fire, discussed above.[112] An example of the second (a simile that considers all aspects) can be found in the following verse:

[108] al-Sakkākī, *al-Miftāḥ*, 460–1. [109] al-Khaṭīb al-Qazwīnī, *al-Īḍāḥ*, 377.
[110] Ibid., 376. [111] Ibid., 377.
[112] See my discussion above of al-Jurjānī's analysis of the verse under "(1) Details."

وقَدْ لاحَ فِي الصُّبْحِ الثُّرَيَّا كَمَا تَرَى　　كَعُنْقُودِ مُلاَّحِيَّةٍ حِينَ نَوَّرا

The Pleiades appeared in the morning as you see
like a cluster of white grapes when plump
~ Abū Qays ibn al-Aslat (pre-Islamic)

In this case, the poet took into account various aspects of the constellation: its shape, quantity, and color, al-Khaṭīb al-Qazwīnī explains.[113]

The utmost and most amazing degree of eloquence achieved through detail, al-Khaṭīb al-Qazwīnī states, is in Ibn al-Muʿtazz's line:

كَأَنّا وضَوْءُ الصُّبْحِ يَسْتَعْجِلُ الدُّجى　　نُطَيِّرُ غُراباً ذا قَوادِمَ جُوْنِ

The morning light hurried the darkness of the night
as if we were shooing away a crow with white wingtips[114]

Al-Khaṭīb al-Qazwīnī explains that the subtle detail in this verse is that "he compared the darkness of the night when the morning light appears in it to the body of a crow, then he specified that the feathers of its wingtips are white."[115] One can imagine the similarity between the image of the beginnings of the morning light penetrating into the night sky and the image of a black crow as it spreads its white-tipped wings to fly away. If one were to scrutinize the verse further, there is another fine detail that adds novelty to it, al-Khaṭīb al-Qazwīnī explains. By describing the morning light as "hurrying" or "urging on" the dark night, the poet conveys the speed with which it is filling the sky. This sense of speed is maintained in the second part of the verse when he says: "shooing away a crow" instead of simply saying "the crow flies away." A bird that is settled in its place and flies away at its own behest will not be as hurried as one that is disturbed and made to fly away, he explains.[116]

The more details are incorporated in a simile and the more aspects are added, the stranger and (hence) more eloquent it is.[117] Based on this criterion, one can judge the relative merit of two similes in terms of the detail they contain. Al-Khaṭīb al-Qazwīnī gives a comparative analysis of several verses, which he copies practically verbatim from al-Jurjānī's *Asrār al-balāgha*. These include the comparison discussed

113 al-Khaṭīb al-Qazwīnī, *al-Īḍāḥ*, 378.
114 al-Jurjānī also thinks highly of the use of detail in this verse (*Asrār*, 162–3).
115 al-Khaṭīb al-Qazwīnī, *al-Īḍāḥ*, 379.
116 Ibid. Al-Qazwīnī's analysis of Ibn al-Muʿtazz's line is taken almost verbatim from al-Jurjānī. Such acts of uncited copying were not unusual (see al-Jurjānī, *Asrār*, 162–3).
117 al-Sakkākī, *al-Miftāḥ*, 462; al-Khaṭīb al-Qazwīnī, *al-Īḍāḥ*, 378.

above of Imruʾ al-Qays's description of a "flaming spear" with ʿAntara's, as well as Bashshār's comparison of swords in the dust of battle to "stars" with al-Mutanabbī's and ʿAmr ibn Kulthūm's renderings of the same image.[118] Speaking of Bashshār's verse (The dust, stirred up over our heads, / and our swords [in its midst] were like a night with shooting stars), which trumps the others, al-Sakkākī highlights the multifaceted nature of the similarity it contains, explaining: "the intention is not to compare the dust to the night and then the swords to the stars. Rather, it is to compare the state resulting from the black dust and the white swords scattered in its midst with the state resulting from the dark night and the stars appearing in it."[119] Such composite, multifaceted images require more thought and contemplation to be grasped than those that revolve around a single aspect.

(2) Rarity in the Combination: Distance Formula

As for the second rule of strange-making, al-Sakkākī and al-Khaṭīb al-Qazwīnī refer to the comparison of violets in a meadow of red hyacinths to "the beginnings of fire at the edges of sulfur" that al-Jurjānī uses to present his "distance formula." They explain that something is striking when it rarely crosses our minds. This can be because it is uncommon in and of itself or because its combination with the thing to which it is compared is rare.[120] Al-Sakkākī explains: "linking fire to the edges of sulfur is not [something that] 'rarely comes to mind' [... in and of itself]. Rather its rarity lies in its [combination] with the talk about violets."[121] The image is pleasing and novel, in other words, because its components are not commonly seen together and their combination is unexpected.

To further illustrate this point, al-Sakkākī narrates the following anecdote about the famous Umayyad poet Jarīr (d. 111/729):[122]

It is related that Jarīr said: ʿAdī [ibn al-Riqāʿ] recited to me [his poem starting with]:

عَرَفَ الدِّيَارَ تَوَهُّماً فَٱعْتَادَهَا. . .

> He knew the encampment [of his beloved] in his imagination and frequented it . . .

[118] al-Khaṭīb al-Qazwīnī, *al-Īḍāḥ*, 381–2. [119] al-Sakkākī, *al-Miftāḥ*, 444.
[120] Ibid., 449; al-Khaṭīb al-Qazwīnī, *al-Īḍāḥ*, 377.
[121] al-Sakkākī, *al-Miftāḥ*, 449. The same sentiment is expressed by al-Khaṭīb al-Qazwīnī in *al-Īḍāḥ*, 359–60.
[122] al-Sakkākī, *al-Miftāḥ*, 450; al-Khaṭīb al-Qazwīnī, *al-Īḍāḥ*, 360.

When he reached the following verse:

تُزجِي أَغَنَّ كَأَنَّ إِبْرَةَ رَوْقِهِ. . .

Urging on a fawn as if the tip of its horn . . .

I pitied him and said: He has stumbled. What can he possibly say [after this] given that he is a rough boorish Bedouin? Then, when he said:

. . . قَلَمٌ أَصابَ مِنَ الدَّوَاةِ مِدَادَها

. . . were a pen that had touched ink in the inkwell

the pity turned into envy.[123]

This anecdote highlights the unexpectedness of the comparison, which Jarīr initially thought would be impossible to carry out successfully. Speaking of the same anecdote, al-Jurjānī asks rhetorically:

Is not the pity in the first instance and the envy in the second only the result of believing when [the poet] first started the comparison that he mentioned something [rare and obscure . . .], for which a good comparison is hard to find, but then when he completed the simile, [Jarīr] realized that he succeeded in finding the closest description from the furthest [possible] subject and discovered something hidden whose place is unknown?[124]

Ibn al-Riqāʿ's simile is striking, therefore, because the two things compared (the fawn's horn and the pen) are so unrelated and yet the similarity the poet reveals between them is so compelling.

(3) Rarity in the *Secundum Comparatum* (*al-Mushabbah Bihi*)

The third rule of strangeness involves the rarity of the image itself to which something is compared. While rarity in the "distance formula" is the result of the unusualness of the *combination* of two otherwise familiar images, rarity in the third rule has to do with the *secundum comparatum* itself being rare. Al-Sakkākī and al-Khaṭīb al-Qazwīnī specify that rarity is the result of a matter being: estimative (*wahmī*), an imaginary composite

[123] Ibn al-Muʿtazz also considered this verse by Ibn al-Riqāʿ of the "marvels (*ʿajāʾib*) of comparison" in his *Kitāb al-badīʿ*, 71. Al-Jurjānī also relates this anecdote. See al-Jurjānī, *Asrār*, 141n146, for a list of medieval references for this oft-cited anecdote.

[124] al-Jurjānī, *Asrār*, 141. The same sentiment is expressed by al-Khaṭīb al-Qazwīnī in *al-Īḍāḥ*, 360.

(*murakkab khayālī*), or an intellected composite (*murakkab ʿaqlī*).[125] Al-Khaṭīb al-Qazwīnī explains that "each of these is a reason for the infrequency with which the *secundum comparatum* crosses the mind."[126] He also adds that a perceptible matter can also be rare due to the "infrequency with which it is perceived through the senses."[127]

To understand what these mean, we have to turn to their discussion of the two parts of a simile (*ṭarafā al-tashbīh*), which are classified as either perceptible through the senses (*maḥsūs*), or intellected through the mind (*ʿaqlī*).[128] The "rarely perceived" and "imaginary composite" types fall under "perceptibles" and the "estimative" and "intellected composite" types fall under the "intellected."[129]

The Perceptible Perceptible matters are those which can be perceived "through one of the five apparent senses."[130] Such things can be compared based on a single similarity, such as color, taste, sound, touch, or smell. These single-faceted comparisons are not counted among the rare and strange similes.[131] However, perceptible matters could be combined in ways that make them less frequent. Detail and rarity overlap in this case. The example al-Khaṭīb al-Qazwīnī discusses to illustrate the "perceptible yet rarely experienced" is one that al-Jurjānī discusses at great length as well. It is a comparison of the sun to a mirror in the hand of a palsied man (والشَّمْسُ كالمِرْآةِ فِي كَفِّ الأَشَلْ).[132] Al-Jurjānī also lists the image among matters that rarely cross one's mind and discusses it primarily to point out the use of "movement" (*ḥaraka*) as a detail-enhancing factor.[133] Al-Khaṭīb al-Qazwīnī also points out the novel effect produced by specifying that the hand belongs to a palsied person, which captures the instability and quivering nature of its reflection.[134] While the source of strangeness in this aspect is the subtle detail this brings to the image, al-Khaṭīb al-Qazwīnī points out that rarity also contributes to the simile's strangeness: "one can spend his whole life and never see the sight of a mirror in

125 al-Sakkākī, *al-Miftāḥ*, 461; al-Khaṭīb al-Qazwīnī, *al-Īḍāḥ*, 377.
126 al-Khaṭīb al-Qazwīnī, *al-Īḍāḥ*, 377.
127 Ibid. Al-Sakkākī does not include this among rare matters.
128 al-Sakkākī, *al-Miftāḥ*, 439.
129 al-Khaṭīb al-Qazwīnī, *al-Talkhīṣ fī ʿulūm al-balāgha*, ed. ʿAbd al-Ḥamīd Hindāwī, 2nd ed. (Beirut: Dār al-Kutub al-ʿIlmiyya, 2009), 62.
130 Ibid.
131 The first rule of "familiar similes" as given by al-Sakkākī states that the similarity in familiar similes is of a single aspect, as we have seen (*al-Miftāḥ*, 460).
132 al-Khaṭīb al-Qazwīnī, *al-Īḍāḥ*, 346–7. The line is by Jabbār ibn Jazʾ (early Islamic).
133 al-Jurjānī, *Asrār*, 144, 164–5. 134 al-Khaṭīb al-Qazwīnī, *al-Īḍāḥ*, 347.

the hand of a palsied person."[135] Therefore, even though the image is composed of perceptible matters combined in a way that forms a clearly perceptible scene, it is rarely – if ever – experienced.[136]

Perceptible matters could also be combined in imaginary ways, such as likening anemonies to "banners of rubies unfurled on lances of peridot," which we have come across in our discussion of al-Jurjānī. While the previous composite image of the "mirror in the hand of a palsied man" belongs to the realm of existing perceptible matters, the "rubies unfurled on lances of peridot" example "is something nonexistent that the comparer conceives of and creates."[137] Speaking of this image al-Jurjānī explains:

> It is not common to take an image of ruby in the form of a flag and underneath it an elongated piece of peridot in the form of lances and stems [. . .]. An additional aspect that makes the anemones simile further from existence is the specification that the banners be "spread or unfurled," when the unfurling of ruby, which is a stone, cannot be imagined to exist.[138]

Although al-Jurjānī speaks of this type of image as nonexistent, he does not explicitly describe it as imaginary (*khayālī*), as al-Sakkākī and al-Khaṭīb al-Qazwīnī do. Speaking of the same example, Fakhr al-Dīn al-Rāzī describes it as a "simile that exists in the imagination (*bi-l-mutakhayyil*) and does not exist in the visible world."[139] He explains that "the nonexistent is [considered] 'imagined' (*mutakhayyal*) when the imagined is produced as a whole in the combination of matters that [otherwise] exist in the visible world individually."[140] This clarifies that the imaginary is a composite image of matters that otherwise exist independently and are perceptible through the senses.

We can conclude, therefore, that what is meant by an "imaginary composite" image (*murakkab khayālī*) is the combination of perceptible matters (like different-colored gemstones) in an imaginary way that cannot exist in reality (making the ruby "unfurl" like a flag over spear-like peridots). While rarity can exist in both types of perceptible composites (the existent yet rare, on the one hand, and the imaginary, on the other), the imaginary composite (*al-murakkab al-khayālī*) possesses greater strangeness because it is even more uncommon.[141]

135 Ibid., 377.
136 This is similar to the comparison of stars to "pearls strewn over a blue carpet," discussed above under al-Jurjānī's treatment of rarity.
137 al-Jurjānī, *Asrār*, 154. 138 Ibid., 155. 139 al-Rāzī, *Nihāyat al-ījāz*, 108. 140 Ibid.
141 al-Jurjānī, *Asrār*, 158.

The Intellected Besides perceptible matters, the *secundum comparatum* can be based on "intellected" matters. These are matters that cannot be perceived through the senses, but are comprehended through the mind (*ʿaql*). These include abstract matters such as psychological states, instincts, and ethical dispositions (e.g., knowledge, anger, forbearance).[142] Intellected meanings include similes such as comparing knowledge to life (two abstract concepts), for example, or justice to a balance (abstract and perceptible).[143] Nevertheless, while *ʿaqlī* is contrasted with matters that can be perceived through the senses, thus pointing to the realm of abstract matter, the term "abstract" does not fully capture the meaning of *ʿaqlī*. In discussing the term as employed by al-Jurjānī, Margaret Larkin translates it as "noetic,"[144] and Kamal Abu Deeb renders it "intellectual."[145] While both translations are plausible, I opt for Smyth's rendering of the term as "intellected."[146] The last captures the important element of intellectual reasoning required in order to derive *ʿaqlī* meanings.

If we look at al-Jurjānī's use of the term *ʿaqlī*, we see that, in addition to its involving an abstract quality, it entails a level of intellectual reasoning and interpretation (*taʾawwul*). The straightforward comparison that does not require interpretation, which he variously refers to as explicit (*ṣarīḥ*), literal (*ḥaqīqī*), or apparent (*ẓāhir*),[147] takes place in the perceived reality of the matter itself. An example of such a straightforward comparison would be comparing the cheek to a rose, as both share the real and physical quality of redness.[148]

The non-straightforward type of comparison, which requires interpretation, on the other hand, takes place in an attribute or judgment associated with the matter being described and does not form a perceptible part of it. This is like comparing eloquent speech to honey in its sweetness. The two are not similar on a physical level, but are likened based on the judgment of speech as "sweet":

142 al-Sakkākī, *al-Miftāḥ*, 441. 143 Ibid., 440.
144 See Larkin, *Theology of Meaning*, ch. 4. 145 Abu Deeb, *Poetic Imagery*, 107.
146 Smyth uses this translation in a different context when he discusses the direct versus indirect levels of signification, in which case the term *ʿaqlī* also points to the logical reasoning required to arrive at secondary levels of signification (Smyth, "Canonical Formulation," 17).
147 al-Jurjānī, *Asrār*, 89–90. He calls it "*tashbīh ṣarīḥ*" (explicit comparison) later in ch. 13.
148 Ibid., 88.

The similarity is not from the aspect of sweetness itself and its genus, but from a necessary consequence and an experience that is renewed in the soul because of it. The intention is to report that the listener finds upon hearing such speech a state similar to that when he tastes the sweetness of honey.[149]

Because the comparison is based on a similarity of attributes, judgments, or consequences associated on a secondary level with the matter being described, and not a material perceptible reality, grasping the similarity requires additional steps of reasoning. Al-Jurjānī explains:

These interpreted similarities (*al-mushābahāt al-muta'awwala*) that the mind extracts from one thing for another are not of the principal[150] apparent [type] of similarities, rather [they belong to] the intellected ones (*shabah 'aqlī*) . . .[151]

This intellected type of comparison is of two types, al-Jurjānī goes on to clarify. It can be "extracted from one thing, like comparing speech to the sweetness of honey, or from several matters from whose combination a similarity can be deduced."[152] The example he gives for the latter is the Quranic verse:

مَثَلُ الَّذِينَ حُمِّلُوا التَّوْرَاةَ ثُمَّ لَمْ يَحْمِلُوهَا كَمَثَلِ الْحِمَارِ يَحْمِلُ أَسْفَارًا

The example of those who were given the Torah and then did not carry on [its teachings] is like the example of a donkey carrying tomes

~ Q62:5

Al-Jurjānī explains that the similarity between those who make no use of the Torah and the donkey lies in the state of the donkey while carrying books and in its not distinguishing them from any other load, oblivious to and making no use of the knowledge they contain.[153] As such, analogy (*tamthīl*), which compares two sets of relationships, is by default of the *'aqlī* type because it requires some deduction of the relationships being compared.

Indeed, the example that al-Sakkākī cites for the composite intellected type of comparison is analogy. He cites verse 24 from Sūrat Yūnus in the Quran in which life and its fleetingness is compared to humans' apparent mastery over earth's cultivation and God's ultimate power to take it away:[154]

149 Ibid.
150 Al-Jurjānī describes the straightforward apparent type of comparison as an "*aṣl*" (principle) and the non-straightforward intellected type as a "*far'*" (branch), hence the description of the former as a "main" comparison in this citation (ibid., 89).
151 Ibid., 90. 152 Ibid. 153 Ibid. 154 al-Sakkākī, *al-Miftāḥ*, 461.

إِنَّمَا مَثَلُ الْحَيَاةِ الدُّنْيَا كَمَاءٍ أَنزَلْنَاهُ مِنَ السَّمَاءِ فَاخْتَلَطَ بِهِ نَبَاتُ الأَرْضِ مِمَّا يَأْكُلُ النَّاسُ وَالأَنْعَامُ حَتَّىٰ إِذَا أَخَذَتِ الأَرْضُ زُخْرُفَهَا وَازَّيَّنَتْ وَظَنَّ أَهْلُهَا أَنَّهُمْ قَادِرُونَ عَلَيْهَا أَتَاهَا أَمْرُنَا لَيْلاً أَوْ نَهَارًا فَجَعَلْنَاهَا حَصِيدًا كَأَن لَّمْ تَغْنَ بِالأَمْسِ كَذَلِكَ نُفَصِّلُ الآيَاتِ لِقَوْمٍ يَتَفَكَّرُونَ.

> It is the case that the example of the worldly life is like water which We send down from the sky; with which the earth's plants mix, from which humans and animals eat, so much so that the earth takes its ornaments and decks itself in beauty and its people think they are masters of it. Our commandment comes by night or day so that We make it harvested [clean], as if it had not flourished [just] the day before. Thus We expound the signs for people who reflect
> ~ Q10:24

As much as we might feel in control of this worldly life of ours, in other words, God has the power to take it away from us from one day to the next. Life is similar to water, which adorns the earth with cultivation to the extent that we might think we are in control of it, but which can also be taken away from us at any moment. In discussing this verse, al-Jurjānī explains how all its sentences are necessary for the analogy to work and that the similarity is an intellected one because what is described as the effect of water cannot be applied to life without some intellectual reasoning and analysis.[155] The composite intellected comparison, therefore, is a composite comparison that requires some interpretation in order to arrive at its meaning. Al-Sakkākī and al-Khaṭīb al-Qazwīnī explicitly identify such intellected composite comparisons with rarity and strangeness.

Finally, estimative (*wahmī*) comparisons also belong to the "intellected" type. Al-Sakkākī states that intellected meanings are either real, such as "psychological states" like intelligence, alertness, knowledge, generosity ... etc., or "hypothetical or discretionary," including descriptions that are "purely conceptual (*taṣawwurī*) and estimative (*wahmī*)."[156] Al-Khaṭīb al-Qazwīnī further explains that "while *wahmī* meanings are not perceptible through any of the five senses, if they were to be perceived, they would be [perceived] through the senses."[157] To illustrate this, he cites a famous verse by Imru' al-Qays in which he states:[158]

(أَيَقْتُلُنِي والمَشْرَفِيُّ مُضاجِعِي)   ومَسْنُونَةٌ زُرْقٌ كَأَنيابِ أَغْوَالِ

> (How can he kill me when the Mashrafiyy [sword] is my bedfellow?)
> And [so are] polished sharp [arrowheads] resembling the canine teeth of ghouls

155 al-Jurjānī, *Asrār*, 96 and 101. 156 al-Sakkākī, *al-Miftāḥ*, 441.
157 al-Khaṭīb al-Qazwīnī, *al-Īḍāḥ*, 336. 158 Ibid. (first hemistich not quoted in *al-Īḍāḥ*).

"Ghoul" is categorized as "intellected" (*ʿaqlī*) because it is a hypothetical creature that has never been perceived through the senses by any human. Thus, the idea of perceiving a ghoul and its canine teeth is a matter that has to be estimated in our mind. Al-Sayyid al-Sharīf explains, speaking of the same ghoul example: "when a person hears that there is a type of animal called 'ghoul' that kills people, the [faculty] of estimation starts inventing the instrument of death for this animal in the shape of canine teeth."[159]

This is similar, al-Khaṭīb al-Qazwīnī explains, to comparing the horribleness of the fruits of the Zaqqūm tree of hell to the devil in the Quran:

طَلْعُهَا كَأَنَّهُ رُؤُوسُ الشَّيَاطِين

Its fruit as if it were the heads of devils[160]

~ Q37:65

The devil is also categorized as an "estimated" (*wahmī*) meaning because it has also never been witnessed by any human, yet one is able to imagine or "estimate" what the devil looks like and the horror of the image.

The separation of imagination and estimation as two distinct faculties is something that Avicenna puts forth in his philosophy. Al-Sakkākī and al-Khaṭīb al-Qazwīnī are undoubtedly influenced by this division in their distinction between imaginary and estimative images. The relationship between the two requires further study, however. The two faculties that Avicenna distinguishes are intertwined and have a complex history. Some later philosophers, including Averroes, reject the distinction altogether and argue for a single faculty of imagination.[161] In fact, Fakhr al-Dīn al-Rāzī classifies both types of comparison, the imaginary and the estimative, under one category of the imagination: comparisons that exist in the "*mutakhayyil*" (imagination) that cannot be seen with the naked eye.[162] Nevertheless, whether we distinguish the estimative from the imaginary

[159] al-Sayyid al-Sharīf al-Jurjānī, *al-Miṣbāḥ*, 556–7.

[160] al-Khaṭīb al-Qazwīnī, *al-Īḍāḥ*, 336. Al-Mubarrad (d. c. 285/898 or 286/899) gives two possible explanations for this comparison: either the fruit of the "*astan*" tree (others say it is "*al-sawm*") are known as "devils' heads" for their ugliness; or that it is a comparison and that God makes believers find the image of devils ugly (i.e., even if they have never seen them) (*al-Kāmil*, 2:996–7). Al-Mubarrad also mentions Imruʾ al-Qays's verse about the ghoul as an example of the use of things that have never been seen in reality. He says: والغول لم يخبر صادق قط أنه رآها (ibid., 999). That indicates that this distinction between imaginary and estimative was already being made in the third/ninth century, though the latter was not described as "*wahmī*" yet.

[161] Deborah Black, "Estimation (*Wahm*) in Avicenna: The Logical and Psychological Dimensions," *Dialogue* 32, no. 2 (1993).

[162] al-Rāzī, *Nihāyat al-ījāz*, 108.

composite image or not, both require intellection and thus contribute to the rarity and strangeness of a simile.

***

We see, therefore, that al-Khaṭīb al-Qazwīnī stresses the comparison's ability to reveal or emphasize through a movement from obscurity to clarity, the unfamiliar to the familiar, the less known to the more known, the perceived through the intellect to the perceived through the senses or instinctually. This process of elucidation (*bayān*) is pleasurable because it provides an experience of discovery, uncovering something hidden. So familiarity is necessary in the *secundum comparatum*, but what causes the pleasure is not familiarity by itself, but the change in one's state of knowledge and awareness from unfamiliarity to familiarity or from the concealed to the apparent. This experience of discovery in the listener that results from the process of revelation that takes place through simile is what makes it aesthetically pleasing. *Bayān* as "elucidation," therefore, is eloquence, not *bayān* as "clarity."

A simile may not always serve to move one's state from the concealed to the apparent, but it can also move the listener by presenting a novel and strange simile instead. In this case, the pleasure arising from simile is due to the unusualness of the combination of its two parts or the rarity of *secundum comparatum* itself. These also slow down the listener's grasp of the image. Strangeness enhances the beauty of simile in general as well, even when the aim is elucidation, by slowing down the process of discovery through adding detail.

Al-Sakkākī and al-Khaṭīb al-Qazwīnī's ideas and examples are clearly drawn from al-Jurjānī, sometimes verbatim, as we have seen. Their taxonomy of familiarity and strangeness, as well as of the different goals of simile, clearly identify al-Jurjānī's discussions within a system that evaluated simile based on its ability to elucidate and its strangeness. What may on the surface seem as tedious categorization in the formalized "science of *bayān*" now clearly has a purpose. Whether the matters compared are perceptible or intellected and whether the similarity is singular or multifaceted affects the degree of strangeness of the simile. Furthermore, human nature's varying degrees of receptiveness to these different forms of gaining knowledge influence a simile's ability to allow the listener to go through an experience of discovery.

CONCLUSION

Terms such as "wonder," "magic," and "splendor" are frequently employed in descriptions of the effect of poetic speech on the listener, going back to as early as the time of the Prophet Muhammad, as we have seen. These descriptions in and of themselves do not amount to a theory of aesthetic experience. However, the attribution of the emotional impact of simile to its ability to elucidate or reveal something about the subject, as well as to its strangeness, does provide us with a logical explanation for its psychological effect. The linking of pleasure to discovery and strangeness suggests that the nature of the aesthetic experience medieval critics expected from eloquent speech was more specifically one of wonder. Their detailed analysis of how discovery and strangeness are achieved in simile amount to a theory of aesthetic experience.

This theory of aesthetic experience is not limited to simile. The emotional impact of other figures of *bayān*, as we will see in Chapter 4, also depends on their ability to "elucidate" in a way that allows for an experience of discovery in the listener. While what they theorize about of simile remains relevant, the mechanism that underlies this process of elucidation in metaphor and metonymy is different. *Bayān* in these figures revolves around the various ways in which signs signify meaning. Therefore, what we turn to next is an inquiry into the aesthetics of the sign. As we will see, the "magic" of "*bayān*" in signs also lies in their ability to move the listener from obscurity to clarity; it does not lie in clarity alone.

4

Metaphor and the Aesthetics of the Sign

The notion of *bayān* as elucidation, as we have seen in Chapter 3, encompasses within it the essence of the aesthetic mechanism of simile. Good similes are ones that result in a movement from obscurity to clarity. This is pleasing because it allows the listener to go through an experience of discovery. However, while simile is approached from a "*bayānī*" perspective, it does not function in exactly the same way as the other components of *bayān*. These come to constitute figurative speech (*majāz*), which encompasses metaphor (*isti'āra*), in addition to a literary device called *kināya*, which approximately corresponds to metonymy.[1] The last figure is not considered "figurative" in nature, as we will see.

These figures are treated as signifiers that signify their meaning indirectly, in ways that have to be intellected. That is, they are treated as signifiers, whose lexical meanings signify further secondary meanings. Such types of signification, as we will see, are inherently more pleasing to the listener, our medieval authors theorize, precisely because they require more pondering and allow for a process of elucidation and discovery to take place that words intended literally do not have the capacity to do. As in simile, the less obvious this process of discovery and the more effort is required on the part of the listener to grasp the intended meaning,

[1] *Kināya* and metonymy do not overlap perfectly. Elsewhere, I have rendered it "implication" and "implied meaning" (Harb, "Form, Content, and Inimitability"). Heinrichs has translated it as "periphrastic expression" in "Rhetorical Figures," in *The Encyclopedia of Arabic Literature*. However, *kināya* shares enough with the debates about metonymy in modern scholarship that I have reverted to translating the figure as metonymy, so not to obscure the commonalities that do exist. Nevertheless, this equation has to be taken with a grain of salt, as the figure has a specific definition in Arabic that does not overlap perfectly with modern Western definitions of metonymy. See below for a detailed description of *kināya*.

the more rewarding the experience. However, while in simile, this experience of discovery results from its comparative nature that elucidates through likening something to something else, figurative speech and metonymy produce an experience of discovery through their processes of signification. Our inquiry in this chapter, therefore, launches us into medieval discussions of the aesthetics of words or compound word units as signifying signs.

ʿABD AL-QĀHIR AL-JURJĀNĪ AND THE ELOQUENCE OF THE WORD

Al-Jurjānī does not grant utterances, in the sense of acoustic signifiers, any role in the beauty of speech except insofar as they should fulfill some basic criteria of acceptability by not being lowly, out-of-date, or incomprehensible. Otherwise, speech does not owe its eloquence "to the ring of its letters or its linguistic appearance, rather to a matter that reaches a person's heart and a benefit the mind ignites from its kindling."[2] Such matters that reach the heart and benefit the mind cannot but depend on the meaning a word signifies, according to al-Jurjānī. A word cannot add beauty to a phrase simply because it sounds good acoustically irrespective of its meaning. Its beauty has to be assessed with respect to the meaning it signifies. Al-Jurjānī, therefore, insists on an understanding of words (*alfāẓ*) in the combined sense of "signifier" and "signified," i.e., as "signs," to borrow terms from Saussure.[3]

However, like Saussure, al-Jurjānī also believes that the relationship between a signifier and signified is an arbitrary one set by linguistic convention. The word "*rajul*" in Arabic in reference to "man", he points out, is not a more eloquent signifier than the word "*ādamī*" for "man" in Persian,

[2] al-Jurjānī, *Asrār*, 4. Al-Jurjānī vehemently denies any role for the sounds of words in eloquence. This is partly due to diverging theological schools of thought about the question of the createdness of the Quran, which Margaret Larkin has discussed in *Theology of Meaning*. Nevertheless, this attitude also fits his aesthetic theory of language. Ibn Sinān al-Khafājī (d. 466/1074), a contemporary of al-Jurjānī's, and a Muʿtazilite, does in fact dedicate a large portion of his treatise on *faṣāḥa* (articulateness) to the sounds of the letters of the alphabet (*Sirr al-faṣāḥa*, 15–25; 66–101). See also van Gelder's extensive study on the aesthetics of sound in classical Arabic literary theory in *Sound and Sense in Classical Arabic Poetry*.

[3] For a detailed discussion of al-Jurjānī's ideas about *lafẓ* and *maʿnā*, see my article "Form, Content, and Inimitability." Alexander Key has made a compelling case against the temptation of mapping classical Arabic concepts onto Saussurian semiotic terminology (see *Language between God and the Poets*, especially 78–83).

for example.[4] Therefore, word choice, even when considering words as "signs," does not in and of itself contribute to eloquence. There is no difference in quality, he points out, between the following invective verse by al-Ḥuṭayʾa (d. after 41/661) and its rewording, which employs different vocabulary to express the same idea in the same grammatical structure:[5]

دَعِ المَكارِمَ لا تَرحَلْ لِبُغْيَتِها وَٱقْعُدْ فَإِنَّكَ أَنتَ الطّاعِمُ الكاسِي

Don't bother with honor! Do not journey in its quest!
Sit down; you are one who [contents himself with] food and clothes[6]

The same verse expressed with synonyms is not more or less beautiful, according to al-Jurjānī:

ذَرِ المَفاخِرَ لا تَذْهَبْ لِمَطْلَبِها وَٱجْلِسْ فَإِنَّكَ أَنْتَ الآكِلُ اللاّبِسِ

Never mind pride! Do not go in its pursuit!
Stay put; you are one who [contents himself with] eating and dressing

Simply replacing a word with its synonym, he argues, does not add anything to the statement.[7]

In order for a word to enhance eloquence, it has to be able to add some meaning to the basic meaning expressed. Words are able to do so when they point to more than their direct lexical signification, adding some implication or suggestion that goes beyond the literal. Al-Jurjānī explains that replacing one word with another does not contribute to eloquence "unless there is some broadening of meaning and figurative expansion

[4] al-Jurjānī, *Dalāʾil*, 44. See also Harb, "Form, Content, and Inimitability," 308–9.

[5] al-Jurjānī, *Dalāʾil*, 487, and see also 259 for the same idea. Elsewhere, al-Jurjānī describes this form of transcription as "*salkh*" (stripping) and considers it a scornful form of plagiarism (ibid., 471).

[6] The story behind this verse and the invective poem of which it is part is widely reported in old sources (for a brief description, see van Gelder, *The Bad and the Ugly: Attitudes towards Invective Poetry (Hijāʾ) in Classical Arabic Literature* (Leiden: Brill, 1988), 24–5). The insult lies in the fact that the poet accuses al-Zibriqān (the target of his invective and a tribe leader during the caliphate of ʿUmar ibn al-Khaṭṭāb (r. 13/634–23/644)) of being satisfied with meeting his basic bodily needs (being fed and clothed) and that he should not even try to go out looking for matters that would bring him honor. This was deemed an insult of the highest order (see al-Ḥutayʾa, *Dīwān al-Ḥutayʾa bi-sharḥ Ibn al-Sikkīt wa-l-Sukkarī wa-l-Sijistānī*, ed. Nuʿmān Amīn Ṭāhā (Cairo: Sharikat Maktabat wa-Maṭbaʿat Muṣṭafā al-Bābī al-Ḥalabī wa-Awladih, 1958), 206–7, 283–93, especially 290).

[7] One could argue, as some medieval critics do, that acoustics do play a role in the beauty of these verses. However, this does not belong to the realm of eloquence (*balāgha*) for al-Jurjānī. Moreover, synonyms often have slightly different connotations which may influence a poet's choice of words. Al-Jurjānī's point here, however, is that choosing a word in and of itself because it accurately expresses what one wants to say reflects one's mastery of the lexicon; it does not reflect an artistic skill.

(*majāz*), and unless what is intended is not the apparent meaning that the words conventionally signify, but another meaning to which their meanings point."[8] He calls this secondary meaning "the meaning of meaning" (*maʿnā al-maʿnā*):[9]

> Speech is of two types: [a] in one you arrive at the intended meaning through the signification (*dalāla*) of the word by itself. [. . .] [b] in the other, you do not reach the intended meaning through the signification of the word itself. Rather, the word signifies its meaning as its place in the lexicon requires, then you find for that meaning a second signification through which you arrive at the intended meaning.[10]

Words as "signs," therefore, do not contribute to the beauty of a phrase as arbitrary signs set by linguistic convention unless they go on to signify other meanings beyond their lexical meaning. Such secondary signification can be achieved through specific kinds of rhetorical figures, namely, metaphor (*istiʿāra*) and figurative speech (*majāz*) more generally, metaphorical analogy (*al-tamthīl bi-l-istiʿāra*), and metonymy (*kināya*).[11] Translating these terms into English is inherently problematic; their precise definitions are fluid and changing in Arabic criticism over the centuries, not to mention the difficulty of trying to map them onto Western terminology, which rarely matches the Arabic understanding of the figures perfectly. In the following, I will briefly review al-Jurjānī's understanding of these figures, especially with respect to their property of signifying a secondary meaning, which is where their beauty lies.

Metaphor, Figurative Speech, and Metonymy

Al-Jurjānī explains that figurative speech (*majāz*) is "any word that is intended to signify in its [particular] context something other than what it [conventionally] signifies for there being some relationship between the

[8] al-Jurjānī, *Dalāʾil*, 265.

[9] Ibid., 263. The concept of *maʿnā al-maʿnā* has been discussed in detail by Larkin in *Theology of Meaning*; and Abu Deeb in *Poetic Imagery*. For extensive investigations of ʿAbd al-Qāhir al-Jurjānī's understandings of meaning, see Mohamed Ait El Ferrane, *Die Maʿnā-Theorie bei ʿAbdalqāhir al-Ǧurǧānī (gestorben 471/1079) Versuch einer Analyse der poetischen Sprache*, Heidelberger orientalistische Studien (Frankfurt am Main: Lang, 1990); Nejmeddine Khalfallah, *La théorie sémantique de ʿAbd al-Qāhir al-Jurjānī (m. 1078)* (Paris: L'Harmattan, 2014); and Key, *Language between God and the Poets*, 196–240.

[10] al-Jurjānī, *Dalāʾil*, 262. Al-Fārābī explains metaphor in similar terms in *Kitāb al-ḥurūf*, 225.

[11] al-Jurjānī, *Dalāʾil*, 66–7, for definitions.

first [signification] and the second."[12] This relationship can be one of similarity, in which case it is a metaphor (*istiʿāra*), such as saying "I saw a lion" to signify a person's bravery by likening him to a lion. Other associations, not based on resemblance, may also link two meanings, such as using the word "hand" to indicate generosity in the statement "his hands abound with me (كَثُرَت أياديه لَدَيّ)." The link in this case results from the fact that the hand is what does the "giving" and not from some similarity between hand and generosity.[13] When you say "I saw a lion", al-Jurjānī states, clarifying the difference, "you want to affirm the quality of lionhood to the man, while you do not intend to affirm, by saying 'he has bestowed a hand on me (لَهُ عِندِي يَدٌ),'[14] some quality of 'handhood' to generosity."[15] Figurative speech (*majāz*) is therefore a larger category than metaphor (*istiʿāra*): "every *istiʿāra* is a *majāz*, but not every *majāz* is an *istiʿāra*."[16] What I am translating as "metaphor" is limited to figurative usage of a word based on a relationship of similarity between its lexical meaning and the intended one.

Kināya also entails the use of a word for a meaning other than its literal signification; however, not figuratively. Instead, this secondary meaning is reached through something the literal meaning implies and of which it is a symptom. Standard examples include: referring to someone as having "a long shoulder strap for his sword's sheath (طَوِيل النِّجَاد)" to imply that he is tall; expressing someone's generosity by describing him as "having abundant ashes under his cauldron (كَثِيرُ رَمَادِ القِدر)," which implies that he provides plentiful food to his guests; and saying "she sleeps in in the morning (نَؤُومُ الضُّحَى)" to convey the idea that a woman is well-off, living in ease and comfort, and is being served, not needing to get up early to do chores. All these examples intend a meaning, which they do not express directly "but arrive at by mentioning another meaning that follows it in existence and is a consequence of it."[17] While the intended meaning is something the direct meaning implies, the direct/literal meaning is also literally accurate in *kināya*: someone who is tall would indeed have a long shoulder strap for his sword's sheath; if a great amount of food is prepared,

[12] al-Jurjānī, *Asrār*, 325.

[13] Ibid., 326–7. Al-Jurjānī goes on to discuss a number of other figurative uses of the word hand, emphasizing that context is the only way to know which indirect meaning is intended (*Asrār*, ch. 21). The non-*tashbīh*-based *majāz* is what later becomes known as "*majāz mursal*" (free or unrestricted figurative speech) (al-Khaṭīb al-Qazwīnī, *al-Īḍāḥ*, 397ff.).

[14] Lane translates this as "I owe him a benefit" (see supplement under "*yad*"). I have kept my translation literal to show the use of the word "hand."

[15] al-Jurjānī, *Asrār*, 373. [16] Ibid., 368. [17] al-Jurjānī, *Dalāʾil*, 66.

the ashes under one's cauldron would indeed be abundant; and if a woman is living a comfortable life, it would indeed follow that she could afford to sleep in in the mornings.[18]

Kināya, therefore, is not considered "figurative" speech because its literal meaning is also accurate. While the ultimate point is to convey the indirect meanings of tallness, generosity, and affluence, the matters that point to these characteristics are also meant literally as symptoms or consequences of the intended meaning. In other words, *kināya* entails referring to something implicitly (e.g., generosity) through indicating a consequence of that thing (e.g., abundant ashes under the cauldron).[19] In contrast, when one calls someone a lion to indicate his bravery, there is no level at which the actual animal is meant literally. Consequently, metaphor (*istiʿāra*) is figurative and part of *majāz*, while metonymy (*kināya*) is not.[20]

Simile, Analogy, and Metaphorical Analogy

Simile (*tashbīh*) does not participate in a process of "indirect signification." In fact, its function is not one of signification at all, whether direct or not. Indeed, this non-significatory character of simile is precisely what distinguishes it from its close cousin, the metaphor.[21] Where to draw the line between simile (*tashbīh*) and metaphor (*istiʿāra*) was debated in medieval

[18] Ibid.

[19] Note here that the whole phrase functions as a "sign" that signifies some other meaning. While many examples of *kināya* can accurately be described as metonyms, others are closer to related figures, including synecdoche and antonomasia (see below). Some aspects of metonymy, in turn, would not apply to *kināya*. The type of figurative speech that is not based on a relationship of similarity, discussed above under *majāz*, often amounts to what we would describe as metonymy or synecdoche in English. It is not considered *kināya*, however, because the association between the lexical meaning and the secondary meaning has to be interpreted figuratively. Significantly, *kināya* in Arabic is by definition not figurative (*majāz*); its lexical meaning is literally accurate, and the intended meaning is something this literal meaning implies through some actual relationship between the two. Indeed, some modern descriptions of metonymy have distinguished it from metaphor in this way, as well (see *The New Princeton Encyclopedia of Poetry and Poetics*, ed. Alex Preminger et al. (Princeton, NJ: Princeton University Press, 1993), 783–5, s.v. "metonymy").

[20] Translating "*majāz*" as "figurative speech" is therefore not inaccurate. However, it can be confusing when distinguished from metonymy (*kināya*), which in English is often considered figurative speech.

[21] Simile is often mistakenly understood to be part of al-Jurjānī's category of "the meaning of meaning," giving it a function of indirect signification (see, for example, Iḥsān ʿAbbās, *Tārīkh al-naqd al-adabī ʿind al-ʿArab: Naqd al-shiʿr min al-qarn al-thānī ḥattā al-qarn al-thāmin al-Hijrī* (Amman: Dār al-Shurūq li-l-Nashr wa-l-Tawzīʿ, 1993), 429). This is not consistent with al-Jurjānī's definition of simile, as we will see.

Arabic literary criticism: Is the article of comparison the only element that differentiates the two figures? Should a phrase that does not employ an article of comparison, such as saying "Zayd is a lion," be considered a metaphor or a simile? For al-Jurjānī, a simile is any statement in which both parts of a comparison, the *primum comparandum* (*mushabbah*) and *secundum comparatum* (*mushabbah bihi*), are mentioned, whether it includes an article of comparison or not:

When you say "Zayd is a lion" or "I saw him a lion," you are making the word of the *secundum comparatum* (*mushabbah bihi*) [i.e., the lion] a predicate (*khabar*) for the *primum comparandum* (*mushabbah*) [i.e., Zayd or him]. A predicate relates something about [the subject] in order [. . .] to affirm either a characteristic [. . .] or a type. [. . .] Since it is impossible in our statement "Zayd is a lion" to be affirming the [applicability of the] species [of the lion] to Zayd in reality, the affirmation that takes place is the similarity between him and the species.[22]

So even though one understands that Zayd is not literally a lion, al-Jurjānī does not consider the statement figurative. This is because it is clear, according to him, that the point of the statement is to declare a similarity to a characteristic associated with the lion as the actual animal. In other words, the word "lion" in that sentence is intended literally to signify the animal. It becomes a metaphor only when the *primum comparandum* (*mushabbah*) is dropped completely and the *secundum comparatum* (*mushabbah bihi*) replaces it and stands in for it, such as saying "a lion is approaching." In this case, the word lion stands in for Zayd. The distinction between metaphor and simile, therefore, lies in their linguistic mechanism. A simile does not function as a sign, but as a statement in which the *primum comparandum* and *secundum comparatum* are intended literally in order to declare a similarity between them, as they are. Whereas a metaphor functions as a signifying sign that stands in the *primum comparandum*'s stead.[23]

Analogy (*tamthīl*) is a kind of simile. Simile is a more general category that encompasses analogy: "every analogy is a simile, but not every simile is an analogy."[24] Instead of locating the similarity in an attribute of a single matter, however, analogy locates it in an attribute extracted from a relationship

[22] al-Jurjānī, *Asrār*, 302.

[23] See ibid., 302–4; al-Jurjānī, *Dalāʾil*, 68. For a more detailed discussion of the distinction between simile and metaphor, see Harb, "Form, Content, and Inimitability," 310–13. This distinction agrees with Ibn Sīnā's differentiation between simile and metaphor (see Chapter 2). Simile continues to be treated as a non-significatory figure later in the science of *bayān*, although some *balāgha* scholars disagree with this assessment (see below).

[24] al-Jurjānī, *Asrār*, 84.

between several matters.[25] Each side of an analogy therefore inevitably requires a sentence to describe the state between matters where the aspect of similarity arises.[26] However, analogy can function as a "signifier" when the compared phrase is omitted and the phrase it is compared to replaces it and "signifies" it as a unit. An example would be saying "I see you placing one foot forward and one back (أراك تقدّمُ رِجْلاً وتُؤخِّرُ أُخْرَى)," as opposed to mentioning both parts of the analogy: "he is in his hesitation like one who is putting one foot forward and one back." In the former, the phrase describing the *secundum comparatum* of the analogy is applied to the subject directly, replacing the description of the actual behavior of hesitation. In this case, the whole phrase "placing one foot forward and one back," as a single unit, functions as a sign that signifies hesitation. When both parts of the analogy are stated, on the other hand, the point of the sentence becomes the declaration of the similarity itself.[27] Employing the *secundum comparatum* of an analogy in place of the *primum comparandum*, therefore, makes it function as a unit like a metaphor in that it signifies something other than its literal meaning. Al-Jurjānī therefore calls it a "metaphorical analogy" (*tamthīl ʿalā ḥadd al-istiʿāra*).[28] A regular analogy, on the other hand, like simile, is a *statement* of similarity.

***

In sum, what al-Jurjānī calls the meaning of meaning (*maʿnā al-maʿnā*) involves an indirect process of signification. It encompasses any speech whose lexical meaning is not what is intended. Rather, the intended meaning is something to which this lexical meaning points. The connection between the lexical and this secondary meaning can be based on various types of association. A metaphor is a kind of indirect signification that is based on an association of similarity. A metaphorical analogy is when the similarity lies in a relationship between matters expressed by a phrase, as opposed to a single word. In this case, the phrase as a unit functions as a metaphorical sign. Associations not based on similarity are still considered figurative speech (*majāz*), but not metaphors (*istiʿāra*). The secondary meaning can also be implied through a nonfigurative, often causal, relationship it has with the lexical meaning, in which case it is *kināya* (metonymy). In all these literary devices, the word or phrase replaces an existing word or phrase that expresses the intended meaning directly, and instead

[25] Ibid., 90. [26] Ibid., 96. [27] See al-Jurjānī, *Dalāʾil*, 68–9.
[28] Ibid., 68. Metaphorical analogy is described by later authors as *majāz murakkab* (compound figurative speech) (al-Khaṭīb al-Qazwīnī, *al-Īḍāḥ*, 438–43).

conveys it indirectly. Simile and a nonmetaphorical analogy do not involve such a process of indirect signification, as we have seen. This distinction is significant because the mechanisms of elucidation that allow *majāz* and *kināya* to produce an experience of discovery in the listener are different from simile and nonmetaphorical analogy. The former lies in their signifying meaning indirectly, while the latter lies in the statement of comparison itself.

Indirect Signification and Eloquence

Al-Jurjānī states: "Everyone agrees that implied meaning is more eloquent than being explicit, allusion is better than spelling [something] out, metaphor has distinction and merit, and that figurative speech is always more eloquent than literal [speech]."[29] Why is that? Al-Jurjānī argues that the distinction that metaphor and metonymy have over literal and explicit speech lies in *the way* they affirm the meaning, not the affirmed meaning itself.[30] The distinction in saying "his ashes are plentiful" does not lie in the fact that it indicates more generosity, but that it indicates generosity through evidence that points to it. The meaning is therefore expressed in a way that renders its expression more secure and forceful.[31] Similarly, when you say "I saw a lion," you imply that the man you saw is indistinguishable from a lion in his bravery and courage. Metaphor, therefore, further affirms the equation between the two things compared by rendering one the other.[32] However, distinction in metaphorical speech is not due to the fact that "metaphor [. . .] necessitates a strong resemblance and having the *primum comparandum* be indistinguishable from the *secundum comparatum*."[33] If this were the case, then spelling out the indistinguishability (by saying "I saw a man equal to a lion in courage, so much so that, were it not for his form, you would have thought you were seeing an [actual] lion") would be as eloquent as saying "I saw a lion."[34] This is not the case. The reason is that the equation between the man and the lion in "I saw a lion" is known by way of meaning (*maʿnā*), whereas in "I saw a man equal to a lion," it is known by way of the words.[35] That is, metaphor requires a mental process of deducing the associations between meanings, while literal speech does not, even if they both express the same degree of indistinguishability.

[29] al-Jurjānī, *Dalāʾil*, 70. [30] Ibid., 71–2 (emphasis added). [31] Ibid., 71. [32] Ibid., 72. [33] Ibid., 448. [34] Ibid., 449. [35] Ibid.

What is significant about metonymy and metaphor is therefore not simply the added affirmation of a meaning, which could just as firmly be spelled out. Rather, it is the way meaning is grasped through them and the fact that "you know the meaning [in both metaphor and metonymy] through reasoning (*al-maʿqūl*), not through the word (*lafẓ*)."[36] The same goes for metaphorical analogy, he goes on to explain. The beauty of *kināya* and *majāz* is hence due to the fact that they require a process of interpretation, analysis (*taʾwīl*), and deduction (*istidlāl*) that direct signification does not.[37] The choice of words, therefore, when their employment remains at a literal level, does not enhance eloquence. However, when words are employed in a way that requires the listener to go through a process of deducing (and discovering) the intended meaning through their lexical meaning, either figuratively or implicitly, the eloquence of speech is elevated. Given that elevated eloquence comes with increased pleasure, I read the attribution of the eloquence of *majāz* and *kināya* to a process of deduction and discovery as a further indication that this pleasure is characterized by wonder.[38]

What Makes One Metaphor Better than Another?

While saying something figuratively is by definition more eloquent than spelling it out, not just any indirect signification necessarily enhances eloquence. Al-Jurjānī distinguishes between "informative" metaphors (*al-istiʿāra al-mufīda*) and "uninformative" ones (*ghayr al-mufīda*). The former is based on some transference of meaning, while the latter is purely acoustic (saying hoof for foot, for example, for the sake of the meter or rhyme).[39] Moreover, there are matters that can render one metaphor better than another. These have to do with increased effort

[36] Ibid., 440. Cf. Key, *Language between God and the Poets*, 220ff., who emphasizes the role of lexical accuracy in al-Jurjānī's conception of metaphorical language.

[37] See al-Jurjānī, *Dalāʾil*, 262–3, 431. In *Asrār al-balāgha*, al-Jurjānī defines *majāz* as "any statement whose meaning you extract through the mind as a result of a kind of interpretation (*taʾawwul*)" (al-Jurjānī, *Asrār*, 356). The term *taʾawwul* is treated in Abu Deeb, "al-Jurjānī's Classification of *Istiʿāra*." Incidentally, the original sense of the word "*majāz*" in early Arabic texts is equivalent to "interpretation." It is only later that it came to denote a figurative kind of expression, as Heinrichs has shown in "The ḥaqîqa-majâz Dichotomy." See also Shukrī al-Mabkhūt's application of the notion of deduction (*istidlāl*) in his interpretation of al-Jurjānī's concept of "meaning of meaning" (*al-Istidlāl al-balāghī* (Beirut: Dār al-Kutub al-Jadīda al-Muttaḥida, 2010), 27–58).

[38] Cf. ʿUṣfūr, *al-Ṣūra al-fanniyya*, 323–8.

[39] al-Jurjānī, *Asrār*, 25–40.

to discovery and increased strangeness and rarity – all wonder-enhancing elements.[40]

Al-Jurjānī explains in his *Dalāʾil* that metaphors range from the common and overused (such as saying "I saw a lion") to the rare and innovative. One of the ways of rendering even a common metaphor strange is through sentence construction, something we will learn more about in Chapter 5. In his discussion of the following hemistich, which we have seen discussed by Ibn Rushd as well, al-Jurjānī emphasizes that the "strangeness" is not due to some unusual similarity it exposes through metaphor, but to its particular sentence structure:[41]

وسَالَتْ بأعناقِ المَطِيِّ الأَباطحُ

as the broad valleys flowed with the necks of camels[42]

~ Kuthayyir ʿAzza (d. 105/723)

He states:

[The poet] did not render [the statement] strange because he made the camels in the speed and ease of their gait resemble water flowing in the valley, for this is a known and obvious similarity. Rather because of the subtlety and detail in a particularity that he conveyed by making "flow" the verb for "valleys" and then following it with [the preposition] "with," and inserting "necks" in between, saying "with the necks of camels" as opposed to "with camels." If the poet said: "the camels flowed in the valleys," it would not be anything [special].[43]

However, poets can also innovate in metaphor by exposing strangeness in the similarity itself, as in the following verse, in which the poet brags about

[40] Abu Deeb also recognizes the role of strangeness in enhancing the pleasure resulting from metaphor. Speaking of metaphor, he says "al-Jurjānī tries to discover the impact of the nature of the dominant trait and its two most important features which determine the emotional and aesthetic effect on the recipient, namely its degree of exaggeration and fusion between the referents of metaphor, and its remoteness and strangeness, which make it more pleasant" ("al-Jurjānī's Classification of *Istiʿāra*," 61). He goes on to explain in a footnote that he means by remoteness and strangeness "the degree of remoteness of *istiʿāra* from plain statement and the degree of the intellectual effort required to perceive it and to comprehend it" (ibid., 61n2).

[41] al-Jurjānī, *Dalāʾil*, 75. The verse is also cited in his discussion of figurative governing of speech (*majāz ḥukmī*) (ibid., 296), which I discuss in Chapter 5.

[42] The first hemistich is: "We took to the choicest of speech between us (أخذنا بأطراف الأحاديث بيننا)." Ibn Rushd discusses this verse as an example of his concept of *taghyīr* (alteration), in *Kitāb al-shiʿr*, 122. See also al-Jurjānī's extensive analysis of this verse and the two that precede it in Kuthayyir's poem in *Asrār*, 21–4.

[43] al-Jurjānī, *Dalāʾil*, 75–6. See ibid., 104–5, for other examples of sentence construction revamping hackneyed old metaphors.

his horse's obedience, stating that he does not need to tether it when he leaves it standing outside while he visits friends:

وَإِذَا احْتَبَى قَرَبُوسُهُ بِعِنَانِهِ   عَلَكَ الشَّكِيمَ إِلَى انْصِرَافِ الزَّائِرِ

And when its saddle binds (*iḥtabā*) itself with its rein [like
a man squatting with the support of a strap]
He chews his [bridle's] bit until the visitor's departure
~ Yazīd ibn Maslama ibn ʿAbd al-Malik (fl. early second/eighth century)

This requires some explanation. The poet, when visiting friends (we learn from the preceding verse not quoted here), can leave the horse with the reins freely resting on the saddle. The horse is so well-behaved that it does nothing except chew the bit in its mouth until the poet (the visitor) completes his visit and decides to leave. The metaphor lies in the word I am loosely translating as "to bind" (*iḥtabā*), which in Arabic refers specifically to the act of drawing one's knees up against the belly while sitting on the ground and holding them in place with one's garment or with a special cloth strap that goes around one's back, providing support when there is nothing to lean on.[44] The word *iḥtabā*, which is impossible to translate as a single word in English, conjures up the image of a man sitting on the floor with his knees bent and bound to his back with his garment or a cloth strap. Al-Jurjānī states that the strangeness in this verse lies in the similarity the poet exposes between the "state of the reins in their placement on the saddle [and] the state of the placement of [the hem of] the garment in relation to the seated person's knees."[45] This similarity certainly requires some contemplation to grasp, which is precisely what renders the strangeness of this metaphor praiseworthy.

Al-Jurjānī goes on to explain that "one of the foundations of excellence in metaphor is when you find that the poet has combined several metaphors, with the aim of matching the shape to the shape to complete the meaning and similarity of what he intends."[46] As an example of this, he cites a famous and much discussed verse from Imruʾ al-Qays's *muʿallaqa*, in which he describes the dark imposing night:

فَقُلْتُ لَهُ لَمَّا تَمَطَّى بِصُلْبِهِ   وَأَرْدَفَ أَعْجَازاً وَنَاءَ بِكَلْكَلِ

[44] The practice is still present today in Hadramawt in Yemen. The strap used for such a form of sitting is called a *ḥabwa*.
[45] al-Jurjānī, *Dalāʾil*, 75. [46] Ibid., 79.

I said to it when it stretched its back
  made its hindquarters follow and sunk its chest[47]

Al-Jurjānī explains that the poet:

gave the night a back with which to stretch, doubled that and gave it hindquarters to go with the back, and tripled it by giving it a chest with which to weigh down, completing for him all components of a body, and [keeping into] consideration what an onlooker would see of its blackness when he looks in front of him, to the back, or if he raises his gaze and stretches it the breadth of the sky.[48]

Later, al-Khaṭīb al-Qazwīnī lists this method of combining metaphors to produce a single image among the strangeness-enhancing techniques of metaphor.[49]

While in the *Dalāʾil* al-Jurjānī discusses metaphor primarily from the aspect of its function as a "meaning of meaning," he provides us with details about the nature of the similarity on which metaphors can be based in his *Asrār.* He explains that metaphors range in materiality from sensed/perceptible truths (*al-maḥsūs*) to abstract/intellected ideas (*al-maʿqūl*).[50] Intellected matters are based on a similarity that lies in a mental image that connects two matters, such as knowledge and light. While light is something that can be physically sensed, knowledge cannot.[51] Al-Jurjānī declares that the intellected type "is the level at which a metaphor reaches its utmost dignity and in which the possibilities for creativity expand as it wishes."[52] Thus, he implies that, like with similes,

47 The word *naʾā*, which I am translating here as "sunk," could mean to weigh down, to raise, or to become distant (Lane, s.v. *n-w-ʾ*). The verse has been interpreted in different ways with all these different meanings. I chose to follow al-Jurjānī's understanding of it as weighing down. In contrast, al-Khaṭīb al-Tibrīzī (d. 502/1109), for example, in his commentary on the *muʿallaqāt* understands it as a camel's "rising" (*Sharḥ al-qaṣāʾid al-ʿashr* (Cairo: Idārat al-Ṭibāʿa al-Munīriyya, 1933), 35–6). Alan Jones translates it as follows: "I said to it when it stretched its loins, and then raised its buttocks behind and then removed its chest" (*Early Arabic Poetry: Selected Poems*, 357). For an overview of the various discussions of this verse in literary criticism, see Heinrichs, *Hand of the Northwind*, 16–25.

48 al-Jurjānī, *Dalāʾil*, 79. While al-Jurjānī emphasizes the strangeness with which the combination of these various elements endows the metaphor, al-Āmidī and al-Qāḍī al-Jurjānī, for example, emphasize the closeness of the resemblance in the metaphor and its truthfulness (*al-Muwāzana*, 1:266; *al-Wasāṭa*, 358). Al-Jurjānī's explanation reflects a concern with an aesthetic of wonder, while al-Āmidī's and al-Qāḍī al-Jurjānī's assessment of the verse, with their concern for its truthfulness and the closeness of the resemblance it proposes, reflects the old-school framework of thinking.

49 al-Khaṭīb al-Qazwīnī, *al-Īḍāḥ*, 425–6.

50 See Chapter 3 for the various definitions of perceptible and intellected matters.

51 al-Jurjānī, *Asrār*, 51–80. Abu Deeb discusses the various types of metaphor from the aspect of the similarity on which they are based in "al-Jurjānī's Classification of *Istiʿāra*," 69–70.

52 al-Jurjānī, *Asrār*, 60.

metaphors based on abstract ideas that need to be imagined are better than ones based on matters readily perceptible through the senses. Ultimately, all the discussions concerning simile, outlined in Chapter 3, apply to metaphor. However, al-Jurjānī clarifies that not all similes work well as metaphors. Similes that require clarification would not be good candidates for omitting the *primum comparandum* altogether.[53] The similarity between the *primum comparandum* and the *secundum comparatum* in a metaphor has to be close and obvious enough.[54]

The act of comparing itself, however, should not be obvious. For a metaphor to have its effect, the listener needs to be able to forget that there is a comparison. If he is reminded of the status of the metaphor as a mere comparison, then it is ugly.[55] In the end, therefore, the similarity itself is not what gives metaphor distinction, rather its beauty lies in its function as an indirect signifier. If you spell it out, it turns ugly. To illustrate this point, al-Jurjānī asks us to consider the metaphors in the following verse:[56]

أَثْمَرَتْ أَغْصَانُ رَاحَتِهِ　　لِجُنَاةِ الحُسْنِ عُنَّابَا

The branches of his hand bore
  jujubes for the harvesters of beauty

~ Ibn al-Muʿtazz (d. 296/908)

He explains:

Don't you see that if you took it upon yourself to expose the similarity and express it explicitly, you would have to say: "the fingers of his hand, which resemble branches, bore fruits, for the seekers of beauty, that look like jujubes because of their [henna-]dyed ends." The ugliness in this is obvious.[57]

The similarity between the metaphor and the original matter it replaces is therefore not necessarily what makes it beautiful. Even comparisons that are ugly when spelled out become beautiful if expressed through metaphor. It is therefore the process of discovering the meaning, rather than the meaning per se, which defines the essence of the beauty of metaphor.

***

Figurative speech and metonymy, therefore, are words or compound word units that signify meaning in an indirect way through logical associations between the literal meaning and the intended meaning. The process of grasping the associations that a poet invokes to get at the intended meaning allows the listener to go through an experience of discovery. This process

[53] Ibid., 230. [54] Ibid., 224–5. [55] al-Jurjānī, *Dalāʾil*, 450. [56] Ibid., 451. [57] Ibid.

of discovery is what renders such indirect signification inherently more pleasing and the reason it enhances eloquence. The less obvious and more arduous the road to discovery, the more wonder-evoking it is.

ʿILM AL-BAYĀN (THE SCIENCE OF ELUCIDATION)

The literary devices discussed by al-Jurjānī under the rubric of "the meaning of meaning" form the basic components of the science of elucidation (*ʿilm al-bayān*), when it becomes formalized as a branch of the science of eloquence (*ʿilm al-balāgha*). We have seen in Chapter 3 that the concept of *bayān* changes in scope over the centuries. It starts out in al-Jāḥiẓ's works meaning anything that functions as a sign, including hand gestures and things in nature. By the time al-Sakkākī uses it as a technical term, it refers to the scholarly inquiry into the aesthetics of linguistic signification.[58] The idea of elucidation and uncovering something hidden, discussed in Chapter 3, remains central. However, it is adapted to describe the process of signification in words – a process whose link with eloquence agrees with al-Jurjānī's aesthetic outlook.

*Definition of the Science of Elucidation (*ʿIlm al-Bayān*)*

The way al-Sakkākī and his commentators describe *ʿilm al-bayān* reveals that the central aspect of the science for them was the process of "intellecting" meaning. Al-Sakkākī, as well as al-Khaṭīb al-Qazwīnī, defines it as the science of "knowing how to convey the same meaning in different ways, by increasing the clarity in the way it is signified or decreasing it."[59] The clarity of a word's signification cannot vary at the level of its lexical signification (*al-dalālāt al-waḍʿiyya*), they go on to explain, because a word at that level corresponds to what it signifies.[60] There is no difference in the clarity of signification between one word and its synonym, as long as the listener knows their meanings. Otherwise, nothing would be understood in the first place. Meanings that the listener has to deduce

[58] Thomas Bauer hence describes *ʿilm al-bayān* as "Referenzrhetorik" (*Rhetorik, außereuropäische: V. Arabische Kultur*, 127).

[59] al-Sakkākī, *al-Miftāḥ*, 249. Al-Khaṭīb al-Qazwīnī's definition is similar (*al-Īḍāḥ*, 326).

[60] The coined signification (*al-dalāla al-waḍʿiyya*) is a signification by correspondence (*dalālat muṭābaqa*) (al-Sakkākī, *al-Miftāḥ*, 437; al-Khaṭīb al-Qazwīnī, *al-Īḍāḥ*, 326). This conception of language and signification as well as the terminology are clearly derived from Arabic philosophy. See, for example, Ibn Sīnā's definition of the relationship between a word and its signification in *al-Ishārāt*, 187.

through various associations, on the other hand, can be more or less clear, depending on the clarity or obscurity of these associations.[61] Such a form of signification is called "intellected signification" (*dalāla ʿaqliyya*).[62]

Counterintuitively, therefore, *ʿilm al-bayān*, which literally means the science of "elucidation" or "clarification," is really about elucidating meaning in an *indirect* way. Wolfhart Heinrichs's description of the science as the "indirect presentation by way of images" and Udo Simon's translation in German as "die Wissenschaft von der (indirekten) Darstellung" are, therefore, among the most accurate.[63] The kinds of speech that present meaning indirectly include figurative speech (*majāz*) – which incorporates metaphor (*istiʿāra*) – and implied meaning (*kināya*). These all function at the level of individual words or word compounds that function as single units, which signify their intended meanings through some association between them and their lexical meanings. Although simile is included as one of the main figures of *bayān*, its inclusion is typically justified for its being the basis of metaphor[64] (more on this below). However, simile does not signify meaning in the same way as the other *bayān* figures. This is because, as we have seen in our discussion of al-Jurjānī, it is a declaration of similarity; not a form of signification founded on the presumed presence of a similarity, like metaphor.[65]

Signification and Deduction

ʿIlm al-bayān, therefore, is not lexicography. That is, it is not the science of how words signify their lexical meanings, something that is set by linguistic convention. Rather, it is the science of a word's signification beyond its lexical meaning in ways that need to be deduced or "intellected." More specifically, it is the study of how words signify meanings through associations between the intended indirect meaning and the literal meaning of a word or group of words. Al-Sakkākī sums this up as follows:

[61] al-Sakkākī, *al-Miftāḥ*, 437. See also Smyth's detailed explanation of the levels of signification in Smyth, "Canonical Formulation," 15–21.

[62] I adopt Smyth's translation of *ʿaqlī* (lit. of the mind) as "intellected," which best conveys the reasoning required in the mind to deduce such secondary meanings of a word, which leads al-Sakkākī to call them "*ʿaqlī*" (through the mind) (Smyth, "Canonical Formulation," 17).

[63] Wolfhart Heinrichs, al-Sakkākī, in EI^2; and *Arabische Dichtung*, 78. Udo Gerald Simon, *Mittelalterliche arabische Sprachbetrachtung zwischen Grammatik und Rhetorik: ʿilm al-maʿānī bei as-Sakkākī* (Heidelberg: Heidelberger Orientverlag, 1993), 61.

[64] See al-Sakkākī, *al-Miftāḥ*, 439; al-Khaṭīb al-Qazwīnī, *al-Īḍāḥ*, 327.

[65] Al-Sakkākī and al-Khaṭīb al-Qazwīnī agree with al-Jurjānī on this distinction and discuss it extensively (al-Sakkākī, *al-Miftāḥ*, 477–80; al-Khaṭīb al-Qazwīnī, *al-Īḍāḥ*, 409–415).

If you know that conveying a single meaning in a variety of forms does not take place except through intellected significations – which constitute the transfer from one meaning to another because of a relationship between them, as when one necessitates the other in some respect – it becomes clear that *'ilm al-bayān* is based on considering the associations between meanings.[66]

Al-Sakkākī develops what al-Jurjānī had started by honing in on these associations between meanings that need to be intellected with the mind. The difference between *majāz* and *kināya* as understood by al-Jurjānī is maintained. Al-Sakkākī and al-Khaṭīb al-Qazwīnī, however, add details to their discussion of the kinds of relationships that can exist in the first place between a signifier and its literal meaning, which shed light on their understanding of the processes of signification.

Al-Sakkākī defines literal meaning (*ḥaqīqa*) as "the word when used for what it was coined, without interpretation (*ta'wīl*) [playing a role] in this coining."[67] These links between signifier and signified (*al-dalīl wa-l-madlūl*) are set arbitrarily by convention.[68] There is nothing in the "sound image" of the signifier that leads one logically to its meaning.[69] One either knows it or does not. However, al-Sakkākī does leave a place for the sounds of the letters of the alphabet in signification and argues that the difference in harshness or softness of the phonemes that make up a word does sometimes influence the meaning a specific "sound image" signifies. For example, he suggests that it is acoustically appropriate that the word "*faṣm*," with an "f," which is a softer-sounding phoneme, denote cracking something without breaking it, while the word "*quṣm*," with the harsher-sounding phoneme "q," denote full breakage. The harsher sound corresponds with a harsher meaning.[70] In

[66] al-Sakkākī, *al-Miftāḥ*, 438.

[67] Ibid., 467. *Haqīqa*, which can also mean "truth," when juxtaposed with *majāz* means literal meaning. For a discussion of this pairing, see Heinrichs, "The ḥaqîqa-majâz Dichotomy." Alexander Key argues for generally interpreting *ḥaqīqa* as "accuracy" in *Language between God and the Poets*. In this case, it would refer to the accurate lexical meaning of a word.

[68] The setter of these connections between the signifier and signified can be (a) the establisher of language, in which case it is lexical (*lughawī*), (b) the jurisprudent, in which case it is legal (*shar'ī*), or (c) it could simply be based on custom (*'urfī*) (al-Sakkākī, *al-Miftāḥ*, 467). *Majāz* (lit. surpassing), in turn, is "going beyond" these meanings as set in the lexicon, in the law, or by custom.

[69] I borrow the term "sound image" from Saussure. For an analysis of theories of signification from a linguistics angle, see Ahmed Moutaouakil, *Réflexions sur la théorie de la signification dans la pensée linguistique arabe* (Rabat: Faculté des Lettres et des Sciences Humaines de Rabat, 1982).

[70] The role of the sounds of letters is something al-Jurjānī categorically dismisses, as we have seen above. His contemporary, Ibn Sinān al-Khafājī, however, dedicates a long chapter to the quality of the various sounds of letters in his *Sirr al-faṣāḥa*. This likely influenced later

the same vein, the morphological forms of words have characteristics that affect the meaning of specific sound images in ways that are more intentional.[71]

Nevertheless, despite the acknowledgment that the relationship between signifier and signified might be less arbitrary than al-Jurjānī would have it, the listener's grasp of this relationship remains something learned, not something that can be logically deduced or "intellected." Moreover, such words signify their meanings by total correspondence (*muṭābaqa*), as opposed to those that signify meaning through some association or relationship, which would amount to more or less than the total correspondence.[72]

Associations between meanings are of two types, they go on to explain. The literal meaning could form a part of the intended meaning, such as "roof" encompassing the concept of "house" (*taḍammun*), or the literal meaning could have an association with something external to it (*iltizām*). External associations of *iltizām* require that the listener be able to infer the relationship in order to arrive at the intended meaning. This inference may be something that passes muster with the rational mind (*ʿaql*), i.e., based on logical associations; or it could be based on the addressee's beliefs, either as a result of custom or otherwise. In this case, "the speaker can entice in his addressee [such an association] because of the soundness of the move in his thought (*dhihn*) from the original concept to the other through that association between the two in his belief."[73] The move from the literal meaning to its associated meaning could either be one from antecedent (*malzūm*) to consequent (*lāzim*) or the other way around.[74] Al-Sakkākī and al-Khaṭīb al-Qazwīnī then

authors such as al-Sakkākī. Before al-Sakkākī, Fakhr al-Dīn al-Rāzī also accounts for sound in his *Nihāyat al-ījāz*. Later commentators, such as al-Taftāzānī, delve into this discussion even further incorporating, among others, "natural" signifiers such as saying "*akh*" for pain, which are not as arbitrary in their signification, thus expanding the understanding of the relationship between signifier and signified (al-Taftāzānī, *al-Muṭawwal*, 507).

[71] al-Sakkākī, *al-Miftāḥ*, 466; al-Khaṭīb al-Qazwīnī, *al-Īḍāḥ*, 394.

[72] al-Sakkākī, *al-Miftāḥ*, 437; al-Khaṭīb al-Qazwīnī, *al-Īḍāḥ*, 326.

[73] al-Sakkākī, *al-Miftāḥ*, 437. Al-Khaṭīb al-Qazwīnī highlights a distinction between *ʿaql* and *dhihn*, both meaning the mind or the intellect (see also *al-Īḍāḥ*, 326). See also definitions in al-Sayyid al-Sharīf al-Jurjānī, *Muʿjam al-taʿrīfāt*, ed. Muḥammad Ṣiddīq al-Minshāwī (Cairo: Dār al-Faḍīla, 2004), 94 and 128.

[74] Al-Sakkākī suggests that *majāz* is a move from antecedent (*malzūm*) to consequent (*lāzim*), while *kināya* is a move from consequent (*lāzim*) to antecedent (*malzūm*) (al-Sakkākī, *al-Miftāḥ*, 438). This does not hold true absolutely as later commentators show (al-Khaṭīb al-Qazwīnī, *al-Īḍāḥ*, 456–7; al-Taftāzānī, *al-Muṭawwal*, 631; al-Sayyid al-Sharīf al-Jurjānī, *al-Miṣbāḥ*, 498).

proceed to describe the main figures of *bayān* based on the kinds of associations they elicit from the listener.

This association could be metonymic (*kināya*), in which case the literal meaning remains in place, but the intended meaning is something that one infers from it; or the association replaces the literal meaning completely, in which case it is figurative speech (*majāz*). As with al-Jurjānī, if the figurativeness is based on a relationship of similarity, it is metaphor (*istiʿāra*). Any other kind of figurative association is called *majāz mursal* (unrestricted figurative speech). *Majāz mursal*, in turn, could include relationships of external associations (*iltizām*) or could encompass the secondary meaning internally (*taḍammun*), such as using the part for the whole (i.e., synecdoche), among others.[75] Metaphorical analogy comes to be described as "compound figurative speech" (*majāz murakkab*) by al-Khaṭīb al-Qazwīnī.[76] The main difference between *kināya* and *majāz* is that the secondary meaning does not negate the accuracy of the literal meaning in the case of *kināya*. Whereas in *majāz*, the literal meaning cannot be taken as literally accurate.

The seeds of all these distinctions can be seen in al-Jurjānī's work. Al-Sakkākī and al-Khaṭīb al-Qazwīnī, however, further distinguish the kinds of relationships that can exist between a primary signification of a word and its secondary meaning. The process of deduction is emphasized to the extent that al-Sakkākī deems it necessary to add a chapter on deduction (*istidlāl*) in his book, in which he applies syllogistic reasoning to these forms of indirect signification.[77] The logical turn is something that has often been lamented by modern scholars as signaling the ossification of the Arabic inquiry into eloquence.[78] However, it is precisely the process of deduction and interpretation that figurative speech and metonymy require which forms the essence of their poeticity, as we will see next.

ʿIlm al-Bayān *and Eloquence*

Know that the masters of eloquence [...] are undivided on [the idea] that figurative speech (*majāz*) is more eloquent than the literal, metaphor (*istiʿāra*)

[75] al-Khaṭīb al-Qazwīnī, *al-Īḍāḥ*, 399–403. [76] Ibid., 438–43.

[77] al-Sakkākī, *al-Miftāḥ*, 607–9. See Shukrī al-Mabkhūt's analysis of *istidlāl* as it applies to *majāz* and *kināya* in al-Sakkākī in *al-Istidlāl al-balāghī*, 84–9.

[78] See, for example, Aḥmad Maṭlūb, *al-Balāgha ʿind al-Sakkākī* (Baghdad: Maktabat al-Nahḍa, 1964); and Shawqī Ḍayf, *al-Balāgha: Taṭawwur wa-tārīkh*, 9th ed. (Cairo: Dār al-Maʿārif, 1995). See al-Mabkhūt's criticism of this characterization of al-Sakkākī and *ʿilm al-balāgha* in *al-Istidlāl al-balāghī*, 68–73.

is more powerful than spelling something out through comparison (*tashbīh*), and that metonymy (*kināya*) is more striking than disclosing through [explicit] statement.[79]

This opinion of al-Sakkākī is indeed voiced unequivocally by all our authors. Why would signifying meaning indirectly contribute to eloquence? Citing al-Jurjānī, al-Khaṭīb al-Qazwīnī reminds us that:

This is not because one of these [forms of signification] conveys something additional to the meaning itself that its counterpart does not. Rather it is because it provides a validation (*ta'kīd*) for the ascription (*ithbāt*) of the meaning that the other does not. The merit of saying "I saw a lion" over saying "I saw a man who is equal to a lion in his courage" is not that the former conveys something extra in the equation between him and the lion in terms of courage that the latter does not. Rather, it is that the former provides a validation of the ascription of this equation to [the lion] that the latter does not. In addition, the merit of saying "he has abundant ashes" over saying "he is very hospitable" is not that the former conveys an additional sense of hospitality that the latter does not; rather, the former provides a validation for the ascription (*ithbāt*) of hospitality to it that the latter does not.[80]

When al-Khaṭīb al-Qazwīnī speaks of "ascribing the meaning (*ithbāt al-ma'nā*)" in this context, he refers to the linguistic process of signification. He is not talking about an external meaning that is being confirmed with more or less evidence. The "validation of the ascription of meaning" he speaks of is in the relationship between a word and what it signifies. This relationship is substantiated in the case of figurative speech and metonymy because there is a deducible association between the primary meaning of a word and the intended meaning. When a word signifies its meaning directly, on the other hand, the connection between signifier and signified is arbitrary, as we have learned. Al-Sakkākī explains that expressing a meaning through figurative speech or metonymy is like "claiming something through evidence. For the presence of the antecedent (*malzūm*) is witness to the presence of the consequent (*lāzim*)."[81] There is nothing added to the overall meaning being signified, in other words, but the way it is signified is more justified in the case of indirect signification.

Al-Sayyid al-Sharīf explains more explicitly that preference is given to figurative speech and metonymy "in terms of the validation and strength of the signification (*dalāla*) [...], not in terms of an increase in the signified (*madlūl*)."[82] Signifying something indirectly through metaphor (or

[79] al-Sakkākī, *al-Miftāḥ*, 523. [80] al-Khaṭīb al-Qazwīnī, *al-Īḍāḥ*, 468.
[81] al-Sakkākī, *al-Miftāḥ*, 523. [82] al-Sayyid al-Sharīf al-Jurjānī, *al-Ḥāshiya*, 408.

figurative speech generally speaking) and metonymy is counterintuitively a more substantiated form of signification, therefore, than direct signification. This is because the signification depends on a logical relationship between the literal meaning and the intended meaning, rather than on one arbitrarily set by convention. What is significant about this with respect to eloquence is not that the signification is firmer but that it is graspable through deduction rather than learned.

Al-Khaṭīb al-Qazwīnī's contemporary, Muḥammad ibn ʿAlī al-Jurjānī,[83] the author of *al-Ishārāt wa-l-tanbīhāt fī ʿilm al-balāgha* (*Pointers and Reminders on the Science of Eloquence*), explains:

> The merit of intellected signification (*al-dalāla al-ʿaqliyya*) over that which is set purely by convention (*al-waḍʿiyya*) [is that in a] signification, when it depends on the handling of the mind, the signified is more striking to the soul, and more pleasing to one's nature.[84]

Elsewhere he asks rhetorically, "Don't you see how the soul finds pleasure in acquired knowledge and not the necessary [ones]."[85] In fact, he criticizes his contemporary, al-Khaṭīb al-Qazwīnī, for basing his definition of *ʿilm al-bayān* on variation in clarity of signification and suggests that a more accurate definition "does not look into intellected significations from the aspect of clarity or lack thereof, rather from the aspect of the soul's pleasure in them."[86]

[83] Not to be confused with ʿAbd al-Qāhir al-Jurjānī.

[84] Muḥammad ibn ʿAlī al-Jurjānī, *al-Ishārāt wa-l-tanbīhāt fī ʿilm al-balāgha*, ed. ʿAbd al-Qādir Ḥusayn (Cairo: Dār Nahdat Misr, 1982), 249.

[85] Ibid., 170. This view has him even exclude associations based on a relationship of encompassment (*taḍammun*), which al-Sakkākī and al-Khaṭīb al-Qazwīnī include as a type of intellected signification. Muḥammad ibn ʿAlī al-Jurjānī says that the relationship of encompassment is "too natural" of an association for the listener to find pleasure in it (ibid.). Nevertheless, most of the associations the main *balāgha* authors discuss are ones based on external relationships of necessity or consequence (*iltizām*).

[86] Ibid., 169. When assessing aesthetic sensibility in al-Sakkākī and al-Khaṭīb al-Qazwīnī's works, it is often assumed that they base their evaluation on clarity. Smyth states, for example, "it is interesting to note [. . .] that al-Sakkākī makes no mention of *istiḥsān* [finding beautiful] in his definition of *al-bayān*. There is, to be sure, variety in *al-bayān*, but it lies in *wuḍū[ḥ]* (clarity) rather than *ḥusn* [beauty]" (Smyth, "Canonical Formulation," 23n28). Beauty, however, does not lie in clarity in and of itself; rather, in the fact that variation in clarity can exist in intellected meanings. Variation in clarity is only possible at the level of intellected signification because it is based on logical associations a poet adduces through metaphor and metonymy. The very fact that there can be variation in the clarity of these associations (as opposed to lexical meaning which entails complete correspondence) and that the intended meaning is one that is deducible through intellectual reasoning is what renders these figures aesthetically pleasing, as we will see.

Even though Muḥammad ibn ʿAlī's *Ishārāt* did not have the same degree of influence as al-Sakkākī's and al-Khaṭīb al-Qazwīnī's works on eloquence, whose definitions of the science of *bayān* were almost always adopted by later commentators, his intervention is revealing. His definition, which attributes aesthetic pleasure to the very process of intellection that indirect signification allows the listener to go through, indicates that what is beautiful about the "validation of ascription of meaning" with which figurative speech and metonymy endow signification is the process of ascription, not the ascription itself. This process of ascription is based on a logical relationship that the listener has to deduce in order to grasp the intended meaning. The pleasure resulting from figurative and implicit expressions, therefore, is due to the experience of discovery (and wonder) these figures by definition allow in the listener. The more delayed this process of discovery is, the more pleasing it is, as we will see in the next section.

Variation in Bayān

Figurative speech and metonymy are by definition more eloquent than direct signification, as we have seen. Indirect signification is inherently wonder-evoking because it allows for an experience of discovery. Like with simile, what enhances this effect of wonder are elements that make the process of discovery less obvious and "slow it down." As Fakhr al-Dīn al-Rāzī states, variation in the eloquence of signifying words summarily amounts to a "difference in the speed and slowness [that] takes place in the grasping of meanings."[87] Indeed, al-Sakkākī and al-Khaṭīb al-Qazwīnī differentiate the quality of the various *bayān* figures in light of their commonness and strangeness, as well as other matters that can delay discovery. In what follows, I will focus on aspects that affect the beauty of metaphor (*istiʿāra*) and metonymy (*kināya*).

Metaphor (*Istiʿāra*)

Al-Khaṭīb al-Qazwīnī classifies metaphor based on various aspects, including its commonness and uniqueness.[88] "Common hackneyed (*al-ʿāmmiyya*

[87] al-Rāzī, *Nihāyat al-ījāz*, 38.

[88] al-Khaṭīb al-Qazwīnī, *al-Īḍāḥ*, 422ff. Other aspects on which al-Khaṭīb al-Qazwīnī bases his classification of metaphor include whether the two things compared can be sensed (*ḥissī*) or are of an abstract nature (*ʿaqlī*) (ibid., 426–9). If we take into account his

al-mubtadhala)" metaphors are so for "the apparentness" of the characteristic uniting the *primum comparandum* and *secundum comparatum*. The less apparent, "unique and strange (*al-khāṣṣiyya al-gharība*)" metaphors, in contrast, are only achievable by those "who rise above the common class, like [...] those metaphors that appear in the revealed text (the Quran)."[89] Strangeness, therefore, is an attribute of excellence in metaphors.

Like al-Jurjānī, al-Khaṭīb al-Qazwīnī explains that (a) strangeness could lie in the similarity itself (like the poet's comparison of his horse's reins on the saddle to a seated person's binding strap, discussed above); (b) the similarity itself could be common but be made strange through the sentence structure (like the "camels' flowing necks in the valley" example, discussed above); (c) strangeness can be attained by combining several metaphors (such as in Imruʾ al-Qays's comparison of the night to a beast discussed above).[90] Al-Sakkākī does not go into the specifics of strangeness in metaphor, but he does say, as does al-Khaṭīb al-Qazwīnī, that the beauty of *istiʿāra* depends on the rules of beauty governing *tashbīh*.[91] So, we can assume, based on our discussion of simile in Chapter 3, that the same strange-making elements applauded in the construction of simile would be commendable in metaphor as well.

However, in the case of metaphor, the act of comparing itself must be masked. While unrestricted figurative speech (*majāz mursal*) and metonymy (*kināya*) are based on a variety of associations that lead the listener from the primary meaning to the secondary, metaphor has a very specific kind of relationship: it makes a claim that two things are so indistinguishable that they belong to the same category. When you call someone a lion you are claiming that the lion species is of two types, al-Sakkākī and al-Khaṭīb al-Qazwīnī explain: the known one, which is known for its power and courage and has a particular form (i.e., the lion as beast); and an unknown one, which has that power and courage but not the same form (i.e., the lion in the form of a brave man).[92] For such a claim to work, the *primum comparandum* or tenor (to use I. A. Richards' terminology) has to be completely out of sight. The less attention you attract to the act of

discussion of these aspects in simile, they would presumably also involve varying degrees of interpretation and thus affect the immediacy of the comprehension of metaphor.

89 Ibid., 422–3. 90 Ibid., 423–9.

91 al-Sakkākī, *al-Miftāḥ*, 497; al-Khaṭīb al-Qazwīnī, *al-Īḍāḥ*, 453.

92 al-Sakkākī, *al-Miftāḥ*, 480; al-Khaṭīb al-Qazwīnī, *al-Īḍāḥ*, 416.

comparison, the firmer is its equation of the two things compared. "Not a whiff" of the comparison in the statement "should be smelled."[93]

It is therefore commendable to add matters that further help the listener forget that the metaphor is in effect a comparison and not the real thing itself. One way of enhancing this illusion is by taking the metaphor literally and building on it. This is called "fostering or development" (*tarshīḥ*), which is defined as adding characteristics or specifications that are appropriate for that which is "borrowed" (*al-mustaʿār minhu*), i.e., the *secundum comparatum* or the vehicle (in I. A. Richards's language).[94] An example of this in the Quran lies in the following verse that sustains a commerce metaphor to describe following the right path:

أُولَٰئِكَ الَّذِينَ اشْتَرَوُا الضَّلَالَةَ بِالْهُدَىٰ فَمَا رَبِحَت تِّجَارَتُهُمْ وَمَا كَانُوا مُهْتَدِينَ

> Those who have bought error [in exchange] for guidance, their transaction did not profit, and they were not guided
>
> ~ Q2:16

Al-Khaṭīb al-Qazwīnī explains that the idea of "'buying' was borrowed for 'choice,' and it was followed up by 'profit' and 'transaction,' which are connected to buying."[95] The original metaphor of buying is therefore reinforced with matters that are associated with it later in the sentence. The basis of such reinforcement is "pretending to forget the comparison and distracting the mind from thinking of it," they explain.[96] Abū Tammām achieves this in the following verse, for example, where he metaphorically treats highness of rank as physical altitude:

ويَصْعَدُ حَتَّى يَظُنَّ الجَهُولُ   بأَنَّ لَهُ حَاجَةً في السَّمَاءِ

> And he rises so [high] that the unsuspecting would think
> that he has some business in the sky[97]

Al-Khaṭīb al-Qazwīnī explains that "were it not that his intention was to pretend to forget (*yatanāsā*) the comparison and be determined to deny it by making him rise in the sky from the aspect of spatial distance, this speech would not have any purpose."[98]

This technique of reinforcing the metaphor through fostering and developing the idea presented by the metaphor includes the rhetorical

93 al-Sakkākī, *al-Miftāḥ*, 497; al-Khaṭīb al-Qazwīnī, *al-Īḍāḥ*, 453.
94 al-Sakkākī, *al-Miftāḥ*, 494; al-Khaṭīb al-Qazwīnī, *al-Īḍāḥ*, 433–4.
95 al-Khaṭīb al-Qazwīnī, *al-Īḍāḥ*, 433–4.
96 al-Sakkākī, *al-Miftāḥ*, 494. See also al-Khaṭīb al-Qazwīnī, *al-Īḍāḥ*, 434.
97 al-Sakkākī, *al-Miftāḥ*, 494; al-Khaṭīb al-Qazwīnī, *al-Īḍāḥ*, 434. 98 Ibid.

figure known as "amazement (*taʿajjub*)," which typically entails an exclamation based on taking a metaphor literally, such as:[99]

قَامَتْ تُظَلِّلُنِي مِنَ الشَّمْسِ   نَفْسٌ أَعَزُّ عَلَيَّ مِنْ نَفْسِي
قَامَتْ تُظَلِّلُنِي ومِن عَجَبٍ   شَمْسٌ تُظَلِّلُنِي مِن الشَّمْسِ

There rose, shading me from the sun
A soul dearer to me than my own
It rose, shading me, and what wonder!
A sun shading me from the sun!

~ Ibn al-ʿAmīd (d. 360/970)[100]

These are examples of literary figures al-Jurjānī discusses under the rubric of "make-believe imagery" (*takhyīl*), which he praises for producing unexpected and innovative images that one would otherwise never imagine.[101] Al-Sakkākī and al-Khaṭīb al-Qazwīnī incorporate them under metaphor as ways of reinforcing the "make-believe" metaphoric claim.

It is also possible to keep the metaphor closer to reality by "elaborating with characteristics appropriate for the [matter] for which it was borrowed (i.e., the *primum comparandum*/tenor)."[102] When one says, for example, "I conversed with a sea, how abundant is his knowledge . . .,"[103] one's mind is immediately brought back to the actual intended meaning, away from the fantasy of the metaphor. This is called "stripping" or "denuding" (*tajrīd*) the metaphor. This type of metaphor is not as effective as the "reinforced" ones, al-Khaṭīb al Qazwīnī explains, because the latter kind confirms the exaggerated likening of the two things compared.[104] It thus follows that concealing the act of comparison as much as possible and affirming the fiction of metaphor is a condition for its beauty.

Metonymy (*Kināya*)

Kināya "is a word with which one intends [something] associated with its meaning with the possibility of intending the meaning [itself] at the [same] time."[105] This is as opposed to figurative speech, where the secondary

[99] al-Sakkākī, *al-Miftāḥ*, 495. Full citation, 479.
[100] These verses are also ascribed to Ibrāhīm ibn Hilāl al-Ṣābiʾ (see Ritter's note in al-Jurjānī, *Asrār*, 280n370; and al-Jurjānī, *Geheimnisse*, 327–8).
[101] See Chapter 1. For al-Jurjānī's discussion of these verses, see *Asrār*, 279–81.
[102] al-Sakkākī, *al-Miftāḥ*, 494. [103] Ibid. [104] al-Khaṭīb al-Qazwīnī, *al-Īḍāḥ*, 433.
[105] Ibid., 456. On *kināya*, see Joseph Dichy, "Kinâya, a tropic device from Medieval Arabic rhetoric, and its impact on discourse theory," in *Proceedings of the 5th Conference of the*

meaning replaces the literal signification of the word.[106] This figure is called *kināya*, al-Sakkākī explains, because "it conceals the explicit way (*wajh al-taṣrīḥ*) [of signification]."[107] He points out that all permutations of the root *k-n-y* "revolve around a sense of the hidden."[108] Concealment is therefore the defining aspect of *kināya*.

Al-Sakkākī describes *kināya* more systematically than al-Jurjānī as well as Fakhr al-Dīn al-Rāzī.[109] He divides it into three types based on the nature of the implicit meaning that is intended. In the first type, the intended meaning implied is the matter itself being described; in the second type, it is a characteristic; and in the third type, it is the attribution of a specific characteristic exclusively to someone or something. Each type, in turn, is described based on its "closeness" or "farfetchedness," with the latter being more praiseworthy.

The first type involves referring to something indirectly with a characteristic that is specific to it. This is similar to what in English we would call "antonomasia," such as saying "[here] comes the hospitable [one]," when you mean Zayd.[110] This example, al-Sakkākī explains, would be a "close" kind of *kināya* for "the apparentness of the identification of hospitability with Zayd." Familiar *kināya*s such as these occur when "it happens that a characteristic of [all available] characteristics has an apparent exclusivity to the specific subject being described."[111] Antonomasia can be made less familiar and "more remote" when several adjectives have to be grouped together in order to restrict the description to a specific subject, such as saying "alive, upright, and with broad nails" in reference to the human species.[112]

International Society for the Study of Argumentation (ISSA), University of Amsterdam, 25–28 June 2002, ed. Frans van Eemeren, et al. (Amsterdam: Sic Sat, 2003).

106 al-Khaṭīb al-Qazwīnī, *al-Īḍāḥ*, 456.

107 al-Sakkākī, *al-Miftāḥ*, 512. Al-Sayyid al-Sharīf clarifies that "it conceals the *signification* (*al-dalāla*)" (*al-Miṣbāḥ*, 687 (emphasis added)).

108 See discussion in *al-Miftāḥ*, 512.

109 Al-Jurjānī does seem to distinguish between different types of *kināya* in *Dalā'il*, 307–14, where he uses several examples that are then employed by al-Sakkākī. Fakhr al-Dīn al-Rāzī only sticks to the standard examples of *kināya* (*Nihāyat al-ījāz*, 160–3). Al-Sakkākī, therefore, seems to be the first to delineate clearly the different types of *kināya*, which are then adopted by al-Khaṭīb al-Qazwīnī and other commentators.

110 This type of *kināya* is also similar to "kenning," which is an expression prevalent in Old Norse poetry that is usually made up of a compound description that takes the place of an ordinary noun either metonymically or metaphorically (see *The New Princeton Encyclopedia of Poetry and Poetics*, 670). I thank Daniel Heller-Roazen for pointing this out to me.

111 al-Sakkākī, *al-Miftāḥ*, 514.

112 Ibid. This definition comes from the Ancient Greeks through Arabic philosophy.

The second type of *kināya*, instead of referring to a thing, aims at conveying a characteristic implicitly through something associated with it or that is a consequence of it. The examples cited above as discussed by al-Jurjānī are all of this type. They vary in closeness and remoteness, however, depending on how many steps are required to reach the intended meaning. Saying "he has a long shoulder strap" is clear and close because its link with tallness is direct. Expressing hospitality by saying "he has an abundance of ashes," on the other hand, is remote because "you move to the intended [meaning] from a distant consequence (*lāzim*) through a series of consequences."[113] Explaining this *kināya*, al-Sakkākī states:

> [One must move in one's reasoning] from the abundance of ashes to the abundance of embers, from the abundance of embers to the frequent burning of wood under cooking pots, from the frequent burning of wood under cooking pots to the abundance of meals, from the abundance of meals to the abundance of eaters, from the abundance of eaters to the abundance of guests, and [finally] from the abundance of guests to [the conclusion] that he is hospitable.[114]

An even remoter example of implicitly conveying the idea of hospitality and generosity is the following verse:[115]

وما يَكُ فِيَّ مِنْ عَيْبٍ فَإنّي   جَبَانُ الكَلْبِ مَهْزُوْلُ الفَصِيلِ

There is no fault in me, for I am one with
a cowardly dog and an emaciated baby camel

~ Unknown[116]

There are two *kināya*s in this verse: cowardly dog and emaciated camel. Al-Sakkākī explains that a cowardly dog is one that does not bark at oncoming strangers. However, given that it is a dog's nature to bark at strangers, its refraining from doing so implies that it is accustomed to seeing strangers flocking to its owner's house. This, in turn, implies that the owner is so known for his hospitality that so many strangers, from near and far, end up seeking his house. The emaciated baby camel leads to a similar implication. Al-Sakkākī explains that the emaciation of a baby camel is due to the loss of its mother because it was slaughtered. Given the degree to which Bedouins prize their camels, al-Sakkākī explains, there must be a very good reason for having slaughtered the mother camel. The only such good reason is to

[113] Ibid., 515. [114] Ibid. [115] Ibid.
[116] The poet is unknown. However, the verse is cited in Abū Tammām's anthology of early poetry known as *Dīwān al-ḥamāsa*. See al-Marzūqī, *Sharḥ Dīwān al-ḥamāsa*, 2:1650.

cook its meat, which in turn is done to provide for guests. The emaciation of the baby camel, therefore, indirectly signifies the length to which the owner is willing to go for the sake of being generous.[117]

The third type of *kināya* involves the exclusive ascription of an attribute. While the first two types intend to indirectly signify the matter itself or a characteristic of that thing or person, the third type of *kināya* aims at implicitly ascribing a characteristic exclusively to someone or something, as in the following verse praising an Umayyad governor by the name of Ibn al-Ḥashraj:

إِنَّ السَّماحَةَ وَالمُروءَةَ وَالنَّدى في قُبَّةٍ ضُرِبَت عَلى ابْنِ الحَشْرَجِ

Munificence, chivalry, and generosity
are in the dome [of the tent] pitched on Ibn al-Ḥashraj
~ Ziyād al-Aʿjam (d. 100/718?)

An explicit way of attributing munificence, chivalry, and generosity to a person would have been to say: "munificence is his . . . etc.," for example.[118] The poet, instead, collected all these attributes in a dome and pitched it on Ibn al-Ḥashraj.[119] In this way, he indirectly ascribed these attributes to the governor, because "if a matter is affirmed in a man's location and his surroundings, it is affirmed in him [as well]."[120] This is not figurative speech because the subject of praise, in whom munificence, chivalry, and generosity are found, would indeed embody the combination of these attributes and he could indeed find himself in a domed tent. While the way this is ascribed to the individual is indirect, one cannot say that it is not possible for it to be accurate at a literal level as well. It remains *kināya*, therefore, and not part of *majāz*.[121]

This form of indirect ascription could also range in degree of subtlety. An example of such added subtlety can be found in the following verse:[122]

والمَجْدُ يَدْعُو أَنْ يَدُومَ لِجِيْدِهِ عِقْدٌ مَساعِي ابْنِ العَمِيدِ نِظَامُهُ

Glory prays for the lasting on its neck
of a necklace whose arrangement is [made up of] Ibn al-ʿAmīd's[123] good deeds
~ Unknown

[117] Ibid. See also al-Khaṭīb al-Qazwīnī, *al-Īḍāḥ*, 459–60. [118] al-Sakkākī, *al-Miftāḥ*, 517.
[119] The dome is placed on the tents of leaders and people of high regard (al-Taftāzānī, *al-Muṭawwal*, 635; al-Sayyid al-Sharīf al-Jurjānī, *al-Miṣbāḥ*, 697).
[120] al-Taftāzānī, *al-Muṭawwal*, 635.
[121] See al-Sayyid al-Sharīf al-Jurjānī, *al-Miṣbāḥ*, 697. [122] al-Sakkākī, *al-Miftāḥ*, 518.
[123] Ibn al-ʿAmīd is probably the famous Buyid vizier Abū al-Faḍl ibn al-ʿAmīd (d. 360/970) or his son and successor, Abū al-Fatḥ ibn al-ʿAmīd (d. 366/976).

The poet indirectly ascribes glory to Ibn al-ʿAmīd by first attributing to him good deeds, which in turn adorn a necklace, which is then made to encircle the neck of glory. Not satisfied with this, the poet takes it even further, making glory pray for this necklace to remain on its neck, thereby "indicating with this that its beautification and guardianship are confined to Ibn al-ʿAmīd."[124] By praying for its permanence, it is also praying for the permanence of Ibn al-ʿAmīd.[125] Al-Sakkākī does not state what about this verse makes it "more subtle." However, there is a lot going on in it. First, besides *kināya*, the verse is based on a reinforced metaphor; al-Khaṭīb al-Qazwīnī explains that the poet compared glory to a human being and gave it a neck, then gave the neck a necklace as a "development" (*tarshīḥ*) on the metaphor.[126] Second, there are two *kināyas* in the verse, as al-Sayyid al-Sharīf points out. The first involves ascribing the quality of glory to Ibn al-ʿAmīd. The second is restricting it exclusively to him.[127] It is, no doubt, this conglomeration of indirect signification, both figuratively and implicitly, that renders the verse particularly beautiful.[128]

After dividing *kināya* into categories based on the nature of the matter that it seeks to imply, al-Sakkākī divides it into types based on the distance between the direct meaning and the indirect meaning implied. When the distance is large and requires several intermediary steps in the logic, it is called "beckoning (*talwīḥ*)," because that means gesturing to someone from afar, as in "his ashes are abundant."[129] If the distance is near but has some degree of obscurity, then it is called a "symbol (*ramz*)." An example of this is calling a fool "wide-bottomed." (Al-Khaṭīb al-Qazwīnī explains that an excessively large bottom or head is a sign of stupidity!)[130] The link between the two, however, while direct, is more obscure. Hence, this type of *kināya* is called a "symbol," because it entails "pointing to something close to you discreetly."[131] If the *kināya* is close and clear, it is called "indication (*īmāʾ*)"

[124] al-Sakkākī, *al-Miftāḥ*, 519. [125] al-Khaṭīb al-Qazwīnī, *al-Īḍāḥ*, 463. [126] Ibid.
[127] al-Sayyid al-Sharīf al-Jurjānī, *al-Miṣbāḥ*, 698.
[128] Given that the attribution of the quality and its restriction to the subject of praise are based on a metaphorical image, it is less obvious how the *kināya* can also hold up at the literal level, except by considering the addressee's role in the metaphor as literally accurate. Were we to take the metaphor literally and accept that glory has a necklace, it is plausible that Ibn al-ʿAmīd would indeed be "decorating it" with his good deeds. This, in turn, implies that he himself is full of glory if glory is decorating itself with his good deeds. The point is that *kināya* refers to what this role implies about him, even if it takes part in a fantastic scenario.
[129] al-Sakkākī, *al-Miftāḥ*, 521. [130] al-Khaṭīb al-Qazwīnī, *al-Īḍāḥ*, 459.
[131] al-Sakkākī, *al-Miftāḥ*, 521.

and "pointing (*ishāra*)." Finally, when the intended, implied meaning is the person or thing itself, as in referring to Zayd, for example, as "the hospitable one" without mentioning his name directly, the *kināya* is best described as "oblique speech (*ta'rīḍ*)."[132] These do not become technical terms that are used to identify different types of *kināya*, but they do represent yet another way of describing the closeness or remoteness of an implication.

Simile as Indirect Signification?

Like simile, expressing something figuratively and implicitly allows for an experience of discovery to take place in the listener. In simile, however, this is the result of its comparative structure, which elucidates through likening one thing to another. Metaphor, figurative speech, and metonymy, on the other hand, are signs that signify their meanings through a logical relationship. Unlike words in their literal state, whose signification is usually arbitrary and whose meanings one simply learns and memorizes, metaphor and metonymy signify their meanings in ways that the listener can deduce based on rational thought. This form of signification, according to our *balāgha* scholars, is the reason *bayān* figures enhance the eloquence of speech.

Simile, in and of itself, is not a "sign" that signifies, but a *statement* of comparison, as al-Jurjānī goes at great lengths to explain.[133] It is therefore not a real *bayān* figure in the sense that it does not signify meaning indirectly as do metaphor and metonymy. Despite this, simile is incorporated into the science of *bayān* as one of its main pillars and the first one to boot. The reason al-Sakkākī and al-Khaṭīb al-Qazwīnī give for this is that it forms the basis of metaphor (*isti'āra*), which is an actual *bayān* figure.[134]

Nevertheless, al-Taftāzānī criticizes al-Sakkākī for justifying the inclusion of simile in *bayān* merely in the service of metaphor and deeming it nonetheless as deserving of its own section and the first topic of *bayān* no less. He states, "you know very well the inconsistency this holds."[135] Later, al-Sayyid al-Sharīf clarifies that this "obvious inconsistency" that al-Taftāzānī points

[132] Ibid.; al-Taftāzānī, *al-Muṭawwal*, 636; al-Sayyid al-Sharīf al-Jurjānī, *al-Miṣbāḥ*, 702. *Ta'rīḍ* is a larger category that could also be used to describe instances of figurative speech (al-Sakkākī, *al-Miftāḥ*, 523).

[133] See discussion above on "Simile, Analogy, and Metaphorical Analogy." See also Harb, "Form, Content, and Inimitability."

[134] See al-Sakkākī, *al-Miftāḥ*, 439; al-Khaṭīb al-Qazwīnī, *al-Īḍāḥ*, 327.

[135] al-Taftāzānī, *al-Muṭawwal*, 515.

out lies in downgrading simile to a mere introduction to metaphor, while at the same time treating it as one of the pillars of *bayān*.[136] He goes on to argue that simile should rightly be part of *bayān* because it is involved in the indirect expression of meaning. Al-Sayyid al-Sharīf compares it to *kināya*, where the literal meaning of word remains, but the intended meaning is something else it implies. Similarly, he continues, when one says, "his face is like the full moon," one does not only intend the literal meaning, but another meaning that the simile implies, which in this case is that the person is beautiful.[137] In this way, simile does function as a way of conveying (a secondary) meaning, affirming that it entails a form of indirect signification in its own right.

Interestingly, Muḥammad ibn ʿAlī al-Jurjānī in his *Ishārāt* even argues that simile is a type of signification just like figurative speech and metonymy because one can express the same idea more explicitly with words that signify the intended meaning directly. He attributes the pleasure that arises from simile to the fact that it delivers its meaning in a way that requires "intellection":

> The truth is that all the types of simile, figurative speech (*majāz*), and metonymy (*kināya*) are one thing. What distinguishes them is what distinguishes a signifier composed of [both] lexical and intellected meanings from purely lexical signification. [The difference lies] in the satisfaction of the soul and the beauty of the occurrence of meaning in it, as a result of the signification (*dalāla*) being occasioned by this [kind of] delivery.[138]

Muḥammad ibn ʿAlī, therefore, groups simile with the other figures of *bayān* and attributes to all of them a kind of signification that communicates meaning in a way that must be intellected. Despite this difference in opinion about whether simile can be treated as a "sign" that signifies a secondary meaning, both approaches ultimately assume a similar aesthetic outcome: *Bayān* figures elucidate meaning in a way that requires deduction; this process of deduction allows for an experience of discovery and hence pleasurable wonder to take place in the listener.

CONCLUSION

Our authors develop an aesthetic theory of signs and signification. Words add to eloquence through distancing their intended meaning. This is

[136] al-Sayyid al-Sharīf al-Jurjānī, *al-Ḥāshiya*, 331. [137] Ibid.
[138] al-Jurjānī, *al-Ishārāt wa-l-tanbīhāt*, 189.

pleasing to the listener because it enables in him an experience of discovery. This again betrays an aesthetic of wonder, which we have seen articulated for other literary figures as well. The figures of *bayān*, however, share a particular mechanism of producing this wonder; that is, indirect signification. The more distant the intended meaning is from a word's literal meaning, the more effort is required to discover it, and hence the more pleasing and wonder-evoking it is.

Ultimately, however, metaphor, figurative speech, and metonymy, which are all words or multi-word clusters that function as single signifying units, cannot stand on their own without being part of a sentence. Al-Jurjānī explains that everything in speech that moves and gives pleasure, from "a nice meaning, wise saying, elegance, metaphor, paronomasia," is ultimately dependent on sentence construction (*naẓm*).[139] This is also where their arguments for the inimitability of the Quran are centered. It is to this that we turn next.

[139] al-Jurjānī, *Dalāʾil*, 85. See also pp. 98–105, where he clarifies that the beauty of a word (*lafẓ*), even when it indirectly signifies its meaning, usually becomes apparent only through its placement in the sentence (*naẓm*).

5

Naẓm, Wonder, and the Inimitability of the Quran

So ʿUmar rose and washed himself and she gave him the page in which was *Ṭā Hā*, and when he had read the beginning he said, "How fine and noble is this speech." [...] At that [he] said, "Lead me to Muhammad so that I may accept Islam."

~ The story of ʿUmar ibn al-Khaṭṭāb's conversion to Islam as told in *Sīrat Ibn Hishām*[1]

THE MIRACLE OF THE QURAN

For the early Muslim community, the Quran was the primary miracle that proved Muhammad's prophethood, akin to Moses' parting of the Red Sea and Jesus' raising of the dead.[2] The Quran's effect on the people who heard it was so great that it had the power, in itself, to compel them to accept Islam, as in the story quoted above of the conversion of ʿUmar ibn al-Khaṭṭāb, who went on to become the second caliph (r. 13/634–23/644) after the death of

1 ʿAbd al-Malik Ibn Hishām, *al-Sīra al-nabawiyya*, ed. Muṣṭafā al-Saqqā, Ibrāhīm al-Ibyārī, and ʿAbd al-Ḥafīz Shalabī, 2nd ed., 4 vols. (Cairo: Maṭbaʿat Muṣṭafā al-Bābī al-Ḥalabī, 1955), 342–6; ʿAbd al-Malik Ibn Hishām, *The Life of Muhammad: A Translation of Isḥāq's Sīrat Rasūl Allāh*, trans. Alfred Guillaume (Karachi; New York: Oxford University Press, 1997), 157.

2 See al-Jāḥiẓ, "Ḥujaj al-nubuwwa," in *Rasāʾil*, ed. ʿAbd al-Salām Muḥammad Hārūn (Beirut: Dār al-Jīl, 1991), especially 3:278–80; Uri Rubin, *Prophets and Prophethood*, in *Encyclopaedia of the Qurʾān*; and more generally on the literature on proofs of prophethood, see Sarah Stroumsa, "The Signs of Prophecy: The Emergence and Early Development of a Theme in Arabic Theological Literature," *The Harvard Theological Review* 78, no. 1/2 (January–April 1985).

Muhammad.[3] The source of this powerful effect was a mystery to people during Muhammad's lifetime, garnering accusations by his enemies that the Prophet was a madman, a possessed poet, a soothsayer (*kāhin*), and a sorcerer.[4] The Quran denied such accusations, which reduced it to humanly producible speech[5] and challenged its opponents to create something like it:[6] "Say: verily, if mankind and the *jinn* united to bring forth the like of this Quran, they would not bring forth the like of it, even if they were supporters of each other" (Q17:88).

According to early Islamic sources, the extraordinary nature of the Quran was obvious to its contemporary audience in Mecca, who had the closest capabilities in eloquence to the Quran.[7] One finds stories even about enemies of the Prophet Muhammad advising their people not to let themselves hear the Quran lest they succumb to its power.[8] Later, with the expansion of Islam to non-Arabic-speaking territories and the passage of time from the period of revelation, Muslim scholars found it necessary to demonstrate the Quran's miraculousness (*iʿjāz*) more systematically for those who did not have the intuitive capacity to recognize and appreciate it.[9]

3 Ibn al-Naqīb (d. 698/1298) recounts some stories of the effect of the Quran on its listeners in *Muqaddimat tafsīr Ibn al-Naqīb fī ʿilm al-bayān wa-l-maʿānī wa-l-badīʿ wa-iʿjāz al-Qurʾān*, ed. Zakariyyā Saʿīd ʿAlī (Cairo: Maktabat al-Khānjī, 1995), 511–18. See stories of listeners of the Quran who were so moved by it that they died in shock as recounted by Abū Isḥāq al-Thaʿlabī (d. 427/1035) in his *Kitāb qatlā al-Qurʾān* (*The Quran's Victims*).

4 See, for example, the story of Walīd ibn al-Mughīra in Ibn Hishām, *al-Sīra al-nabawiyya*, 270–1.

5 See Quran 8:31; 15:6; 21:5; 25:4–5; 37:36; 38:7; 74:24–5. See Issa J. Boullata, "The Rhetorical Interpretation of the Quran, *Iʿjaz* and Related Topics," in *Approaches to the Quran*, ed. Andrew Rippin (Oxford; New York: Clarendon Press; Oxford University Press, 1988), 140.

6 See ibid. The Quran's so-called challenge verses additionally include: Q2:23–4; 10:38; 17:88; 52:34.

7 Al-Bāqillānī, for example, explains that in order to recognize the inimitability of the Quran, one has to have a high degree of eloquence (al-Bāqillānī, *Iʿjāz al-Qurʾān*, ed. al-Sayyid Aḥmad Ṣaqr (Cairo: Dār al-Maʿārif, 1954), 34–8). He argues that if the people at the time of Muhammad could not challenge the Quran, with their high eloquence, later generations have no chance (ibid., 10, and also 380–1). In modern scholarship, Navid Kermani proposes a social and anthropological explanation for the perception of the Quran as a miracle at the time of its revelation as well (*Gott ist schön: Das ästhetische Erleben des Koran* (Munich: C.H. Beck, 1999), chs. 1 and 2).

8 Maḥmūd al-Sayyid Shaykhūn, *al-Iʿjāz fī naẓm al-Qurʾān* (Cairo: Maktabat al-Kulliyyāt al-Azhariyya, 1978), 11. See stories about how they secretly would go and listen to the Quran at night in Bint al-Shāṭiʾ, *al-Iʿjāz al-bayānī li-l-Qurʾān* (Cairo: Dār al-Maʿārif, 1971), 46–7.

9 Shaykhūn, *al-Iʿjāz fī naẓm al-Qurʾān*, 13; al-Bāqillānī, *Iʿjāz al-Qurʾān*, 171–2.

The miraculousness of the Quran lay, summarily, in its contradicting the usual course of nature in a way that is humanly irreplicable.[10] The inability of anyone to live up to the challenge to create something like it, put forth in the text itself, was proof to early Muslims that the Quran is of divine origin.[11] Why exactly attempts to challenge the Quran failed was subject to debate in the centuries that followed the rise of Islam.[12] Among the theories proposed by medieval authors, one held that there was nothing inimitable about the Quranic text per se, but that God blocked humans from being able to produce something like it, an opinion known as *ṣarfa* (turning away/incapacitation).[13] Another cited the accurate predictions contained in the Quran about the future as a proof of its miraculousness.[14] Yet another situated its miraculousness in the inimitability of its eloquence.[15] The last opinion argued that the Quran achieves a degree of eloquence that is humanly impossible to attain. This opinion

[10] al-Bāqillānī, *Iʿjāz al-Qurʾān*, 33–8.

[11] While there were attempts to challenge the Quran, there was a consensus in the Muslim community that they failed. The most notable attempts were by Musaylima, a rival of the Prophet during his lifetime (see ibid., 238–40). Later Ibn al-Muqaffaʿ (d. c. 139/756–7), the famous Persian translator and one of the shapers of early Arabic prose writing, is said to have attempted to challenge the style of the Quran (see Josef van Ess, "Some Fragments of the *Muʿāraḍat al-Qurʾān* Attributed to Ibn al-Muqaffaʿ," in *Studia Arabica et Islamica: Festschrift for Iḥsān ʿAbbās on his Sixtieth Birthday*, ed. Wadad al-Qadi (Beirut: American University of Beirut, 1981)). For further information on imitations of the Quran, see Sarah Stroumsa, *Freethinkers of Medieval Islam: Ibn al-Rāwandī, Abū Bakr al-Rāzī and Their Impact on Islamic Thought* (Leiden: Brill, 1999), 137–9.

[12] For an overview of the history of the debates on *iʿjāz*, see Naʿīm al-Ḥimṣī, *Fikrat iʿjāz al-Qurʾān min al-baʿtha al-nabawiyya ilā ʿaṣrinā al-ḥāḍir*, 2nd ed. (Beirut: Muʾassasat al-Risāla, 1980).

[13] Abū Isḥāq Ibrāhīm ibn Sayyār al-Naẓẓām (d. between 220/835 and 230/845), for example, was famously a proponent of this argument. His works on *iʿjāz* are lost, however. While initially the idea of *ṣarfa* seemed to negate other theories about the Quran being inimitable in its eloquence, later theologians, such as al-Rummānī, did not consider the theories of *ṣarfa* and inimitability mutually exclusive and cited both as proofs of the miraculousness of the Quran (see al-Rummānī, *al-Nukat*, 75). *Ṣarfa* was an argument adopted primarily by Muʿtazilites (see Muṣṭafā Ṣādiq al-Rāfiʿī, *Iʿjāz al-Qurʾān wa-l-balāgha al-nabawiyya*, 3rd ed. (Beirut: Dār al-Kitāb al-ʿArabī, 2005); and Bint al-Shāṭiʾ, *al-Iʿjāz al-bayānī li-l-Qurʾān*). The differing theological considerations certainly affected how various scholars demonstrated the miraculousness of the Quran, which is something discussed in detail by Larkin, *Theology of Meaning*; and Darwīsh al-Jundī, *Naẓariyyat ʿAbd al-Qāhir fī al-naẓm* (Cairo: Maktabat Nahḍat Miṣr, 1960), 13–46.

[14] See, for example, al-Bāqillānī, *Iʿjāz al-Qurʾān*, 48–50.

[15] Other aspects of *iʿjāz* discussed by medieval authors also include the Quran's revelation of unknown ancient events of the past, as well as the comprehensiveness of the laws it contains (Shaykhūn, *al-Iʿjāz fī naẓm al-Qurʾān*, 22–4). Scientific *iʿjāz* also comes to be discussed in later centuries (see al-Ḥimṣī, *Fikrat iʿjāz*, 91, and 8–9, who credits al-Ghazālī with having started the idea of scientific *iʿjāz*).

ultimately becomes the dominant theory and is the one that concerns us here.[16]

The concern with the eloquence of the Quran motivated the development of a scholastic enterprise dedicated to the aesthetic inquiry into linguistic beauty. The scholars involved in this enterprise sought to detail and classify the aspects of language that contribute to its beauty in order to identify what specifically was inimitable about the Quran. While the whole religion was at stake, the proof ultimately did not depend on the truth of the message held within the Quran. Rather, it depended on its aesthetic superiority. What was inimitable about the Quran did not lie in its message, which could after all be reproduced by humans. Instead, its inimitability lay in the way it conveyed its message (i.e., its form), regardless of its content.

Scholars of *iʿjāz* were interested in poetry, therefore, even when its subjects were unsacred. However, given that it represented the loftiest example of humanly produced eloquence, they sought to show that it did not reach the same level of eloquence as the Quran. Thus, they had to develop a single comprehensive understanding of literary aesthetics that could be used as a yardstick to which both human and Quranic speech could be held up. As I will argue in this chapter, this yardstick also depended on the ability of speech to evoke wonder in the listener. The main way wonder is evoked in the Quran, however, is through the particular ways in which its phrases are constructed, something they call *naẓm*.[17] The explanations for the eloquence of sentence structure add yet another component to the medieval Arabic aesthetic theory of wonder.

THE MIRACLE AND WONDER

Besides the failure to challenge the Quran, its miraculousness, as we have seen, was attested by the extraordinary impact it had on its listeners. Al-

[16] While authors might disagree about which of these theories to include, the inimitability of the Quran's eloquence seems to have been a unanimously held viewpoint, as argued by Bint al-Shāṭiʾ. Even when it comes to *ṣarfa*, which places the miracle in divine intervention rather than the inimitability of the eloquence of the text itself, a thorough appreciation of eloquence remains necessary to recognize that such an inhibition has taken place. This is something that Ibn Sinān al-Khafājī argues in *Sirr al-faṣāḥa*, 4.

[17] It is difficult to accurately render the word "*naẓm*" in English. As we will see later in the chapter, it involves linguistic composition at the level of single sentences. It is not concerned, for example, with compositional aspects of larger units, such as narrative or plot. Note also that the concept of *naẓm* under discussion in this chapter is unrelated to *naẓm* in the sense of "versification" or "verse" as opposed to *nathr* (prose).

Khaṭṭābī (d. 386/996 or 388/998), the author of one of earliest surviving treatises on *iʿjāz*, even suggests that the Quran's effect alone is indicative of its miraculousness.[18] The Quran itself also describes its effect on humans as causing their skin to shudder: "God revealed the best speech [in the form] of a book, consistent and iterative, from which shudders the skin of those who fear their lord" (Q39:23). Even the jinn who hear the Quran call it "a wonder": "a group of the jinn listened and said we have indeed heard a wondrous Quran (*Qurʾānan ʿajaban*)" (Q72:1).

The fact that this impact arises from its eloquence is attested by statements about the aesthetic experience that eloquent speech produces. For example, al-Bāqillanī (d. 403/1013) states in his treatise on the inimitability of the Quran:

> When speech reaches high levels [of eloquence] its effect on the heart and hold on the soul is of the kind that amazes (*yudhhil*) and elates, causes distress and pleasure, entices and frustrates, makes one laugh and cry, saddens and brings joy, calms and perturbs, stirs one's emotions and delights (*yushjī wa-yuṭrib*). It agitates one's sentiments and attracts the ear towards it. [...] It has subtle paths to the soul and fine entries into the heart. [...] Its effect is wondrous (*ʿajīb*) and its elements novel (*badīʿ*).[19]

ʿAbd al-Qāhir al-Jurjānī uses similar adjectives to describe eloquent speech throughout his *Dalāʾil al-iʿjāz*, including that it dazzles (*yubhir*) and fills one with wonder (*hayba*) and amazement (*rawʿa*).[20]

Given that they locate the Quran's inimitability primarily in its *naẓm*, one can conjecture that *naẓm* is what "dazzles" and "fills one with wonder." In the following pages, I will analyze precisely this: How can the composition of a sentence evoke wonder? I will first look at al-Jurjānī's treatment of *naẓm* in his *Dalāʾil al-iʿjāz*. I will then look at its development in the works of al-Sakkākī and al-Khaṭīb al-Qazwīnī, where the study of *naẓm* becomes the subject of a third branch of the science of eloquence, called the science of [conveying] meanings (*ʿilm al-maʿānī*). While the science of *bayān* focused on how words or groups of words signify their

[18] al-Khaṭṭābī, *Bayān iʿjāz al-Qurʾān*, in *Thalāth rasāʾil fī iʿjāz al-Qurʾān*, ed. Muḥammad Khalafallāh and Muḥammad Zaghlūl Sallām (Cairo: Dār al-Maʿārif, 1976), 70.

[19] al-Bāqillānī, *Iʿjāz al-Qurʾān*, 419.

[20] al-Jurjānī, *Dalāʾil*, 388. The psychological bent of works on *iʿjāz* has been noted in modern scholarship, namely, by Muḥammad Khalafallah in "Naẓariyyat ʿAbd al-Qāhir"; and "ʿAbdalqâhir's Theory in His 'Secrets of Eloquence': A Psychological Approach," *Journal of Near Eastern Studies* 14, no. 3 (July 1955). See also Muḥammad Zaghlūl Sallām, *Athar al-Qurʾān fī taṭawwur al-naqd al-ʿArabī* (Cairo: Maktabat al-Shabāb, 1952); and Abu Deeb, *Poetic Imagery*.

intended meaning, the science of meanings focuses on how the syntax of a sentence and its construction convey meaning. Relying on the principle of discovery discussed in Chapter 3, which al-Jurjānī articulates in *Asrār al-balāgha*, I will suggest that the aesthetics of *naẓm* revolve around the manipulation of sentence structures in such a way as to make the "discovery" of their meaning less straightforward and less obvious. That is, the more time, effort, and thought it takes to grasp the meaning of a statement, the more pleasurable and wonder-evoking is its discovery.

***

How do medieval scholars distinguish between Quranic wonder and that produced by a good line of poetry? There is a fine line that had to be drawn between a marvel (*ʿajība*), which – though extraordinary – remains within the grasp of human achievement, and a miracle (*muʿjiza*), which surpasses human powers and can only originate from the Divine. However, my goal here is not to determine where they draw this line or to judge how successfully they do so. Rather, I am interested in understanding their reasoning and in identifying the underlying aesthetic criteria motivating their argument for the miraculousness of the Quran. Whether the reader is convinced by their arguments or not is beside the point. What interests me here is understanding how they establish the relationship between eloquence and the experience of wonder it produces. In other words, I am looking at these medieval theorizations of *iʿjāz* purely from an aesthetic perspective, leaving the theological debates and beliefs aside. This is not to say that the various theological schools of thought that the medieval scholars adhered to did not influence their argumentation and conclusions, as Margaret Larkin has shown. However, leaving theological debates aside, I seek to uncover the aesthetic reasoning underlying their claims.

The concept of *naẓm* has not received the same kind of attention in modern scholarship on classical Arabic literary theory that other aspects of eloquence, such as *badīʿ*, have enjoyed.[21] While the focus of poetic criticism centers on *badīʿ*, Quranic criticism complements it by adding the

[21] Studies on subcategories of *naẓm*, in particular the concept of "*ījāz*" (conciseness), are more plentiful. See, for example, Mukhtār ʿAṭiyya, *al-Ījāz fī kalām al-ʿArab wa-naṣṣ al-iʿjāz: Dirāsa balāghiyya* (Alexandria: Dār al-Maʿrifa al-Jāmiʿiyya, 1997). And more recently, Ibrāhīm Ṭāha, *al-Ījāz fī al-mawrūth al-balāghī wa-l-Qurʾān al-karīm* (Beirut: al-Muʾassasa al-ʿArabiyya li-l-Dirāsāt wa-l-Nashr, 2012). Otherwise, one finds brief discussions of the concept of *naẓm* in surveys of literary criticism, such as in ʿAbbās, *Tārīkh al-naqd al-adabī*, 419–38. See also Aḥmad Abū Zayd, *Muqaddima fī al-uṣūl al-fikriyya li-l-balāgha wa-iʿjāz al-Qurʾān* (Rabat: Dār al-Amān, 1989), 51–122; Abu Deeb, *Poetic Imagery*, 24–103; Kermani, *Gott ist schön*, 253–84; Ait El Ferrane, *Die Maʿnā-Theorie*.

component of linguistic composition. It is therefore important to incorporate it into the inquiry into medieval Arabic aesthetics. Modern scholars who have investigated *naẓm* and *ʿilm al-maʿānī* have typically approached it – and rightly so – from the perspective of linguistics, pragmatics, and grammar.[22] Simply deciphering this quite technical field of study is a feat in and of itself. In this chapter, I seek to build on the work of these scholars who have tackled this area to investigate the link between these technical discussions and eloquence, and more specifically, wonder. I will not seek to provide comprehensive overviews of all the various linguistic components of *naẓm* and its subsequent development into *ʿilm al-maʿānī*.[23] However, through select examples I seek to show that their understanding of eloquence in sentence construction results from linguistic and syntactical structures that allow for an experience of discovery that is otherwise not possible.

Al-Jurjānī shows how paying attention to the implications of syntactical choices can add nuance and meaning to a sentence. This added meaning,

[22] Antonella Ghersetti, for example, provides a pragmatic analysis of al-Jurjānī's concept of *naẓm* in her unpublished dissertation, "Per una rilettura in chiave pragmatica di *Dalāʾil al-iʿǧāz* di ʿAbd al-Qāhir al-Ǧurǧānī" (PhD Dissertation, Università degli Studi di Firenze, 1998). See also Ahmad Sweity, "Al-Jurjaanii's Theory of *naZm* (discourse arrangement): A Linguistic Perspective" (PhD Dissertation, University of Texas at Austin, 1992). On pragmatics and *ʿilm al-maʿānī*, see the work of Pierre Larcher, including "Information et performance en science arabo-islamique du langage" (PhD Dissertation, Université de Paris 3, 1980); "Éléments pragmatiques dans la théorie grammaticale arabe postclassique," in *Studies in the History of Arabic Grammar, II*, ed. Michael G. Carterand Kees Versteegh (Amsterdam and Philadelphia: J. Benjamins, 1990); "Une pragmatique avant la pragmatique: 'médiévale,' 'arabe' et 'islamique,'" *Histoire Epistémologie Langage* 20, no. 1 (1998); and "Arabic Linguistic Tradition II: Pragmatics," in *The Oxford Handbook of Arabic Linguistics*, ed. Jonathan Owens (Oxford: Oxford University Press, 2013). See also Majdī Bin Ṣūf, *ʿIlm al-adab ʿind al-Sakkākī: Baḥth fī intiẓām al-taṣawwurāt al-lisāniyya fī Miftāḥ al-ʿulūm* (Tunis: Miskīliyānī li-l-Nashr, 2010). On grammar and pragmatics, see Michael Carter, "Pragmatics and Contractual Language in Arabic Grammar and Legal Theory," in *Approaches to Arabic Linguistics: Presented to Kees Versteegh on the Occasion of His Sixtieth Birthday*, ed. E. Ditters and H. Motzki (Leiden: Brill, 2007); and Jonathan Owens, "Arabic Syntactic Research," in *Syntax – Theory and Analysis: An International Handbook, Vol. 1*, ed. Tibor Kiss and Artemis Alexiadou (Berlin: De Gruyter Mouton, 2015). On the relationship between grammar and *balāgha*, see Ramzi Baalbaki, "The Relation between *Naḥw* and *Balāġa*: A Comparative Study of the Methods of Sībawayhi and Ǧurǧānī," *Zeitschrift für arabische Linguistik* 11 (1983).

[23] For an overview of *naẓm* according to al-Jurjānī, see Max Weisweiler, "ʿAbdalqāhir al-Curcānī's Werk über die Unnachahmlichkeit des Korans und seine syntaktisch-stilistischen Lehren," *Oriens* 11, no. 1/2 (1958). For studies of *ʿilm al-maʿānī*, see Simon, *Mittelalterliche arabische Sprachbetrachtung*; and Herbjørn Jenssen, *The Subtleties and Secrets of the Arabic Language: Preliminary Investigations into al-Qazwīnī's Talkhīṣ al-Miftāḥ* (Bergen: Centre for Middle Eastern and Islamic Studies, 1998).

conveyed obliquely through subtle manipulations of sentence structures, enhances the eloquence of a phrase because it requires interpretation and deduction. This added meaning is later identified in the science of *maʿānī* as a correspondence with the requirements of the context. That is, the way a sentence is constructed can give information about the context for which it was pronounced. Going against the expectations generated by a particular context further enhances eloquence, as we will see.

EARLY ARGUMENTS

Various definitions of eloquence and its subcategories were proposed by scholars concerned with the question of the inimitability of the Quran starting from the third/ninth century. Some of these clearly drew from the field of poetic criticism, which was emerging at the time, or at least they had to contend with their discussions of rhetorical figures (*badīʿ*). What developed as a concern unique to the question of *iʿjāz*, however, was sentence construction (*naẓm*).

The linguistic composition of the Quran seems to have already been the basis of al-Jāḥiẓ's (d. 255/868) proof of its inimitability. Though this work is now lost, the title alone, *Fī al-iḥtijāj li-naẓm al-Qurʾān wa-salāmatihi min al-ziyāda wa-l-nuqṣān (The Argument for the Composition (Naẓm) of the Quran and Its Freedom from Superfluity and Lack)*, suggests as much.[24] This is confirmed by statements in al-Jāḥiẓ's surviving works, such as: "in this revealed book of ours, what points to the fact that it is truthful is its innovative composition (*naẓmuhu l-badīʿ*), the like of which no human can produce."[25]

The earliest surviving treatises on *iʿjāz* from the tenth century also ultimately prioritized composition, despite the variation in their approaches and organization of the material. Al-Rummānī (d. 384/994),

[24] See Wolfhart Heinrichs, *Naẓm*, in *EI*^{2}. See also Gustave E. von Grunebaum, *A Tenth-Century Document of Arabic Literary Theory and Criticism: The Sections on Poetry of Bâqillânî's Iʿjâz al-Qurʾân* (Chicago: University of Chicago Press, 1950), xvi, especially n15. It seems, however, that there were others before al-Jāḥiẓ who had discussed the question of *naẓm* in the Quran, as evidenced by al-Bāqillānī's comment that al-Jāḥiẓ "did not add anything to what other theologians had said before him" (*Iʿjāz al-Qurʾān*, 7).

[25] al-Jāḥiẓ, *al-Ḥayawān*, 4:90. We do not know what al-Jāḥiẓ really meant by *naẓm*. But Saʿd ʿAbd al-ʿAẓīm Muḥammad has tried to deduce that through collecting all of al-Jāḥiẓ's statements about *naẓm* in his surviving works. These include elements that later become standard parts of discussions of *naẓm*, such as word order and sentence structure, concision (*ījāz*), and ellipsis, among others (see al-Jāḥiẓ and Saʿd ʿAbd al-ʿAẓīm Muḥammad, *Naẓm al-Qurʾān* (Cairo: Maktabat al-Zahrāʾ, 1995)).

in his *al-Nukat fī iʿjāz al-Qurʾān* (*The Subtleties of the Inimitability of the Quran*), divided eloquence into ten aspects, incorporating *badīʿ* figures such as paronomasia, as well as metaphor and simile, as central components of eloquence. However, in the end, he placed the Quran's inimitability in its composition (*taʾlīf*).[26]

Later, al-Bāqillānī argued that, while *badīʿ* might add beauty to the Quranic text, it is not what makes it inimitable.[27] This is for two reasons: not all Quranic verses employ them, yet every single verse is supposed to be inimitable; furthermore, he points out that they represent an artistic skill that humans can learn and excel in with practice.[28] Instead, al-Bāqillānī placed the inimitability of the Quran's eloquence squarely in its sentence structures and composition (*al-naẓm wa-l-taʾlīf*) and the consistency of the high quality of composition throughout the text.[29]

[26] al-Rummānī, *al-Nukat*, 107. For a translation, see *Three Treatises on the Iʿjaz of the Qur'an: Qur'anic Studies and Literary Criticism*, ed. Muḥammad Khalafallāh Aḥmad and Muḥammad Zaghlūl Sallām, trans. Issa J. Boullata (Reading, England: Garnett Publishing, 2014), 54–92). See summary of al-Rummānī's text in Andrew Rippin and Jan Knappert, eds., *Textual Sources for the Study of Islam* (Chicago: University of Chicago Press, 1990), 49–59. The ten parts of eloquence according to al-Rummānī are: "conciseness, simile (*tashbīh*), metaphor (*istiʿāra*), harmony in the sounds of words and letters, analogous endings of speech divisions, paronomasia, morphology (*taṣrīf*), metonymy (which he calls *taḍmīn*), hyperbole, and elucidation (*bayān*)" (al-Rummānī, *al-Nukat*, 76). It is worth noting that al-Rummānī discusses composition under the heading of "*bayān*," showing how broadly the term was employed in this early period. He also lists factors other than eloquence as evidence for the miraculousness of the Quran. These include: "the lack of imitation even though there is an abundance of reason and a great need to make the attempt; the challenge put forth to everyone; the prevention from imitation by God; the true predictions about coming events; the Quran being out of the ordinary, contradicting custom; and the analogy of the Quran to all other miracles" (Rippin and Knappert, *Textual Sources*, 49; al-Rummānī, *al-Nukat*, 75).

[27] al-Bāqillānī, *Iʿjāz al-Qurʾān*, 161–2 and 416–18. Nevertheless, al-Bāqillānī goes to great lengths to describe the various *badīʿ* figures found in poetry and the Quran alike and acknowledges their beautifying effect (ibid., 106–70). See von Grunebaum, *A Tenth-Century Document*, for a translation of the relevant sections on literary figures. Metaphor, however, and other *bayān* figures are already treated differently from other *badīʿ* figures and do form a basis for inimitability (al-Bāqillānī, *Iʿjāz al-Qurʾān*, 430). Simile, significantly, is excluded (ibid., 417; see also Harb, "Form, Content, and Inimitability," 315). For a discussion of al-Bāqillānī's views on *iʿjāz* in *Iʿjāz al-Qurʾān* as well as his other works, see Sallām, *Athar al-Qurʾān*, 267ff.

[28] al-Bāqillānī, *Iʿjāz al-Qurʾān*, 162 and 168–9. *Bayān* and other aspects of *iʿjāz*, instead, cannot be gained with learning and practice (ibid., 431–3).

[29] Ibid., 75. On consistency of eloquence throughout the Quran, see ibid., 54–5. Besides its eloquence, al-Bāqillānī also cites as evidence of the miraculousness of the Quran: the true predictions contained in it and the fact that the Prophet was illiterate and could not have known all the information conveyed in it about the past were it not for divine instruction (ibid., 48–51). Al-Bāqillānī also looks at the novelty of the Quran as a genre that does not

Naẓm also formed a major component of al-Khaṭṭābī's argument in his *Bayān iʿjāz al-Qurʾān* (*Exposing the Inimitability of the Quran*). He states: "the Quran became inimitable because it brought forth the most articulate utterances (*lafẓ*) in the best order of composition (*naẓm*) containing the most correct meanings (*maʿnā*)."[30] He delineates three aspects of speech: the utterance (*lafẓ*), meaning (*maʿnā*), and something that ties them together in an order (i.e., *naẓm*).[31] He discusses each of these aspects, but puts particular emphasis on *naẓm*:

> As for the forms of *naẓm*, the need to study and look at them carefully is greater because it is the harness of utterances and the reins of meanings, and with it the parts of speech are organized and made to fit in harmony with each other so that it produces an image in the soul (*ṣūra fī al-nafs*) through which elucidation (*bayān*) is achieved.[32]

While the case for *iʿjāz* drew on contemporary discussions of poetry in the third/ninth and fourth/tenth centuries, the medieval scholars' arguments ultimately rested on *naẓm* rather than *badīʿ*. The concern with the inimitability of the Quran thus added a new aspect of eloquence to the inventory of components analyzed by literary critics. A more comprehensive description of *naẓm*, however, did not take place until the following century with ʿAbd al-Qāhir al-Jurjānī's treatise on the inimitability of the Quran entitled *Dalāʾil al-iʿjāz* (*The Signs of the Inimitability of the Quran*).[33]

ʿABD AL-QĀHIR AL-JURJĀNĪ

Al-Jurjānī locates the source of beauty in speech in three elements: (a) the idea itself, (b) the individual words chosen in the phrase that expresses it,

fit any of the existing poetic or literary forms of the time: it is neither poetry nor prose (ibid., 51ff.).

30 al-Khaṭṭābī, *Bayān iʿjāz al-Qurʾān*, 27. See English translation in al-Khaṭṭābī, al-Rummānī, and al-Jurjānī, *Three Treatises on the Iʿjaz of the Qur'an: Qur'anic Studies and Literary Criticism*.

31 al-Khaṭṭābī, *Bayān iʿjāz al-Qurʾān*, 27. See also Sallām, *Athar al-Qurʾān*, 256–7.

32 al-Khaṭṭābī, *Bayān iʿjāz al-Qurʾān*, 36. Sallām also points out the fact that al-Khaṭṭābī gives precedence to *naẓm* (Sallām, *Athar al-Qurʾān*, 263). The language of al-Khaṭṭābī here contains the kernels of al-Jurjānī's concept of *naẓm* and *ṣūrat al-maʿnā* (image of meaning), which I will discuss below. For discussions of al-Khaṭṭābī's influence on al-Jurjānī, see ibid., 248, and the editors' introduction to al-Khaṭṭābī, al-Rummānī, and ʿAbd al-Qāhir al-Jurjānī, *Thalāth rasāʾil fī iʿjāz al-Qurʾān*, ed. Muḥammad Khalafallāh and Muḥammad Zaghlūl Sallām (Cairo: Dār al-Maʿārif, 1976), 14. Heinrichs says al-Khaṭṭābī may be called al-Jurjānī's "precursor in matters of *naẓm*" (Heinrichs, *Naẓm*).

33 On al-Bāqillānī's influence on al-Jurjānī, see, Shadhā Jarrār, *Muwāzana bayn madhhabay al-Bāqillānī wa-l-Jurjānī fī kitābayhimā Iʿjāz al-Qurʾān wa-Dalāʾil al-iʿjāz* (Amman: Amānat ʿAmmān, 2005).

and (c) the way these words are strung together (i.e., *naẓm*).[34] All these elements come together to create a unique image or form of a given idea, something he calls *ṣūrat al-maʿnā* (the image or form of meaning). When it comes to the inimitability of the Quran, al-Jurjānī argues explicitly that it does not lie in its content. It is not the ideas of the Quran themselves that have broken the laws of nature and rendered it extraordinary. People could reproduce the ideas expressed in the Quran in their own words, after all.[35] He argues instead that the miraculousness of the Quran lies in the manner in which the ideas are expressed, i.e., its form. The challenge to produce something like it is therefore a challenge to imitate its form.

Given that content is taken out of the equation, the remaining elements that bestow beauty on speech are individual words and *naẓm*. Individual words or word units, as we have seen in Chapter 4, contribute to eloquence when they signify their meaning indirectly. Individual words, therefore, have the capacity to affect the final "image of meaning" when they express that meaning through metaphor (*istiʿāra*) or figurative speech (*majāz*) and metonymy (*kināya*). However, *naẓm* takes precedence as an inevitable component of eloquence on which metaphor and metonymy depend.[36] While the inimitability of the Quran also lies in its use of metaphors, figurative speech in general, and meanings that are implied through *kināya* instead of expressed explicitly, *naẓm* constitutes the primary aspect that renders the Quran inimitable.[37]

Naẓm

Al Jurjānī preliminarily explains that *naẓm* is nothing more than "obeying the rules of syntax."[38] However, as he goes on to clarify, it involves something more than simply using grammar properly:

[It is not simply] knowing that the "and" is for combining, the "then" for indicating a sequence, [. . .] the "when" for this, and the "if" for that. Rather, it is to have the

[34] See Harb, "Form, Content, and Inimitability."

[35] al-Jurjānī, *Dalāʾil*, 257; ʿAbd al-Qāhir al-Jurjānī, "al-Risāla al-shāfiya fī wujūh al-iʿjāz," in *Dalāʾil al-iʿjāz*, ed. Maḥmūd Muḥammad Shākir (Cairo: Maktabat al-Khānjī, 2004), 602–10.

[36] al-Jurjānī, *Dalāʾil*, 393.

[37] Note that al-Jurjānī excludes simile from the aspects which render the Quran inimitable. This is because he understands simile as a statement of an idea (i.e., content), not form (I argue this in "Form, Content, and Inimitability").

[38] al-Jurjānī, *Dalāʾil*, 81.

ability when composing poetry or a letter to choose well and know the place of each matter.[39]

Elsewhere he defines *naẓm* as "heeding the meanings of syntax (*tawakhkhī maʿānī al-naḥw*), its principles, differences, and [various] aspects."[40] Therefore, *naẓm* involves being aware of how the syntax and grammatical construction of a sentence affect its overall meaning.

The eloquence of *naẓm* is not simply the proper use of grammar. Rather, it is the use of grammar in a way that requires deduction. Just as individual words employed for their literal meaning do not play any role in eloquence, as we have seen, because they do not require deduction or interpretation, eloquence at the level of the sentence also cannot be attributed to the mere correctness of grammar. That is because "the avoidance of a [grammatical] mistake [...] does not require careful inspection, good reflection, strong intellect, and acute awareness."[41] Al-Jurjānī emphasizes that distinctiveness (*maziyya*) in speech is "without a doubt" something that requires "thought and examination."[42] Elsewhere he elaborates:

Knowledge of grammar is common to all Arabs and it is not something that is deduced through thought or that requires reflection. For there is not one person more knowledgeable than another of the fact that the subject is in the nominative, the object is in the accusative, and the governed noun of a possessive construction is in the genitive.[43] Neither is this something that requires keen intelligence and strong intellect. Rather, the [kind of situation] where [intellect] is necessary is knowing [for example] what to attribute "subjectness" (*al-fāʿiliyya*) to in the case where its attribution is conveyed figuratively (through *majāz*). Such as in the Almighty saying: "their transaction did not profit (فَمَا رَبِحَت تِجَارَتُهُم)" (Q2:16),[44] and as in al-Farazdaq saying:

سَقَتْهَا خُرُوقٌ في المَسَامِعِ ...

Ear-piercing [fame] watered [his camels]...[45]

[39] Ibid., 250. [40] Ibid., 452. [41] Ibid., 98. [42] Ibid., 395.

[43] "فليس أحدهم بأعلم من غيره بأن إعراب الفاعل الرفع أو المفعول النصب والمضاف إليه الجر" (ibid.).

[44] See Chapter 3, my discussion of metaphor under "Variation in *Bayān*" for this verse.

[45] The idea of this hemistich, which I discuss in more detail below, is that the renown of the tribe to whom these camels belong was enough to make other tribes give them precedence at the watering-hole. What I am translating as "ear-piercing [fame]" (*khurūq fī al-masāmiʿ*) literally means "piercings in the ears." I follow Abū Mūsā's understanding of it as meaning the widespread fame of the poet's camel that "pierced the ears" of the people, which is also implied in al-Mubarrad's (d. c. 285/898 or 286/899) discussion of the verse (Muḥammad Muḥammad Abū Mūsā, *Khaṣāʾiṣ al-tarākīb: Dirāsa taḥlīliyya li-masāʾil ʿilm al-maʿānī* (Cairo: Maktabat Wahba, 1996), 129–30; al-Mubarrad, *al-Kāmil*, 1:101). However, one could also understand it as literal piercings in the ears of the camels that indicated to whom they belonged. See my discussion of the verse in what follows.

And the likes of that, which makes something the subject through subtle interpretation (*ta ʾwīl*) and by way of nuance. This does not result from one's knowledge of grammatical cases, rather [from knowledge] of the description that leads to these grammatical cases.[46]

I will discuss the examples he mentions here shortly, but we can generally understand from this passage that *naẓm*, unlike grammar, involves sentence structures that require a certain intellectual effort to interpret. The use of proper grammar conveys an idea adequately, but what gives speech distinctiveness is a concern with and awareness of the attributes and implications of certain grammatical constructions, which require interpretation. This is the way in which differences in the quality of the final "image of meaning" (*ṣūrat al-maʿnā*) arise.

Grammatical constructions can themselves be figurative, as we will see in the next section, thus requiring deduction to grasp the meaning. This syntactical figurativeness is distinct from the kind of figurativeness in individual words we encountered in Chapter 4 in the science of *bayān*, as I will clarify below. Otherwise, sentence construction can impart meaning and give nuance through manipulations of grammatical structures, such as: (a) changing the placement of a word in a sentence, (b) omitting a grammatical entity that should otherwise be included, (c) the deliberate employment of a definite noun as opposed to indefinite, (d) the employment of conjunctions or lack thereof, and (e) the use of function words like *inna*, a corroborative particle that has the sense of "indeed," or "in fact."[47] All these manipulations convey some additional meaning in a way that requires deduction, as we will see in the following.

Figurativeness in Naẓm

In the passage quoted above, among the examples al-Jurjānī provides of syntactical constructions that require "subtle deduction" is the figurative attribution of an action to a subject, something he calls *majāz ḥukmī* (figurative governing [of speech]).[48] The Quranic verse 2:16 ("their transaction did not profit") that al-Jurjānī cites above provides an example of such figurative attribution because the verb "to profit" is figuratively

46 al-Jurjānī, *Dalāʾil*, 395–6.

47 For a comprehensive presentation of the various aspects of *naẓm* in al-Jurjānī's work, see Weisweiler, "ʿAbdalqāhir al-Curcānī's Werk."

48 al-Jurjānī, *Dalāʾil*, 293–303. In the *Asrār* he describes *majāz ḥukmī* variously as *isnād majāzī* (figurative attribution), *majāz ʿaqlī* (intellected figurative speech), and *majāz fī al-jumla* (figurativeness in the sentence) (*Asrār*, 338ff).

ascribed to "their transaction." That is, while "their transaction" is made to be the subject of the verb grammatically, in reality it is "those who have bought error [in exchange] for guidance," mentioned earlier in the verse, who have not profited from this transaction. Elsewhere he asks rhetorically: "to whom is the merit, distinction, and difference not obvious between the Almighty saying 'their transaction did not profit' and saying 'they did not profit in their transaction'?"[49]

To illustrate this further, al-Jurjānī provides a verse by the Umayyad poet al-Farazdaq (d. 110/728):[50]

يَحْمِي إذَا آخْتُرِطَ السُّيُوفُ نِسَاءَنا ضَرْبٌ تَطِيرُ لَهُ السَّواعِدُ أَرْعَلُ

Strong blows to which arms come flying
protect – if swords are drawn – our women

Al-Jurjānī exclaims the obviousness of the splendor of this verse when compared to its literal presentation, which would make explicit the actual subject as "we" instead of attributing the act of protection to the "strong blows," as in saying: "We protect – if swords are drawn – our women with strong blows to which arms come flying."[51] It is the syntactical construction, which figuratively attributes the verb "to protect" to the "strong blows," that bestows splendor on the verse, not a figurative usage of words as signifiers. The word "protect" is intended literally, after all.

The same mechanism is at play in the other verse by al-Farazdaq he refers to in his description of *naẓm* quoted above. The verse in full states:[52]

سَقَتْهَا خُرُوقٌ في المَسَامِعِ لَمْ تَكُنْ عِلاطاً ولا مَخْبُوطَةً في المَلاغِمِ

Ear-piercing [fame] watered [his camels]; they did not
have any marks on their necks and were not branded on the mouth

To borrow from the third/ninth-century philologist's, al-Mubarrad's, explanation of the verse, "the owners of the watering-hole knew to whom [the camels] belonged. Therefore, what they had heard mentioned about their owners of their might and power [was enough] to provide for [the camels], so that they did not need a mark [to identify them]."[53] The poet, therefore, figuratively attributes the action of "giving water" to

[49] al-Jurjānī, *Dalāʾil*, 295.
[50] Ibid.; al-Farazdaq, *Sharḥ Dīwān al-Farazdaq*, ed. Īliyyā al-Ḥāwī, 2 vols. (Beirut: Dār al-Kitāb al-Lubnānī, Maktabat al-Madrasa, 1983), 2:319.
[51] al-Jurjānī, *Dalāʾil*, 295.
[52] Ibid., 396 and 293–4, for al-Jurjānī's discussion of the verse. The verse does not appear in al-Farazdaq's *Dīwān*, however. Al-Mubarrad cites it in *al-Kāmil*, 1:101.
[53] al-Mubarrad, *al-Kāmil*, 1:101.

the camels' (and their owner's) fame, when in reality it is the owners of the watering-hole who provided the water. Al-Jurjānī emphasizes that it is the grammatical attribution of subjectness to – what amounts to – "fame" that requires examination, not a figurative use of the word "to water," the meaning of which remains literal.

The Meanings of Syntax vs. the Meaning of Meaning

What is the difference between this kind of *majāz* here, which results from a figurative grammatical construction (i.e., the meaning of syntax), and the kind of figurative speech we encountered in Chapter 4, which takes place in the signification of words (i.e., the meaning of meaning)? Both entail the conveying of meaning in a figurative way. However, the literal counterpart of each is different. In *naẓm*, the literal meaning which is to be interpreted figuratively results from an interpretation of the grammatical structure that the author constructs. As a result, al-Jurjānī describes it as "intellected *majāz*" (*majāz ʿaqlī*) because the literal reading itself of the grammatical structure requires interpretation. In individual words, on the other hand, the literal meaning that is to be interpreted figuratively is set by convention. As a result al-Jurjānī identifies it as "lexical *majāz*" (*majāz lughawī*) because the literal reading is set by the lexicon.[54]

An example of the intellected type of figurative speech is the phrase: "spring decorated [the gardens] (وَشَّى الرَّبِيعُ)."[55] The literal meaning that has to be interpreted figuratively is the attribution of the action of decorating to something that cannot possibly be its subject: a nonliving thing such as the spring. This attribution is something that has to be deduced in the first place by judging the syntactical relationship between the two words in the sentence. It is not set by linguistic convention but is produced in that particular phrase by rendering spring the subject of the action. The literal meaning in this case is a kind of meaning that has to be "intellected" in the first place (i.e., figuring out what is the subject of the sentence). The listener then must proceed to further interpret this intellected attribution to understand the intended meaning that "the spring was the cause for

[54] Al-Jurjānī discusses the two types of figurative speech in great detail at the end of his *Asrār* (p. 324ff.). The subtle difference between the two is discussed in chapter 25 of the *Asrār* (pp. 376–83).

[55] Ibid., 378.

the existence of flowers, which resemble embellishments."[56] Al-Jurjānī therefore calls this type of *majāz*, which arises in the sentence, *ʿaqlī* (intellected) because the literal meaning of the grammatical construction is already something that has to be "intellected." The literal meaning in *majāz lughawī*, on the other hand, is set by the lexicon; we cannot arrive at the meaning of the sound image "lion," for example, through reasoning, as we have seen in Chapter 4, because it is arbitrarily set by convention.[57] While both types of figurative speech require interpretation (*taʾwīl*), therefore, the literal meaning is intellected in one case and lexical in the other.[58]

Later commentators disagree about whether to classify the intellected type of figurative speech (*majāz ʿaqlī*) separately under the science of meanings (*ʿilm al-maʿānī*) or together with the other type of *majāz* under the science of elucidation (*ʿilm al-bayān*). Al-Sakkākī classifies both under *ʿilm al-bayān*.[59] Al-Khaṭīb al-Qazwīnī criticizes him for this and classifies the intellected type under *ʿilm al-maʿānī*, where he adds a discussion on "intellected literal [meaning]" (*ḥaqīqa ʿaqliyya*), which entails grammatical constructions intended literally, and "intellected figurative [meaning]" (*majāz ʿaqlī*), which entails figurative syntactical relations, such as the ones discussed here.[60] Regardless of later classification, the distinction al-Jurjānī makes between the two types of *majāz* sheds light on the difference between the function of words as signs and the mechanisms of conveying meaning through sentence construction. The secondary meaning in the former depends on processes of indirect signification, i.e., the "meaning of meaning." The secondary meaning in the latter depends on syntactical processes of meaning production, i.e., the "meanings of syntax."[61]

[56] Ibid. Al-Jurjānī's choice of example is a bit confusing because it also employs a lexical *majāz* in the word "decorated." Nevertheless, the point of the example is to show its figurative attribution to "spring."

[57] See ibid., 347. In other words, there is no logical connection between the signifier that sounds out the word "lion" and the animal it signifies. This is an arbitrary relationship agreed upon by convention. See al-Jurjānī's discussion of this matter in *Dalāʾil*, 44–6.

[58] See al-Jurjānī's response to the claim that both types of *majāz* are "intellected" (*Asrār*, 379–81). Margaret Larkin also discusses the difference between *majāz ʿaqlī* and *lughawī* in chapter 4 of *Theology of Meaning*, especially 87ff. Her focus, however, is on al-Jurjānī's theological outlook and she believes that what is at stake is a question of essence vs. attributes (ibid., 105–9). What is at stake from an aesthetic point of view is two different ways of expressing meaning indirectly.

[59] al-Sakkākī, *al-Miftāḥ*, 503–9. [60] al-Khaṭīb al-Qazwīnī, *al-Īḍāḥ*, 107–8.

[61] Al-Jurjānī therefore also assigns the former to the individual word (*fī al-mufrad*) and the latter to the sentence (*fī al-jumla*) (*Asrār*, 324–51). This does not mean that verbs cannot function metaphorically in themselves as signifiers, such as saying, for example, "his eyes

*Sentence Construction (*Naẓm*) and Eloquence*

Constructing a sentence in a way that figuratively attributes an action to a subject therefore is one way for speech to necessitate "thought and examination" and thus "add distinction (*maziyya*)."[62] There are many other features of sentence construction that can similarly relate additional information in a way that requires interpretation, such as word order, ellipsis, and the employment of various particles. In the following, I will focus on a select number of these features, which al-Jurjānī discusses in *Dalāʾil al-iʿjāz* in order to give the reader a sense of what they entail, highlighting how al-Jurjānī explains their eloquence. Given that many of these *naẓm*-based features are unique to the linguistic structure of the Arabic language, the translations will more often than not fail to convey the beauty al-Jurjānī is trying to expose in the Arabic construction. Nevertheless, what concerns us more is the reasoning behind his explanations of its beauty.

Pre- and Post-positioning

Pre- and post-positioning (*taqdīm wa-taʾkhīr*)[63] entails changing the order in which parts of speech are typically arranged, such as placing the predicate (*khabar*) before the subject of a sentence (*mubtadaʾ*), or the object (*mafʿūl bihi*) before the subject of a verb (*fāʿil*). Al-Jurjānī explains that many a time when you are pleased by some poetry and you search for the source of this pleasure, "you find that the reason it delighted and appealed to you is that something was made to come first and that the words were switched around from one place to another."[64] The effect of this phenomenon on the meaning of a phrase is discussed by grammarians as early as Sībawayh (d. 177/793), who wrote the first book on Arabic grammar in the second/eighth century. An example of pre- and post-positioning that is commonly cited is saying "Zayd killed the Khārijite" versus "[it was] the Khārijite whom Zayd killed," a difference which in Arabic can easily be rendered by pre-positioning the object and post-positioning the subject while

spoke to me." There is no level at which speaking can be intended literally in the phrase. Metaphor can be in the noun (*ismiyya*), that is, or in the verb (*fiʿliyya*) (ibid., 42–51).

62 al-Jurjānī, *Dalāʾil*, 395–6.

63 Al-Jurjānī discusses pre- and post-positioning throughout *Dalāʾil al-iʿjāz*, but primarily pp. 106–45.

64 Ibid., 106.

maintaining the declensions that indicate their grammatical role: *qatala Zaydun al-khārijiyya* vs. *qatala al-khārijyya Zaydun*.[65] The point of the first sentence is reporting that Zayd is the one who did the killing. "The place of surprise," as Fakhr al-Dīn al-Rāzī explains, "is the emanation of killing from Zayd, not its befalling the victim."[66] Whereas the second sentence emphasizes that the victim of the killing was a Khārijite.[67]

Al-Jurjānī goes on to explain, however, that most people assume that the only benefit of placing a word earlier in a sentence is emphasis.[68] Inverting the word order has implications for the meaning of a statement as well, he reminds us. He asks us to consider the Quranic verse that says:

قُلْ أَغَيْرَ اللّٰهِ أَتَّخِذُ وَلِيًّا

Say: Other than God [how] shall I take [anyone] as protector?

~ Q6:14

Al-Jurjānī explains that the verse has a "beauty, distinctiveness, and grandeur that does not exist if [the object] came later, as in: 'Say: Shall I take [anyone] other than God as protector? (قُلْ أَأَتَّخِذُ غيرالله وليًا).'"[69] This is because,

By [mentioning the object first], you are giving the sense of saying: Can there be any other than God that could be taken as a protector? How could any sane person allow himself to do something like that? Can there be ignorance more ignorant than that and blindness blinder than that? None of this is conveyed with "who shall I take as protector other than God" and that is because the verb is taken as is, without any additional [connotations].[70]

[65] Note that there are two kinds of pre- and post-positioning: one that maintains the syntactic value of the word, as in the example here where Zayd remains the subject even when the word order changes; another that changes the syntactical value of the word. Fakhr al-Dīn al-Rāzī explains that pre- and post-positioning can either be intentional, so that you pre-position the predicate (*khabar*) or the object (*maf'ūl*). Alternatively, it could come about not with the intention of post-positioning or pre-positioning. A different order could result in different grammatical values, for example saying: "Zayd is going (*Zayd al-munṭaliq*)" vs. "He who is going is Zayd (*al-Munṭaliq Zayd*)." The first word in each of the sentences is always the subject (*mubtada'*). The meaning changes, as a result, with the change in word placement (al-Rāzī, *Nihāyat al-ījāz*, 181). Kees Versteegh calls *taqdīm* "fronting" and clarifies that in one kind of fronting "you do not shift [words] from their syntactic position . . .," the other kind of fronting "is when there is no underlying postposing, but you shift the constituent from its former status to a new and different status, and a new and different declension" ("A New Semantic Approach to Linguistics: al-Jurjânî and as-Sakkâkî on Meaning," in *Landmarks in Linguistic Thought: The Arabic Linguistic Tradition*, ed. Kees Versteegh (London: Routledge, 1997), 115).

[66] al-Rāzī, *Nihāyat al-ījāz*, 181.

[67] The Khārijites were a group of early Islamic dissidents, hence the example!

[68] al-Jurjānī, *Dalā'il*, 107–8. [69] Ibid., 121. [70] Ibid., 122.

Changing the order of words in a sentence, therefore, can add meaning to the statement, much more than mere "emphasis."

What is it, however, that makes adding meaning through a change in word order more distinct and eloquent than spelling it out in a more typical and straightforward way? In his discussion of another Quranic verse, al-Jurjānī points out the "splendor" of stating the word "partners" before "jinn":

وَجَعَلوا لِلَّهِ شُرَكاءَ الجِنَّ

They made partners of God, the jinn

~ Q6:100[71]

If you state it afterwards and say: "They made the jinn partners of God (وجعلوا الجنّ شركاء لِلَّهِ)," he explains, this "splendor and beauty" is lost. The reason for this is that the former has an additional meaning that the latter construction does not have. Both statements convey the general meaning that they made the jinn partners of God and worshiped them as they did God. However, placing the word "partners" first conveys the additional meaning that "there should not be any partners to God, whether among the jinn or otherwise."[72] Placing the word "partners" second, on the other hand, gives the impression that it is the fact that the jinn specifically were made partners that is problematic, not polytheism in and of itself.[73] If you wanted to add the meaning achieved in the Quranic verse to the latter construction, you would have to say: "they made the jinn partners of God, and God should not have any partner neither jinn nor any other."[74] The difference in eloquence between this long statement and what the short verse was able to convey concisely through its particular construction is clear, he states. The merit of the construction of the Quranic verse, therefore, lies in the fact that "meaning is added without adding words."[75] In other words, additional meaning is conveyed implicitly simply through a manipulation of the order of words in a phrase, making the listener go through additional steps of reasoning to arrive at the meaning rather than spelling it out for him.

In addition, bringing attention to something earlier in a sentence before actually explaining it can give the effect of concealment (*iḍmār*). Consider, for example, the Quranic verse:

[71] The accusative form in Arabic makes it clear that the jinn is an object.
[72] al-Jurjānī, *Dalāʾil*, 286. [73] Ibid., 287. [74] Ibid., 288. [75] Ibid.

فَإِنَّهَا لَا تَعْمَى الْأَبْصَارُ وَلَكِن تَعْمَى الْقُلُوبُ الَّتِي فِي الصُّدُورِ

For indeed, it is not the case with them that eyes become blind, but
the hearts that are in the chests become blind

~ Q22:46

Al-Jurjānī explains that mentioning the subject ahead of time in an obscure form, by saying "it is ... the case with them that" (*fa-innahā*) without clarification, gives the statement grandeur, nobility, and splendor in a way that we would not find if we were to say: "for indeed (*fa-inna*) eyes do not become blind (فإنّ الأبصار لا تعمى)."[76] Although it is difficult to see the elegance of a particle attached to a pronoun (*innahā*) in English when its meaning would have to be translated with a whole phrase (it is the case with them that . . .), al-Jurjānī argues that such constructions add splendor. This is because "obscuring followed by an explanation is grander than [simply] mentioning something [directly] without introducing it [first] obscurely."[77] While in the previous example, the listener's thought is activated because changing the order of words adds something to the meaning implicitly, in this case the listener's interest is piqued and his curiosity about the meaning is stimulated through an initial obscuration that is elegantly producible in Arabic through the employment of *innahā*. In both cases, a manipulation of the order of words makes the path to the meaning less direct than saying it plainly.

This becomes even clearer in al-Jurjānī's discussion of the following verse by Abū Tammām, in which the poet describes the powers of the pen:

لُعَابُ الأَفَاعِي القَاتِلاتِ لُعَابُهُ وَأَرْيُ الجَنَى اشْتَارَتْهُ أَيْدٍ عَوَاسِلُ

The saliva of killer vipers is its saliva
and the harvested honey gathered by honey-collecting hands[78]

If one were to interpret the meaning as it appears on the surface and thus take the first phrase, "the saliva of the vipers," as the subject and the second, "its saliva," as the predicate, "you would spoil the meaning and impede the image that [the poet] intended with it."[79] The poet meant to liken the ink of his pen and its deleterious powers to the deadly saliva of vipers, on the one hand. At the same time, he meant to liken its power to generate joy and pleasure to honey. This meaning can only be achieved by taking the second phrase ("its saliva") as a post-positioned subject of the verse. (This is an unusual construction since the subject (*mubtadaʾ*) in

[76] Ibid., 132. The verse is also discussed under the uses of *inna* (ibid., 317–18).
[77] Ibid., 132. [78] Ibid., 371. [79] Ibid.

a nominal sentence typically comes first in a sentence.) Otherwise, you would be likening the venomous saliva of the snakes (instead of the ink) to honey.[80] The listener therefore has to go through a process of reasoning and deduction to realize what is being likened to what – a process that a straightforward and ordinary sentence construction would not require. He goes on to explain that "there is no speech [. . .], in which the predicate is made to come first, that does not complicate matters for you: you cannot know that the predicate was made to precede without going back to the meaning and considering it carefully."[81]

Ellipsis

Another aspect of sentence construction that can induce "thought and examination" is ellipsis (*ḥadhf*).[82] Ellipsis entails excluding a part of speech that should typically be included in a sentence such as the subject or object. It is an aspect of *naẓm*, al-Jurjānī declares, that:

> entails subtle ways, delicate paths, and wondrous matters, akin to magic. For you see in it that not stating [something] is more revealing than stating it, remaining silent about a meaning adds to the conveying of that meaning. You find yourself most articulate when you do not articulate and most elucidating when you do not elucidate.[83]

Al-Jurjānī explains that choosing *not* to mention a part of speech focuses the meaning on the aspect you intend to convey. For example, you can say: "Zayd hit ʿAmr," "Zayd hit," or "hitting took place." In the first case, you are affirming that the object of the hitting was ʿAmr. In the second, you are affirming that Zayd is the subject of hitting. In the third case, you are emphasizing the fact that hitting took place, regardless of who did it and to whom.[84] Depending on what your intention is, refraining from mentioning information can direct the listener's attention to the point you desire to make.

In the following Quranic verses relating a story about Moses, for example, the object "the flock of sheep" is omitted in four instances:[85]

[80] Ibid., 371–2.
[81] Ibid., 373. Al-Khaṭīb al-Qazwīnī discusses Abū Tammām's verse in the chapter concerning the subject (*al-musnad ilayh*) and describes it as inversion (*qalb*) (*al-Īḍāḥ*, 165).
[82] Al-Jurjānī discusses ellipsis in *Dalāʾil*, 146–72. [83] Ibid., 146. [84] Ibid., 153–4.
[85] Ibid., 161.

وَلَمَّا وَرَدَ مَاءَ مَدْيَنَ وَجَدَ عَلَيْهِ أُمَّةً مِّنَ النَّاسِ يَسْقُونَ وَوَجَدَ مِن دُونِهِمُ امْرَأَتَيْنِ تَذُودَانِ قَالَ مَا
خَطْبُكُمَا قَالَتَا لَا نَسْقِي حَتَّىٰ يُصْدِرَ الرِّعَاءُ وَأَبُونَا شَيْخٌ كَبِيرٌ فَسَقَىٰ لَهُمَا ثُمَّ تَوَلَّىٰ إِلَى الظِّلِّ

> And when he came upon the water of Madyan he found by it a large group of people watering and found beside them two women holding back. He said: what is the matter? They said: we do not water until the shepherds leave and our father is an old man. So he watered on their behalf and then proceeded to the shade.
>
> ~ Q28:23–4

The complete meaning would be: "he found a large group of people watering [their flocks]," "two women holding back [their flocks]," "they said: we do not water [our flocks]," and "he watered [their flocks] . . ." The ellipsis serves to focus the listener's attention on the action of giving water. What was being watered, whether sheep or camels or otherwise, is irrelevant in this context.[86] Even though the verbs "to water" (*yasqī*) and "to hold back" (*dhāda*) are transitive and grammatically require an object, omitting it clarifies more than stating it.

In another example, ellipsis serves a different purpose: instead of focusing the attention of the listener, it serves to generalize the meaning in the following verse:[87]

إذا بَعُدَتْ أَبْلَتْ وإن قَرُبَتْ شَفَتْ　　فهِجْرانُها يُبْلِي ولُقْيانُها يَشْفِي

> If she moves away, she ails; and if she comes close, she heals
> For her departure ails and her encounter heals
>
> ~ al-Buḥturī (d. 284/897)

Al-Jurjānī explains that one understands that the intended meaning is that: "if she moves away [from me], she ails [me], and if she comes close [to me] she heals [me]." The ellipses, he explains, add the sense that this characteristic is part of her nature and that it is the effect she has on any person she encounters or leaves.[88] Here again, the implicit augmentation of meaning, without explicitly spelling it out, adds to the beauty of the verse. Ellipsis, therefore, evokes an added meaning, which would otherwise not be conveyed.

Finally, ellipses can also produce the effect of obscuring followed by clarification (like the one mentioned earlier through changing the word order). For example:[89]

[86] Ibid. [87] Ibid., 162. [88] Ibid. [89] Ibid., 163.

لَوْ شِئْتَ لَمْ تُفْسِدْ سَمَاحَةَ حَاتِمٍ　　كَرَماً وَلَمْ تَهْدِمْ مَآثِرَ خَالِدِ

If you desired, you would not damage Ḥātim's munificence
with your generosity and you would not destroy the good deeds of Khālid

~ al-Buḥturī (d. 284/897)

The poet praises the addressee by claiming that he is capable of ruining, through his generosity and good deeds, the legendary reputations of Ḥātim and Khālid.[90] Ellipsis takes place here because the object of desire is not mentioned right away after "if you desired" but revealed in the answer to the conditional phrase. The original phrase would be: "if you desired not to damage Ḥātim's munificence, you would not damage it." The phrase is then altered by dispensing with the object of desire in the first instance given that it is mentioned later in the sentence, rendering the phrase the shape it is, in terms of "beauty and strangeness" (*al-ḥusn wa-l-gharāba*).[91] Al-Jurjānī goes on to explain that this is because: "clarification, if it comes after obscuration and after exciting [one's curiosity] for it, is ever more pleasing and dignified than if it was not preceded with what excites [the curiosity]."[92]

The effect of obscuring through ellipsis is reiterated by many rhetoricians after al-Jurjānī.[93] One of the more elaborate explanations of the idea can be found in Badr al-Dīn al-Zarkashī's (d. 794/1392) *al-Burhān fī ʿulūm al-Qurʾān* (*The Proof in the Sciences of the Quran*). Among the benefits of ellipsis, he lists the effect of making something more magnificent and

[90] Ḥātim is in reference to Ḥātim al-Ṭāʾī, a pre-Islamic figure famous for his generosity. Khālid is said to be a reference to Khālid ibn Sudūs ibn Aṣbaʿ (or Aṣmaʿ) al-Nabhānī according to early commentators (see al-Buḥturī, *Dīwān*, 1:508n11). Khālid was known for having hosted the famous pre-Islamic poet Imruʾ al-Qays but having failed to protect his belongings, an incident the poet proceeded to mock in a poem (see *Dīwān Imriʾ al-Qays*, 135–6). Nevertheless, Imruʾ al-Qays also praised him in another poem (see ibid., 90). Some manuscripts of al-Buḥturī's *Dīwān* introduce the poem to which the verse quoted here belongs as a panegyric, others as reproach (see editor's footnote to poem in *Dīwān al-Buḥturī*, 1:507). Given the story of Khālid and Imruʾ al-Qays, the tone is likely more satirical than serious.

[91] al-Jurjānī, *Dalāʾil*, 163. [92] Ibid., 164.

[93] Muḥammad ibn ʿAlī al-Jurjānī, the author of *al-Ishārāt wa-l-tanbīhāt*, also states this idea that ellipsis requires the mind to work harder to get to the meaning, in his chapter on the "subject" (*al-musnad ilayh*): "when the subject is obscured through ellipsis, the soul pains for its ignorance of it. If the soul notices a related [word] that reminds it of it, it experiences pleasure for knowing it. And pleasure resulting after pain is more intense than immediate pleasure" (*al-Ishārāt wa-l-tanbīhāt*, 33). Al-Khaṭīb al-Qazwīnī mentions "clarification after obscuring" as an effect of omitting the object, especially of a verb that expresses desire (such as in the example discussed by al-Jurjānī here) (*al-Īḍāḥ*, 198).

exalted (*al-tafkhīm wa-l-iʿẓām*). He attributes this to the ability of ellipsis to obscure, causing the mind "to wander in every direction, and yearn for what is intended, falling short of grasping it. In such a case, the status of [the obscure matter] is elevated and its place in the soul raised."[94] He goes on to explain that the mind's searching for the omitted matter increases pleasure: "For the more difficult it is to get at the omitted [matter], the better and more intense the pleasure."[95] He goes on to quote Ḥāzim al-Qarṭājannī, the philosophically bent literary critic whom we encountered in Chapter 2, who says:

> ellipsis is found beautiful as long as it does not cause problems in the meaning, given the strength of [the evidence] pointing to it. [...] So [when a word] is omitted the evidence [provided by] the context (*al-ḥāl*) must suffice. The mind is left to wander among the matters about the context that the context itself affords not to mention. With this aim, [ellipsis] produces an effect in the places in which the production of wonder and awe (*al-taʿajjub wa-l-tahwīl*) in the soul is intended.[96]

This passage by al-Zarkashī is significant because it explicitly recounts the experience of the listener when confronted with obscurity and correlates the difficulty of the search for clarity with the degree of pleasure resulting from its discovery, in line with al-Jurjānī's "principle of discovery," which we encountered in Chapter 3. Even more telling is his quotation from al-Qarṭājannī's *Minhāj*, which must come from the lost first part of the book,[97] where he directly links this experience with the "production of *wonder and awe*."

However, as al-Qartājannī also insists, this effect is only possible when the context provides enough information for the omitted matter to be revealed. Otherwise, ellipsis is not advised, as in the following verse discussed by al-Jurjānī:[98]

فَلَم يُبْقِ مِنِّي الشَّوْقُ غَيْرَ تَفَكُّرِي   فَلَوْ شِئْتُ أَنْ أَبْكِي بَكَيْتُ تَفَكُّرا

Yearning has left nothing in me but thoughts
[Even] if I wanted to cry, I would cry thoughts
~ Abū al-Ḥasan al-Jawharī (d. after 377/987)

The poet in this case mentions the object of the wanting ("to cry") and rightly so. He does not omit it and say "if I wanted, I would cry thoughts"

[94] Badr al-Dīn al-Zarkashī, *al-Burhān fī ʿulūm al-Qurʾān*, ed. Muḥammad Abū al-Faḍl Ibrāhīm (Cairo: Dār al-Turāth, 1957), 3:104.
[95] Ibid., 3:105. [96] Ibid., 3:105–6.
[97] The passage is added by the editor at the end of the printed edition of *al-Minhāj* as preserved by al-Zarkashī. (al-Qarṭājannī, *Minhāj*, 391.)
[98] al-Jurjānī, *Dalāʾil*, 167.

as al-Buḥturī did in his verse discussed above in which he said: "If you desired, you would not damage Ḥātim's munificence." Not omitting the object of wanting in al-Jawharī's verse is better because the answer to the conditional phrase ("if I wanted") does not aim at illuminating the object of the "wanting" initially expressed, as in al-Buḥturī's verse. Rather it aims at illuminating the unusual object of the *crying*, i.e., thoughts.[99] It is not that the poet wanted to cry "thoughts," it is that his thoughts were so all-consuming that even if he tried to cry, nothing other than his worries and thoughts would come out.

Refraining from omitting an object is preferable, therefore, when the object is itself unusual. In another example, the poet's declaration that he would "cry blood" for a deceased he is elegizing is also not a good candidate for omitting the object of desire:[100]

وَلَوْ شِئْتُ أَنْ أَبْكِي دَمَاً لَبَكَيْتُهُ   عَلَيْهِ وَلكِنْ سَاحَةَ الصَّبْرِ أَوْسَعُ

And if I wanted to cry blood I would have done so
for him, but the realm of patience is greater
~ Abū Yaʿqūb al-Khuraymī (d. 214/829)

Al-Jurjānī explains that given the "strange novelty" of a person "desiring to cry blood," stating the object is better than omitting it in order to "cement the idea in the soul of the listener and please him with it."[101]

In sum, ellipsis can – counterintuitively – serve to convey an additional meaning. It can also obscure something artificially to allow for an experience of discovery in the listener. This enhances the eloquence of speech and the effect it has on the listener. However, if a matter is strange or novel in and of itself, then stating it does the job of moving the listener.

The Different Kinds of Predicates

Al-Jurjānī also discusses the various forms the predicate can take and their effect on meaning, including the effect of having it be a definite or indefinite word.[102] For example, by making the predicate definite, such as saying "Zayd is *the* generous [person]" or "ʿAmr is *the* brave [person]," one

[99] Ibid. [100] Ibid., 164. [101] Ibid.
[102] For al-Jurjānī's discussion of the effects of the different kinds of predicates, see ibid., 173–221.

implies that Zayd and ʿAmr are the epitomes of generosity and bravery: "You divert the speech to an image that makes one imagine that generosity and bravery do not exist except in [that person]."[103] The use of definite predicates can also serve to imply that something is an already known and established fact, on which the poet then proceeds to build an idea. For example:[104]

هُوَ الرَّجُلُ المَشْروكُ في جُلِّ مالِهِ وَلٰكِنَّهُ بِالمَجْدِ والحَمْدِ مُفْرَدُ

He is the man who has equals in abundance of wealth
But in glory and praiseworthiness he is singular

~ Ibn al-Rūmī (d. 283/896)

In this case, the use of the definite noun does not convey the sense that he is the epitome of a certain quality, as its use in the first examples does. Instead, it gives the sense that the poet is talking about someone the listener is already familiar with: he is that person we all know who has peers as wealthy as him. The poet with such a construction makes the listener "imagine something in his mind that he had never seen or known before, and then uses it as if it were something known and seen."[105] He then proceeds to contrast this quality of being one of many in terms of his wealth with the singularity of his glory and praiseworthiness. Of this last kind of usage of a definite predicate, al-Jurjānī states: "this is a remarkable art that has a place of majesty and nobility, and is of eloquence's magic, to which an explanation cannot do justice. The crux of it lies in revision [. . .] and thorough contemplation."[106] It is therefore the subtle implied meaning that the intentional employment of the definite article can impart that is eloquent. Here again, what al-Jurjānī emphasizes is the fact that this sort of added meaning is not obvious or explicit but requires thought and contemplation.

Detachment and Conjunction (*al-Faṣl wa-l-Waṣl*)

Something as seemingly insignificant as the employment of the conjunction "and" or lack thereof can also have a significant effect on meaning.[107] Al-Jurjānī states that knowing when to connect sentences with each other and when to keep them separate is "one of the secrets of eloquence."[108] Its importance is so great that some have equated eloquence with "knowing

[103] Ibid., 179. [104] Ibid., 183. [105] Ibid., 184. [106] Ibid., 183.
[107] For al-Jurjānī's discussion of *al-faṣl wa-l-waṣl*, see ibid., 222–48. [108] Ibid., 222.

when to connect and separate."[109] Indeed, the topic later receives its own dedicated chapter within the field of *ʿilm al-maʿānī*. Al-Jurjānī explains its importance as being: "due to the mysteriousness and subtlety of its ways, and because one cannot reach distinction [in this aspect] without having [first] perfected the other [aspects] of eloquence."[110]

One of the benefits of separating sentences by not using a conjunction is that it can give an effect similar to what we would today produce with a semicolon. That is, it indicates that the subsequent sentence is an explanation of some sort. For example:

زَعمتُم أنَّ إخوتَكُم قُرَيْشٌ لَهُمْ إلفٌ وَلَيْسَ لَكُمْ إلافُ

You claim that [the tribe of] Quraysh are your brothers;
They have an alliance [that protects them] and you do not have [any] alliances[111]

~ Musāwir ibn Hind (pre-/early Islamic)

The poet satirizes the tribe of Asad in this verse for claiming to be related to the powerful Meccan tribe of Quraysh.[112] However, the fact that Quraysh's alliances do not apply to them reveals the unfoundedness of their claim. Al-Jurjānī explains that by separating the two sentences, the poet implies that someone had asked the question: "So what do you say of their allegation and claim?" In other words, the second hemistich presupposes that someone asked for proof of his doubt in their claim. If the two phrases were connected and the poet would have said instead: "you claimed that Quraysh are your brothers *and* they have an alliance and you do not," he would have simply been stating: "you claimed that Quraysh are your brothers and you lied." In this case, the statement does not imply a question doubting the poet's declaration, to which he proceeds to give an answer.[113]

Another similar example might clarify this further:[114]

قَالَ لِي: كَيْفَ أَنْتَ؟ قلتُ: عَلِيلُ سَهَرٌ دائِمٌ وَحُزْنٌ طَوِيلُ

[109] Ibid. This definition of *balāgha* is mentioned by al-Jāḥiẓ in his *al-Bayān wa-l-tabyīn*, where he attributes it to the Persians (see *al-Bayān wa-l-tabyīn*, 1:88).

[110] al-Jurjānī, *Dalāʾil*, 222.

[111] *Ilāf* and *ilf* signify "A writing of security, written by the king for people, that they may be secure in his territory" (Lane, s.v. *a-l-f*). Lane cites this same verse as an example of usage of this meaning and I quote his translation here to show the full meaning of the verse: "Ye asserted [that your brothers are Ḳureysh; i.e.,] *that ye are like Ḳureysh*: but how should ye be like them? for *they have* [*an alliance whereby they are protected in*] the *trade* of El-Yemen and Syria; and *ye have not* that [*alliance*]."

[112] al-Jurjānī, *Dalāʾil*, 236n3. [113] Ibid., 236–7. [114] Ibid., 238.

> He said to me: how are you? I said: unwell;
> Endless wakefulness and drawn-out sadness
>
> ~ Unknown

The commencement of a new statement in the second hemistich without a conjunction renders it an answer to an implied question. One imagines someone having asked at the end of the first hemistich: "What is wrong? What is the cause of your distress?" To which the poet responds: "Endless wakefulness ... etc."[115] Through a simple syntactical choice of including or excluding a particle of conjunction, therefore, one can add meaning to a sentence implicitly, without adding words.

Inna

The final feature of *nazm* I will discuss here is the use of the word *inna*, a "corroborative particle," as Edward Lane describes it in his lexicon, "corroborating the predicate."[116] It can often be rendered in English as "indeed," or "in fact." Certain punctuation marks, such as a colon, could often convey the focalizing sense of *inna.*[117] Affirmation through *inna* can also have subtle ways of adding to the meaning, even though many assume such function words do not add anything. Al-Jurjānī relates an anecdote about the philosopher al-Kindī (d. after 256/870) showing that even he – as intelligent and educated as he was – did not know the difference between using "*inna*" and refraining from its use. I quote it in full here because it will be relevant for our discussion of *ʿilm al-maʿānī* later as well:

> It is said that [...] the philosopher al-Kindī went to Abū al-ʿAbbās [Thaʿlab][118] and said to him: I find in the speech of Arabs meaningless fillers (*ḥashw*)! [...] I find them saying "ʿAbdallāh is standing (عبدُ الله قائمٌ)," then "Indeed, ʿAbdallāh is standing (إنّ عبدَ الله قائمٌ)," and "Actually, ʿAbdallāh is standing (إنّ عبدَ الله لَقائمٌ)." The words are repeated and the meaning is identical. Abū al-ʿAbbās said: rather, the meanings are different because of a difference in the words. Saying "ʿAbdallāh is standing (عبد الله قائم)" is [simply] relating information about his standing, saying "Indeed, ʿAbdallāh is standing (إنّ عبد الله قائمٌ)" is an answer to an inquirer's question, and saying "Actually, ʿAbdallāh is standing (إنّ عبد الله لقائمٌ)" is an answer to a denier's denial.[119]

115 Ibid. 116 Ibid., 315–27. Lane and Lane-Poole, *An Arabic-English Lexicon*, 1:109.
117 I thank Geert Jan van Gelder for pointing this out to me.
118 The famous grammarian and author of *Qawāʿid al-shiʿr* (*The Fundaments of Poetry*), a short treatise on poetic elements. He died in 291/904.
119 al-Jurjānī, *Dalāʾil*, 315.

While all these statements appear on the surface to be conveying the same meaning, each is in fact presenting a different "image" or "form" of that meaning. Through the employment of words as seemingly insignificant as "indeed" and "actually," one relates information implicitly about the degree of doubt the addressee has expressed about one's claim. One can imagine the use of *inna* in the second phrase posed in the Kindī example to be an answer to the question: "Is he standing?" and in the third to the claim: "He is not standing." It is therefore particularly good to use "*inna*" when relating something doubtful or unusual, such as in the following verse:[120]

عَلَيْكَ بِاليأْسِ مِنَ النَّاسِ　　إنَّ غِنَى نَفْسِك فِي الياسِ

Let yourself be despaired of people:
　Verily (*inna*), your soul's enrichment [lies] in despair
~ Abū Nuwās (d. c. 198/813)

Al-Jurjānī explains: "you see the goodness of its placement and its agreeableness to the soul. This is so only because most people do not go after despair and do not give up hope and greed."[121] The use of *inna*, therefore, works so well in Abū Nuwās's verse because he is making an unusual claim, which he expects the listener to doubt. In our final example, the poet tactfully uses "*inna*" to enhance sarcasm:[122]

جَاءَ شَقيقٌ عارِضاً رُمْحَهُ　　إنَّ بَني عَمِّكَ فيهِم رِماحْ

Shaqīq[123] came, showing off his spear
　By the way (*inna*), your cousins [also] have spears[124]
~ Ḥajl ibn Naḍla (pre-Islamic)

The meaning of the verse is that the addressee came, proudly displaying his spear for everyone to see as if it were an indication of his bravery and as if no one else with a spear could do the same. The poet then satirically affirms that others also have spears.[125] The affirmation using *inna* (which I render

[120] Ibid., 325. [121] Ibid. [122] Ibid., 326.

[123] The verse is also cited in al-Jāḥiẓ, *al-Bayān wa-l-tabyīn*, 3:340. The editor's footnote there explains that *shaqīq*, meaning "brother," is a name. Al-Taftāzānī also takes it as a name of a man in *al-Muṭawwal*, 188.

[124] I am taking some liberty in translating *inna* as "by the way." However, this is the sense that its use in this context has. Udo Simon translates the sense into German nicely by adding the expression "aber auch": Unter den Söhnen deines Onkels gibt es (aber auch) Lanzen!" (*Mittelalterliche arabische Sprachbetrachtung*, 86). Van Gelder has also suggested to me the use of parentheses: "Shaqīq came, showing off his spear (your cousins [also] have spears)." While this is a more elegant translation, I adhere to translating the particle explicitly to highlight its grammatical place.

[125] al-Jurjānī, *Dalāʾil*, 326.

as "by the way" in this example) adds to the satire, since it highlights that the addressee seems to have questioned this obvious fact.[126]

Al-Jurjānī discusses many more of the different nuances that can be achieved through the careful use of *inna*, as well as other function words. The general mechanism that characterizes them is the ability to convey a sense or a meaning implicitly without spelling it out. Words like *inna* have many ways of achieving this.

Naẓm *and Wonder*

Al-Jurjānī regularly cites in the *Dalāʾil* the emotional impact a statement has on the listener as an indicator of its eloquence and explains that the goal in the study of *balāgha* (and hence the inimitability of the Quran) is to understand what causes one statement to be more moving than the other.[127] He says: "One statement cannot be better than another without it having some effect (*taʾthīr*) [...] that the other does not have."[128] Elsewhere he explains: "while two statements can have the same intended meaning, one can beautify and decorate this meaning and produce a particularity that creates an effect (*taʾthīr*) that the other does not."[129]

At the same time, we have seen from the selections discussed above that *naẓm* entails shaping the syntactical structure of a sentence in such a way that it conveys an additional meaning indirectly or implicitly. This can be achieved though the attribution of a verb to its subject figuratively, through word order, ellipsis, the use or lack of use of definite articles and other function words such as conjunctions and "indeed," among others. Eloquence arises when these features add a subtle meaning in a way that compels the listener to think and examine it in order to grasp it. Al-Jurjānī therefore understands the aesthetic mechanism of *naẓm* in a manner that is consistent with his "principle of discovery," which he puts forth in his discussion of simile, as we have seen in Chapter 3; sentence construction can add beauty to speech by conveying additional meaning indirectly, which can only be "discovered" after examination. The possibility of discovering an added subtlety in the meaning is precisely what produces pleasure in the listener. The nature of the effect that eloquent *naẓm* has on

[126] The verse is discussed by al-Sakkākī and al-Khaṭīb al-Qazwīnī as an example of "putting forth speech contrary to the expectations of the context" (*al-Miftāḥ*, 263; *al-Īḍāḥ*, 95). See my discussion of this in what follows.

[127] al-Jurjānī, *Dalāʾil*, 85. [128] Ibid., 258. [129] Ibid., 423.

the soul and the explanations al-Jurjānī gives for the pleasure the listener feels as a result of it are hence also characterized by an aesthetic of wonder.

NAẒM AFTER AL-JURJĀNĪ

While al-Jurjānī uses a mix of Quranic and poetic examples to illustrate his points, later authors apply his principles more systematically to the Quran. One of the most notable examples is al-Zamakhsharī (d. 538/1144), who in his Quranic exegesis entitled *al-Kashshāf* (*The Revealer*) regularly points out the nuances implied by the particular sentence structures of the Quran, à la al-Jurjānī.[130] Otherwise, al-Jurjānī's successors completely reorganize his material on *naẓm* and greatly develop the concept in the science of meanings (*ʿilm al-maʿānī*), as we will see in this section.

I have emphasized in my discussion of al-Jurjānī's treatment of *naẓm* that sentence structure can contribute to eloquence by obliquely bestowing an additional sense on the basic meaning. Al-Sakkākī goes on to identify more specifically the character of this "added meaning," describing it as "a correspondence with the requirements of the context (*muṭābaqa li-muqtaḍā al-ḥāl*)," as we will see. The discussion of the eloquence of *naẓm* therefore shifts focus from the production of a secondary meaning through sentence construction to the nature of the relationship between a phrase and its implicit context. Al-Sakkākī and his commentators elaborate further on this correspondence with the context, pointing out that it can either be in accordance with the apparent expectations (*ʿalā muqtaḍā al-ẓāhir*) or diverge from them (*ʿalā khilāf muqtaḍā al-ẓāhir*) in order to produce certain effects, adding another layer of complexity to the theory of wonder.

*The Science of Meanings (*ʿIlm al-Maʿānī*)*

While the commentators on al-Sakkākī's *Miftāḥ al-ʿulūm*, starting with al-Khaṭīb al-Qazwīnī, were only concerned with the section of his book on the science of eloquence (*ʿilm al-balāgha*), al-Sakkākī's endeavor in the *Miftāḥ* was more comprehensive. His project incorporated all literary

130 For an analysis of al-Zamakhsharī's thought, especially with regard to al-Jurjānī's influence, see Badri Najib Zubir, *Balāghah as an Instrument of Qurʾān Interpretation: A Study of Al-Kashshāf* (Kuala Lumpur: International Islamic University Malaysia, 2008).

disciplines (*anwāʿ al-adab*), including prosody, as well as morphology and syntax.[131] In the introduction to the whole work, al-Sakkākī explains that the original point of studying the literary arts is to be able to "avoid mistakes in the speech of the Arabs."[132] In an effort to achieve this goal, he explains that he has to deal with the aspects of language where mistakes tend to be made. These, he states, can happen at three levels: "(1) in the individual word (*al-mufrad*), (2) in composition (*taʾlīf*), (3) in the correspondence of constructed [speech] (*al-murakkab*) with what it must be uttered for."[133]

He goes on to explain that morphology (*ʿilm al-ṣarf*) deals with the first (i.e., individual words), syntax (*ʿilm al-naḥw*) with the second (i.e., composition), whereas *ʿilm al-maʿānī* and *bayān* deal with the last (i.e., the correspondence).[134] What is significant here is al-Sakkākī's distinction between the science of syntax and the science of meanings (*ʿilm al-maʿānī*). While the subject matter of syntax is composition (*taʾlīf*) itself, the purview of *ʿilm al-maʿānī* goes beyond mere composition. As al-Sakkākī explains, it looks at the relationship between composed speech and the purpose for which it is uttered. This is also how he later defines the science of meanings:

Know that *ʿilm al-maʿānī* entails tracing the characteristics of the structures of speech (*khawāṣṣ tarākīb al-kalām*) in conveying information (*fī al-ifāda*) and what comes with it of appreciation (*istiḥsān*) and the like. [This is in order] to avoid, by

[131] See al-Sakkākī, *al-Miftāḥ*, 37. He also has chapters on the logical sciences of "definition and deduction" (*al-ḥadd wa-l-istidlāl*) and prosody, all of which he sees as a necessary complement to both the science of meanings and *bayān*. He excludes lexicography, which would otherwise also be part of the "literary arts" (ibid.).

[132] Ibid., 39.

[133] Ibid., 40 "كون المركب مطابقا لما يجب أن يتكلم له". This is a refinement of previous descriptions of linguistic communication, which limit it to words, their meanings, and the way the words are strung together (e.g., al-Khaṭṭābī, discussed above, and even al-Jurjānī).

[134] Ibid. The fact that al-Sakkākī pairs *ʿilm al-bayān* with *ʿilm al-maʿānī* as a science dealing with the correspondence with the context should be taken with a grain of salt. *Bayān*, as we have seen in Chapter 4, deals with the signification of words, not with a correspondence. In fact, al-Taftāzānī points out, "there is no given situation that requires evoking a comparison, metaphor, or metonymy" (*al-Muṭawwal*, 168). Al-Khaṭīb al-Qazwīnī is clearer in distinguishing the purposes of the two sciences. He describes *balāgha* as being based on [a] avoiding errors in the delivery of the intended meaning and the ability to distinguish articulate speech from inarticulate speech, which is achieved through knowledge of the language, morphology, and syntax or intuitively, and it is what is free of conceptual complexity. Point [a] (avoiding errors in delivery of the intended meaning) is studied in *ʿilm al-maʿānī*; and (avoiding conceptual complexity) is studied in *ʿilm al-bayān* (*al-Īḍāḥ*, 83).

studying them, mistakes in making speech correspond to that which the context necessitates mention.[135]

Al-Sakkākī clarifies that what he means by "the characteristics of the structures of speech" is "what one understands from a given construction [. . .]."[136] He goes on to explain that what he means by "what one understands from a given construction" is the ability to:

grasp from the construction "Indeed, Zayd is leaving" (إنّ زيدا منطلقٌ) that the intention is to remove any doubt and refute any denial [about Zayd's leaving]; and from the construction "Zayd is leaving" (زيدٌ منطلقٌ) that it follows that the intention is merely to report the information (*ikhbār*); or from – say – "he is leaving" (منطلقٌ) omitting [the explicit mention of] the subject, that it follows that the aim is to be brief while providing a subtle meaning that its position indicates.[137]

Or put more simply, al-Khaṭīb al-Qazwīnī – who criticizes the convolutedness of al-Sakkākī's description – defines *ʿilm al-maʿānī* as:

[135] al-Sakkākī, *al-Miftāḥ*, 247 "اعلم أن علم المعاني هو تتبع خواص تراكيب الكلام في الإفادة ، وما يتصل بها من الاستحسان وغيره ، ليحترز بالوقوف عليها عن الخطأ في تطبيق الكلام على ما يقتضي الحال ذكره". Some commentators understood al-Sakkākī's phrase, which I am translating here as "what comes with it of appreciation (*istiḥsān*) and the like" as meaning "beautification" and referring to rhetorical figures (i.e., *badīʿ*). Al-Sayyid al-Sharīf criticizes this interpretation, and clarifies that it is the beauty of the sentence construction itself that is meant. He says explicitly "attributing *istiḥsān* to rhetorical embellishments is incorrect because these embellishments have no place in the avoiding [of mistakes] mentioned [. . .] how should it be part of *ʿilm al-maʿānī*? [. . .] The correct [understanding] is to attribute *istiḥsan* to its literal meaning (*mafhūmihi al-ḥaqīqī*) [. . .] That is, the construction that is tied to a specific characteristic – such as an affirming predicate, for example – which could be found beautiful from one speaker in one state, and be understood as intentional. Or it could be not found beautiful from another in that state for our distrust in [that person's abilities]. His [particular phrasal construction] is thus not considered intentional, but coincidental (hence not beautiful)" (*al-Miṣbāḥ*, 16–17). In other words, if a sentence happens to match the context in its construction by coincidence, it does not reflect any intentional meaning by the speaker. However, making the construction of a sentence correspond to the context intentionally is something that the listener appreciates and admires.

[136] al-Sakkākī, *al-Miftāḥ*, 248. Cf. Simon, *Mittelalterliche arabische Sprachbetrachtung*, 60.

[137] al-Sakkākī, *al-Miftāḥ*, 248. The "subtle meaning" of suppressing the mention of the subject could be that the addressee knows who you are talking about or some other meaning discussed under the chapter on suppressing the subject, as al-Sayyid al-Sharīf explains in his commentary on the *Miftāḥ* (*al-Miṣbāḥ*, 25). Cf. Udo Simon's translation (*Mittelalterliche arabische Sprachbetrachtung*, 60–1). He understands "the subtle meaning that its position indicates" as the external context giving meaning to the statement: ". . . worauf die dazugehörige Situation eine Andeutung gibt" (p. 61). But it is the statement itself that provides this subtle meaning, as al-Sayyid al-Sharīf's comment clarifies.

The science through which one knows the states of Arabic speech with which the requirements of the context can be matched.[138]

What al-Jurjānī describes as the "meanings of syntax" in his definition of *naẓm*, therefore, is here specified as "a correspondence with the requirements of the context."[139] Furthermore, this correspondence with the context (*taṭbīq li-muqtaḍā al-ḥāl*) is for al-Sakkākī a meaning added to the basic idea being conveyed, just as in al-Jurjānī's treatment of *naẓm*. Al-Sakkākī differentiates between these two levels of speech, calling the basic meaning "*aṣl al-maʿnā*":

Sometimes [a situation only] necessitates [a] what does not require for its fulfillment [anything] more than lexical significations (*dalālāt waḍʿiyya*) and words (*alfāẓ*) as they are, whose arrangement (*naẓm*) simply for their composition (*taʾlīf*) is distinguished from mere crowing (*naʿīq*). This is what is called in grammar "the basic meaning" (*aṣl al-maʿnā*). We consider this here (i.e., in the science of eloquence) at the level of animal sounds. Other [times a situation] necessitates that which for its fulfillment requires more.[140]

In other words, there is a basic meaning that can be conveyed using words as they are at their literal level and with a composition that is indistinguishable from sounds produced by animals except for its arrangement in some order. This order is nothing more than simply following the rules of grammar. In his definition of the science of syntax he states:

[*ʿilm al-naḥw*] is to aim at knowing how to combine words (*kalim*) together in order to deliver the basic meaning (*aṣl al-maʿnā*) outright, according to measures extracted from examining the speech of the Arabs (*kalām al-ʿArab*).[141]

This – we might say – is a nonliterary form of expression, which aims at simply relaying basic information. A situation may not require more than this. Other times it may require something additional in its execution, as al-Sakkākī tells us. What the science of meanings is concerned with is this additional sense that a sentence construction conveys.[142] This is also what renders speech literary and eloquent.

138 al-Khaṭīb al-Qazwīnī, *al-Īḍāḥ*, 84 "هو علم يعرف به أحوال اللفظ العربي التي بها يطابق مقتضى الحال".

139 Al-Khaṭīb al-Qazwīnī explicitly equates *naẓm* with the correspondence with the context (ibid., 81).

140 al-Sakkākī, *al-Miftāḥ*, 250. See also al-Sayyid al-Sharīf al-Jurjānī, *al-Miṣbāḥ*, 32–3; as well as al-Khaṭīb al-Qazwīnī, *al-Īḍāḥ*, 82, where he also compares the mere correct usage of grammar to animal sounds for those of eloquence.

141 al-Sakkākī, *al-Miftāḥ*, 125.

142 Aḥmad Maṭlūb calls this additional sense that is the subject of the science of meanings "secondary meaning" (*Asālīb balāghiyya: al-Faṣāḥa, al-balāgha, al-maʿānī* (Kuwait:

The New Conceptualization of Naẓm

Al-Sakkākī and his commentators analyze the various elements of syntax that can be the source of such added meanings in a more systematic fashion than al-Jurjānī.[143] Significantly, they analyze them with respect to the implied context. With al-Khaṭīb al-Qazwīnī, the science of meanings becomes standardized into an eight-part taxonomy of syntactical constructions and parts of speech, whose different aspects can effect a change in the meaning.[144] These are:

(1) the kind of predication itself (*al-isnād al-khabarī*);
(2) the subject (*al-musnad ilayh*);
(3) the predicate (*al-musnad*);
(4) things relating to the verb (namely the object and the subject);
(5) restriction (*qaṣr*), which deals with the use of function words such as *innamā* and *illā* that serve to limit and restrict the information to something specific;
(6) performative (*inshā'*),[145] non-informational statements, such as questions, wishes, and commands;
(7) conjunction and disjunction; and finally

Wikālat al-Maṭbū'āt, 1979–80), 85). See also al-Sayyid Aḥmad al-Hāshimī, *Jawāhir al-balāgha fī al-ma'ānī wa-l-bayān wa-l-badī'* (Beirut: al-Maktaba al-'Aṣriyya, 1999?), 46n3. Modern scholars sometimes misleadingly describe *'ilm al-ma'ānī* as a "study of syntax" (e.g., Smyth, "Canonical Formulation," 7). It is important to note that *'ilm al-ma'ānī* deals with secondary meaning resulting from syntax (*ma'ānī al-naḥw*), not syntax itself.

143 The first attempt to (re)organize al-Jurjānī's material on *naẓm* was by Fakhr al-Dīn al-Rāzī, who follows a scheme different from al-Sakkākī's and that of his commentators. For Fakhr al-Dīn al-Rāzī's influence on al-Sakkākī, see Maṭlūb, *al-Sakkākī*, 248–59.

144 This eight-part division is established by al-Khaṭīb al-Qazwīnī (*al-Īḍāḥ*, 85). This becomes the standard taxonomy followed by later commentators (e.g., al-Taftāzānī and al-Sayyid al-Sharīf). It is a modification of al-Sakkākī's classification, who divides speech into two types: the informational statement or assertion (*khabar*) and the request (*ṭalab*). Al-Sakkākī then divides the discussion of *khabar* into four parts: (a) the kind of predication (*al-isnād al-khabarī*); (b) the subject; (c) the predicate (which includes a discussion of the verb); (d) conjunction and disjunction (*al-faṣl wa-l-waṣl*) and conciseness and elaboration (*al-ījāz wa-l-iṭnāb*). Though he has a different organization, he covers the same topics that al-Khaṭīb al-Qazwīnī then reorganizes into the standard eight-part taxonomy. For a description of al-Khaṭīb al-Qazwīnī's structuring of language, see Jenssen, *Subtleties and Secrets*, 61.

145 *Inshā'* (lit. production or creation) is al-Khaṭīb al-Qazwīnī's term for what al-Sakkākī calls "*ṭalab*" (request). It is a relatively late linguistic category that appears as a counterpart to "*khabar*" (informational statement). The two are analogous to J. L. Austin's distinction between "constative" statements that "describe an action, an event, or a fact (e.g., John came)" and "performative" ones, which typically involve the expression of a wish or a command that does not have a correspondence with an outside reality (see Daniela Rodica Firanescu, "Speech Acts," in *Encyclopedia of Arabic Language and Linguistics*, ed.

(8) conciseness and elaboration.[146]

These eight aspects of speech can be subjected to the conditions we have come across in al-Jurjānī's work, such as pre- and post-positioning, ellipsis, rendering a word definite or indefinite, and so on, that can add nuance to the basic meaning. This nuance has to do with the context or situation (*ḥāl*) for which the phrase is uttered.

Returning to al-Kindī's inquiry into the apparent redundancies in language discussed above, al-Sakkākī and al-Khaṭīb al-Qazwīnī incorporate the anecdote within the first chapter of their discussion of *ʿilm al-maʿānī*, which deals with the various "types of predication" (*isnād ikhbārī*). They describe the different statements as representing different ways of relating information about a subject. The first, "ʿAbdallāh is standing (عبد الله قائم)," is an "initiatory" kind of predication (*ibtidāʾī*), with no preconceived assumptions about the knowledge of the addressee. The second, "Indeed (*inna*), ʿAbdallāh is standing (إنّ عبد الله قائمٌ)," is a response to an inquiry (*ṭalabī*) that serves to remove any confusion. The third, "Actually (*inna* … *la*), ʿAbdallāh is standing (إنّ عبد الله لقائمٌ)," is a response to a denial (*khabar inkārī*).[147]

This is not different from al-Jurjānī's interpretation. However, it is a reconceptualization. While al-Jurjānī discusses it simply under the effect of using *inna* (indeed) on the meaning of a sentence, *ʿilm al-maʿānī* incorporates it under the generalized category of "types of predication," and defines these types with respect to the situation for which they are uttered. The relationship with the context becomes a defining aspect of the inquiry

Kees Versteegh (Leiden: Brill, 2009); and Larcher, "Une pragmatique avant la pragmatique"). *Inshāʾ* is therefore typically translated as "performative."

146 Al-Khaṭīb al-Qazwīnī explains the logic behind these eight aspects of sentence construction as follows: "Speech is either informative (*khabar*) or performative (*inshāʾ*). This is because it is associated either with an external [matter], which it [consequently] corresponds to or not, or it does not have an external [matter with which to correspond]. The former is informative (*khabar*), and the latter is performative (*inshāʾ*). The informative [statement], in turn, is constituted of a predication (*isnād*), that which it is predicated upon (*musnad ilayh*), and the predicate (*al-musnad*). These three aspects are the first three entries. Then, the predicate can have dependents if it is a verb, something related to it, or has the meaning of a verb, such as agent nouns (*ism al-fāʿil*) and the like. This is the fourth entry. Then the predication and the dependency each could either be with a restriction (*qaṣr*) or without one. This is the fifth entry. The performative is the sixth. Then, a sentence when combined with another is attached to the first either with a conjunction or without. This is the seventh entry. The words of eloquent speech either exceed the original intention for some useful [added meaning], or they do not exceed it. This is the eighth entry" (*al-Īḍāḥ*, 85). Cf. Jenssen's translation of a similar passage from al-Khaṭīb al-Qazwīnī's shorter commentary, *al-Talkhis* (Jenssen, *Subtleties and Secrets*, 61). See also Larcher, "Arabic Linguistic Tradition II: Pragmatics," 190–1, where he describes this division as well.

147 al-Khaṭīb al-Qazwīnī, *al-Īḍāḥ*, 93.

into sentence construction in the science of meanings. *ʿIlm al-maʿānī* proceeds to systematically and comprehensively map out the Arabic language and all the possible implications about the context its sentence constructions can produce.

This has been compared to pragmatics in modern linguistics.[148] However, rather than being a purely linguistic endeavor, the motivation behind studying the science of meanings is an aesthetic one. It is one of the branches of the science of eloquence and it is through it that we can gain an appreciation of the inimitable quality of the Quran.[149] A phrase's ability to convey meaning about the context for which it was uttered, the addressee, and the purpose of enunciation through its syntactical construction is precisely what distinguishes eloquent speech from mere composition. In other words, the ultimate point of describing the pragmatic aspects of the Arabic language for our medieval authors is to understand and appreciate eloquence.

The Unexpected

The above examples of the three types of predication, as al-Sakkākī notes and al-Khaṭīb al-Qazwīnī confirms, represent speech that is put forth on the basis of the apparent expectations of the context (*ʿalā muqtaḍā al-ẓāhir*). However, speech can also intentionally diverge from the apparent expectations presented by the context in order to achieve a particular effect or an additional meaning. This is produced in the case of predication, for example, by treating the knower as if he does not know and addressing him with an "initiatory" statement, or constructing speech in a way that treats a non-inquirer as an inquirer, or non-denier as a denier.[150]

[148] See especially the work of Pierre Larcher. See also Mohamed M. Yunis Ali's work on linguistics in the Islamic context in general, including *Medieval Islamic Pragmatics: Sunni Legal Theorists' Models of Textual Communication* (Surrey, UK: Curzon, 2000).

[149] al-Khaṭīb al-Qazwīnī, *al-Talkhīṣ*, 5.

[150] al-Sakkākī, *al-Miftāḥ*, 259–63; al-Khaṭīb al-Qazwīnī, *al-Īḍāḥ*, 93–6. Al-Sayyid al-Sharīf says the various constructions of the types of predication result in nine combinations that produce speech that is contrary to the apparent expectations (*al-Miṣbāḥ*, 75). This is based on three possible states of knowledge in the addressee: freedom of mind (*khuluww al-dhihn*), that is, a mind without any knowledge to make a judgment; hesitation (*taraddud*); and denial (*inkār*) (ibid., 74). The initiatory statement is compatible with an addressee who lacks any knowledge about the situation, but when used for an addressee who knows the information or who has either of the other two states of knowledge (hesitation and denial), the statement is contrary to the apparent expectation, and so on, for the other types of predication.

Al-Khaṭīb al-Qazwīnī comments, "Taking this path is a branch of eloquence that contains subtlety and obscurity (*diqqa wa-ghumūḍ*)."[151]

As an example of a predicative construction that does not match expectation, al-Khaṭīb al-Qazwīnī discusses verses 15 and 16 from Sūra 23 in the Quran:

ثُمَّ إِنَّكُم بَعْدَ ذَٰلِكَ لَمَيِّتُونَ * ثُمَّ إِنَّكُمْ يَوْمَ الْقِيَامَةِ تُبْعَثُونَ

> Then you are actually (*inna-kum*) after that all dead (*la-mayyitūn*). Then you indeed (*inna-kum*), on the day of resurrection, will be resurrected.

He explains that death is affirmed in the first verse using the denial (*inkārī*) form of predication, (*inna* ... *la-*, which I try to render in English using the expression "actually"), even though it is something that no one would deny. Whereas, the second verse affirms resurrection less emphatically through the employment of the inquiry (*ṭalabī*) form of predication (*inna*, which I try to render in English with "indeed"), even though, in this case, resurrection is something that could be denied. Given the expected degree of certainty the addressee might have about the occurrence of death, on the one hand, and resurrection, on the other, one would expect the inverse: the "initiatory" or "inquiry" form of predication to be used in the first instance and the "denial" form in the second.

Al-Khaṭīb al-Qazwīnī explains that treating the undeniable as if it were being denied in the first verse, places the addressee at the level of those who ignore the certainty of death through their "excessive inattention and abandonment of working for that which comes after."[152] Whereas treating the deniable as if it were merely met with uncertainty in the second verse implies, as al-Khaṭīb al-Qazwīnī describes it, that:

> The evidence for [resurrection] is [so] apparent that it does not merit being denied. Rather one either admits it or [at most] hesitates in doing so. The addressee is therefore treated among the ranks of those who are uncertain, in order to highlight the plainness of the signs, encouraging them to inspect them more carefully.[153]

[151] al-Khaṭīb al-Qazwīnī, *al-Īḍāḥ*, 94.

[152] Ibid., 96. That is also why the verse uses the adjective "dead" (*mayyitūn*) and not the phrase "you will die" (*tamūtūn*), to affirm it as a done deed (ibid.). In a similar vein, al-Khaṭīb al-Qazwīnī explains that the use of the past tense or an active participle (*ism fāʿil*) or passive participle (*ism mafʿūl*) can be used to express a future event that has not yet happened in order to emphasize its certainty (see below) (ibid., 164).

[153] Ibid., 96.

In both cases, going against the presumed state of certainty in the addressee implies an admonishment of the addressee and an exhortation to think more deeply about his state of knowledge and behavior.

Other forms of putting forth speech in unexpected ways are discussed or hinted at throughout their examination of *ʿilm al-maʿānī*. Al-Sakkākī reminds the reader on several occasions that, while the mechanisms of language that he describes assume a concordance with the apparent expectations of the context, going contrary to expectation enhances eloquence:

> You know, from what has preceded, that putting speech forth *not* in accordance with the apparent needs [of the context] is the path of the eloquent, often forged by replacing one kind with another in one of the considerations. Remember this.[154]

Al-Khaṭīb al-Qazwīnī groups four types of syntactical devices that are based on unexpected correspondence at the end of his chapter on the subject (*al-musnad ilayh*).[155] These include using an unexpected verb tense, such as the past tense for a future event to affirm its certainty,[156] and inverting a grammatical relationship (*qalb*), such as treating the subject as the object and vice versa.[157] In addition, he includes a literary device called *iltifāt* (lit. turning), which entails the shifting of the grammatical person (i.e., apostrophe). Finally, he includes a device that can be described as wit. I will discuss these last two devices in more detail so to give a broader sense of how expectations arise from a context and, in turn, what renders a sentence construction unexpected (*ʿala khilāf muqtaḍā al-ẓāhir*).

Apostrophe (*Iltifāt*)

Apostrophe (*iltifāt*) is a literary device already listed among the *badīʿ* figures compiled by Ibn al-Muʿtazz (d. 296/908) in his *Kitāb al-badīʿ* (*The Book of*

[154] al-Sakkākī, *al-Miftāḥ*, 346 (emphasis added).

[155] al-Khaṭīb al-Qazwīnī, *al-Īḍāḥ*, 154–68. Even though al-Khaṭīb al-Qazwīnī groups several types of unexpected correspondence under the heading of the grammatical "subject," al-Taftāzānī points out that they do not all concern the subject, but grants that al-Khaṭīb al-Qazwīnī was on a roll and listed many of them there! (*al-Muṭawwal*, 294.)

[156] al-Khaṭīb al-Qazwīnī, *al-Īḍāḥ*, 164. This is similar to the use of the adjective "dead" in Q23:15 discussed above to highlight the certainty of the future event.

[157] An example of inverting the grammatical relationship (*qalb*) is saying "I displayed the camel to the watering trough" (عرضت الناقة على الحوض), instead of the other way around, "I displayed the watering trough to the camel" (al-Sakkākī, *al-Miftāḥ*, 312; al-Khaṭīb al-Qazwīnī, *al-Īḍāḥ*, 165). The inversion of this phrase seems to have been common in Bedouin speech, according to al-Khaṭīb al-Qazwīnī. The inverted phrase is cited in lexicons as well (see Lane, s.v. ʿ-r-ḍ).

Rhetorical Figures).[158] It consists of switching pronouns between first person (*ḥikāya* or *takallum*), second person (*khiṭāb*), and third person (*al-ghayba*). Medieval Arab writers regarded this kind of shift in grammatical person as one of the beautifying aspects of language.[159] Al-Khaṭīb al-Qazwīnī explains that this is the case because speech is moved from one mode to another, which is "more stimulating to the eagerness of the listener and induces more alertness than if it were in one mode (*uslūb*)."[160] Al-Sakkākī points out that this subtle figure, which is appreciated only by the sharpest of minds, "dresses [speech] with the distinction of glory and splendor and bequeaths the listener more emotion and excitement."[161] While al-Sakkākī also lists it as a *badīʿ* figure, his main treatment of the device takes place in *ʿilm al-maʿānī*, where he discusses it as an example of contradicting the expectations set by the context.

What constitutes the context, however, was not always agreed upon. In their discussion of the following three verses by Imruʾ al-Qays, al-Sakkākī and al-Khaṭīb al-Qazwīnī disagree about how many changes in grammatical person take place. The disagreement, as we will see, stems from their different conceptions of what should constitute the context: the text itself or the external context it implies. Here are the lines as translated by van Gelder:[162]

تَطاوَلَ لَيلُكَ بِالأَثمُدِ   وَنامَ الخَلِيُّ وَلَم تَرقُدِ
وَباتَ وَباتَت لَهُ لَيلَةٌ   كَلَيلَةِ ذي العائِرِ الأَرمَدِ
وَذَلِكَ مِن نَبَإٍ جاءَني   وَخُبِّرتُهُ عَن أَبي الأَسوَدِ

Long was your night at al-Athmud:
  The carefree one slept but you did not slumber
He spent a night and it passed for him
  As does a night for someone with sore and inflamed eyes:

[158] Ibn al-Muʿtazz, *Kitāb al-badīʿ*, 58–9.

[159] Abdel Haleem points out that the German Orientalist Theodor Nöldeke (d. 1930) regarded the pronominal shifts in the Quran as mistakes and described them as happening "in an unusual and not beautiful way (nicht schöner Weise)." Abdel Haleem correctly points out that, quite to the contrary, this stylistic feature was among the "remarkable things and exquisite subtleties" of the Quran, quoting Ibn al-Athīr ("Grammatical Shift for Rhetorical Purposes: *Iltifāt* and Related Features in the Quran," *Bulletin of the School of Oriental and African Studies* 55, no. 3 (1992): 407).

[160] al-Khaṭīb al-Qazwīnī, *al-Īḍāḥ*, 160; al-Sakkākī, *al-Miftāḥ*, 296.

[161] al-Sakkākī, *al-Miftāḥ*, 299.

[162] Ibid., 298–9; al-Khaṭīb al-Qazwīnī, *al-Īḍāḥ*, 159; Imruʾ al-Qays, *Dīwān Imriʾ al-Qays*, ed. Muṣṭafā ʿAbd al-Shāfī, 5th ed. (Beirut: Dār al-Kutub al-ʿIlmiyya, 2004), 53; Geert Jan van Gelder, "The Abstracted Self in Arabic Poetry," *Journal of Arabic Literature* 14 (1983): 25.

That is because of tidings that came to me
That have been told to me, about Abū al-Aswad
~ Imru' al-Qays (d. c. 550 CE)

Al-Sakkākī explains that the above verses contain three shifts in grammatical person: the use of the second person in the first verse, the third person in the second, and finally the first in the last verse. Al-Khaṭīb al-Qazwīnī disagrees with this, arguing that only two shifts take place in the second and third verses and that the opening verse is simply setting up the grammatical person, not shifting from any previously set point of view.[163] Al-Sakkākī, instead, considers the grammatical person in the first verse already a shift because it is not the same as the actual subject being spoken about, which is the "I." As al-Taftāzānī further clarifies, the poet addresses himself in the second person when the more obvious way of phrasing it would have been in the first person, opening the poem with "my night" instead of "your night."[164] One must presume, however, in this case, that the unexpectedness of the pronoun used in the first verse can only be appreciated retroactively after reading the verses that follow and discovering the actual subject of the poem. While al-Khaṭīb al-Qazwīnī considers the immediate textual context, therefore, al-Sakkākī and al-Taftāzānī consider the overall context the text implies.

Nevertheless, it is the unexpectedness that lies at the crux of this figure. Al-Taftāzānī emphasizes that the shifting in grammatical pronoun has to happen in an unexpected way in order to catch the attention of the listener, otherwise any shift in grammatical person would count as *iltifāt*, such as saying "I am Zayd, you are 'Amr, and we are men, you are men . . ."[165] Al-Sayyid al-Sharīf confirms this idea, arguing that whether the shift is literal (*taḥqīqī*), as al-Khaṭīb al-Qazwīnī would have it, or presumptive (*taqdīrī*), as al-Sakkākī would have it, *iltifāt* serves the same purpose: exciting the listener by proceeding in an unexpected manner.[166] It is this deliberate divergence from the apparent expectations set by the text, whether literal or presumed, therefore, that gives *iltifāt* its aesthetic quality.

163 al-Khaṭīb al-Qazwīnī, *al-Īḍāḥ*, 159–60. See van Gelder's discussion of the figure of *iltifāt*, including a discussion of these verses as treated by al-Sakkākī in "The Abstracted Self in Arabic Poetry." See also Geert Jan van Gelder, "The Qur'an in *Kitāb al-Badī'* by Ibn al-Mu'tazz (d. 296/908)," in *The Qur'an and Adab*, ed. Nuha Alshaar (Oxford: Oxford University Press/Institute of Ismaili Studies, 2017), 182–4.

164 al-Taftāzānī, *al-Muṭawwal*, 286. 165 Ibid., 287.

166 al-Sayyid al-Sharīf al-Jurjānī, *al-Ḥāshiya*, 165.

Wit (*al-Uslūb al-Ḥakīm*)

Another kind of speech that goes against the expectations of the context is something called "*al-uslūb al-ḥakīm*" (the shrewd way), which one could translate summarily as "wit."[167] It involves "responding to the addressee with what he does not expect by putting forth speech contrary to his intent."[168] The example al-Sakkākī and al-Khaṭīb al-Qazwīnī cite amounts to a play on double meaning between two speakers. The story goes as follows: Al-Ḥajjāj, the Umayyad governor of Iraq, tells a Kharijite rebel named al-Qabaʿtharā, threatening to arrest him:[169] "I will throw you in chains (*adham*) (لأحملنّك على الأدهم)" and al-Qabaʿtharā responds: "[you are] like a prince who gifts black horses [*adham*] and white ones [*ashhab*] (مِثل الأميرِ يحمل على الأدهم والأشهب)." By playing on the word *adham*, which means black but can refer to a black horse or metal chains (for their blackness), the Kharijite deliberately (mis)interprets the governor's phrase as meaning "I will place you on a black horse (*adham*)" instead of "in chains," turning his threat into a promise. In this way, al-Khaṭīb al-Qazwīnī explains, he showed in the subtlest of ways that he who has the character of a generous sultan should give freely (*yuṣfid*), rather than shackle (*yaṣfid*). (Al-Khaṭīb al-Qazwīnī himself adding his own play on words in his explanation!) The story goes on and the wit continues when al-Ḥajjāj tries to correct the Kharijite, clarifying that he meant "*ḥadīd*" (iron). Al-Qabaʿtharā responds that it is better for the [horse] to be *ḥadīd* rather than *balīd* (i.e., strong rather than weak).[170]

While it is obvious from the context what the governor intended with the words *adham* and *ḥadīd*, the Kharijite intentionally misinterprets them to distort the governor's threats. *Al-Uslūb al-ḥakīm* is, therefore, the art of deliberately interpreting the context in a way that is inconsistent with the obvious intention of the addressee in order to arrive at a different meaning. Al-Sakkākī exclaims that it can "stimulate the listener's excitement which the dictates of the solemn one had taken away, and put him forth in a state of enchantment."[171] Indeed, so powerful is this device that he credits it

167 Al-Jurjānī only briefly discusses *al-uslūb al-ḥakīm* in a different context and describes it as misleading reasoning (*mughālaṭa*) (*Dalāʾil*, 138). Al-Jāḥiẓ discusses this in *al-Bayān wa-l-tabyīn*, 2:147.

168 al-Khaṭīb al-Qazwīnī, *al-Īḍāḥ*, 162; al-Sakkākī, *al-Miftāḥ*, 435–6.

169 al-Sakkākī, *al-Miftāḥ*, 436. Al-Khaṭīb al-Qazwīnī identifies him as al-Qabaʿtharā (*al-Īḍāḥ*, 162).

170 al-Khaṭīb al-Qazwīnī, *al-Īḍāḥ*, 163.

171 al-Sakkākī, *al-Miftāḥ*, 436.

with having softened al-Ḥajjāj's stance toward al-Qabaʿtharā so much that he let him go.[172]

Granted, this lack of correspondence with the obvious or apparent intentions of the addressee in this case is achieved through a play with double meaning and not necessarily through a manipulation of sentence structure per se, yet it further exposes what is meant by a lack of correspondence with the expectations of the context. In this case, the expectation is created through the interlocutor's speech presented in the narrative. Wit only arises through the interplay between the two speakers, one of whom creates an expectation, which is subsequently broken by the other.

***

In sum, expectations are created either through common sense and experience external to the text (e.g., death is a certainty) or through the text itself, in which case it is produced through syntax or an interlocutor's speech within a narrative. In other words, expectations may be presumed to already be in place in the reader or listener external to the text, or they have to be established within the text in order for them to be broken. That is, the expected can be context- or co-text-dependent. Either way, the effect on the listener depends on producing something unexpected.

Al-Sakkākī proclaims that constructing speech in such a way is particularly moving to the soul:

> This type – I mean producing speech not in accordance with apparent expectations – when it takes its hold on keen beholders, it cheers the soul, amazes the ear, moves the faculties, and excites the mind. It is for a reason that you find the masters of eloquence (*balāgha*), and the fighting horsemen in its shooting range [who are aiming at] the mark of elucidation (*bayān*), abounding in this craft in their debates.[173]

Producing speech that goes contrary to expectations can happen in many ways other than those discussed here. Al-Sakkākī points out how performative phrases (e.g., questions, wishes, or commands) can appear contrary to expectation when: (a) the actual intention is an informational/assertive statement (*khabar*), or (b) the other way around, an assertive statement can be used in place of a performative speech act.[174] Generalizing (*al-taghlīb*) is another form of unexpected phrasing.[175] In addition, obscuring the apparent and vice versa, making apparent the obscure through the use of demonstrative pronouns in the place of regular pronouns, are also forms of

172 Ibid.

173 Ibid., 263. Cf. al-Sayyid al-Sharīf's explanation of this passage in *al-Miṣbāḥ*, 86–7.

174 al-Sakkākī, *al-Miftāḥ*, 431–5; see also 413. 175 Ibid., 611.

speech that contradict what one would expect were speech constructed in a more straightforward way.[176]

Producing speech in an unexpected way does not mean it ceases to be "in accordance with the requirements of the context (*ʿalā muqtaḍā al-ḥāl*)." Even if produced in an unexpected way, speech would still have to correspond with the context. Al-Sayyid al-Sharīf spells this out, explaining that:

> [What is meant with] the apparent expectation (*muqtaḍā al-ẓāhir*) is the apparent expectation *of the context* (*muqtaḍā ẓāhir al-ḥāl*). Its counterpart is what contradicts the apparent expectations (*ʿalā khilāf muqtaḍā al-ẓāhir*). Both of them are requirements *of the context* (*muqtaḍā al-ḥāl*).[177]

The Science of Meanings and Eloquence

Al-Sakkākī and al-Khaṭīb al-Qazwīnī explain eloquence (*balāgha*) as the "correspondence with the requirements of the context." Eloquence is, therefore, defined by how the composition of a sentence corresponds with the specific situation for which it is uttered. On a basic level, this is fairly convincing if not obvious: it makes sense that eloquence necessitates having the addressee, the occasion, the situation, and the textual context in mind when constructing sentences. However, this limits the definition of eloquence to criteria of correctness and properness. This alone does not make speech beautiful and certainly does not explain the miraculousness of the Quran. What is significant about the correspondence of speech to the context with respect to eloquence is, rather, the fact that it is achieved indirectly, implicitly, and sometimes in unexpected ways.

Part of al-Sakkākī's definition of *ʿilm al-maʿānī*, as we have seen, has him describe it as "tracing the characteristics of speech structures (*khawāṣṣ tarākīb al-kalām*) in conveying information (*fī al-ifāda*)."[178] He clarifies that what he means by "the characteristics of speech structures" is "what one understands from a given construction, in a way that is a consequence (*lāzim*) of it [. . .]."[179] It is, therefore, not something explicitly expressed in the sentence, but a meaning that arises as a result of the construction of the sentence.

Arriving at this secondary meaning requires some process of deduction and examination. In fact, al-Sakkākī complements the science of eloquence

[176] Ibid., 294–5; al-Khaṭīb al-Qazwīnī, *al-Īḍāḥ*, 154–5.
[177] al-Sayyid al-Sharīf al-Jurjānī, *al-Miṣbāḥ*, 74 (emphasis added).
[178] al-Sakkākī, *al-Miftāḥ*, 247.
[179] Ibid., 248. Cf. Udo Simon's translation, *Mittelalterliche arabische Sprachbetrachtung*, 60.

with a chapter on the "science of definition and deduction" (*al-ḥadd wa-l-istidlāl*),[180] which he views as necessary for understanding and appreciating the science of meanings.[181] Al-Sakkākī describes deduction that occurs under the umbrella of the science of meanings as "tracing the characteristics of the composition of speech *in deduction*."[182] This is in contrast to the definition of *ʿilm al-maʿānī*, which entails "tracing the characteristics of the composition of speech in *conveying meaning*."[183] Deduction, therefore, is the work the listener has to do to interpret the eloquent speech. He treats the basic structure of a sentence (subject + predicate) as a kind of syllogism. He adapts logic to language by applying syllogistic reasoning to the processes of ascribing a predicate to its subject. As a result, al-Sakkākī defines deduction as "the [process through which] one acquires the affirmation of the predicate to the subject."[184] The bulk of al-Sakkākī's chapter on logic proceeds to describe the various possible subject–predicate constructions as forms of syllogism.[185] How syllogistic logic applies in practice to the various constructions discussed in the science of meanings has yet to be clarified.[186]

Most medieval commentators on al-Sakkākī's *Miftāḥ* ignore this section completely. A brief discussion of deduction by al-Sayyid al-Sharīf in his commentary on the *Miftāḥ* sheds some light on the topic. He explains that only some aspects of the science of eloquence are based on [pure] deduction (*istidlāl*), while the rest relies on rhetorical associations (*munāsabāt khuṭābiyya*).[187] Later, discussing al-Sakkākī's definition of *ʿilm al-maʿānī* above, he argues that when he talks about "the characteristics of speech" he ought to have addressed the subject of "rhetorical characteristics" versus "deductive" ones, defining the former as based on "customary associations or presumptive relationships" (*al-munāsabāt al-ʿurfiyya wa-l-ʿalāqāt al-ẓanniyya*) and the latter on "categorical relationships" (*ʿalāqāt*

[180] al-Sakkākī, *al-Miftāḥ*, 544–616. [181] Ibid., 37, 543, and 548.
[182] Ibid., 544 (emphasis added). [183] Ibid., 247 (emphasis added). [184] Ibid., 548.
[185] Ibid., 548ff.
[186] Shukrī al-Mabkhūt makes an interesting attempt to apply syllogistic deduction to *ʿilm al-maʿānī*, but he does not engage with al-Sakkākī's chapter on *istidlāl* in *al-Istidlāl al-balāghī*. Manuela E. B. Giolfo and Wilfrid Hodges have looked at al-Sakkākī's chapter on *istidlāl* but from the perspective of logic and not with respect to how it would apply in practice to *ʿilm al-maʿānī*. Nevertheless, their inquiry reveals new aspects of Fakhr al-Dīn al-Rāzī's influence on al-Sakkākī ("The System of the Sciences of the Arabic Language by al-Sakkākī: Logic as a Complement of Rhetoric," in *Approaches to the History and Dialectology of Arabic in Honor of Pierre Larcher*, ed. Manuel Sartori, Manuela E. B. Giolfo, and Philippe Cassuto (Leiden: Brill, 2017)).
[187] al-Sayyid al-Sharīf al-Jurjānī, *al-Miṣbāḥ*, 10.

qaṭʿiyya).[188] He also tells us that the rhetorical characteristics are more common in speech than purely deductive ones.[189]

Unpacking the details of what the application of this to speech would look like is beyond the scope of this study. What concerns us here is the fact that the secondary meaning that a sentence produces through its particular construction has to be "intellected" or "deduced" through some sort of reasoning and association, whether verifiable or simply based on custom and belief. Even though many modern scholars have lamented al-Sakkākī's rigid application of logic to the study of eloquence, the fact that he thinks logical reasoning is necessary for appreciating eloquence and the miraculousness of the Quran is telling. It is a reflection of the underlying mechanism that is at play in sentence construction, which in turn is the basis of its eloquence: beauty arises from the experience of examination and subsequent discovery that the listener goes through when grasping the "meanings of syntax."

CONCLUSION. THE MIRACLE

In sum, both *naẓm* and *ʿilm al-maʿānī* deal with the secondary meanings that are produced through sentence construction. In the case of al-Jurjānī, he distinguishes between the original basic idea and the final product with the concept of *ṣūrat al-maʿnā* (the image of meaning). The same basic meaning can be expressed in ways that result in different "images" of that meaning. The main component influencing this final image, as we have seen, is *naẓm*. Al-Sakkākī and his commentators identify more systematically the effect of *naẓm* on the final "image of meaning" as concerning a secondary meaning it conveys about the context. They further specify the nature of this correspondence with the context, pointing out that it can be produced in expected or unexpected ways.

As we have seen, al-Jurjānī highlights the process of examination and contemplation that *naẓm* requires from the listener and locates eloquence in it. A similar mechanism is at play in the science of meanings. What renders the "correspondence with the context" eloquent is that such correspondence is achieved obliquely and indirectly

[188] Ibid., 21–2. Al-Sakkākī does mention rhetorical associations as opposed to deductive ones in passing (*al-Miftāḥ*, 317–18).

[189] al-Sayyid al-Sharīf al-Jurjānī, *al-Miṣbāḥ*, 22. The treatment of rhetorical and poetic syllogisms after Ibn Rushd has yet to be thoroughly investigated.

through manipulations of syntax and sentence structures, requiring thought and examination in order to be grasped. In other words, eloquent sentence constructions convey meaning about the situation in which they were pronounced in a way that requires deduction. Such obliqueness, in turn, allows for an experience of discovery in the listener. The pleasure the listener experiences, therefore, is the result of discovery. This again points to an aesthetic of wonder. The effect of wonder can be enhanced even further by adding the element of the unexpected. The experience of discovery and the element of the unexpected thus provide the rationale for the marvelous effect of the Quran.

Eloquence ranges in degrees with that of the Quran being the highest, our critics explain.[190] Presumably the more wonder-evoking a statement is, the better. From the basic principles of discovery that al-Jurjānī sets out in his *Asrār*, we know that the more effort to discovery, the more rewarding is the result. One would expect, therefore, that the more a sentence conveys meaning obliquely, the better. This indeed seems to be the case as one would observe from al-Sakkākī's discussion of the "degrees of eloquent speech." In order to illustrate how far the Quran is from the basic meaning (*aṣl al-maʿnā*), he analyzes a short phrase from the Quran's narration of the prophet Zechariah pleading to God in his old age, saying:

إِنِّي وَهَنَ الْعَظْمُ مِنِّي

Indeed, it is the case with me that the bone in me has withered

~ Q19:4

He shows how the phrase (which I translate awkwardly as such to capture all the syntactical aspects he discusses) is eight degrees of eloquence more elevated than its basic meaning (*aṣl al-maʿnā*), which is simply: [1] "I have become old (قد شخت)."[191] By way of conclusion, I will relate his discussion of it here.

Al-Sakkākī delineates how in each additional level a secondary meaning is conveyed indirectly either through indirect signification or through sentence construction. The first enhancement takes place by specifying the effect of old age on the body by saying: [2] "my body has become weak" (ضعف بدني). Thus, old age is implied by one of its

190 al-Khaṭīb al-Qazwīnī, *al-Īḍāḥ*, 82.

191 al-Sakkākī, *al-Miftāḥ*, 397. Cf. German translation of passage in Simon, *Mittelalterliche arabische Sprachbetrachtung*, 283–4.

symptoms. This represents a second level of eloquence. The third level entails the use of bones as a *kināya* (synecdoche, in this case) for the body: [3] "my body's bones have withered" (وهنت عظام بدني). These first two enhancements involve the use of *kināya*, which is the purview of the science of *bayān*. The following enhancements involve manipulations of sentence structures and are therefore the purview of the science of meanings. The fourth level entails further affirmation by constructing the phrase as the predicate of a nominal sentence: [4] "It is the case with me that my body's bones have withered" (أنا وهنت عظام بدني).[192] This, as we have seen above, produces the effect of obscuration followed by clarification.[193] At the fifth level, you add "*inna*" (indeed), which we have seen renders the statement an affirmation in response to an inquirer: [5] "Indeed, it is the case with me that, my body's bones have withered" (إني وهنتْ عظام بدني).[194] The sixth level constitutes expressing the subject in general terms first ("the bones"), then adding the detail, "in my body": [6] "Indeed, it is the case with me that the bones in my body have withered" (إني وهنت العظام من بدني). While stating something in general terms first then specifying it might add length to a statement, such constructions add emphasis, al-Sakkākī points out, by delaying the clarifying detail.[195] The seventh level involves the removal of the intermediary word, "body," presumably because it is unnecessary and the meaning stays intact without it: [7] "Indeed, it is the case with me that the bones in me have withered" (إني وهنت العظام مني). Finally, what

[192] Simon translates this construction into German in a similar fashion: "Was mich angeht, so sind meine Knochen schwach geworden" (*Mittelalterliche arabische Sprachbetrachtung*, 284). The Hindāwī edition of the *Miftāḥ*, which I cite here, has the word "*taqrīb*" (approximation) instead of "*taqrīr*" (confirmation or affirmation) in al-Sakkākī's discussion of this level. This is likely a mistake. The Zarzūr edition renders it the latter (*Miftāḥ al-'ulūm*, ed. Na'īm Zarzūr (Beirut: Dār al-Kutub al-'Ilmiyya, 1983), 286). This is also al-Khaṭīb al-Qazwīnī's reading of the term (*al-Īḍāḥ*, 294).

[193] I have discussed al-Jurjānī's treatment of such constructions earlier in this chapter under "Pre- and Post-positioning." Al-Sakkākī does not mention this effect explicitly in this context and only suggests an effect of added affirmation. However, in his discussion of placing the obscure in the place of the apparent (وضع المضمر موضع المظهر) earlier in the *Miftāḥ*, he points out that it has the effect of cementing an idea more firmly in the listener's mind because the initial announcement of the topic with the obscure pronoun ("I", in this case, which I am translating here as "it is the case with me") makes the listener eager to listen for the clarification and more ready to receive it. This is a form of producing speech contrary to expectation (al-Sakkākī, *al-Miftāḥ*, 294–5).

[195] al-Sakkākī, *al-Miftāḥ*, 394–5. Stating the general first then specifying it is akin to clarification after obscuration. In fact, al-Sakkākī uses the same example in his discussion of both cases (ibid., 394–5; compare with 294: نعم رجلا زيد).

elevates it to the eighth degree of eloquence is the use of the singular (the bone) to imply the totality (all bones).[196] With this level, we reach the construction as it appears in the Quranic verse: [8] "Indeed, it is the case with me that the bone in me has withered" (إنِّي وَهَنَ الْعَظْمُ مِنِّي).

[196] Al-Sakkākī makes this point in *al-Miftāḥ*, 318, as well.

Epilogue

Faṣāḥa, Balāgha, *and Poetic Beauty*

Faṣāḥa and *balāgha*, which roughly correspond to "articulateness" and "eloquence" respectively, are two terms employed in Arabic to describe the quality of speech. Definitions of the terms in classical Arabic texts often entailed descriptions such as being free of mistakes, correctness and purity of language, clarity, and making speech correspond to the context properly. How does this fit with an aesthetic of wonder, which locates poetic beauty in qualities such as indirectness, inexplicitness, strangeness, and unexpectedness?

While in earlier criticism, *faṣāḥa* and *balāgha* were frequently employed interchangeably, with time they came to refer to two different aspects of the quality of speech. ʿAbd al-Qāhir al-Jurjānī, for example, did not distinguish between them in his works. His contemporary, Ibn Sinān al-Khafājī, however, begins to differentiate the two terms, specifying that "*faṣāḥa* is limited to the description of words (*alfāẓ*), [while] *balāgha* is not a description of words except [insofar as they relate to] meaning (*maʿānī*)."[1] By the time *ʿilm al-balāgha* became standardized as a science, the term *faṣāḥa*, which literally means clarity and purity, comes to refer more or less to a person's knowledge and correct usage of the Arabic language. *Faṣāḥa*, as al-Sakkākī explains, entails the clarity of speech, its freedom from convolutedness, and the use of pure genuine Arabic.[2] The term *balāgha*, on the other hand, which holds the literal sense of "reaching" or "attaining," comes to refer to a person's ability to make meaning reach the listener. Al-Sakkākī defines *balāgha* as:

[1] al-Khafājī, *Sirr al-faṣāḥa*, 60.
[2] al-Sakkākī, *al-Miftāḥ*, 526.

the speaker's [ability] to deliver in conveying meanings a degree of specification by giving the characteristics of composition (*khawāṣṣ al-tarākīb*) [the attention] they deserve, [as well as] the employment of the various types of simile, figurative speech, and metonymy, for their [proper] purposes.[3]

In other words, articulateness (*faṣāḥa*) involves the proper use of grammar and the lexicon, whereas eloquence (*balāgha*) entails the use of grammar and lexicon in literary ways.

Al-Khaṭīb al-Qazwīnī discusses the distinction between articulateness (*faṣāḥa*) and eloquence (*balāgha*) more extensively right at the beginning of his commentary. Articulateness (*faṣāḥa*) is when the chosen vocabulary is clear and "its usage among the Bedouins is well attested in their Arabic,"[4] while at the same time being "devoid of dissonance [among its] letters, strangeness, and inconsistencies with linguistic standards."[5] It also entails that speech "be free of weakness in composition, dissonance between words [i.e., heavy on the tongue and difficult to pronounce], and convolutedness [either in composition or signification]."[6] Articulateness (*faṣāḥa*), therefore, encompasses five aspects, which I number here so as to refer back to them later:

(1) purity and familiarity of vocabulary,
(2) consistency with standard linguistic forms,
(3) the proper use of grammar,
(4) clarity and straightforwardness in (a) composition and (b) signification, and
(5) harmony of sounds.

Eloquence (*balāgha*), on the other hand, is the "correspondence [of speech] to the requirements of the context given its articulateness (*faṣāḥa*)."[7] *Balāgha*, therefore, is a larger category than *faṣāḥa* and subsumes it: "Everything eloquent (*balīgh*) is articulate (*faṣīḥ*) and not

[3] Ibid.

[4] al-Khaṭīb al-Qazwīnī, *al-Īḍāḥ*, 74. The language of Bedouin Arabs was seen as the repository of pure Arabic language uncontaminated by too much contact with foreign languages compared to the Arabic spoken in urban centers like Baghdad.

[5] Ibid., 72. Strangeness (*gharāba*) in word choice is something to be avoided. It refers to rough, harsh-sounding, and obscure words, even if they are genuine pure Bedouin Arabic words (see ibid., 73).

[6] Ibid., 74. Convolutedness in composition is described as "*ta ʿqīd lafẓī*" and in signification as "*ta ʿqīd ma ʿnawī*." It becomes clear from the description of each that what is meant by the former is the wording and syntax, whereas the latter is the associations produced through indirect signification, such as through metaphor and metonymy (see ibid., 75–8).

[7] Ibid., 80.

everything articulate (*faṣīḥ*) is eloquent (*balīgh*)."[8] As a result, eloquence (*balāgha*) depends on two aspects:

(i) the ability "to avoid mistakes in conveying the intended meaning"[9] (thus successfully corresponding to the context), and
(ii) the ability "to distinguish between speech that is articulate (*faṣīḥ*) or not."[10]

The ability to distinguish speech in terms of its articulateness (*faṣāḥa*) (aspect (ii) of *balāgha*), in turn, is learned through various linguistic sciences and through the senses, al-Khaṭīb al-Qazwīnī explains. Aspect (1) of *faṣāḥa* delineated above (the ability to distinguish proper words from strange ones) is learned in lexicography (*ʿilm matn al-lugha*), (2) distinguishing between correct linguistic forms and those inconsistent with the standards is the purview of morphology (*ʿilm al-ṣarf*), (3) recognizing weak composition and (4a) convoluted wording lies in the realm of grammar (*ʿilm al-naḥw*).[11] The ability to recognize (5) dissonance in sound and heaviness in pronunciation, on the other hand, takes place through the senses (*yudrak bi-l-ḥiss*).[12]

What remains is the ability to avoid convolutedness in the *signification* of meanings (aspect 4b of *faṣāḥa*). This becomes the purview of the science of elucidation (*ʿilm al-bayān*), as we have seen in Chapter 4. Finally, the distinguishing aspect of eloquence, after we take account of all other defining features of *faṣāḥa*, rests on aspect (i) of al-Khaṭīb al-Qazwīnī's definition of *balāgha*: correspondence with the context. The "correspondence of speech to the requirements of the context" is the subject of the science of meanings (*ʿilm al-maʿānī*), as we have seen in Chapter 5.

As a result, the science of eloquence (*ʿilm al-balāgha*) ends up encompassing these last two remaining sciences, which the other sciences do not cover.[13] This is despite the fact that the definition of *balāgha*, beyond *faṣāḥa*, remains centered on "the correspondence with the requirements of the situation," which does not apply to *bayān*. As al-Taftāzānī points

[8] Ibid., 83.
[9] Ibid.
[10] Ibid.
[11] Ibid.; see clarification in al-Taftāzānī, *al-Muṭawwal*, 163–4.
[12] al-Khaṭīb al-Qazwīnī, *al-Īḍāḥ*, 83.
[13] From al-Khaṭīb al-Qazwīnī's overview it appears that *bayān* would in fact be part of *faṣāḥa*, but is incorporated under *balāgha* because it is not covered in the other sciences. This reinforces the attitude already evident in ʿAbd al-Qāhir al-Jurjānī's treatment of metaphor, metonymy, and *naẓm*, that *bayān* figures are secondary to sentence construction in achieving eloquence. Indeed, the Quran's inimitability lies primarily in the latter, according to our authors.

out, "there is no given situation that requires evoking a simile, metaphor, or metonymy."[14] At the same time, al-Taftāzānī explains that *bayān* is an added consideration after taking into account how speech corresponds with the context.[15]

The remaining rhetorical figures, which are not covered under *bayān*, are allocated to *ʿilm al-badīʿ* (the science of rhetorical figures), which comes to form the third branch of *balāgha*. The science of *badīʿ*, in turn, al-Khaṭīb al-Qazwīnī explains, focuses on "the ways of beautifying (*taḥsīn*) speech, after taking into account its correspondence with the context and the clarity of signification (*dalāla*)"[16] (i.e., the matters studied in the science of meanings (*ʿilm al-maʿānī*) and the science of elucidation (*ʿilm al-bayān*), respectively). Rhetorical figures, therefore, are features added to speech after its articulateness is ensured, its sentence is constructed in a way that corresponds to the context, and its metaphors and metonymies are attended to.

If one were to stop at this definition of eloquence here, one would conclude that eloquence in *ʿilm al-balāgha* depended on accuracy (of corresponding to the context) and clarity (of signification). However, what I have tried to show through my analysis of the components of each of the three branches of *ʿilm al-balāgha* is that the underlying *aesthetic* revolves around the ability of speech to convey meaning indirectly, implicitly, and in unexpected ways. Whether through the construction of the sentence, indirect signification, or rhetorical figures, what renders speech beautiful is its ability to make the listener go through an experience of discovery. While clarity and conveying the intended meaning are ultimately the stated goals of eloquent speech, this is the case given the assumed aesthetic principle that meaning is *not* conveyed in a straightforward way in eloquent speech. Clarity and correspondence are emphasized as goals of eloquence given that poetic beauty requires distancing and obscuring, which enhance the wonder effect.

ʿIlm al-bayān concerns the aesthetics of elucidating meaning through words that signify their intended sense *indirectly* and *inexplicitly*. *ʿIlm al-maʿānī* concerns the aesthetics of conveying information about the context *implicitly* through manipulations of the syntactical structures of a sentence. *ʿIlm al-badīʿ*, I have argued in Chapter 1, involves literary

[14] al-Taftāzānī, *al-Muṭawwal*, 168.
[15] Ibid., 166.
[16] al-Khaṭīb al-Qazwīnī, *al-Īḍāḥ*, 477 "علم يعرف به وجوه تحسين الكلام، بعد رعاية تطبيقه على مقتضى الحال ووضوح الدلالة".

devices that produce the unexpected or present information in non-straightforward ways. Medieval *balāgha* scholars' concern with "avoiding mistakes," therefore, should not derail our understanding of their aesthetic sensibility. Clarity and correctness are the limits of what is otherwise an assumed aesthetic of indirectness, implicitness, and unexpectedness.

Conclusion

Zakariyyā al-Qazwīnī in the introduction to his cosmography, *ʿAjāʾib al-makhlūqāt* (*The Wonders of Creations*), argues that *everything* in the world is wonder-evoking. It is merely our familiarity with the world that strips away its wonder.[1] Only when something appears out of the ordinary is one in awe of it. Over the course of this book, we have seen how poetry can recover this sense of wonder by rendering the familiar strange. Through the correct manipulation of sentence construction, the employment of metaphor and metonymy, as well as simile and other rhetorical figures, poetry and eloquent speech replicate experiences of novelty, unexpectedness, strangeness, and obscurity that force the listener to slow down and contemplate in order to grasp the unfamiliar or unobvious meaning, producing a sense of wonder. This ability to evoke wonder in the listener is the main underlying criterion for evaluating poeticity in classical Arabic literary theory beginning in the fifth/eleventh century. This new aesthetic represents an adaptation of the critical discourse to the aesthetics of the new style of poetry that developed in the early Abbasid period. The presence of this aesthetic outlook across disciplines, as we have seen, reflects the prevalence of this view of poetics and exposes an elegant widespread theory of literary aesthetics.

Wonder as the defining aesthetic experience of poetic language is not always explicitly announced in classical Arabic literary theory. The delight one experiences from poetry is described in medieval treatises with a wide

[1] al-Qazwīnī, *ʿAjāʾib al-makhlūqāt*, 31–5.

range of adjectives. However, through an analysis of the causes to which medieval scholars ascribed the pleasure one experiences from beautiful speech, I have argued that poetic beauty is defined by an experience of wonder. I use the concept of wonder as an umbrella term to describe the effect of the various linguistic mechanisms detailed in medieval works that render speech eloquent. Wonder not only describes the emotional experience one has when faced with something obscure, strange, or unexpected, but it also entails the impetus to contemplate and explain this obscure, strange, or unexpected meaning. The moment one grasps the image or idea a poet presents to us is a moment of sudden discovery and awareness that fills the listener with joy and wonder. As we have learned, the more effort this journey of discovery requires, the more pleasure one experiences upon its completion.

This experience of wonder is the aesthetic basis for literary judgment throughout medieval discussions of the various components of eloquence after the fourth/tenth century. The explanations provided by medieval critics of how this experience is produced amounts to a theory of aesthetic experience in language, i.e., it provides generalizable principles that explain why language is moving and pleasurable. This, in turn, gives us access to tangible criteria of literary judgment that are unique to Arabic literary forms but universal in their basic premises and principles.

In Chapter 1, we have seen how the aesthetics of rhetorical figures were defined by their capacity to delay the grasping of meaning through various techniques of deception, trickery, and obscuration, which lead to unexpected meanings. The beauty of simile, as we have seen in Chapter 3, also depended on its capacity of producing an experience of discovery in the listener by compelling him to search for the similarity between the two things compared. The more arduous this search, we also learned, the more rewarding the discovery. As a result, elements that slow down the grasping of a simile were analyzed and human nature's receptiveness to various ways of gaining knowledge were theorized. Such delaying strategies include the use of detail, rarity, strangeness, matters that require intellection (as opposed to being perceptible through the senses), and having the similarity be multifaceted (as opposed to entailing only one aspect). While simile is a figure of *bayān* (elucidation), its beauty lies in the experience of discovery, not its clarity in and of itself. The other *bayān* figures, which include metaphor and metonymy (*kināya*), also allow for such an experience of discovery, as we have seen in Chapter 4. These figures inherently carry the capacity of making the listener labor through a process of intellectual reasoning in order to deduce the intended meaning expressed figuratively in metaphor or implicitly in *kināya*. This process of deduction that the listener must go through when faced with indirect signification is inherently more moving than the experience one has when words signify their meaning explicitly. This is because the former allows for an experience of discovery that the latter does not. Finally, sentences are eloquent when constructed in a way that implicitly conveys information about the context in either expected or unexpected ways. Here again, as we have seen in Chapter 5, the more steps one has to go through in order to grasp the full nuance of a sentence, the more beautiful it is.

The aesthetic of wonder was perhaps always present intuitively in the poets and their audiences, but the critics did not always articulate poetic beauty in these terms. The discourse in the poetic criticism of the third/ninth and fourth/tenth centuries was framed primarily by a concern with truthfulness and falsehood, on the one hand, and naturalness and artificiality, on the other. Spurred by the innovations and fantastic imagery that abounded in the new (*muḥdath*) style of Abbasid poetry, critics debated whether the best poetry is the most truthful or the most false. While opinions varied, the general tolerance for fantastic imagery was low and poetic beauty was ascribed to the closeness of imagery to literal accuracy, its straightforwardness, and its familiarity given an established canon of images. As I have argued in Chapter 1, this truth–falsehood binary that shaped the old school of criticism is replaced by an aesthetic of wonder. In this new aesthetic paradigm, truthfulness and falsehood cease to be ascribed a role in poetic beauty. Instead, aspects that lead to an experience of discovery and wonder are credited for the beauty of poetic speech. This not only allowed for the articulation of the aesthetics of *muḥdath* poetry, but it also provided a more comprehensive conception of aesthetics: one that could explain the beauty of the old style of poetry as well as the new, in addition to the Quran.

A similar shift in paradigm takes place with the reception of Aristotle's *Poetics* in Arabic philosophy. As discussed in Chapter 2, the Islamicate world inherited a classification of the *Poetics* from late antiquity that placed it among the logical sciences. Arabic philosophy provided a new interpretation for the poetic as part of the logical sciences through the concept of *takhyīl* (the make-believe acknowledgment of the truth of the conclusion of a proposition). Unlike earlier attempts in late antiquity that differentiated the poetic syllogism from its counterparts by its falsehood, Arabic philosophy distinguished it by the emotional impact the make-believe conclusion of a simile or metaphor has on the soul. Their explanations of the impact of poetic speech on the soul also depended on wonder-evoking features such as discovery, rarity, and the defamiliarization of speech through alteration. Thus, a common conceptual framework of literary beauty began to emerge at the turn of the fifth/eleventh century across poetic criticism, philosophy, and works on eloquence and the inimitability of the Quran.

TIMING OF NEW AESTHETIC

There is no clear-cut temporal boundary between what I am describing as the old school of criticism and the beginning of the new school. I point to the turn of the fifth/eleventh century as the critical turning point because this new aesthetic framework is most clearly visible in the works of Ibn Sīnā (d. 428/1037) in the philosophical tradition and ʿAbd al-Qāhir al-Jurjānī (d. 471/1078 or 474/1081) in *balāgha*.[2] However, the old-school framework continued to exist in works of criticism written in the fifth/eleventh century, namely, in the works of al-Marzūqī (d. 421/1030) and Ibn Rashīq (d. 456/1063–4 or later). Moreover, traces of the new-school framework are visible in earlier works (e.g., al-Fārābī in philosophy, the early works on *bayān* and *iʿjāz al-Qurʾān*, and even in Ibn al-Muʿtazz's *Kitāb al-badīʿ*, if we consider the act of identifying discovery-based linguistic structures as *badīʿ* in itself as implicitly betraying an aesthetic of wonder).[3] While the new school of criticism could not have appeared without the foundation earlier works in poetic criticism, grammar, *bayān*, and philosophy had laid down, tracing the origins of the wonder framework in these works is beyond the scope of this book. I have merely taken the first steps in exposing this new aesthetic paradigm that seems to emerge uniformly across disciplines. This new paradigm is clearly different from the discourse of the old school of criticism, which has received much more attention in scholarship to date. How long this wonder paradigm

[2] Thomas Bauer has recently argued for thinking of the fifth/eleventh century as an intellectual and historical boundary between a "formative period" (first/seventh–fifth/eleventh century), still influenced by late antiquity and a new "post-formative" era (sixth/twelfth–thirteenth/nineteenth century), in which specialized sciences developed (Bauer, *Warum es kein islamisches Mittelalter gab*, 140). This would roughly fit our analysis here, which points to the fifth/eleventh century as a turning point in aesthetic theory. However, when it comes to *balāgha*, he counts al-Jurjānī as part of the "formative period" of late antiquity (ibid., 127). Although he points out the advancements al-Jurjānī forged in *balāgha* with respect to his predecessors (ibid., 126), he considers al-Sakkākī's *Miftāḥ* as marking the "surprisingly late end" of this formative period for the field of *balāgha* (ibid., 127). Given the profound aesthetic shift, which is already established by al-Jurjānī, however, I believe a strong case can be made for considering the "post-formative" era in the field of *balāgha* as beginning with him in the fifth/eleventh century, just as in logic it begins back with Ibn Sīnā (ibid., 131).

[3] See end of Chapter 1.

remains the dominant aesthetic outlook in later works has also yet to be investigated. It certainly continues to shape the discourse in the scholastic science of *balāgha* up to at least the eight/fourteenth century. However, the presence of alternative aesthetic outlooks in contemporaneous criticism as well as later attitude shifts has yet to be seen.[4]

ART FOR ART'S SAKE?

One of the fascinating outcomes of this aesthetic of wonder is that the value of poetic speech is located in aspects intrinsic to the poetic utterance. Unlike the old-school framework, it does not depend on an assessment of poetry's relationship with an external reality or its adherence to the conventions of a literary heritage. Social, political, and even theological concerns are not taken into consideration in their assessment of the poetic and the eloquent. Though the motivation behind the aesthetic inquiry might be religious (e.g., the question of the inimitability of the Quran), their analysis revolves around abstract linguistic matters and is decontextualized not only from the external nonpoetic context, but also from the immediate larger *poetic* context from which an excerpt is taken. Does this aesthetic of wonder then reflect an attitude of "art for art's sake"? On one level, one could say yes: Arabic critics could be said to view poetry as an end in itself that needed no further justification. Although this view of aesthetics has been suspect in the West, it is not an unjustifiable view to hold. Nevertheless, much was at stake with beautiful poetic language and its assessment as such. Poetry's social and political functions are well attested in the medieval Arabic context. Moreover, the Quran's inimitability depended on its extraordinary aesthetic quality.

Furthermore, the power of poetic speech to move the listener itself was given functions beyond aesthetic appreciation. The profound effect of the Quran was credited with the power to move people into submitting to Islam in countless medieval anecdotes. The philosophers also saw in the power of poetry to move the listener a means to educate the general public and sway their emotions, endowing it with civil purposes (*aghrāḍ madaniyya*).[5] Moreover, the active mind and the seeking of knowledge

[4] Most notably, Ḍiyāʾ al-Dīn ibn al-Athīr, in whose works Avigail Noy recognizes a continuity with pre-Jurjānian literary theory and a "viable alternative to the theories of al-Jurjānī," might very well complicate the story I have presented in this book (Noy, "The Emergence of *ʿIlm al-Bayān*," 203–306).

[5] See, for example, Ibn Sīnā, *al-Shiʿr*, 25.

(of which the poetic was a part) were necessary components for humans' attainment of happiness and perfection, according to the philosophers.[6] The fifth-/eleventh-century mystical theologian al-Ghazālī (d. 505/1111), who famously argued against the soundness of philosophy as a means of gaining all types of knowledge, sees that "the perception of beauty leads to God" and that "pleasure is a form of cognition" and to "enjoy is to know."[7] Speaking of al-Ghazālī, Doris Behrens-Abouseif explains: "There is a parallel between man's perception of God's creation and his perception of art. Just as beautiful calligraphy or a wall painting inspires us to reflect upon the artist's talent, so the wonders of the world induce us to think of Him who designed it."[8] The same can be said about the perception of poetic speech, which with an aesthetic of wonder certainly induces the listener's reflection on the meaning behind it. Although mystical poetry is never the subject of literary criticism as such, the aesthetic of wonder with the layers of deduction it entails fits well with the kind of cognitive rapture that mystical poetry seeks to achieve.

IS IT FOR EVERYONE?

While the aesthetic experience of wonder is first and foremost an emotional experience, it results from a cognitive process of deduction that can be quite complex. Can everyone experience it then? Al-Jurjānī states that while poets play with riddles and obscuration, the Quran's inimitability does not depend on such methods of disguise and concealment, otherwise it would not be described as "clear Arabic (*ʿArabī mubīn*)."[9] Nevertheless, al-Sakkākī states that the appreciation of eloquence depends on having a literary sensibility and natural taste (*dhawq*) for it. However, one can use the mind to cultivate one's taste, though it requires much practice, talent, and intelligence.[10] Excellent knowledge of the Arabic language would of course be a prerequisite, which is not a given in a multiethnic, multilingual Islamic empire. Moreover, the intellectual activity that such an

[6] See, for example, Abū Naṣr al-Fārābī, *al-Siyāsa al-madaniyya (also known as Mabādiʾ al-mawjūdāt)*, ed. Fawzī Mitrī Najjār (Beirut: al-Maṭbaʿa al-Kāthūlīkiyya, 1964), 22.

[7] Cited in Behrens-Abouseif, *Aesthetics*.

[8] Ibid.

[9] al-Jurjānī, *Asrār*, 326, in reference to Q26:195, which states that the Quran was revealed in a "clear Arabic tongue."

[10] al-Sakkākī, *al-Miftāḥ*, 257 and 263.

aesthetic often demands of its listeners assumes an audience of highly educated elites, as Matthew Keegan has argued.[11]

BEYOND ARABIC LITERATURE

Besides revealing some concrete aspects of classical Arabic aesthetic values, this theory of wonder developed in Arabic can also inform our understanding of other literatures written in the Islamicate context, including medieval Persian, Hebrew, and even Ottoman literatures. Medieval Persian poetry, for example, was greatly influenced by the forms, genres, and styles of Arabic poetry. Persian criticism was also very much influenced by its Arabic counterpart. Furthermore, Persian poetry went through a shift in poetic style from a more classical style (*sabk-e Khurasānī*) that flourished in the fourth/tenth and fifth/eleventh centuries to a more manneristic and embellished style (*sabk-e ʿIraqī*), which started crystallizing in the sixth/twelfth century: a shift similar to the one that took place in Arabic with *muḥdath* poetry. Given these parallels, one might expect to see a similar concern with wonder as a poetic effect in the medieval Persian critical tradition. Further research is needed to determine whether the aesthetic of wonder as exhibited in literary theory has any direct bearing on other artistic realms, including art, architecture, and music. However, enough parallels do exist that suggest the possibility of its application more broadly.[12]

Finally, the medieval Arabic theorization of wonder and the mechanisms through which it is evoked bear a resemblance to some Western theories of aesthetics, including those of the eighteenth-century Swiss thinker Johann Jakob Breitinger, who in his principal work *Critische Dichtkunst* rejects the classical principles of mimesis and whose understanding of wonder presents an astounding resemblance to that of al-Jurjānī.[13] Parallels can also be drawn between Arabic theory and the twentieth-century school of

[11] Keegan, "Throwing the Reins."

[12] The philosophical concept of *takhyīl*, for example, is applied to music as well in medieval Arabic philosophy (see Yaron Klein, "Imagination and Music: *Takhyīl* and the Production of Music in al-Fārābī's *Kitāb al-mūsīqī al-kabīr*," in *Takhyīl: The Imaginary in Classical Arabic Poetics*, ed. Geert Jan van Gelder and Marlé Hammond (Cambridge, UK: Gibb Memorial Trust, 2008)). Wonder has also been the subject of analysis in the context of Islamic art (see Saba, "Abbasid Lusterware and the Aesthetics of *ʿAjab*," and Berlekamp, *Wonder, Image, and Cosmos in Medieval Islam*).

[13] See Johannes Wankhammer, "Cultures of Sense: Science, Aesthetics, and the Art of Attention in the Eighteenth Century" (PhD Dissertation, Cornell University, 2016), 85–91.

Russian Formalism. Like Arabic theory, Russian Formalism was concerned with the intricacies contained within linguistic structures and verbal signification (instead of an extra-linguistic reality) that render language poetic. For the Formalist, just like for the Arab theorist of the new school of criticism, "the poet's job was defined as manipulation of language rather than as representation of reality."[14] As a result, like the new school of classical Arabic literary theory, they engaged closely with linguistics and semiotics.[15] Interestingly, the Russian Formalists arrive at a conclusion about literariness that resonates with Arabic theory, with the concepts of *ostranenie* (strange-making or defamiliarization) and "de-automatization," as developed by Viktor Sklovskij.[16] The French literary theorist Michael Riffaterre's semiotic approach to poetry also shares affinities with the Arabic concern with *bayān* and discovery. His idea of "indirection," which he considers central to poeticity, involves producing meaning "by displacing, distorting, or creating [further] meaning."[17] Moreover, he contends, "the harder it is to force the reader to notice the indirection and to lead him step by step through distortion, away from mimesis, the longer the detour must be and the more developed the text."[18] These similarities, however, would need to be more carefully studied in relation to their respective literary and historical contexts. Nevertheless, the striking parallels suggest that the theory in its Arabic context can also inform our understanding of aesthetics beyond Arabic literature.

[14] Victor Erlich, *Russian Formalism: History, Doctrine*, 3rd ed. (New Haven: Yale University Press, 1981), 190.

[15] See, for example, Roman Jakobson, "Closing Statement: Linguistics and Poetics," in *Style in Language*, ed. Thomas A. Sebeok (Cambridge, MA: MIT Press, 1960); and Erlich, *Russian Formalism*, 179.

[16] Erlich, *Russian Formalism*, 180–1. Viktor Shklovskiĭ and Alexandra Berlina, *Viktor Shklovsky: A Reader*, trans. Alexandra Berlina (New York: Bloomsbury Academic, 2017).

[17] Michael Riffaterre, *Semiotics of Poetry* (Bloomington, IN: Indiana University Press, 1978), 2.

[18] Ibid., 19.

Bibliography

ʿAbbās, Iḥsān. *Malāmiḥ yūnāniyya fī al-adab al-ʿArabī*. Beirut: al-Muʾassasa al-ʿArabiyya li-l-Dirāsāt wa-l-Nashr, 1977.

Tārīkh al-naqd al-adabī ʿind al-ʿArab: Naqd al-shiʿr min al-qarn al-thānī ḥattā al-qarn al-thāmin al-Hijrī. Amman: Dār al-Shurūq li-l-Nashr wa-l-Tawzīʿ, 1993.

Abdel Haleem, M. A. S. "Grammatical Shift for Rhetorical Purposes: *Iltifāt* and Related Features in the Quran." *Bulletin of the School of Oriental and African Studies* 55, no. 3 (1992): 407–32.

Abu Deeb, Kamal. *al-Adab al-ʿajāʾibī wa-l-ʿālam al-gharāʾibī fī kitāb al-ʿAẓma wa-fann al-sard al-ʿArabī*. Beirut: Dār al-Sāqī, 2007.

"al-Jurjānī's Classification of *Istiʿāra* with Special Reference to Aristotle's Classification of Metaphor." *Journal of Arabic Literature* 2 (1971): 48–75.

al-Jurjānī's Theory of Poetic Imagery. Warminster: Aris & Phillips, 1979.

"Literary Criticism." In *ʿAbbasid belles-lettres*, edited by Julia Ashtiany, T. M. Johnstone, J. D. Latham, R. B. Serjeant, and G. Rex Smith, 339–87. The Cambridge History of Arabic Literature. Cambridge: Cambridge University Press, 1990.

Abū Mūsā, Muḥammad Muḥammad. *Khaṣāʾiṣ al-tarākīb: Dirāsa taḥlīliyya li-masāʾil ʿilm al-maʿānī*. Cairo: Maktabat Wahba, 1996.

Abū Nuwās. *Dīwān*. Edited by Ewald Wagner and Gregor Schoeler. 5 vols. Wiesbaden: Franz Steiner Verlag, 1958–2003.

Abū Tammām. *Dīwān Abī Tammām bi-sharḥ al-Khaṭīb al-Tibrīzī*. Edited by Muḥammad ʿAbduh ʿAzzām. 4 vols. Cairo: Dār al-Maʿārif, 1957–65.

Abū Zayd, Aḥmad. *Muqaddima fī al-uṣūl al-fikriyya li-l-balāgha wa-iʿjāz al-Qurʾān*. Rabat: Dār al-Amān, 1989.

Adonis. *al-Shiʿriyya al-ʿArabiyya*. Beirut: Dār al-Ādāb, 1985.

al-Thābit wa-l-mutaḥawwil: Baḥth fī al-ittibāʿ wa-l-ibdāʿ ʿind al-ʿArab. 7th ed. 3 vols. Beirut: Dār al-Sāqī, 1994.

Ait El Ferrane, Mohamed. *Die Maʿnā-Theorie bei ʿAbdalqāhir al-Ǧurǧānī (gestorben 471/1079) Versuch einer Analyse der poetischen Sprache*. Heidelberger orientalistische Studien. Frankfurt am Main: Lang, 1990.

Ajami, Mansour. "Al-Marzūqī's Treatment of 'Amūd al-Shi'r (The Essentials of Poetry)." PhD Dissertation, Columbia University, 1976.

"'*Amūd al-shi'r*': Legitimization of a Tradition." *Journal of Arabic Literature* 12 (1981): 30–48.

The Alchemy of Glory: The Dialectic of Truthfulness and Untruthfulness in Medieval Arabic Literary Criticism. Washington, DC: Three Continents Press, 1988.

The Neckveins of Winter: The Controversy over Natural and Artificial Poetry in Medieval Arabic Literary Criticism. Studies in Arabic Literature, vol. 9. Leiden: E.J. Brill, 1984.

al-'Alawī, Yaḥyā ibn Ḥamza. *al-Ṭirāz al-mutaḍammin li-asrār al-balāgha wa-'ulūm ḥaqā'iq al-i'jāz*. Cairo: Dār al-Kutub al-Khidaywiyya, 1914.

Ali, Mohamed M. Yunis. *Medieval Islamic Pragmatics: Sunni Legal Theorists' Models of Textual Communication*. Surrey, UK: Curzon, 2000.

al-Āmidī, Abū al-Qāsim. *al-Muwāzana bayn shi'r Abī Tammām wa-l-Buḥturī*. Edited by Aḥmad Ṣaqr, vol. 1–2. 4th ed. 2 vols. Cairo: Dār al-Ma'ārif, 1961–5.

al-Muwāzana bayn shi'r Abī Tammām wa-l-Buḥturī. Edited by 'Abd Allāh Ḥamad Muḥārib, vol. 3, i–ii. Cairo: Maktabat al-Khānjī, 1990.

Aouad, Maroun, and Gregor Schoeler. "Le syllogisme poétique selon al-Fārābī: un syllogisme incorrect de la deuxième figure." *Arabic Sciences and Philosophy* 12 (2002): 185–96.

Arberry, Arthur John. *Arabic Poetry: A Primer for Students*. Cambridge: Cambridge University Press, 1965.

Aristotle. *The Complete Works of Aristotle*. Edited and translated by Jonathan Barnes, vol. 2. Bollingen Series 71.2. Princeton, NJ: Princeton University Press, 1984.

Poetics: Editio Maior of the Greek Text with Historical Introductions and Philological Commentaries. Edited by Leonardo Tarán and Dimitri Gutas. Leiden: Brill, 2012.

Ashtiany, Julia. "The Muwāzana of al-Āmidī." DPhil Dissertation, University of Oxford, 1983.

al-'Askarī, Abū Hilāl. *Kitāb al-ṣinā'atayn*. Edited by 'Alī Muḥammad al-Bijāwī and Muḥammad Abū al-Faḍl Ibrāhīm. Cairo: 'Īsā al-Bābī al-Ḥalabī, 1952.

al-Aṣma'ī. *al-Aṣma'iyyāt*. Edited by Aḥmad Muḥammad Shākir and 'Abd al-Salām Hārūn. Cairo: Dār al-Ma'ārif, 1963.

al-'Asqalānī, Ibn Ḥajar. *al-Fatḥ al-bārī bi-sharḥ Ṣaḥīḥ al-Bukhārī*. Edited by 'Abd al-'Azīz ibn 'Abd Allāh ibn Bāz, Muḥammad Fu'ād 'Abd al-Bāqī, and Muḥibb al-Dīn al-Khaṭīb. 13 vols. Cairo: al-Maktaba al-Salafiyya, 1979.

Athamina, Khalil. "*Lafẓ* in Classical Poetry." In *Israel Oriental Studies XI: Studies in Medieval Arabic and Hebrew Poetics*, edited by Sasson Somekh, 47–56. Leiden: Brill, 1991.

'Aṭiyya, Mukhtār. *al-Ījāz fī kalām al-'Arab wa-naṣṣ al-i'jāz: Dirāsa balāghiyya*. Alexandria: Dār al-Ma'rifa al-Jāmi'iyya, 1997.

'Ayyād, Shukrī Muḥammad. *Kitāb Arisṭūṭālis fī al-shi'r*. Cairo: Dār al-Kātib al-'Arabī, 1967.

Baalbaki, Ramzi. "The Relation between *Naḥw* and *Balāġa*: A Comparative Study of the Methods of Sībawayhi and Ǧurǧānī." *Zeitschrift für Arabische Linguistik* 11 (1983): 7–23.

Badawī, ʿAbd al-Raḥmān. *Fann al-shiʿr*. Cairo: Maktabat al-Nahḍa al-Miṣriyya, 1953.

al-Bāqillānī. *Iʿjāz al-Qurʾān*. Edited by al-Sayyid Aḥmad Ṣaqr. Cairo: Dār al-Maʿārif, 1954.

Bauer, Thomas. "In Search of 'Post-Classical Literature': A Review Article." *Mamlūk Studies Review* 11, no. 2 (2007): 137–67.

"Rhetorik, außereuropäische: V. Arabische Kultur." In *Historisches Wörterbuch der Rhetorik*, edited by Gert Ueding, 113–40. Tübingen: Max Niemeyer Verlag, 2007.

Warum es kein islamisches Mittelalter gab: das Erbe der Antike und der Orient. Munich: C.H. Beck, 2018.

Behrens-Abouseif, Doris. "Aesthetics." In *Encyclopaedia of Islam, THREE*, Part 2010–12, edited by Gudrun Krämer, Denis Matringe, John Nawas, and Everett Rowson, 25–35. Leiden: Brill, 2010.

Beauty in Arabic Culture [Schönheit in der arabischen Kultur]. Princeton, NJ: Markus Wiener Publishers, 1999.

Behzadi, Lale. *Sprache und Verstehen: al-Ǧaḥiẓ über die Vollkommenheit des Ausdrucks*. Wiesbaden: Harrassowitz, 2009.

Berlekamp, Persis. *Wonder, Image, and Cosmos in Medieval Islam*. New Haven, CT: Yale University Press, 2011.

Bin Ṣūf, Majdī. *ʿIlm al-adab ʿind al-Sakkākī: Baḥth fī intiẓām al-taṣawwurāt al-lisāniyya fī Miftāḥ al-ʿulūm*. Tunis: Miskīliyānī li-l-Nashr, 2010.

bin Tyeer, Sarah R. *The Quran and the Aesthetics of Premodern Arabic Prose*. London: Palgrave Macmillan, 2016.

Bint al-Shāṭiʾ. *al-Iʿjāz al-bayānī li-l-Qurʾān*. Cairo: Dār al-Maʿārif, 1971.

Black, Deborah. "Aesthetics in Islamic Philosophy." In *Routledge Encyclopedia of Philosophy*, vol. 1, edited by Edward Craig, 75–9. London and New York: Routledge, 1998.

"Estimation (*Wahm*) in Avicenna: The Logical and Psychological Dimensions." *Dialogue* 32, no. 2 (1993): 219–58.

Logic and Aristotle's "Rhetoric" and "Poetics" in Medieval Arabic Philosophy. Leiden: E.J. Brill, 1990.

Bonebakker, Seeger Adrianus. "Ibn Abi'l-Iṣbaʿ's Text of the *Kitāb al-badīʿ* of Ibn al-Muʿtazz." *Israel Oriental Studies* 2 (1972): 83–91.

"Poets and Critics in the Third Century A.H." In *Logic in Classical Islamic Culture*, edited by G. E. von Grunebaum, 85–111. Wiesbaden: Harrasowitz, 1970.

"Reflections on the *Kitāb al-badīʿ* of Ibn al-Muʿtazz." In *Atti del terzo congresso di studi arabi e islamici (Ravello, 1966)*, 191–209. Naples: Istituto Universitario Orientale, 1967.

Some Early Definitions of the Tawriya and Ṣafadī's Faḍḍ al-Xitām ʿan al-Tawriya wa-'l-istixdām. The Hague and Paris: Mouton & Co., 1966.

Boullata, Issa J. "The Rhetorical Interpretation of the Quran, *Iʿjaz* and Related Topics." In *Approaches to the Quran*, edited by Andrew Rippin, 139–57. Oxford; New York: Clarendon Press; Oxford University Press, 1988.

al-Buḥturī. *Dīwān al-Buḥturī*. Edited by Ḥasan Kāmil al-Ṣayrafī. Cairo: Dār al-Maʿārif, 1963–4.

al-Bukhārī. *Ṣaḥīḥ al-Bukhārī*. Damascus, Beirut: Dār Ibn Kathīr, 2002.

Bürgel, J. Christoph. "Die beste Dichtung ist die lügenreichste: Wesen und Bedeutung eines literarischen Streites des Arabischen Mittelalters im Lichte komparatistischer Betrachtung." *Oriens* 23–24 (1974): 7–102.

The Feather of Simurgh: The "Licit Magic" of the Arts in Medieval Islam. New York: New York University Press, 1988.

Bynum, Caroline Walker. "Wonder." *The American Historical Review* 102, no. 1 (1997): 1–26.

Cachia, Pierre J. "Arabic Literature." In *Encyclopaedia of Islam, THREE*, edited by Kate Fleet, Gudrun Krämer, Denis Matringe, John Nawas, and Everett Rowson. Brill Online, 2007.

The Arch Rhetorician or the Schemer's Skimmer: A Handbook of Late Arabic badīʿ Drawn from ʿAbd al-Ghanī an-Nābulsī's Nafaḥāt al-azhār ʿalā nasamāt al-asḥār. Wiesbaden: Harrassowitz, 1998.

Cantarino, Vicente. *Arabic Poetics in the Golden Age: Selection of Texts Accompanied by a Preliminary Study*. Leiden: Brill, 1975.

Carter, Michael. "Pragmatics and Contractual Language in Arabic Grammar and Legal Theory." In *Approaches to Arabic Linguistics: Presented to Kees Versteegh on the Occasion of His Sixtieth Birthday*, edited by E. Ditters and H. Motzki, 25–44. Leiden: Brill, 2007.

Colla, Elliott. *Conflicted Antiquities: Egyptology, Egyptomania, Egyptian Modernity*. Durham; London: Duke University Press, 2007.

D'Ancona, Cristina. "Aristotle and Aristotelianism." In *Encyclopaedia of Islam, THREE*, edited by Kate Fleet, Gudrun Krämer, Denis Matringe, John Nawas, and Everett Rowson. Brill Online, 2008.

Dahiyat, Ismail M. *Avicenna's Commentary on the Poetics of Aristotle: A Critical Study with an Annotated Translation of the Text*. Leiden: E.J. Brill, 1974.

Ḍayf, Shawqī. *al-Balāgha: Taṭawwur wa-tārīkh*. 9th ed. Cairo: Dār al-Maʿārif, 1995.

Dhū al-Rumma. *Dīwān Dhī al-Rumma: Sharḥ Abī Naṣr al-Bāhilī*. Edited by ʿAbd al-Quddūs Abū Ṣāliḥ. 3 vols. Beirut: Muʾassasat al-Īmān, 1982.

Dichy, Joseph. "Kinâya, a Tropic Device from Medieval Arabic Rhetoric, and Its Impact on Discourse Theory." In *Proceedings of the 5th Conference of the International Society for the Study of Argumentation (ISSA), University of Amsterdam, 25–28 June 2002*, edited by Frans van Eemeren, J. Anthony Blair, Charles A. Willard and A. Francisca Snoeck Henkemans, 237–41. Amsterdam: Sic Sat, 2003.

Drory, Rina. "Three Attempts to Legitimize Fiction in Classical Arabic Literature." *Jerusalem Studies in Arabic and Islam* 18 (1994): 146–64.

El Sadda, Hoda. "Figurative Discourse in Medieval Arabic Criticism." *Alif: Journal of Comparative Poetics* 12, "Metaphor and Allegory in the Middle Ages" (1992): 95–109.

Erlich, Victor. *Russian Formalism: History, Doctrine*. 3rd ed. New Haven: Yale University Press, 1981.

van Ess, Josef. "Some Fragments of the *Muʿāraḍat al-Qurʾān* Attributed to Ibn al-Muqaffaʿ." In *Studia Arabica et Islamica: Festschrift for Iḥsān ʿAbbās on His*

Sixtieth Birthday, edited by Wadad al-Qadi, 151–63. Beirut: American University of Beirut, 1981.

Fakhreddine, Huda J. *Metapoesis in the Arabic Tradition: From Modernists to Muḥdathūn*. Leiden: Brill, 2015.

al-Fārābī, Abū Naṣr. *Iḥṣāʾ al-ʿulūm*. Edited by ʿUthmān Amīn. 3rd ed. Cairo: Maktabat al-Anjlū al-Miṣriyya, 1968.

"Jawāmiʿ al-shiʿr (Kitāb al-shiʿr)." In *Talkhīs kitāb Arisṭuṭālis fī al-shiʿr*, edited by Muḥammad Salīm Sālim, 171–5. Cairo: Maṭābiʿ al-Ahrām al-Tijāriyya, 1971.

Kitāb al-ḥurūf. Edited by Muḥsin Mahdī. Beirut: Dār al-Mashriq, 1986.

al-Manṭiqiyyāt li-l-Fārābī. Edited by Muḥammad Taqī Dānish Pazhūh. Qum: Manshūrāt Maktabat Āyatullah al-ʿUẓmā al-Marʿashī al-Najafī, 1987.

"Qawl al-Fārābi fī al-tanāsub wa-l-taʾlīf." In *al-Manṭiqiyyāt li-l-Fārābī*, edited by Muḥammad Taqī Dānish Pazhūh, 1, 504–6. Qum: Manshūrāt Maktabat Āyatullah al-ʿUẓmā al-Marʿashī al-Najafī, 1987.

al-Siyāsa al-madaniyya (also known as Mabādiʾ al-mawjūdāt). Edited by Fawzī Mitrī Najjār. Beirut: al-Maṭbaʿa al-Kāthūlīkiyya, 1964.

al-Fārābī, Abū Naṣr, and A. J. Arberry. "Fārābī's Canons of Poetry." *Rivista degli Studi Orientali* 17 (1938): 266–78.

al-Fārābī, Abū Naṣr, and Muḥsin Mahdī. "Kitāb al-shiʿr." *Shiʿr* 12 (1959): 90–5.

al-Farazdaq. *Sharḥ Dīwān al-Farazdaq*. Edited by Īliyyā al-Ḥāwī. 2 vols. Beirut: Dār al-Kitāb al-Lubnānī, Maktabat al-Madrasa, 1983.

Firanescu, Daniela Rodica. "Speech Acts." In *Encyclopedia of Arabic Language and Linguistics*, edited by Kees Versteegh, vol. 4, 328–34. Leiden: Brill, 2009.

Fisher, Philip. *Wonder, the Rainbow, and the Aesthetics of Rare Experiences*. Cambridge, MA: Harvard University Press, 1998.

van Gelder, Geert Jan. "The Abstracted Self in Arabic Poetry." *Journal of Arabic Literature* 14 (1983): 22–30.

The Bad and the Ugly: Attitudes towards Invective Poetry (hijāʾ) in Classical Arabic Literature. Leiden: Brill, 1988.

Badīʿ. In *Encyclopaedia of Islam, THREE*, edited by Kate Fleet, Gudrun Krämer, Denis Matringe, John Nawas, and Everett Rowson. Brill Online, 2009.

Beyond the Line: Classical Arabic Literary Critics on the Coherence and Unity of the Poem. Leiden: E.J. Brill, 1982.

Classical Arabic Literature: A Library of Arabic Literature Anthology. New York: New York University Press, 2013.

"'A Good Cause': Fantastic Etiology (*Ḥusn al-Taʿlīl*) in Arabic Poetics." In *Takhyīl: The Imaginary in Classical Arabic Poetics*, edited by Geert Jan van Gelder and Marlé Hammond, 221–37. Cambridge, UK: Gibb Memorial Trust, 2008.

"The Lamp and Its Mirror." In *Takhyīl: The Imaginary in Classical Arabic Poetics*, edited by Geert Jan van Gelder and Marlé Hammond, 265–73. Cambridge, UK: Gibb Memorial Trust, 2008.

"The Qurʾan in *Kitāb al-Badīʿ* by Ibn al-Muʿtazz." In *The Qur'an and Adab: The Shaping of Literary Traditions in Classical Islam*, edited by Nuha Alshaar, 173–89. Oxford: Oxford University Press/Institute of Ismaili Studies, 2017.

Sound and Sense in Classical Arabic Poetry. Wiesbaden: Harrassowitz, 2012.

Ta'adjdjub. In *Encyclopaedia of Islam, Second Edition*, edited by P. Bearman, Th. Bianquis, C. E. Bosworth, E. van Donzel, and W. P. Heinrichs. Brill Online, 2012.

van Gelder, Geert Jan, and Marlé Hammond, eds. *Takhyīl: The Imaginary in Classical Arabic Poetics*. Cambridge, UK: Gibb Memorial Trust, 2008.

al-Ghāzī, 'Allāl. "Taṭawwur muṣṭalaḥ 'al-takhyīl' fī naẓariyyat al-naqd al-adabī 'ind al-Sijilmāsī." *Majallat kulliyyat al-ādāb wa-l-'ulūm al-insāniyya bi-Fās* 4 (1988): 285–334.

Ghersetti, Antonella. "Per una rilettura in chiave pragmatica di *Dalā'il al-i'ǧāz* di 'Abd al-Qāhir al-Ǧurǧānī." PhD Dissertation, Università degli Studi di Firenze, 1998.

Giolfo, Manuela E. B., and Wilfrid Hodges. "The System of the Sciences of the Arabic Language by al-Sakkākī: Logic as a Complement of Rhetoric." In *Approaches to the History and Dialectology of Arabic in Honor of Pierre Larcher*, edited by Manuel Sartori, Manuela E. B. Giolfo and Philippe Cassuto, 242–66. Leiden: Brill, 2017.

Goldziher, Ignaz. "Alte und neue Poesie im Urtheile der arabische Kritiker." In *Abhandlungen zur arabischer Philologie*, 1, 122–76. Leiden: E.J. Brill, 1896.

Gonzalez, Valerie. *Beauty and Islam: Aesthetics in Islamic Art and Architecture*. London: I.B. Tauris in association with the Institute of Ismaili Studies, 2001.

Graziosi, Barbara. "On Seeing the Poet: Arabic, Italian and Byzantine Portraits of Homer." *Scandinavian Journal of Byzantine and Modern Greek Studies* 1 (2015): 25–47.

Greenblatt, Stephen. *Marvelous Possessions: The Wonder of the New World*. Chicago: University of Chicago Press, 1991.

Gruendler, Beatrice. "Fantastic Aesthetics and Practical Criticism in Ninth-Century Baghdad." In *Takhyīl: The Imaginary in Classical Arabic Poetics*, edited by Geert Jan van Gelder and Marlé Hammond, 196–220. Cambridge, UK: Gibb Memorial Trust, 2008.

Medieval Arabic Praise Poetry: Ibn al-Rūmī and the Patron's Redemption. London; New York: Routledge, 2003.

"Modernity in the Ninth Century: The Controversy around Abū Tammām." *Studia Islamica* 112, no. 1 (2017): 131–48.

von Grunebaum, Gustave E. "The Aesthetic Foundation of Arabic Literature." *Comparative Literature* 4, no. 4 (1952): 323–40.

Bayān. In *Encyclopaedia of Islam, Second Edition*, edited by P. Bearman, Th. Bianquis, C. E. Bosworth, E. van Donzel, and W. P. Heinrichs. Brill Online, 2012.

Kritik und Dichtkunst. Wiesbaden: Harrassowitz, 1955.

A Tenth-Century Document of Arabic Literary Theory and Criticism: The Sections on Poetry of Bâqillânî's I'jâz al-Qur'ân. Chicago: University of Chicago Press, 1950.

Gutas, Dimitri. "The Empiricism of Avicenna." *Oriens* 40 (2012): 391–436.

Greek Thought, Arabic Culture: The Graeco-Arabic Translation Movement in Baghdad and Early 'Abbāsid Society (2nd–4th/8th–10th Centuries). London: Routledge, 1998.

"Paul the Persian on the Classification of the Parts of Aristotle's Philosophy: A Milestone between Alexandria and Bagdâd." *Der Islam* 60 (1983): 231–67.

Halliwell, Stephen, and Aristotle. *Aristotle's Poetics*. Chicago: University of Chicago Press, 1998.

Hamarneh, Walid. "Arabic Theory and Criticism." In *The Johns Hopkins Guide to Literary Theory and Criticism*, edited by Michael Gorden, Martin Kreiswirth and Imre Szeman, 55–62. Baltimore and London: The Johns Hopkins University Press, 2004.

"The Reception of Aristotle's Theory of Poetry in Arab-Islamic Medieval Thought." In *Poetics East and West*, edited by Milena Doleželová-Velingerová, 183–201. Toronto: Toronto Semiotic Circle, Victoria College in the University of Toronto, 1989.

Hamori, Andras. "Anthologies, Arabic Literature (Pre-Mongol Period)." In *Encyclopaedia of Islam, THREE*, edited by Kate Fleet, Gudrun Krämer, Denis Matringe, John Nawas, and Everett Rowson. Brill Online, 2007.

Harb, Lara. "Beyond the Known Limits: Ibn Dāwūd al-Iṣfahānī's Chapter on 'Intermedial' Poetry." In *Arabic Humanities, Islamic Thought: A Festschrift for Everett K. Rowson*, edited by Shawkat Toorawa and Joseph Lowry, 122–49. Leiden: Brill, 2017.

"Form, Content, and the Inimitability of the Qurʾān in ʿAbd al-Qāhir al-Jurjānī's Works." *Middle Eastern Literatures* 18, no. 3 (2015): 301–21.

al-Hāshimī, al-Sayyid Aḥmad. *Jawāhir al-balāgha fī al-maʿānī wa-l-bayān wa-l-badīʿ*. Beirut: al-Maktaba al-ʿAṣriyya, 1999?

von Hees, Syrinx. "The Astonishing: A Critique and Re-reading of ʿAjāʾib Literature." *Middle Eastern Literatures* 8, no. 2 (2005): 101–20.

Enzyklopädie als Spiegel des Weltbildes: Qazwinis Wunder der Schöpfung: Eine Naturkunde des 13. Jahrhunderts. Wiesbaden: Harrassowitz, 2002.

Heinemann, Arnim, John L. Meloy, Tarif Khalidi, and Manfred Kropp, eds. *Al-Jāḥiẓ: A Muslim Humanist for Our Time*. Würzburg: Ergon Verlag, 2009.

Heinrichs, Wolfhart. *Arabische Dichtung und Griechische Poetik: Ḥāzim al-Qarṭāğannīs Grundlegung der Poetik mit Hilfe Aristotelischer Begriffe*. Beirut: Franz Steiner Verlag, 1969.

"Die antike Verknüpfung von phantasia und Dichtung bei den Arabern." *Zeitschrift der Deutschen Morgenländischen Gesellschaft* 128 (1978): 252–98.

The Hand of the Northwind: Opinions on Metaphor and the Early Meaning of Istiʿāra in Arabic Poetics. Abhandlungen für die Kunde des Morgenlandes. Wiesbaden: Kommissionsverlag Franz Steiner, 1977.

"*Istiʿāra* and *Badīʿ* and Their Terminological Relationship in Early Arabic Literary Criticism." *Zeitschrift für Geschichte der Arabisch-Islamischen Wissenschaften* 1 (1984): 180–211.

"Literary Theory: The Problem of Its Efficiency." In *Arabic Poetry: Theory and Development*, edited by G. E. von Grunebaum. Third Giorgio Levi della Vida Biennial Conference. Wiesbaden: Harrassowitz, 1973.

"Mannerism in Arabic Poetry: A Structural Analysis of Selected Texts by Stefan Sperl (Review)." *Middle East Journal* 45, no. 4 (1991): 698–9.

Mubālagha. In *Encyclopaedia of Islam, Second Edition*, edited by P. Bearman, Th. Bianquis, C. E. Bosworth, E. van Donzel, and W. P. Heinrichs. Brill Online, 2012.

Naẓm. In *Encyclopaedia of Islam, Second Edition*, edited by P. Bearman, Th. Bianquis, C. E. Bosworth, E. van Donzel, and W. P. Heinrichs. Brill Online, 2012.

"On the Genesis of the *ḥaqîqa-majâz* Dichotomy." *Studia Islamica* 59 (1984): 111–40.

"Paired Metaphors in *Muḥdath* Poetry." *Occasional Papers of the School of Abbasid Studies* 1 (1986): 1–22.

"Rhetorical Figures." In *Encyclopedia of Arabic Literature*, edited by Julie Scott Meisami and Paul Starkey, 156–62. London; New York: Routledge, 1998.

al-Sakkākī. In *Encyclopaedia of Islam, Second Edition*, edited by P. Bearman, Th. Bianquis, C. E. Bosworth, E. van Donzel, and W. P. Heinrichs. Brill Online, 2012.

al-Sidjilmāsī. In *Encyclopaedia of Islam, Second Edition*, edited by P. Bearman, Th. Bianquis, C. E. Bosworth, E. van Donzel, and W. P. Heinrichs. Brill Online, 2012.

"Ta'jīb." In *Encyclopedia of Arabic Literature*, edited by Julie Scott Meisami and Paul Starkey, 754–5. London; New York: Routledge, 1998.

"Takhyīl: Make-Believe and Image Creation in Arabic Literary Theory." In *Takhyīl: The Imaginary in Classical Arabic Poetics*, edited by Geert Jan van Gelder and Marlé Hammond, 1–14. Cambridge, UK: Gibb Memorial Trust, 2008.

al-Ḥimṣī, Na'īm. *Fikrat i'jāz al-Qur'ān min al-ba'tha al-nabawiyya ilā 'aṣrinā al-ḥāḍir*. 2nd ed. Beirut: Mu'assasat al Risāla, 1980.

Hussein, Taha. "al-Bayān al-'Arabī min al-Jāḥiẓ ilā 'Abd al-Qāhir." Introduction to Pseudo-Qudāma ibn Ja'far, *Naqd al-nathr*, edited by Taha Hussein and A. H. al-'Abbādī, 1–32. Cairo: al-Maṭba'a al-Amīriyya, 1941.

al-Ḥutay'a. *Dīwān al-Ḥutay'a bi-sharḥ Ibn al-Sikkīt wa-l-Sukkarī wa-l-Sijistānī*. Edited by Nu'mān Amīn Ṭāhā. Cairo: Sharikat Maktabat wa-Maṭba'at Muṣṭafā al-Bābī al-Ḥalabī wa-Awladih, 1958.

Ibn Abī al-Iṣba'. *Taḥrīr al-taḥbīr fī ṣinā'at al-shi'r*. Edited by Ḥifnī Muḥammad Sharaf. Cairo: al-Majlis al-A'lā li-l-Shu'ūn al-Islāmiyya, Lajnat Iḥyā' al-Turāth al-Islāmī, 1963.

Ibn al-Athīr, Ḍiyā' al-Dīn. *al-Mathal al-sā'ir fī adab al-kātib wa-l-shā'ir*. Edited by Aḥmad al-Ḥūfī and Badawī Ṭabāna. 4 vols. Cairo: Maktabat Nahḍat Miṣr, 1959–65.

Ibn Hishām, 'Abd al-Malik. *The Life of Muhammad: A Translation of Isḥāq's Sīrat Rasūl Allāh*. Translated by Alfred Guillaume. Karachi; New York: Oxford University Press, 1997.

al-Sīra al-nabawiyya. Edited by Muṣṭafā al-Saqqā, Ibrāhīm al-Ibyārī, and 'Abd al-Ḥafīz Shalabī. 2nd ed. 4 vols. Cairo: Maṭba'at Muṣṭafā al-Bābī al-Ḥalabī, 1955.

Ibn al-Mu'tazz. *Dīwan Ibn al-Mu'tazz*. Beirut: Dār Ṣādir, 1961.

Kitāb al-badī'. Edited by Ignatius Kratchkovsky. 3rd ed. Beirut: Dār al-Masīra, 1982.

Ibn al-Nadīm, Muḥammad ibn Isḥāq. *Kitāb al-fihrist*. Edited by Muḥammad Riḍā Tajaddud. Tehran: Amīr Kabīr, 1987.

Ibn al-Naqīb. *Muqaddimat tafsīr Ibn al-Naqīb fī ʿilm al-bayān wa-l-maʿānī wa-l-badīʿ wa-iʿjāz al-Qurʾān*. Edited by Zakariyyā Saʿīd ʿAlī. Cairo: Maktabat al-Khānjī, 1995.

Ibn al-Ṭiqṭaqā. *al-Fakhrī*. Edited by Hartwig Derenbourg. Paris: Bouillon, 1895.

Ibn Khallikān. *Wafayāt al-aʿyān*. Edited by Iḥsān ʿAbbās. Beirut: Dār Ṣādir, 1968.

Ibn Mālik, Badr al-Dīn. *al-Miṣbāḥ fī al-maʿānī wa-l-bayān wa-l-badīʿ*. Edited by Ḥusnī ʿAbd al-Jalīl Yūsuf. Cairo: Maktabat al-Ādāb, 1989.

Ibn Manẓūr. *Lisān al-ʿArab*. Beirut: Dār Ṣādir, 1955.

Ibn Qutayba. *al-Shiʿr wa-l-shuʿarāʾ*. Edited by Aḥmad Muḥammad Shākir. 2nd ed. Cairo: Dār al-Maʿārif, 1967.

Ibn Rashīq al-Qayrawānī. *al-ʿUmda fī maḥāsin al-shiʿr wa-ādābih wa-naqdih*. Edited by Muḥammad Muḥyīddīn ʿAbd al-Ḥamīd. 5th ed. 2 vols. Beirut: Dār al-Jīl, 1981.

Ibn Rushd. *Averroes' Middle Commentary on Aristotle's Poetics*. Translated by Charles E. Butterworth. Princeton, NJ: Princeton University Press, 1986.

Averroes' Three Short Commentaries on Aristotle's "Topics," "Rhetoric," and "Poetics" (Jawāmiʿ li-kutub Arisṭūṭālīs fī al-jadal wa-l-khaṭāba wa-l-shiʿr). Edited and translated by Charles E. Butterworth. Albany: State University of New York Press, 1977.

Talkhīṣ al-Khaṭāba. Edited by Muḥammad Salīm Sālim. Cairo: al-Majlis al-Aʿlā li-l-Shuʾūn al-Islāmiyya, Lajnat Iḥyāʾ al-Turāth al-Islāmī, 1967.

Talkhīṣ kitāb al-shiʿr. Cairo: Markaz Taḥqīq al-Turāth, 1986.

Ibn Sīnā. *al-Ishārāt wa-l-tanbīhāt, with the Commentary of Naṣīr al-Dīn al-Ṭūsī*. Edited by Sulaymān Dunya. 3 vols. Cairo: Dār al-Maʿārif, 1960.

Kitāb al-majmūʿ aw al-Ḥikma al-ʿarūḍiyya fī maʿānī al-shiʿr. Edited by Muḥammad Salīm Sālim. Cairo: Maṭbaʿat Dār al-Kutub, 1969.

Kitāb al-najāt. Edited by Majid Fakhrī. Beirut: Dār al-Āfāq, 1982.

al-Shifāʾ, al-Manṭiq 4: al-Qiyās. Edited by Ibrāhīm Madkūr and Saʿīd Zāyid. Cairo: al-Hayʾa al-ʿĀmma li-Shuʾūn al-Maṭābiʿ al-Amīriyya, 1964.

al-Shifāʾ, al-Manṭiq 8: al-Khaṭāba. Edited by Muḥammad Salīm Sālim. Cairo: al-Maṭbaʿa al-Amīriyya, 1954.

al-Shifāʾ, al-Manṭiq 9: al-Shiʿr. Edited by ʿAbd al-Raḥmān Badawī. Cairo: al-Dār al-Miṣriyya li-l-Taʾlīf wa-l-Tarjama, 1966.

Ibn Ṭabāṭabā, Abū al-Ḥasan. *ʿIyār al-shiʿr*. Edited by ʿAbd al-ʿAzīz ibn Nāṣir al-Māniʿ. Riyad: Dār al-ʿUlūm, 1985.

Ibn Wahb, Isḥāq. *al-Burhān fī wujūh al-bayān*. Edited by Aḥmad Maṭlūb and Khadīja al-Ḥadīthī. Baghdad: Maṭbaʿat al-ʿĀnī, 1967.

Imruʾ al-Qays. *Dīwān Imriʾ al-Qays*. Edited by Muṣṭafā ʿAbd al-Shāfī. 5th ed. Beirut: Dār al-Kutub al-ʿIlmiyya, 2004.

Ismāʿīl, ʿIzzuddīn. *al-Usus al-jamāliyya fī al-naqd al-ʿArabī: ʿArḍ wa-tafasīr wa-muqārana*. 3rd ed. Cairo: Dār al-Fikr al-ʿArabī, 1974.

Jacobi, Renate. "Abbasidische Dichtung (8.-13. Jhdt.)." In *Grundriss der arabischen Philologie. Band II: Literaturwissenschaft*, edited by Helmut Gätje, 41–57. Wiesbaden: Ludwig Reichert Verlag, 1987.

"Dichtung und Lüge in der arabischen Literaturtheorie." *Der Islam* 49 (1972): 85–99.
al-Jāḥiẓ. *al-Bayān wa-l-tabyīn*. Edited by ʿAbd al-Salām Hārūn. 7th ed. 4 vols. Cairo: Maktabat al-Khānjī, 1998.
"Ḥujaj al-nubuwwa." In *Rasāʾil*, edited by ʿAbd al-Salām Muḥammad Hārūn, 3, 221–82. Beirut: Dār al-Jīl, 1991.
Kitāb al-ḥayawān. Edited by ʿAbd al-Salām Hārūn. 8 vols. Beirut: Dār al-Jīl, 1996.
Rasāʾil al-Jāḥiẓ. Edited by ʿAbd al-Salām Hārūn. 4 vols. Beirut: Dār al-Jīl, 1991.
al-Jāḥiẓ, and Saʿd ʿAbd al-ʿAẓīm Muḥammad. *Naẓm al-Qurʾān*. Cairo: Maktabat al-Zahrāʾ, 1995.
Jakobson, Roman. "Closing Statement: Linguistics and Poetics." In *Style in Language*, edited by Thomas A. Sebeok, 350–77. Cambridge, MA: MIT Press, 1960.
Jarrār, Shadhā. *Muwāzana bayn madhhabay al-Bāqillānī wa-l-Jurjānī fī kitābayhimā Iʿjāz al-Qurʾān wa-Dalāʾil al-iʿjāz*. Amman: Amānat ʿAmmān, 2005.
Jenssen, Herbjørn. *The Subtleties and Secrets of the Arabic Language: Preliminary Investigations into al-Qazwīnī's Talkhīṣ al-Miftāḥ*. Bergen: Centre for Middle Eastern and Islamic Studies, 1998.
Jones, Alan. *Early Arabic Poetry: Selected Poems*. 2nd ed. Reading, UK: Ithaca Press, 2011.
al-Jundī, Darwīsh. *Naẓariyyat ʿAbd al-Qāhir fī al-naẓm*. Cairo: Maktabat Nahḍat Miṣr, 1960.
al-Jurjānī, ʿAbd al-Qāhir. *Asrār al-balāgha*. Edited by Hellmut Ritter. Istanbul: Government Press, 1954.
Dalāʾil al-iʿjāz. Edited by Maḥmūd Muḥammad Shākir. 5th ed. Cairo: Maktabat al-Khānjī, 2004.
Die Geheimnisse der Wortkunst (Asrār al-balāgha) des ʿAbdalqāhir al-Jurjānī [*Asrār al-balāgha*]. Translated by Hellmut Ritter. Wiesbaden: In Kommission bei Franz Steiner, 1959.
"al-Risāla al-shāfiya fī wujūh al-iʿjāz." In *Dalāʾil al-iʿjāz*, edited by Maḥmūd Muḥammad Shākir, 575–628. Cairo: Maktabat al-Khānjī, 2004.
al-Jurjānī (al-Qāḍī), ʿAlī ibn ʿAbd al-ʿAzīz. *al-Wasāṭa bayn al-Mutanabbī wa-khuṣūmih*. Edited by Muḥammad Abū al-Faḍl Ibrāhīm and ʿAlī Muḥammad al-Bajāwī. Beirut: al-Maktaba al-ʿAṣriyya, 2006.
al-Jurjānī (al-Sayyid al-Sharīf), ʿAlī ibn Muḥammad. *al-Ḥāshiya ʿalā al-Muṭawwal*. Edited by Rashīd Aʿraḍī. Beirut: Dār al-Kutub al-ʿIlmiyya, 2007.
al-Miṣbāḥ fī sharḥ al-Miftāḥ. Edited by Yüksel Çelik. PhD Dissertation, Marmara University, Istanbul, 2009.
Muʿjam al-taʿrīfāt. Edited by Muḥammad Ṣiddīq al-Minshāwī. Cairo: Dār al-Faḍīla, 2004.
al-Jurjānī, Muḥammad ibn ʿAlī. *al-Ishārāt wa-l-tanbīhāt fī ʿilm al-balāgha*. Edited by ʿAbd al-Qādir Ḥusayn. Cairo: Dār Nahḍat Miṣr, 1982.
Kahwaji, S. *ʿIlm al-Djamāl*. In *Encyclopaedia of Islam, Second Edition*, edited by P. Bearman, Th. Bianquis, C. E. Bosworth, E. van Donzel, and W. P. Heinrichs. Brill Online, 2012.

Keegan, Matthew. "Commentarial Acts and Hermeneutical Dramas: The Ethics of Reading al-Ḥarīrī's *Maqāmāt*." PhD Dissertation, New York University, 2017.

"Throwing the Reins to the Reader: Hierarchy, Jurjānian Poetics, and al-Muṭarrizī's Commentary on the *Maqāmāt*." In "ʿAbd al-Qāhir al-Jurjānī," edited by Alexander Key. Special issue, *Journal of Abbasid Studies* 5 (2018): 105–45.

Kemal, Salim. "Aristotle's *Poetics*, the Poetic Syllogism, and Philosophical Truth in Averroes's Commentary." *The Journal of Value Inquiry* 35 (2001): 391–412.

The Poetics of Alfarabi and Avicenna. Leiden: E.J. Brill, 1991.

Kennedy, Philip F. *Abu Nuwas: A Genius of Poetry*. Oxford: Oneworld, 2005.

The Wine Song in Classical Arabic Poetry: Abū Nuwās and the Literary Tradition. Oxford; New York: Clarendon Press; Oxford University Press, 1997.

Kenseth, Joy, ed. *The Age of the Marvelous*. Hanover, NH: Hood Museum of Art, 1991.

Kermani, Navid. *Gott ist schön: Das ästhetische Erleben des Koran*. Munich: C.H. Beck, 1999.

Key, Alexander. *Language between God and the Poets: Maʿnā in the Eleventh Century*. Berkeley, CA: University of California Press, 2018.

al-Khafājī, Ibn Sinān. *Sirr al-faṣāḥa*. Edited by ʿAbd al-Mutaʿāl al-Ṣaʿīdī. Cairo: Maktabat wa-Maṭbaʿat Muḥammad ʿAlī Ṣubayḥ, 1953.

Khalafallah, Muhammad. "ʿAbdalqâhir's Theory in His 'Secrets of Eloquence': A Psychological Approach." *Journal of Near Eastern Studies* 14, no. 3 (July 1955): 164–7.

"Naẓariyyat ʿAbd al-Qāhir fī Asrār al-balāgha." *Majallat kulliyyat al-ādāb, Alexandria* 2 (1944): 14–82.

Khalfallah, Nejmeddine. *La théorie sémantique de ʿAbd al-Qāhir al-Jurjānī (m. 1078)*. Paris: L'Harmattan, 2014.

al-Khaṭṭābī. "Bayān iʿjāz al-Qurʾān." In *Thalāth rasāʾil fī iʿjāz al-Qurʾān*, edited by Muḥammad Khalafallāh and Muḥammad Zaghlūl Sallām, 19–65. Cairo: Dār al-Maʿārif, 1976.

al-Khaṭṭābī, al-Rummānī, and ʿAbd al-Qāhir al-Jurjānī. *Thalāth rasāʾil fī iʿjāz al-Qurʾān*. Edited by Muḥammad Khalafallāh and Muḥammad Zaghlūl Sallām. Cairo: Dār al-Maʿārif, 1976.

Three Treatises on the Iʿjaz of the Qur'an: Qur'anic Studies and Literary Criticism. Translated by Issa J. Boullata. Edited by Muḥammad Khalaf-Allāh Aḥmad and Muḥammad Zaghlūl Sallām. Reading, England: Garnett Publishing, 2014.

Kilito, Abdelfattah. *al-Adab wa-l-gharāba: Dirāsāt bunyawiyya fī al-adab al-ʿArabī*. Beirut: Dār al-Ṭalīʿa, 1983.

"Sur le métalangage métaphorique des poéticiens arabes." *Poétique* 38 (1979): 162–74.

Kirby, John T. "Aristotle on Metaphor." *The American Journal of Philology* 118, no. 4 (1997): 517–54.

Klein, Yaron. "Imagination and Music: *Takhyīl* and the Production of Music in al-Fārābī's *Kitāb al-mūsīqī al-kabīr*." In *Takhyīl: The Imaginary in Classical

Arabic Poetics, edited by Geert Jan van Gelder and Marlé Hammond, 179–95. Cambridge, UK: Gibb Memorial Trust, 2008.

Landau, Justine. "Naṣīr al-Dīn Ṭūsī and Poetic Imagination in the Arabic and Persian Philosophical Tradition." In *Metaphor and Imagery in Persian Poetry*, edited by Ali Asghar Seyed-Gohrab, 15–66. Leiden; Boston: Brill, 2012.

Lane, Edward William, and Stanley Lane-Poole. *An Arabic-English Lexicon*. Beirut: Librairie du Liban, 1968.

Larcher, Pierre. "Arabic Linguistic Tradition II: Pragmatics." In *The Oxford Handbook of Arabic Linguistics*, edited by Jonathan Owens, 185–212. Oxford: Oxford University Press, 2013.

"Éléments pragmatiques dans la théorie grammaticale arabe postclassique." In *Studies in the History of Arabic Grammar, II*, edited by Michael G. Carter and Kees Versteegh, 193–214. Amsterdam and Philadelphia: J. Benjamins, 1990.

"Information et performance en science arabo-islamique du langage." PhD Dissertation, Université de Paris-3, 1980.

"Mais qu'est-ce donc que la *balâgha*?" In *Literary and Philosophical Rhetoric in the Greek, Roman, Syriac, and Arabic Worlds*, edited by Frédérique Woerther, 197–213. Hildesheim; Zürich; New York: Georg Olms Verlag, 2009.

"Une pragmatique avant la pragmatique: 'médiévale,' 'arabe' et 'islamique.'" *Histoire Epistémologie Langage* 20, no. 1 (1998): 101–16.

Larkin, Margaret. *The Theology of Meaning: ʿAbd al-Qāhir al-Jurjānī's Theory of Discourse*. New Haven, CT: American Oriental Society, 1995.

Larsen, David. "Meaning and Captivity in Classical Arabic Philology." In "ʿAbd al-Qāhir al-Jurjānī," edited by Alexander Key. Special issue, *Journal of Abbasid Studies* 5 (2018): 177–228.

Llewelyn, John. "On the Saying that Philosophy Begins in Thaumazein." *Afterall: A Journal of Art, Context, and Inquiry* 4 (2001): 48–57.

al-Maʿarrī, Abū al-ʿAlāʾ. *Muʿjiz Aḥmad: Sharḥ Dīwān Abī al-Ṭayyib al-Mutanabbī*. Edited by ʿAbd al-Majīd Diyāb. Cairo: Dār al-Maʿārif, 1988.

al-Mabkhūt, Shukrī. *al-Istidlāl al-balāghī*. 2nd ed. Beirut: Dār al-Kutub al-Jadīda al-Muttaḥida, 2010.

Mandūr, Muḥammad. *al-Naqd al-manhajī ʿind al-ʿArab*. Cairo: Nahḍat Miṣr, 2004.

al-Mānīʿ, Suʿād. "Mafhūm muṣṭalaḥ 'al-majāz' ʿind al-Sijilmāsī fī ʿalāqatihi bi-muṣṭalaḥ 'al-takhyīl.'" *Majallat abḥāth al-yarmūk, Silsilat al-ādāb wa-l-lughawiyyāt* 17, no. 1 (1999): 89–137.

Margoliouth, D. S. *Analecta orientalia ad poeticam aristoteleam* [in Latin, Arabic, and Syriac.]. Hildesheim; New York: G. Olms, 2000.

al-Marzūqī, Abū ʿAlī Aḥmad ibn Muḥammad ibn al-Ḥasan. *Sharḥ Dīwān al-ḥamāsa*. Edited by Aḥmad Amīn and ʿAbd al-Salām Hārūn. Beirut: Dār al-Jīl, 1991.

Maṣlūḥ, Saʿd. *Ḥāzim al-Qarṭājannī wa-naẓariyyat al-muḥākāt wa-l-takhyīl fī al-shiʿr*. Cairo: ʿĀlam al-Kutub, 1980.

Maṭlūb, Aḥmad. *Asālīb balāghiyya: al-Faṣāḥa, al-balāgha, al-maʿānī*. Kuwait: Wikālat al-Maṭbūʿāt, 1979–80.

al-Balāgha ʿind al-Sakkākī. Baghdad: Maktabat al-Nahḍa, 1964.

al-Qazwīnī wa-shurūḥ al-talkhīṣ. Baghdad: Maktabat al-Nahḍa, 1967.

Mavroudi, Maria. "Greek Language and Education under Early Islam." In *Islamic Cultures, Islamic Contexts: Essays in Honor of Professor Patricia Crone*, edited by Behnam Sadeghi, Asad Q. Ahmed, Robert Hoyland, and Adam Silverstein, 295–342. Leiden: Brill, 2015.

Meisami, Julie Scott. "Arabic Poetics Revisited." *Journal of the American Oriental Society* 112, no. 2 (1992): 254–68.

Structure and Meaning in Medieval Arabic and Persian Poetry: Orient Pearls. London; New York: Routledge, 2003.

Miller, Jeannie. "*Bayān*, Gesture, and Genre: Self-Positioning in al-Jurjānī's Introductions." In "ʿAbd al-Qāhir al-Jurjānī," edited by Alexander Key. Special issue, *Journal of Abbasid Studies* 5 (2018): 58–104.

Minsaas, Kirsti. "Poetic Marvels: Aristotelian Wonder in Renaissance Poetics and Poetry." In *Making Sense of Aristotle: Essays in Poetics*, edited by Øivind Andersen and Jon Haarberg, 145–71. London: Duckworth & Co., 2001.

Montgomery, James E. *Al-Jāḥiẓ: In Praise of Books*. Edinburgh Studies in Classical Arabic Literature. Edited by Wen-chin Ouyang and Julia Bray. Edinburgh: Edinburgh University Press, 2013.

"Al-Jāḥiẓ's *Kitāb al-Bayān wa-l-Tabyīn*." In *Writing and Representation in Medieval Islam*, edited by Julia Bray, 91–152. London; New York: Routledge, 2006.

Moraux, Paul. *Les listes anciennes des ouvrages d'Aristote*. Louvain: Éditions Universitaires de Louvain, 1951.

Mottahedeh, Roy P. "*ʿAjāʾib* in *The Thousand and One Nights*." In *The Thousand and One Nights in Arabic Literature and Society*, edited by Richard C. Hovannisian and Georges Sabagh, 29–39. Cambridge; New York: Cambridge University Press, 1997.

Moutaouakil, Ahmed. *Réflexions sur la théorie de la signification dans la pensée linguistique arabe*. Rabat: Faculté des Lettres et des Sciences Humaines de Rabat, 1982.

Mubārak, Fāṭima. *al-ʿAjab fī adab al-Jāḥiẓ: Dirāsa sīmyāʾiyya fī Kitāb al-ḥayawān*. Tunis: al-Dār al-Tūnisiyya li-l-Kitāb, 2015.

al-Mubarrad. *al-Kāmil*. Edited by Muḥammad Aḥmad al-Dālī. 3rd ed. 4 vols. Beirut: Muʾassassat al-Risāla, 1997.

al-Mufaḍḍaliyyāt. Edited by Aḥmad Muḥammad Shākir and ʿAbd al-Salām Muḥammad Hārūn. Cairo: Dār al-Maʿārif, 1963.

Muhanna, Elias. *The World in a Book: al-Nuwayri and the Islamic Encyclopedic Tradition*. Princeton, NJ: Princeton University Press, 2018.

al-Musawi, Muhsin J. *The Medieval Islamic Republic of Letters: Arabic Knowledge Construction*. Notre Dame, IN: University of Notre Dame Press, 2015.

al-Mutanabbī. *Dīwān Abī al-Ṭayyib al-Mutanabbī*. Edited by ʿAbd al-Wahhāb ʿAzzām. Cairo: Lajnat al-Taʾlīf wa-l-Tarjama wa-l-Nashr, 1944.

al-Mutanabbī, and al-Wāḥidī. *Dīwān Abī al-Ṭayyib al-Mutanabbī wa-fī athnāʾ matnih sharḥ al-Imām al-ʿAllāma al-Wāḥidī*. Edited by Fridericus Dieterici. Berlin: n.p., 1861.

al-Muẓaffar al-Ḥusaynī. *Naḍrat al-ighrīḍ fī nuṣrat al-qarīḍ*. Edited by Nuhā ʿĀrif al-Ḥasan. Damascus: Majmaʿ al-Lugha al-ʿArabiyya, 1976.

Nallino, Carlo A. "Del Vocabolo Arabo '*Niṣbah*' (con '*ṣād*')." *Rivista degli Studi Orientali* 8, no. 1/4 (1919/1920): 637–46.

Noy, Avigail. "The Emergence of *'Ilm al-Bayān*: Classical Arabic Literary Theory in the Arabic East in the 7th/13th Century." PhD Dissertation, Harvard University, 2016.

Ouyang, Wen-chin. *Literary Criticism in Medieval Arabic-Islamic Culture: The Making of a Tradition*. Edinburgh: Edinburgh University Press, 1997.

Owens, Jonathan. "Arabic Syntactic Research." In *Syntax – Theory and Analysis: An International Handbook, Vol. 1*, edited by Tibor Kiss and Artemis Alexiadou, 99–133. Berlin: De Gruyter Mouton, 2015.

Pontani, Filippomaria. "Inimitable Sources: Canonical Texts and Rhetorical Theory in the Greek, Latin, Arabic and Hebrew Traditions." In *Canonical Texts and Scholarly Practices: A Global Comparative Approach*, edited by Anthony Grafton and Glenn W. Most, 224–52. Cambridge: Cambridge University Press, 2016.

Puerta Vílchez, José Miguel. *Aesthetics in Arabic Thought: From Pre-Islamic Arabia through al-Andalus*. Leiden: Brill, 2017.

al-Qarṭājannī, Abū al-Ḥasan Ḥāzim. *Minhāj al-bulaghā' wa-sirāj al-udabā'*. Edited by M. al-Ḥabīb Ibn al-Khawja. Beirut: Dār al-Gharb al-Islāmī, 1981.

al-Qasṭallī, Ibn Darrāj. *Dīwān*. Edited by Maḥmūd 'Alī Makkī. Damascus: Manshūrāt al-Maktab al-Islāmī, 1961.

al-Qawāsimī, Bassām al-'Afw. "al-Hawl al-mu'jib fī al-qawl bi-l-mūjib li-Ṣalāḥ al-Dīn al-Ṣafadī (d. 764AH): Dirāsa naqdiyya taḥlīliyya." *Majallat al-jāmi'a al-islāmiyya (Silsilat al-dirāsāt al-insāniyya)* 19, no. 1 (Jan 2011): 957–86.

al-Qazwīnī (al-Khaṭīb), Jalāl al-Dīn. *al-Īḍāḥ fī 'ulūm al-balāgha*. Edited by Muḥammad 'Abd al-Mun'im Khafājī. 3rd ed. Beirut: Dār al-Kitāb al-Lubnānī, 1971.

al-Talkhīṣ fī 'ulūm al-balāgha. Edited by 'Abd al-Ḥamīd Hindāwī. 2nd ed. Beirut: Dār al-Kutub al-'Ilmiyya, 2009.

al-Qazwīnī, Zakariyyā. *'Ajā'ib al-makhlūqāt wa-gharā'ib al-mawjūdāt*. Edited by Fārūq Sa'd. Beirut: Dār al-Āfāq al-Jadīda, 1973.

Qudāma ibn Ja'far, Abū al-Faraj [pseudo]. *Naqd al-nathr*. Edited by Taha Hussein and 'Abd al-Ḥamīd al-'Abbādī. Cairo: Dār al-Kutub al-Miṣriyya, 1933.

Qudāma ibn Ja'far, Abū al-Faraj. *Naqd al-shi'r*. Edited by Muḥammad 'Abd al-Mun'im Khafājī. Beirut: Dār al-Kutub al-'Ilmiyya, n.d.

Rabbat, Nasser. "*'Ajīb* and *Gharīb*: Artistic Perception in Medieval Arabic Sources." *The Medieval History Journal* 9, no. 1 (2006): 99–113.

al-Rāfi'ī, Muṣṭafā Ṣādiq. *I'jāz al-Qur'ān wa-l-balāgha al-nabawiyya*. 3rd ed. Beirut: Dār al-Kitāb al-'Arabī, 2005.

al-Rāzī, Fakhr al-Dīn. *Nihāyat al-ījāz fī dirāyat al-i'jāz*. Edited by Nasrullah Hacimüftüoğlu. Beirut: Dār Ṣādir, 2004.

Reinert, Benedikt. "Der Concetto-Stil in den islamischen Literaturen." In *Neues Handbuch der Literaturwissenschaft (Band 5: Orientalisches Mittelalter)*, edited by Wolfhart Heinrichs, 366–408. Wiesbaden: AULA-Verlag, 1990.

al-Ma'ānī wa'l-bayān. In *Encyclopaedia of Islam, Second Edition*, edited by P. Bearman, Th. Bianquis, C. E. Bosworth, E. van Donzel, and W. P. Heinrichs. Brill Online, 2012.

Riffaterre, Michael. *Semiotics of Poetry*. Bloomington, IN: Indiana University Press, 1978.

Rippin, Andrew, and Jan Knappert, eds. *Textual Sources for the Study of Islam*. Chicago: University of Chicago Press, 1990.

al-Rūbī, Ulfat Kamāl. *Naẓariyyat al-shiʿr ʿind al-falāsifa al-muslimīn: Min al-Kindī ḥattā Ibn Rushd*. Beirut: Dār al-Tanwīr, 1983.

Rubin, Uri. "Prophets and Prophethood." In *Encyclopaedia of the Qurʾān*, vol. 4, edited by Jane Dammen McAuliffe, 289–306. Leiden: Brill, 2004.

al-Rummānī. "al-Nukat fī iʿjāz al-Qurʾān." In *Thalāth rasāʾil fī iʿjāz al-Qurʾān*, edited by Muḥammad Khalafallāh and Muḥammad Zaghlūl Sallām, 73–113. Cairo: Dār al-Maʿārif, 1976.

Saba, Matthew D. "Abbasid Lusterware and the Aesthetics of *ʿAjab*." *Muqarnas* 29 (2012): 187–212.

al-Saʿdī, Ibn Nubāta. *Dīwān*. Edited by ʿAbd al-Amīr Mahdī Ḥabīb al-Ṭāʾī. Baghdad: Dār al-Ḥurriyya, 1977.

al-Ṣafadī, Ṣalāḥ al-Dīn. *al-Hawl al-muʿjib fī al-qawl bi-l-mūjib*. Edited by Muḥammad ʿAbd al-Majīd Lāshīn. Cairo: Dār al-Āfāq al-ʿArabiyya, 2005.

al-Sakkākī, Abū Yaʿqūb. *Miftāḥ al-ʿulūm*. Edited by ʿAbd al-Ḥamīd Hindāwī. Beirut: Dār al-Kutub al-ʿIlmiyya, 2000. [Edition cited in book.]

Miftāḥ al-ʿulūm. Edited by Naʿīm Zarzūr. Beirut: Dār al-Kutub al-ʿIlmiyya, 1983.

Sallām, Muḥammad Zaghlūl. *Athar al-Qurʾān fī taṭawwur al-naqd al-ʿArabī*. Cairo: Maktabat al-Shabāb, 1952.

Schoeler, Gregor. Der poetische Syllogismus: Ein Beitrag zum Verständnis der "logischen" Poetik der Araber. In *Zeitschrift der Deutschen Morgenländischen Gesellschaft*, 43–91. N.p., 1983.

Einige Grundprobleme der autochthonen und der aristotelischen arabischen Literaturtheorie: Ḥāzim al-Qarṭāğannīs Kapitel über die Zielsetzungen der Dichtung und die Vorgeschichte der ihm dargelegten Gedanken. Wiesbaden: Kommissionsverlag Franz Steiner GMBH, 1975.

The Genesis of Literature in Islam: From the Aural to the Read. Edited and translated by Shawkat M. Toorawa. Revised ed. Edinburgh: Edinburgh University Press, 2009.

"The 'Poetic Syllogism' Revisited." *Oriens* 41 (2013): 1–26.

Schrier, O. J. "The Syriac and Arabic Versions of Aristotle's 'Poetics.'" In *The Ancient Tradition in Christian and Islamic Hellenism*, edited by G. Endress and R. Kruk, 259–78. Leiden: Research School CNWS, 1997.

Sellheim, Rudolf. *Materialien zur arabischen Literaturgeschichte*. 2 vols. Wiesbaden: Franz Steiner, 1976–87.

Sells, Michael. "The Qasida and the West: Self-Reflective Stereotype and Critical Encounter." *al-ʿArabiyya* 20 (1987): 307–24.

Shaykhūn, Maḥmūd al-Sayyid. *al-Iʿjāz fī naẓm al-Qurʾān*. Cairo: Maktabat al-Kulliyyāt al-Azhariyya, 1978.

Shinar, P. Ibn Wahb. In *Encyclopaedia of Islam, Second Edition*, edited by P. Bearman, Th. Bianquis, C. E. Bosworth, E. van Donzel, and W. P. Heinrichs. Brill Online, 2012.

Shklovskiĭ, Viktor, and Alexandra Berlina. *Viktor Shklovsky: A Reader.* Translated by Alexandra Berlina. New York: Bloomsbury Academic, 2017.

al-Sijilmāsī. *al-Manzaʿ al-badīʿ fī tajnīs asālīb al-badīʿ.* Edited by ʿAllāl al-Ghāzī. Rabat: Maktabat al-Maʿārif, 1980.

Simon, Udo Gerald. *Mittelalterliche arabische Sprachbetrachtung zwischen Grammatik und Rhetorik: ʿilm al-maʿānī bei as-Sakkākī.* Heidelberg: Heidelberger Orientverlag, 1993.

Singer, Alan, and Allen Dunn, eds. *Literary Aesthetics: A Reader.* Oxford, UK; Malden, MA: Blackwell, 2000.

Smyth, William. "The Canonical Formulation of *ʿIlm al-Balāghah* and al-Sakkākī's *Miftāḥ al-ʿUlūm.*" *Der Islam* 72 (1995): 7–24.

"Controversy in a Tradition of Commentary: The Academic Legacy of al-Sakkākī's *Miftāḥ al-ʿulūm.*" *Journal of the American Oriental Society* 112, no. 4 (1992): 589–97.

"Some Quick Rules Ut Pictura Poesis: The Rules for Simile in *Miftāḥ al-ʿUlūm.*" *Oriens* 33 (1992): 215–29.

Sperl, Stefan. *Mannerism in Arabic Poetry: A Structural Analysis of Selected Texts (3rd Century AH/9th Century AD–5th Century AH/11th Century AD).* Cambridge; New York: Cambridge University Press, 1989.

Stetkevych, Suzanne Pinckney. *Abū Tammām and the Poetics of the ʿAbbāsid Age.* Leiden: E.J. Brill, 1991.

"Toward a Redefinition of 'Badīʿ' Poetry." *Journal of Arabic Literature* 12 (1981): 1–29.

Stroumsa, Sarah. *Freethinkers of Medieval Islam: Ibn al-Rāwandī, Abū Bakr al-Rāzī and Their Impact on Islamic Thought.* Leiden: Brill, 1999.

"The Signs of Prophecy: The Emergence and Early Development of a Theme in Arabic Theological Literature." *The Harvard Theological Review* 78, no. 1/2 (January–April 1985): 101–14.

Suleiman, Yasir. "*Bayān* as a Principle of Taxonomy: Linguistic Elements in Jāḥiẓ's Thinking." In *Studies on Arabia in Honour of Professor G. Rex Smith*, edited by J. F. Healey and V. Porter, 273–95. Oxford: Oxford University Press, 2002.

al-Ṣūlī, Abū Bakr. *Akhbār Abī Tammām.* Edited by Muḥammad ʿAbduh ʿAzzām, Khalīl Maḥmūd ʿAsākir, and Naẓīr al-Islām al-Hindī. 3rd ed. Beirut: Dār al-Āfāq al-Jadīda, 1980.

al-Ṣūlī, Muḥammad ibn Yaḥyā. *The Life and Times of Abū Tammām.* Translated by Beatrice Gruendler. Library of Arabic Literature. New York: New York University Press, 2015.

al-Suyūṭī. *al-Muzhir fī ʿulūm al-lugha wa-anwāʿihā.* Edited by Muḥammad Aḥmad Jād al-Mawlā, Muḥammad Abū al-Faḍl Ibrāhīm, and ʿAlī Muḥammad al-Bajāwī. 3rd ed. 2 vols. Cairo: Maktabat Dār al-Turāth, n.d.

Sweity, Ahmad. "Al-Jurjaanii's Theory of NaZm (Discourse Arrangement): A Linguistic Perspective." PhD Dissertation, University of Texas at Austin, 1992.

Ṭabāna, Badawī. *al-Bayān al-ʿArabī: Dirāsa fī taṭawwur al-fikra al-balāghiyya ʿind al-ʿArab wa-manāhijihā wa-maṣādirihā al-kubrā*. Cairo: Maktabat al-Anjlū al-Miṣriyya, 1958.

al-Taftāzānī, Saʿd al-Dīn. *al-Muṭawwal: Sharḥ Talkhīṣ Miftāḥ al-ʿulūm*. Edited by ʿAbd al-Ḥamīd Hindāwī. 3rd ed. Beirut: Dār al-Kutub al-ʿIlmiyya, 2013.

Ṭāhā, Ibrāhīm. *al-Ījāz fī al-mawrūth al-balāghī wa-l-Qurʾān al-karīm*. Beirut: al-Muʾassasa al-ʿArabiyya li-l-Dirāsāt wa-l-Nashr, 2012.

Talib, Adam. *How Do You Say "Epigram" in Arabic? Literary History at the Limits of Comparison*. Leiden: Brill, 2018.

al-Thaʿālibī, Abū Manṣūr. *Yatīmat al-dahr fī maḥāsin ahl al-ʿaṣr*. Edited by Muḥammad Muḥyī al-Dīn ʿAbd al-Ḥamīd. 4 vols. Cairo: al-Maktaba al-Tijāriyya, 1956.

Yatīmat al-dahr fī maḥāsin ahl al-ʿaṣr. Edited by Mufīd Muḥammad Qumayḥa, vol. 5, *Tatimmat al-Yatīma*. Beirut: Dār al-Kutub al-ʿIlmiyya, 1983.

al-Tibrīzī (al-Khaṭīb). *Sharḥ al-qaṣāʾid al-ʿashr*. Cairo: Idārat al-Ṭibāʿa al-Munīriyya, 1933.

The New Princeton Encyclopedia of Poetry and Poetics. Edited by Alex Preminger and T. V. F. Brogan; (associate editors) Frank J. Warnke, O. B. Hardison, Jr., and Earl Miner. Princeton, NJ: Princeton University Press, 1993.

Toorawa, Shawkat. *Ibn Abī Ṭāhir Ṭayfūr and Arabic Writerly Culture: A Ninth-Century Bookman in Baghdad*. London: Routledge Curzon, 2005.

ʿUmar ibn Abī Rabīʿa. *Sharḥ Dīwān ʿUmar ibn Abī Rabīʿa al-Makhzūmī*. Edited by Muḥammad Muḥyī al-Dīn ʿAbd al-Ḥamīd. Cairo: Maṭbaʿat al-Saʿāda, 1952.

ʿUṣfūr, Jābir. *al-Ṣūra al-fanniyya fī al-turāth al-naqdī wa-l-balāghī ʿind al-ʿArab*. 3rd ed. Beirut: al-Markaz al-Thaqāfī al-ʿArabī, 1992.

Vagelpohl, Uwe. *Aristotle's Rhetoric in the East: The Syriac and Arabic Translation and Commentary Tradition*. Leiden: Brill, 2008.

Vasalou, Sophia. *Wonder: A Grammar*. Albany, NY: State University of New York Press, 2015.

Versteegh, Kees. *The Arabic Language*. New York: Columbia University Press, 1997.

"A New Semantic Approach to Linguistics: al-Jurjânî and as-Sakkâkî on Meaning." In *Landmarks in Linguistic Thought: The Arabic Linguistic Tradition*, edited by Kees Versteegh, 115–26. London: Routledge, 1997.

Wankhammer, Johannes. "Cultures of Sense: Science, Aesthetics, and the Art of Attention in the Eighteenth Century." PhD Dissertation, Cornell University, 2016.

Weisweiler, Max. "ʿAbdalqāhir al-Curcānī's Werk über die Unnachahmlichkeit des Korans und seine syntaktisch-stilistischen Lehren." *Oriens* 11, no. 1/2 (1958): 77–121.

al-Zabīdī. *Tāj al-ʿarūs min jawāhir al-qāmūs*. Kuwait: Maṭbaʿat Ḥukūmat al-Kuwayt, 1965–2001.

Zadeh, Travis. *Mapping Frontiers across Medieval Islam: Translation, Geography, and the ʿAbbāsid Empire*. London; New York: I.B. Tauris, 2011.

"The Wiles of Creation: Philosophy, Fiction, and the *ʿAjāʾib* Tradition." *Middle Eastern Literatures* 13, no. 1 (April 2010): 21–48.

al-Zarkashī, Badr al-Dīn. *al-Burhān fī ʿulūm al-Qurʾān*. Edited by Muḥammad Abū al-Faḍl Ibrāhīm. Cairo: Dār al-Turāth, 1957.

Zubir, Badri Najib. *Balāghah as an Instrument of Qurʾān Interpretation: A Study of Al-Kashshāf*. Kuala Lumpur: International Islamic University Malaysia, 2008.

"Departure from Communicative Norms in the Qur'an: Insights from al-Jurjānī and al-Zamakhsharī." *Journal of Qur'anic Studies* 2, no. 2 (2000): 69–81.

Index

Abbasid era
  classicism during, xii, 16, 34
  criticism during (*See* old school of criticism)
  poetry during (*See* Arabic poetry; *muḥdath*)
Abū Bishr Mattā ibn Yūnus (d. 328/940), 78, 79, 83–4
Abu Deeb, Kamal, 43, 49–50, 148, 181
Abū Firās al-Ḥamdānī, (d. 357/968), 47–8
Abū Nuwās (d. 199/813), 14, 36–7, 57, 59, 231
  innovative poetry of, 26
Abū Tammām (d. 232/845), 14, 16, 31, 32, 36–7, 65, 117, 153, 194. *See also* *badīʿ*; *muḥdath*
accuracy. *See ḥaqīqa*
adab, xiii
aesthetic experience, 3–4
  in Arabic literary theory, 257–8
  wonder as, 10–11, 257–8
    as cognitive, 262–3
    as emotional, 262–3
aesthetic judgment, 3–4
aesthetic object, 3–4
aesthetic pleasure, Aristotle on, 95
aesthetics (as concept), 3–6. *See also* new aesthetic
  in Arabic classical literary theory, 22–4
  in Arabic poetry, 22–4
  beauty and, 3, 4, 139
  development of, 3
  European context for, 4
  poetic speech and, 4
  the sublime and, 4
  of wonder, 259–60
ʿajab. *See* wonder
ʿajāʾib (marvels), as genre, 7–9
al-Aʿjam, Ziyād (d. 100/718?), 198
ʿalā khilāf muqtaḍā al-ẓāhir. *See muqtaḍā al-ẓāhir*
al-Akhṭal (d. c. 92/710), 30
Alfarabius. *See* al-Fārābī, Abū Naṣr
alfāẓ. *See lafẓ*
allusion (*ishāra*)
  as physical gesture, 136–7
  al-Sijilmāsī on, 124, 127–8
  as type of *kināya*, 199–200
alteration. *See taghyīr*
amazement and wonderment (*taʿajjub*), 5. *See also* wonder
  in Aristotelian Arabic poetics, 89, 91, 94, 96, 99–100, 114
  al-Jurjānī, ʿAbd al-Qāhir, on, 145–6
  as reinforcement of metaphor, 194–5
  as rhetorical figure (*badīʿ*), 10–11, 45–6, 53–4, 55–6
    wonder as aesthetic experience, as distinct from, 5, 10–11
Al-Āmidī, Abū al-Qāsim (d. 370/980 or 371/981), 15–16, 31–3
  on Abū Tammām, 32
  on al-Buḥturī, 31–2
  on preference of style, 32–3
  on truthfulness, 37, 40–2
ʿamūd al-shiʿr. *See* fundaments of poetry

Other Titles in the Series

Agricultural Innovation in the Early Islamic World: The Diffusion of Crops and Farming Techniques, 700–1100, Andrew M. Watson
Muslim Tradition: Studies in Chronology, Provenance and Authorship of Early Ḥadīth, G. H. A. Juynboll
Social History of Timbuktu: The Role of Muslim Scholars and Notables 1400–1900, Elias N. Saad
Sex and Society in Islam: Birth Control before the Nineteenth Century, B. F. Musallam
Towns and Townsmen of Ottoman Anatolia: Trade, Crafts and Food Production in an Urban Setting 1520–1650, Suraiya Faroqhi
Unlawful Gain and Legitimate Profit in Islamic Law: Riba, Gharar and Islamic Banking, Nabil A. Saleh
Men of Modest Substance: House Owners and House Property in Seventeenth-Century Ankara and Kayseri, Suraiya Faroqhi
Roman, Provincial and Islamic Law: The Origins of the Islamic Patronate, Patricia Crone
Economic Life in Ottoman Jerusalem, Amnon Cohen
Mannerism in Arabic Poetry: A Structural Analysis of Selected Texts (3rd Century AH/9th Century AD–5th Century AH/11th Century AD), Stefan Sperl
The Rise and Rule of Tamerlane, Beatrice Forbes Manz
Popular Culture in Medieval Cairo, Boaz Shoshan
Early Philosophical Shiism: The Ismaili Neoplatonism of Abū Yaʿqūb al-Sijistānī, Paul E. Walker
Indian Merchants and Eurasian Trade, 1600–1750, Stephen Frederic Dale
Palestinian Peasants and Ottoman Officials: Rural Administration around Sixteenth-Century Jerusalem, Amy Singer
Arabic Historical Thought in the Classical Period, Tarif Khalidi
Mongols and Mamluks: The Mamluk–Īlkhānid War, 1260–1281, Reuven Amitai-Preiss
Knowledge and Social Practice in Medieval Damascus, 1190–1350, Michael Chamberlain
The Politics of Households in Ottoman Egypt: The Rise of the Qazdağlis, Jane Hathaway
Hierarchy and Egalitarianism in Islamic Thought, Louise Marlow
Commodity and Exchange in the Mongol Empire: A Cultural History of Islamic Textiles, Thomas T. Allsen
State and Provincial Society in the Ottoman Empire: Mosul, 1540–1834, Dina Rizk Khoury
The Mamluks in Egyptian Politics and Society, Thomas Philipp and Ulrich Haarmann (eds.)
The Delhi Sultanate: A Political and Military History, Peter Jackson
European and Islamic Trade in the Early Ottoman State: The Merchants of Genoa and Turkey, Kate Fleet
The Ottoman City between East and West: Aleppo, Izmir, and Istanbul, Edhem Eldem, Daniel Goffman, and Bruce Masters

The Politics of Trade in Safavid Iran: Silk for Silver, 1600–1730, Rudolph P. Matthee
The Idea of Idolatry and the Emergence of Islam: From Polemic to History, G. R. Hawting
A Monetary History of the Ottoman Empire, Şevket Pamuk
Classical Arabic Biography: The Heirs of the Prophets in the Age of al-Ma'mūn, Michael Cooperson
Empire and Elites after the Muslim Conquest: The Transformation of Northern Mesopotamia, Chase F. Robinson
Poverty and Charity in Medieval Islam: Mamluk Egypt, 1250–1517, Adam Sabra
Culture and Conquest in Mongol Eurasia, Thomas T. Allsen
Christians and Jews in the Ottoman Arab World: The Roots of Sectarianism, Bruce Masters
Arabic Administration in Norman Sicily: The Royal Diwan, Jeremy Johns
Law, Society and Culture in the Maghrib, 1300–1500, David S. Powers
Revival and Reform in Islam: The Legacy of Muhammad al-Shawkānī, Bernard Haykel
Tolerance and Coercion in Islam: Interfaith Relations in the Muslim Tradition, Yohanan Friedmann
Guns for the Sultan: Military Power and the Weapons Industry in the Ottoman Empire, Gábor Ágoston
Marriage, Money and Divorce in Medieval Islamic Society, Yossef Rapoport
The Empire of the Qara Khitai in Eurasian History: Between China and the Islamic World, Michal Biran
Domesticity and Power in the Early Mughal World, Ruby Lal
Power, Politics and Religion in Timurid Iran, Beatrice Forbes Manz
Postal Systems in the Pre-Modern Islamic World, Adam J. Silverstein
Kingship and Ideology in the Islamic and Mongol Worlds, Anne F. Broadbridge
Justice, Punishment and the Medieval Muslim Imagination, Christian Lange
The Shiites of Lebanon under Ottoman Rule, 1516–1788, Stefan Winter
Women and Slavery in the Late Ottoman Empire, Madeline Zilfi
The Second Ottoman Empire: Political and Social Transformation in the Early Modern World, Baki Tezcan
The Legendary Biographies of Tamerlane: Islam and Heroic Apocrypha in Central Asia, Ron Sela
Non-Muslims in the Early Islamic Empire: From Surrender to Coexistence, Milka Levy-Rubin
The Origins of the Shi'a: Identity, Ritual, and Sacred Space in Eighth-Century Kufa, Najam Haider
Politics, Law, and Community in Islamic Thought: The Taymiyyan Moment, Ovamir Anjum
The Power of Oratory in the Medieval Muslim World, Linda G. Jones
Animals in the Qur'an, Sarra Tlili
The Logic of Law Making in Islam: Women and Prayer in the Legal Tradition, Behnam Sadeghi
Empire and Power in the Reign of Süleyman: Narrating the Sixteenth-Century Ottoman World, Kaya Şahin
Law and Piety in Medieval Islam, Megan H. Reid

Women and the Transmission of Religious Knowledge in Islam, Asma Sayeed
The New Muslims of Post-Conquest Iran: Tradition, Memory, and Conversion, Sarah Bowen Savant
The Mamluk City in the Middle East: History, Culture, and the Urban Landscape, Nimrod Luz
Disability in the Ottoman Arab World, 1500–1800, Sara Scalenghe
The Holy City of Medina: Sacred Space in Early Islamic Arabia, Harry Munt
Muslim Midwives: The Craft of Birthing in the Premodern Middle East, Avner Giladi
Doubt in Islamic Law: A History of Legal Maxims, Interpretation, and Islamic Criminal Law, Intisar A. Rabb
The Second Formation of Islamic Law: The Ḥanafī School in the Early Modern Ottoman Empire, Guy Burak
Sexual Violation in Islamic Law: Substance, Evidence, and Procedure, Hina Azam
Gender Hierarchy in the Qurʾān: Medieval Interpretations, Modern Responses, Karen Bauer
Intellectual Networks in Timurid Iran: Sharaf al-Dīn ʿAlī Yazdī and the Islamicate Republic of Letters, Ilker Evrim Binbaş
Authority and Identity in Medieval Islamic Historiography: Persian Histories from the Peripheries, Mimi Hanaoka
The Economics of Ottoman Justice: Settlement and Trial in the Sharia Courts, Metin Coşgel and Boğaç Ergene
The Mystics of al-Andalus: Ibn Barrajān and Islamic Thought in the Twelfth Century, Yousef Casewit
Muhammad's Heirs: The Rise of Muslim Scholarly Communities, 622–950, Jonathan E. Brockopp
The First of the Modern Ottomans: The Intellectual History of Ahmed Vasif, Ethan Menchinger
Non-Muslim Provinces under Early Islam: Islamic Rule and Iranian Legitimacy in Armenia and Caucasian Albania, Alison Vacca
Women and the Making of the Mongol Empire, Anne F. Broadbridge
Slavery and Empire in Central Asia, Jeff Eden
Christianity in Fifteenth-Century Iraq, Thomas A. Carlson
Child Custody in Islamic Law: Theory and Practice in Egypt since the Sixteenth Century, Ahmed Fekry Ibrahim
Ibadi Muslims of North Africa: Manuscripts, Mobilization and the Making of a Written Tradition, Paul M. Love Jr.
Islamic Law of the Sea: Freedom of Navigation and Passage Rights in Islamic Thought, Hassan S. Khalilieh
Law and Politics under the Abassids: An Intellectual Portrait of al-Juwayni, Sohaira Z. M. Siddiqui
Friends of the Emir: Non-Muslim State Officials in Premodern Islamic Thought, Luke B. Yarbrough
The Crisis of Kingship in Late Medieval Islam: Persian Emigres and the Making of Ottoman Sovereignty, Christopher Markiewicz
Collective Liability in Islam: The ʿĀqila and Blood Money Payments, Nurit Tsafrir

Printed in Great Britain
by Amazon

20237431R00183